Lecture Notes in Artificial Intelligence   1582

Subseries of Lecture Notes in Computer Science
Edited by J. G. Carbonell and J. Siekmann

Lecture Notes in Computer Science

Edited by G. Goos, J. Hartmanis and J. van Leeuwen

Springer

Berlin
Heidelberg
New York
Barcelona
Hong Kong
London
Milan
Paris
Singapore
Tokyo

Alain Lecomte   François Lamarche
Guy Perrier (Eds.)

Logical Aspects of Computational Linguistics

Second International Conference, LACL '97
Nancy, France, September 22-24, 1997
Selected Papers

 Springer

Series Editors

Jaime G. Carbonell, Carnegie Mellon University, Pittsburgh, PA, USA
Jörg Siekmann, University of Saarland, Saarbrücken, Germany

Volume Editors

Alain Lecomte
Université Pierre Mendès France (Grenoble 2)
1251 avenue Centrale, BP 47
F-38040 Grenoble Cedex, France
E-mail: Alain.Lecomte@upmf-grenoble.fr

François Lamarche
Guy Perrier
LORIA (Nancy)
615 rue du Jardin Botanique, BP 101
F-54602 Villers lès Nancy Cedex, France
E-mail: {Lamarche,Perrier}@loria.fr

Cataloging-in-Publication data applied for

Die Deutsche Bibliothek - CIP-Einheitsaufnahme

Logical aspects of computational linguistics : second international conference ;
selected papers / LACL '97, Nancy, France, September 22 - 24, 1997. Alain
Lecomte ... (ed.). - Berlin ; Heidelberg ; New York ; Barcelona ; Hong Kong ;
London ; Milan ; Paris ; Singapore ; Tokyo : Springer, 1999
  (Lecture notes in computer science ; Vol. 1582 : Lecture notes in artificial
  intelligence)
  ISBN 3-540-65751-7

CR Subject Classification (1998): F.4, F.3, I.2.7, I.2.3, J.5

ISBN 3-540-65751-7 Springer-Verlag Berlin Heidelberg New York

© Springer-Verlag Berlin Heidelberg 1999
Printed in Germany

Typesetting: Camera-ready by author
SPIN 10703147   06/3142 – 5 4 3 2 1 0   Printed on acid-free paper

Preface

This volume contains invited and selected papers of the Second International Conference on Logical Aspects of Computational Linguistics, held in Nancy, France, 22-24 September 1997.[1] Several perspectives are adopted in this volume and we will classify them according to their school of thought or to the main domain to which they seem to contribute. For instance, two invited papers, out of a total of four[2], are included, one by Jim LAMBEK and another by Denis BOUCHARD. LAMBEK's paper belongs to the logical tradition also represented in this volume by other contributions based on type theory, like the one by S. Shaumyan and P. Hudak [3]. It was a great honour to welcome Professor LAMBEK at this colloquium as the founding father of a new discipline, *language analysis by means of type theory*. All the participants knew how deeply indebted they have been to him since his first seminal papers of the early sixties on syntactic calculus. Besides his activities in pure mathematics, LAMBEK has continued to explore type logical systems, consistently looking for maximal simplicity. Here, he presents a new calculus: a bilinear formalism (therefore similar to the classical systems of linear logic) where multiplicative conjunction and disjunction are collapsed into a single operation/connector. What is appealing is the kind of rigourous and simple model that he can obtain for complex phenomena like verbal inflection. He can even give an account of what is analyzed in terms of Chomsky's theory of traces.

Denis BOUCHARD's contribution is completely different: it provides a purely linguistic analysis of *adjectival modification*, but this analysis must be recast in a more general perspective because it is treated like a case study in order to test the assumptions of the chomskyan minimalist program. Bouchard's purpose is to draw all the conclusions that can be drawn from the minimalist assumptions. He can therefore give us some guidelines for going deeper into a theory of language, and particularly for chosing adequate minimal concepts. He focuses here on the opposition between French and English relative to the question of word order in noun-adjective associations.

These two invited papers perfectly illustrate the theoretical situation of this conference between *logic* and *linguistics*. More precisely, we know that generative linguistics is oriented more and more towards operations of feature checking and

---

[1] The proceedings of the first conference, edited by Christian Retoré, were also published by Springer as volume 1328 of the LNCS/LNAI series. The reader may find in it a survey of works connecting logic and linguistics.

[2] The other two invited papers were : one by Michael MOORTGAT, published elsewhere, and another by Yves LAFONT, a tutorial on Linear Logic and its phase semantics.

[3] Of course all the papers connected to categorial grammars could be said to belong to this tradition. We put emphasis on these papers here because they advocate the use of pure type-logical systems.

merging that can be thought of in terms of resource consumption and categorial selection. On the other hand, we know that contemporary logic has provided us with so-called resource conscious logics, like linear logic, and of course Lambek grammars. It was therefore natural and profitable to mix researchers coming from these various fields.

Another classification may be provided. It distinguishes papers according to their main domain of enquiry: philosophical, mathematical and foundational, linguistic-oriented, computational and applicational. The philosophical perspective concerns the philosophy of language and addresses the question of the place of logic with regards to language. This question is very controversial. Some authors (and Chomsky amongst them) argue that because *language is not logic*, all the convergence points between logical investigations and linguistic ones are mere accidents. For them, linguistic systems must be described by independent means and tools, logical formalization being spurious. This is of course not the attitude adopted here. Some contributors argue, on the contrary, that the system of language is very similar to Logic. For instance, S. SHAUMYAN and P. HUDAK present ideas that can be traced to the works of Haskell B. Curry on *combinatory logic*. Their view remains parallel to Montague's who claimed in 1970 that "there is no important theoretical difference between natural languages and the artificial languages of logicians." Of course, if we think of linguistics as an ordinary science, there is no reason to reject the idea of a mathematical formalization, and if that is the case, it seems natural that such a formalization be addressed by a particular branch of mathematics (not necessarily the same one that is used, say, for physics). Mathematical logic seems at present to be the best candidate for that, if only because it has taken the notion of language as one of its objects and has derived from it several suggestions for analysing language. Since it is not certain that we understand the same thing under the two notions of language, the linguistic and the logical, it seems the philosophical question will still remain open for a long time.

We can hope for more success by adopting a more technical perspective. A foundation for studying aspects of linguistics including categories and operations for combining signs can be found in the mathematics of categorial systems as they originate from Ajduckiewicz. Many authors in this volume share the view that modern techniques make it possible to generalize old categorial systems to new ones which are able to deal with several dimensions of signs at the same time. One basis for doing that consists in introducing several arbitrary products with their residuals, according to a line mainly explored by M. Moortgat, D. Oehrle and N. Kurtonina, but also by M. Hepple, G. Morrill. It is taken up in this volume by M. KANDULSKI, who demonstrates the strong equivalence of Ajduckiewicz and Lambek grammars when using these arbitrary products (we already had results from Buszkowski on the equivalence of Lambek and Ajduckiewicz grammars in the standard case). Such results must be classified among others concerning the generative capacity of grammars based on logical systems (and therefore categorial grammars). When we show that Ajduckiewicz and Lambek grammars are equivalent to context-free ones and therefore equivalent to each other, we show that at least we don't lose anything when working in the logical framework compared to, say, a phrase structure grammar approach. But moreover, with the ability to use several products and thus to superpose several calculi onto a single one, we of course enrich the structural descriptions.

Another way of dealing with multi-dimensionality is *fibring*. In the past, there have been several attempts to combine a feature logic and a categorial one, as in the CUG and UCG models. The interest in Head Driven Phrase Structure Grammars has lead to reversing the perspective and N. FRANCEZ proposes a conception according to which the categorial information "leaves-within" feature terms. Such technical approaches show us the rich power of logical techniques as soon as we dare to escape from strict orthodoxy and strict "logicism." Of course, pure logicians can be frightened by the simple project of mixing several logics, but here the linguists are acting like physicists in making many trials and attempts before obtaining a "realistic" view of the field.

Another particularly relevant technical application of logics to computational linguistics concerns the use of automata for checking well-formedness with regards to some kind of theory expressed by a set of constraints. The principle and parameters approach provides such a theory. F. MORAWIETZ and T. CORNELL explore the power of automata for *monadic second order logic* in this perspective. By doing so, they implicitly show that the chomskyan theoricisation is far from being out of the reach of logical investigation.

It is then interesting to see the impact of such logical investigations on the linguistic theory itself, this being the "linguistics-oriented" perspective in this volume, which is represented by works by H. HENDRIKS and D. HEYLEN.

It initially seems very strange that the logical framework is able to provide a very new and adequate tool for studying intonation, a dimension which seems to belong only to the phonological interpretation of a sentence. H. HENDRIKS shows the complexity of the phenomenon, which is not only part of phonology but also of *information packaging*. Traditional approaches to prosody based on the notion of constituent as defined in ordinary phrase structure grammars fail to provide a correct account of the association between intonational marks (like *pitch accent*) and the informational content. The proof-theoretic approach works better because it makes it possible to deal with multi-component signs in such a way that a syntactic analysis, a semantical form and a prosodic one are obtained at the same time. For instance, "intonation and word order are dealt with at one and the same level." Such results are direct applications of well-known techniques from proof theory, like the Curry-Howard homomorphism.

The notion of *underspecification* has received much interest in computational linguistics for several years. It crucially occurs in the resolution of agreement problems. Johnson and Bayer have already shown that unification-based grammars give a less rich account of agreement than Lambek grammars. D. HEYLEN

goes further on this topic by showing how to more generally solve feature checking problems by entirely logical means. This involves the introduction of dual
modalities, box and diamond, with their *residuation logic*. Each mode *i* represents some morphosyntactic feature, and underspecification is dealt with by
assuming general modes that are related to specific instances by inclusion postulates.

Another kind of "linguistics-oriented" paper is provided by T. CORNELL who
tries to give formal representations of minimalist grammars (as they have been
defined by E. Stabler). After papers on the derivationalist view, CORNELL develops a representational one, keeping in mind the idea that the two views must
always coexist simultaneously and that they stand in respect to each other like
a deductive system and its proof representation. The derivationalist view could
be compared to the (Gentzen) sequent presentation of a calculus and the representationalist one to its proof net syntax. By doing so, it can be shown that the
approach in terms of movement and the one in terms of chains are not contradictory but complementary.

Logic is also applied to computation and implementation. Besides the paper by SHAUMYAN and HUDAK already mentioned, which shows the use of the
programming language *Haskell* in order to implement applicative grammars,
the reader will find a paper by J. HODAS, introducing the use of the language
Lolli, based on linear logic. As it has been shown by D. Miller, linear logic can
be used for programming according to different paradigms, which we can refer
to as proof reduction (by means of the Curry-Howard homomorphism and the
interpretation it provides in functional terms) and proof search (or logic programming). *Lolli* uses the later possibility and thus allows the implementation
of logical grammars similar to DCGs. HODAS uses primitives of linear logic (ex-
ponentials and additive conjunction for instance) in a very innovative way in
order to have derivations taking unbounded dependencies into account and to
block some unwanted derivations. The trick consists in using rules which have
nested implications. These implications are used locally, as they license empty
nps in case of unbounded dependencies. But an np (for instance an np enclosed
in a subject np) can be blocked from extraction (and therefore not realizable
by an empty string) simply by marking it with the exponential "!". We actually
know that in this case, the "resource" can be produced only if all the consumed
formulae are also marked with the same exponential, but the nested implicative
formula allowing an empty np is not marked and therefore the deduction fails.

Questions of implementation are also treated by M. VILARES, M. A. ALONSO
and D. CABRERO, who question efficiency of the DCG model and propose logical
automata for parsing with DCGs according to an LALR method. Strategies for
executing definite clause grammars are still often expressed directly as symbolic
manipulations of terms and rules using backtracking, which does not constitute
an adequate basis for efficient implementations. The strategy proposed by the

three authors is based on an evolution of the notion of *logical push-down automaton* introduced by B. Lang, "a push-down automaton that stores logical atoms and substitutions on its stack, and uses unification to apply transitions."

Finally, a fruitful application of constructive type theory to the analysis of mathematical language is suggested by Z. LUO and P. C. CALLAGHAN. This work is related to others on the same topic, like Ranta and Coscoy's, using different proof development systems (Alf, Coq or Lego). They all aim at using natural language in order to interact with proof systems. Of course, that necessitates a deep exploration of the language of mathematics (here called mathematical vernacular). The novelty of this paper is its treatment of *coercion* and *subtyping*.

***

On behalf of the Program Committee, I wish to thank the participants for the pleasant and stimulating atmosphere during the meeting. The Committee is especially grateful to the aforementioned invited speakers. I also wish to thank the two institutions that co-organized this event, namely INRIA-Lorraine and CRIN-CNRS, as well as the sponsors of this event: France-Télécom CNET, Xerox Research Center Europe, l'Institut National Polytechnique de Lorraine, l'Université Henri Poincaré, La Région Lorraine and La Communauté Urbaine du Grand Nancy.

More personally, I deeply thank the members of the Program Committee and the Organizing Committee, listed overleaf, for their hard work and support, and let us not forget the research project without which nothing would have happened *Calligramme*.[4]

I particularly thank François Lamarche, who proofread this preface and had to work hard to improve the presentation of some of the papers; Christian Retoré, who provided me with some templates from the first edition (LACL'96); and Guy Perrier, who was a very efficient organizer of this conference.

Grenoble, December 1998   Alain Lecomte (*Chairman*)

---

[4] *Calligramme, Logique linéaire, réseaux de démonstration et grammaires catégorielles* (INRIA-Lorraine and CRIN-CNRS): D. Bechet, Ph. de Groote, F. Lamarche, A. Lecomte, J.-Y. Marion, G. Perrier, V. Antoine (secretary) and C. Retoré.

Programme Committee

Bob Carpenter — Bell Laboratories
Marc Dymetman — Rank-Xerox Research Center, Grenoble
Claire Gardent — Universität des Saarlandes, Saarbrücken
Philippe de Groote — INRIA-Lorraine & CRIN-CNRS, Nancy
Seth Kulick — University of Pennsylvania
François Lamarche — INRIA-Lorraine & CRIN-CNRS, Nancy
Alain Lecomte (Chair) — Université Grenoble 2 & INRIA-Lorraine
Michael Moortgat — OTS, Universiteit Utrecht
Glyn V. Morrill — Universitat Politècnica de Catalunya, Barcelona
Aarne Ranta — Universities of Helsinki & Tampere
Patrick Saint-Dizier — IRIT-Toulouse
Edward Stabler — UCLA, Los Angeles
Eric Villemonte de la Clergerie — INRIA-Rocquencourt

Organizing Committee

Valérie Antoine, Denis Bechet, Anne-Lise Charbonnier,
François Lamarche, Guy Perrier (Chair), Armelle Savary
INRIA-Lorraine & CRIN-CNRS, Nancy

Table of Contents

Invited papers

Selected papers

Type Grammar Revisited

J. Lambek

McGill University

To Claudia Casadio, who persuaded me that there is something to categorial grammar after all.

Abstract. A *protogroup* is an ordered monoid in which each element a has both a left proto-inverse a^ℓ such that $a^\ell a \leq 1$ and a right proto-inverse a^r such that $aa^r \leq 1$. We explore the assignment of elements of a free protogroup to English words as an aid for checking which strings of words are well-formed sentences, though ultimately we may have to relax the requirement of freeness. By a *pregroup* we mean a protogroup which also satisfies $1 \leq aa^\ell$ and $1 \leq a^r a$, rendering a^ℓ a left adjoint and a^r a right adjoint of a. A pregroup is precisely a poset model of classical non-commutative linear logic in which the tensor product coincides with it dual. This last condition is crucial to our treatment of passives and Wh-questions, which exploits the fact that $a^{\ell\ell} \neq a$ in general. Free pregroups may be used to recognize the same sentences as free protogroups.

1 Protogroups

Traditional dimensional analysis assigns to each quantity of classical mechanics a type, usually called *dimension*, $L^a T^b M^c$, where a, b, and c are integers and L, T and M stand for *length, time* and *mass* respectively. (We shall ignore the later attempt to incorporate electro-magnetic quantities by allowing fractional exponents.) These types form a free Abelian group and the well-foundedness (though of course not the correctness) of a physical equation can be verified by checking that the two sides of the equation have the same type.

A seductive idea, which has occured to many people, is to apply a similar technique to natural languages such as English, using a free (non-commutative) group of what might be called syntactic types. Having assigned types to words, one would expect to be able to decide whether given strings of words are sentences, by checking that the product of their types is s, the type of a sentence. This naïve attempt breaks down as soon as one realizes that every element of a group has a unique inverse, whereas syntax would seem to require a distinction between the left inverse a^ℓ and the right inverse a^r of a. Unfortunately, if $a^\ell a = 1 = aa^r$, it follows that

$$a^\ell = a^\ell 1 = a^\ell aa^r = 1a^r = a^r.$$

Now, if we assign type $\mathbf{n}$ to *John*, presumably we should assign type $\mathbf{nn}^\ell$ to *poor* so that *poor John* has type $\mathbf{nn}^\ell \mathbf{n} = \mathbf{n}1 = \mathbf{n}$. But, if $\mathbf{n}^\ell = \mathbf{n}^r$, *poor* would have type 1, meaning that it could pop up anywhere in a sentence.

To get around this difficulty, we define a *protogroup* to be an ordered monoid, that is a semigroup with a unity element 1 and a partial order rendering multiplication order preserving, such that each element a has two "proto-inverses" a^ℓ and a^r satisfying $a^\ell a \leq 1$ and $aa^r \leq 1$ respectively. If the order is discrete, a protogroup is just a group.

For mathematical purposes, at first sight without linguistic significance, it is convenient to consider also the following equations:

$$(E) \qquad 1^r = 1, \quad a^{\ell r} = a, (ab)^r = b^r a^r; \quad 1^\ell = 1, \quad a^{r\ell} = a, \quad (ab)^\ell = b^\ell a^\ell,$$

as well as the implications:

$$(I) \qquad\qquad \text{if } a \leq b \text{ then } b^\ell \leq a^\ell \text{ and } b^r \leq a^r.$$

Note, however, that in general $a^{\ell\ell} \neq a$ and $a^{rr} \neq a$. While we do not incorporate these conditions into the definition of a protogroup, they will reappear in Section 6 as giving rise to "pregroups". We mention them now for motivating why the following construction describes a protogroup.

Given a poset (= partially ordered set) A, we construct the *free protogroup* $F(A)$ as follows. For the moment we shall write

$$\cdots a^{(-2)}, \ a^{(-1)}, \ a^{(0)}, \ a^{(1)}, \ a^{(2)}, \cdots$$

for

$$\cdots a^{\ell\ell}, \ a^\ell, \ a, \ a^r, \ a^{rr}, \cdots$$

Then an element of $F(A)$ has the form

$$\alpha = a_1^{(n_1)} \cdots a_k^{(n_k)},$$

where the $a_i \in A$ and the $n_i \in \mathbb{Z}$.

Multiplication is defined by concatenation and proto-inverses are defined thus:

$$\alpha^r = a_k^{(n_k+1)} \cdots a_1^{(n_1+1)},$$
$$\alpha^\ell = a_k^{(n_k-1)} \cdots a_1^{(n_1-1)}.$$

The equations (E) ensure that proto-inverses have to be defined in this way.

Finally we define $\alpha \leq \beta$ to mean that there is a sequence

$$\alpha = \alpha_1, \alpha_2, \cdots, \alpha_m = \beta$$

of elements of $F(A)$, where α_i and α_{i+1} are related as follows:

Case 1. $\qquad\qquad \alpha_i = \gamma a^{(n)} \delta, \gamma b^{(n)} \delta = \alpha_{i+1},$

where n is even and $a \leq b$ in A or n is odd and $b \leq a$ in A, in view of (I).

Case 2. $\qquad\qquad \alpha_i = \gamma a^{(n)} a^{(n+1)} \delta, \alpha_{i+1} = \gamma\delta.$

In case 1 we shall call the step from α_i to α_{i+1} an *induced step*, in case 2 we call it a *contraction*.

A *generalized contraction* has the form

$$\gamma a^{(n)} b^{(n+1)} \delta \leq \gamma \delta,$$

where n is even and $a \leq b$ in A or n is odd and $b \leq a$ in A. This may be justified by interposing either $\gamma a^{(n)} a^{(n+1)} \delta$ or $\gamma b^{(n)} b^{(n+1)} \delta$ between the two sides of the inequality.

We claim that, without loss in generality, it may be assumed that no induced step immediately precedes a generalized contraction. There are essentially two cases:

Case *A*.
Say $\delta = \delta' c^m \delta''$
and $\gamma a^{(n)} b^{(n+1)} \delta' c^{(m)} \delta'' \leq \gamma a^{(n)} b^{(n+1)} \delta' d^{(m)} \delta'' \leq \gamma \delta' d^{(m)} \delta''$,

then we may replace the intermediate term by $\gamma \delta' c^{(m)} \delta''$. (The case $\gamma = \gamma' c^{(m)} \gamma''$ is treated similarly.)

Case *B*.
$$\gamma a^{(n)} c^{(n+1)} \delta \leq \gamma b^{(n)} c^{(n+1)} \delta \leq \gamma \delta,$$

where either n is even and $a \leq b \leq c$ or n is odd and $c \leq b \leq a$. Then we may delete the intermediate term altogether. (The case when the intermediate term is $\gamma a^{(n)} d^{(n+1)} \delta$ is treated similarly.)

We thus have the following:

Proposition 1. *If $\alpha \leq \beta$ in $F(A)$ then there exists a string γ such that $\alpha \leq \gamma$ by generalized contractions only and $\gamma \leq \beta$ by induced steps only.*

The following sketch of a small part of English grammar is very provisional. I have several times been forced to make revisions and there is no reason to suppose that further revision will not be needed. I thought it best not to hide my false starts, but to discuss the reasons for abandoning them.

2 Typing the English verb

2.1 Intransitive verbs

Originally, the English verb, like that in other European languages, had six persons, three singular and three plural. The old second person associated with the pronoun *thou* is now obsolete; even the Quaker *thee* takes the third person singular. Taking advantage of this fact, we shall assume from now on that there are three types of personal pronouns: π_1, π_2 and π_3. Provisionally, the second person will also do for other plurals. Thus

I has type π_1,
you, we, they have type π_2,
he, she, it, one have type π_3.

Sometimes the person is irrelevant, so we shall introduce the type π and postulate:

$$\pi_1 \leq \pi, \ \pi_2 \leq \pi, \ \pi_3 \leq \pi.$$

We shall also assume that there are two tenses, present and past, and we shall ignore the subjunctive. Accordingly we distinguish two types of declarative sentences (or statements): s_1 in the present tense and s_2 in the past tense. Sometimes the tense of a statement is irrelevant, then we just assign it type s and postulate:

$$s_1 \leq s, \ \ s_2 \leq s.$$

Given an intransitive verb such as *go*, we consider three non-finite forms:

the infinitive *go* of type **i**,
the present participle *going* of type $\mathbf{p}_1$,
the past participle *gone* of type $\mathbf{p}_2$.

There are also, in principle, six finite forms, of which only three are distinct, making up the 3×2 conjugation matrix

$$\begin{bmatrix} go & go & goes \\ went & went & went \end{bmatrix}.$$

(The analogous matrix in French has 6×7 entries.) The corresponding types are given by $\pi_k^r s_i$, when $k = 1, 2$ or 3 and $i = 1$ or 2. For example, *he goes* has type

$$\pi_3(\pi_3^r s_1) = (\pi_3 \pi_3^r)s_1 \leq 1s_1 1 = s_1,$$

making it a statement in the present tense.

To emphasize a statement, one makes use of the auxiliary verb *do*, as in *he does go*, which leads us to assign the type $\pi_3^r s_1 i^\ell$ to *does* so that

$$\pi_3(\pi_3^r s_1 i^\ell)i = (\pi_3 \pi_3^r)s_1(i^\ell i) \leq 1s_1 1 = s_1.$$

The conjugation matrix for *do* is

$$\begin{bmatrix} do & do & does \\ did & did & did \end{bmatrix}$$

with types $\pi_k^r s_i i^\ell$, the subscript k ranging from 1 to 3, the subscript i from 1 to 2.

2.2 Inflectors

Suppose we want to type the adverb *quietly* as in *goes quietly, going quietly, gone quietly*, etc. Unless we want to assign different types to each of these occurrences of the adverb, we are led to say that it modifies the infinitive *go*, as in *I want to go quietly*, hence has type $i^r i$, and that somehow the forms *goes, going, gone* etc are obtained from the infinitive. Elsewhere I had suggested that these forms should be analyzed as

$$C_{13} \; go, \quad \text{Part } go, \quad \text{Perf } go,$$

where C_{13}, Part and Perf are what I called "inflectors", standing for the present tense third person, the present participle and the past (= perfect) participle respectively.

We can incorporate this idea into the present context by typing

C_{ik} with $\pi_k^r \mathbf{s}_i \mathbf{i}^\ell$,
Part with $\mathbf{p}_1 \mathbf{i}^\ell$,
Perf with $\mathbf{p}_2 \mathbf{i}^\ell$.

This is consistent with the old types for *goes, going* and *gone*, since for instance

$$(\pi_3^r \mathbf{s}_1 \mathbf{i}^\ell)\mathbf{i} \leq \pi_3^r \mathbf{s}_1.$$

The old types are still valid, but the new types make explicit the relation between the verb form and the infinitive and they imply the old types.

2.3 Transitive verbs

A transitive verb like *see* requires an object, as in *I saw her*. We shall use o for the type of objects and assign type o to the accusative form of the pronouns: *me; you, us, them; him, her, it, one*. We are thus led to assign type $\pi_1^r \mathbf{s}_2 \mathbf{o}^\ell$ to *saw* in *I saw her*. The conjugation matrix of a transitive verb then has types $\pi_k^r \mathbf{s}_i \mathbf{o}^\ell$, the person of the object being irrelevant. There are also non-finite forms of types $\mathbf{io}^\ell$, $\mathbf{p}_1 \mathbf{o}^\ell$ and $\mathbf{p}_2 \mathbf{o}^\ell$. If we analyze *saw* as C_{21} *see*, we assign to it the type

$$(\pi_1^r \mathbf{s}_2 \mathbf{i}^\ell)(\mathbf{io}^\ell) \leq \pi_1^r \mathbf{s}_2 \mathbf{o}^\ell$$

as required.

2.4 Auxiliary verbs

Let us take a look at the modal verbs *may, can, will, shall* and *must*. It is convenient to say that the first four of them have past tenses *might, could, would* and *should*. In view of such sentences as *he may go, I might go*, we are tempted to assign to *may* the type $\pi_k^r \mathbf{s}_1 \mathbf{i}^\ell$ and to *might* the type $\pi_k^r \mathbf{s}_2 \mathbf{i}^\ell$, where k ranges from 1 to 3. But this assignment will have to be revised presently.

The word *have*, in addition to being a transitive verb, can also act as a perfect auxiliary, as in *I have gone*, where it must have type $\pi_1^r \mathbf{s}_1 \mathbf{p}_2^\ell$. Altogether, the conjugation matrix

$$\begin{bmatrix} have & have & has \\ had & had & had \end{bmatrix}$$

will have types $\pi_k^r s_i p_2^\ell$. Whereas the transitive verb *have* also has three non-finite forms (*have, having, had*), the perfect auxiliary only has the infinitive *have*. At first sight we are tempted to assign to it the type $i p_2^\ell$, but this would permit the non-sentence

$$^* he\ does\ have\ gone.$$

Therefore we shall assign to the infinitive *have* the type $j p_2^\ell$ instead, which will rule this out. However, we do wish to admit

$$I\ may\ go,\quad she\ may\ have\ gone,$$

so we postulate $i \le j$ and retype *may* with $\pi^r s_1 j^\ell$ and *might* with $\pi^r s_2 j^\ell$. Since $\pi_k \le \pi$ and $i \le j$, we thus obtain e.g.

$$\pi_1(\pi^r s_1 j^\ell) i \le (\pi \pi^r) s_1 (j^\ell j) \le s_1.$$

We may say that i is the type of infinitives of intransitive main verbs, while j is the type of all infinitival intransitive verb phrases. To account for the conjugation of the auxiliary verbs *have* and *be*, we should retype C_{ik} with $\pi_k^r s_i j^\ell$, Part with $p_1 j^\ell$ and Perf with $p_2 j^\ell$.

Forms of the verb *be* can be used as progressive auxiliaries or as passive auxiliaries, as in

$$I\ am\ going,\quad he\ was\ seen\ -\ ,$$

where the dash represents a Chomskian trace. (The notion of trace is not really necessary for our analysis; we only refer to it to facilitate comparison with generative-transformational grammars.) Here *am* should have type $\pi_1^r s_1 p_1^\ell$ and *was* should have type $\pi_3^r s_2 o^{\ell\ell} p_2^\ell$, as is verified by the calculations:

$$\pi_1(\pi_1^r s_1 p_1^\ell) p_1 \le (\pi_1 \pi_1^r) s_1 (p_1^\ell p_1) \le s_1,$$

$$\pi_3(\pi_3^r s_2 o^{\ell\ell} p_2^\ell)(p_2 o^\ell) \le (\pi_3 \pi_3^r) s_2 (o^{\ell\ell}(p_2^\ell p_2) o^\ell) \le s_2.$$

Note that the double ℓ in $o^{\ell\ell}$ signals the presence of a Chomskian trace.

Altogether, the conjugation matrix

$$\begin{bmatrix} am & are & is \\ was & were & was \end{bmatrix}$$

is assigned the types $\pi_k^r s_i p_1^\ell$ for the progressive auxiliary and $\pi_k^r s_i o^{\ell\ell} p_2^\ell$ for the passive auxiliary.

The progressive auxiliary also has an infinitive *be* of type $j p_1^\ell$, as witnessed by *I may be going* of type

$$\pi_1(\pi s_1 j^\ell)(j p_1^\ell) p_1 \le s_1,$$

and a past participle *been* of type $p_2 p_1^\ell$, as witnessed by *I have been going* of type

$$\pi_1(\pi_1^r s_1 p_2^\ell)(p_2 p_1^\ell) p_1 \le s_1.$$

It does not have a present participle, in view of the non-sentence

$$*I\ am\ being\ going.$$

The passive auxiliary has an infinitive *be* of type $\mathbf{jo}^{\ell\ell}\mathbf{p}_2^\ell$, as witnessed by *I may be seen*– of type

$$\pi_1(\pi^r\mathbf{s}_1\mathbf{j}^\ell)(\mathbf{jo}^{\ell\ell}\mathbf{p}_2^\ell)(\mathbf{p}_2\mathbf{o}^\ell) \le \mathbf{s}_1.$$

(We ignore here the optional agent as in *seen by her.*) It also has a present participle *being* of type $\mathbf{p}_1\mathbf{o}^{\ell\ell}\mathbf{p}_2^\ell$, as witnessed by *I am being seen* – of type

$$\pi_1(\pi_1^r\mathbf{s}_1\mathbf{p}_1^\ell)(\mathbf{p}_1\mathbf{o}^{\ell\ell}\mathbf{p}_2^\ell)(\mathbf{p}_2\mathbf{o}^\ell) \le \mathbf{s}_1,$$

and a past participle *been* of type $\mathbf{p}_2\mathbf{o}^{\ell\ell}\mathbf{p}_2^\ell$, as witnessed by *I have been seen* - of type

$$\pi_1(\pi_1^r\mathbf{s}_1\mathbf{p}_2^\ell)(\mathbf{p}_2\mathbf{o}^{\ell\ell}\mathbf{p}_2^\ell)(\mathbf{p}_2\mathbf{o}^\ell) \le \mathbf{s}_1.$$

These type assignments also justify

I have been going, I may have been going, I have been seen –,

and even

I have been being seen –,

although many people might doubt the sentencehood of the latter. Our type assignments do not justify

$$*I\ do\ be\ going,\ *I\ do\ be\ seen\ -,\ *I\ have\ had\ gone.$$

However, the passive can also be expressed with the help of *get* instead of *be*, and *I do get seen* – sounds alright and suggests the type $\mathbf{io}^{\ell\ell}\mathbf{p}_2^\ell$ for *get*.

2.5 Bitransitive verbs

A word should be said about doubly transitive verbs such as *give*, *teach* and *tell*, as in

I gave him books, she taught me English, she told me she is going.

Here *books* and *English* are direct objects of type $\mathbf{o}$, but *him* and *me* are indirect objects of type $\mathbf{o}'$, say. We are led to assign to the infinitives *give* and *teach* the type $\mathbf{io}^\ell\mathbf{o}'^\ell$ and to *tell* also the type $\mathbf{is}^\ell\mathbf{o}'^\ell$. To recognize that any expression of type $\mathbf{o}$ may serve as an indirect object we postulate $\mathbf{o} \le \mathbf{o}'$.

Formerly the indirect object was in the dative case and the direct object in the accusative, but in modern English these two cases have coalesced. It is a peculiarity of English that the indirect object can become the subject in passive sentences:

he was given – *books, I was taught* – *English, I was told* – *she is going.*

8

To account for these passives, we must assign new types to the passive auxiliary *be*, as summarized by the following metarule (apologies to Gazdar):

Corresponding to any verb of type $\mathbf{i}x^{\ell}\mathbf{o}'^{\ell}$, the passive auxiliary *be* may have type $\mathbf{j}x^{\ell}\mathbf{o}'^{\ell\ell}x^{\ell\ell}\mathbf{p}_2^{\ell}$.

In our examples $x = \mathbf{o}$ or $\mathbf{s}$; but, taking $x = 1$, we recapture the earlier type of *be* in Section 2.4.

Semantically, the bitransitive verbs may all be viewed as indicating causation. Thus, the above sample sentences are roughly equivalent to:

I let him have books, she made me learn English, she let me know she is going.

They may all be rephrased with the help of the preposition *to*:

I gave books to him, she taught English to me, she told that she is going to me.

(For the complementizer *that* see Section 4.2 below.) These alternative statements may also be passivized as follows:

> *books were given – to him,*
> *English was taught – to me,*
> *that she is going was told – to me.*

The above metarule may be amended to account for these alternative passives, but we shall refrain from doing so here.

3 Questions

3.1 Negation

Interrogative sentences, as I shall use the term here, are tied to the notion of negation: to ask whether a statement holds is to choose between it and its negation. The easiest way to introduce grammatical negation is to assign to the word *not* the type xx^{ℓ}, where $x = \mathbf{i}, \mathbf{j}, \mathbf{p}_1$ or $\mathbf{p}_2$. This will justify the following sentences:

> *he does not go,* with *does* of type $\pi_3^r \mathbf{s}_1 \mathbf{i}^{\ell}$,
> *he is not going,* with *is* of type $\pi_3^r \mathbf{s}_1 \mathbf{p}_1^{\ell}$,
> *I was not seen –,* with *was* of type $\pi_1^r \mathbf{s}_2 \mathbf{o}^{\ell\ell} \mathbf{p}_2^{\ell}$,
> *he has not gone,* with *has* of type $\pi_3^r \mathbf{s}_1 \mathbf{p}_2^{\ell}$,
> *he will not be going,* with *will* of type $\pi^r \mathbf{s}_1 \mathbf{j}^{\ell}$.

It will explain why the optional contracted forms

> *doesn't, isn't, wasn't, hasn't, won't*

also have the types of

> *does, is, was, has, will*

respectively. It does not explain why the spelling *cannot* is obligatory.

3.2 Interrogatives

We shall distinguish between interrogative sentences of types q_1 in the present tense and q_2 in the past tense. If the tense is irrelevant, we make use of type q and postulate $q_1 \leq q$ and $q_2 \leq q$. The quickest way to summarize the so-called interrogative transformation in English in the present context is with the help of the following metarule, which assigns new types to *does, is, was*, etc:

If the finite form V of an auxiliary verb has type $\pi_k^r s_i x^\ell$, where $x = i, j, p_1$ or p_2, then V (with rising intonation) may be assigned the type $q_i x^\ell \pi_k^\ell$.

For example, this metarule will account for the following questions:

does he go?	with *does* of type $q_1 i^\ell \pi_3^\ell$,
is he going?	with *is* of type $q_1 p_1^\ell \pi_3^\ell$,
was I seen –?	with *was* of type $q_2 o^{\ell\ell} p_2^\ell \pi_1^\ell$,
has he gone?	with *has* of type $q_1 p_2^\ell \pi_3^\ell$,
will he be going?	with *will* of type $q_1 j^\ell \pi^\ell$.

It will also account for:

does he not go?

is he not going?

etc. However, to account for

doesn't he go?

isn't he going?

etc, we must allow the contracted forms *doesn't, isn't*, etc as values for V in the metarule. Indeed, in Section 6 below, we shall assign to them exactly the same types as to *does, is*, etc.

The types q_i may be useful in handling other inversions, though without rising intonation, for example:

Seldom does he sleep, never did he yawn.

Here we may assign type $s_i q^\ell$ to *seldom* and *never*, $i = 1$ or 2.

3.3 Wh-questions

We shall now look at questions such as *whom does he see –?*

I realize that many people, even some linguists, say *who* instead of *whom*, but I shall follow Inspector Morse in distinguishing between the two. (To account for the distinction between *whom* or *who* and *what* we would have to subdivide type π_3 into animate versus inanimate, something I hesitate to do in this preliminary sketch of English grammar.)

We shall take the view that a Wh-question is a request to complete a statement, present or past, and is itself without tense. We assign type q' to all questions, interrogative as well as Wh-questions, hence we must postulate $q \leq q'$.

Noting that *does he see* has type

$$(q_1 i^\ell \pi_3^\ell)\pi_3(i o^\ell) \leq q_1 o^\ell,$$

we are led to assign type $q' o^{\ell\ell} q_1^\ell$ to *whom*, so that *whom does he see – ?* has type

$$(q' o^{\ell\ell} q_1^\ell)(q_1 o^\ell) = q'(o^{\ell\ell}(q_1^\ell q_1)o^\ell) \leq q'.$$

But *whom* also occurs in *whom did he see –?*, which suggests also type $q' o^{\ell\ell} q_2^\ell$ for *whom*. These two type assignments may be combined into $q' o^{\ell\ell} q^\ell$, if we recall that $q_k \leq q$.

Surprisingly, the same type assignment will work for *whom did she say she saw -?* Here *she saw* has type $s_2 o^\ell \leq s o^\ell$ and *did she say* has type $q_2 s^\ell \leq q s^\ell$, so we may calculate

$$(q' o^{\ell\ell} q^\ell)(q_2 s^\ell)(s_2 o^\ell) \leq q'(o^{\ell\ell}(q^\ell q_2)(s^\ell s_2)o^\ell) \leq q'.$$

The situation is a little more complicated for the nominative form *who*. To account for *who is/was going?* we are led to assign to *who* the type $q' s^\ell \pi_3$. However, in *who did she say - is going?*, *did she say* has type $q_2 s^\ell$, *is going* has type $\pi_3^r s_1$, hence we require *who* to have type $q' s^\ell \pi_3 s^{\ell\ell} q^\ell$ so that we can calculate

$$(q' s^\ell \pi_3 s^{\ell\ell} q^\ell)(q_2 s^\ell)(\pi_3^r s) \leq q'.$$

Fortunately, this second type assignment is now stable, it will also account for

$$\text{who did she say he believes – is going?}$$

as it is easily calculated that

$$(q' s^\ell \pi_3 s^{\ell\ell} q^\ell)(q_2 s^\ell)(s_1 s^\ell)(\pi_3^r s) \leq q'.$$

We can thus handle unbounded dependencies. However, it is known that some constraints are necessary, as one does not wish to admit

$$\text{*whom did she see John and –?}$$

and similar non-sentences. I still hope to find a reason why these are ruled out.

Unfortunately, the above non-sentence will receive type q' if *and* is here given type $o^r o o^\ell$. Perhaps it is relevant to observe that this non- sentence will have type $q' o^{\ell\ell} o^\ell o o^r o o^\ell$ at the penultimate stage of its type calculation and that one must defer the contractions $o^{\ell\ell} o^\ell \leq 1$ and $o^\ell o \leq 1$ until after the contraction $o o^r \leq 1$ has been carried out.

Note that we cannot say *who am going?* and *who are going?*, so *who* does not have type $q' s^\ell \pi_1$ or $q' s^\ell \pi_2$. Concerning the confusion between *who* and *whom*, even Inspector Morse would not approve of the butler announcing:

$$\text{*whom shall I say – is calling?}$$

3.4   Discontinuous dependencies

Unfortunately, we are not quite finished with the type assignment to *whom*. It remains to consider such questions as:

whom did you see – yesterday?
whom did you see – with Jane?
whom did you see – when you left?

We shall assume that the adverb *yesterday*, the propositional phrase *with Jane* and the subordinate clause *when you left* all have type $\mathbf{i}^r\mathbf{i}$ (as did *quietly* in Section 2.2). Then we must assign to *whom* the new type $\mathbf{q}'\mathbf{i}^\ell\mathbf{io}^{\ell\ell}\mathbf{q}^\ell$, so that *whom did you see* - before an adverbial phase has type

$$(\mathbf{q}'\mathbf{i}^\ell\mathbf{io}^{\ell\ell}\mathbf{q}^\ell)(\mathbf{q}_2\mathbf{i}^\ell\pi^\ell)\pi_2(\mathbf{io}^\ell)$$

$$\leq \mathbf{q}'\mathbf{i}^\ell\mathbf{io}^{\ell\ell}\mathbf{i}^\ell\mathbf{io}^\ell \leq \mathbf{q}'\mathbf{i}^\ell\mathbf{io}^{\ell\ell}\mathbf{o}^\ell \leq \mathbf{q}'\mathbf{i}^\ell\mathbf{i}.$$

In the absence of an adverbial phrase, we are justified in contracting $\mathbf{i}^\ell\mathbf{i} \leq 1$; in other words, the new type implies the old. But, if an adverbial phrase follows, this contraction should be delayed, to permit the following argument:

$$(\mathbf{q}'\mathbf{i}^\ell\mathbf{i})(\mathbf{i}^r\mathbf{i}) \leq \mathbf{q}'\mathbf{i}^\ell\mathbf{i} \leq \mathbf{q}'.$$

Yet another type assignment is required to handle

whom did you teach – English?

Here *whom* should have type $\mathbf{q}'x^\ell\mathbf{o}''^{\ell\ell}x^{\ell\ell}\mathbf{q}^\ell$, where $x = \mathbf{o}$. A similar type assignment will justify

whom did you ask – whether he is leaving?

and

whom did you ask – to leave?

where we should take $x = \overline{\mathbf{q}}$ and $x = \overline{\mathbf{i}}$ respectively, anticipating sections 4.2 and 4.4. However, there seems to be no reason for invoking an indirect object here, so *whom* should have type $\mathbf{q}'x^\ell\mathbf{o}^{\ell\ell}x^{\ell\ell}\mathbf{q}^\ell$. We recapture the original type of *whom* by taking $x = 1$.

A further complication arises when we allow both generalizations simultaneously, as in

whom did you teach – English yesterday?

for example. We shall ignore this here. Evidently, the longer the type of *whom* becomes, the less confidence we have in the present approach. Perhaps we should try to formulate an appropriate metarule instead.

4 Typing the noun phrase

4.1 Mass nouns versus count nouns.

We shall use $\mathbf{n}$ as the type of names and other singular noun phrases. We postulate

$$\mathbf{n} \leq \pi_3, \quad \mathbf{n} \leq \mathbf{o}$$

to ensure that names can occupy the subject or object position of a sentence. We will use $\hat{\mathbf{n}}$ for plural noun phrases, such as *many people*, and postulate $\hat{\mathbf{n}} \leq \pi_2$, $\mathbf{n} \leq \mathbf{o}$.

Most noun phrases are made up from nouns preceded by determiners, such as articles, quantifiers or numerals. We distinguish three types of nouns:

mass nouns of type $\mathbf{m}$, e.g. *water, pork*;
count nouns of type $\mathbf{c}$, e.g. *apple, pig*;
plurals of type $\mathbf{p}$, e.g. *police, pigs*.

Typical determiners are *much* of type $\mathbf{nm}^\ell$, *one* of type $\mathbf{nc}^\ell$ and *many* of type $\mathbf{np}^\ell$, as in:

much pork, one pig, many pigs.

Many determiners have several types, in fact the article *the* has all three of the above. Mass nouns and plurals can have zero determiners, which we will express with the help of two postulates:

$$\mathbf{m} \leq \mathbf{n}, \quad \mathbf{p} \leq \hat{\mathbf{n}}.$$

But we don't have $\mathbf{c} \leq \mathbf{n}$, to the consternation of many Slavs!

The types $\mathbf{c}$ and $\mathbf{m}$ are not rigidly attached to the associated nouns. Some type shifting may occur accompanied by a corresponding shift in meaning. For example, while *beer* usually has type $\mathbf{m}$ and *man* almost always has type $\mathbf{c}$, one may order *two beers* in a tavern and a cannibal may *prefer man to pork*.

Sometimes names can also be used as count nouns, as in

six Nguyens were registered in my course.

This is not the case for other noun phrases and suggests that $\mathbf{n}$ should really be split into two types.

Most plurals arise from count nouns by adding a morpheme $+s$, e.g. *pigs* may be analyzed as *pig* $+s$, which seems to suggest the morpheme $+s$ has type $\mathbf{c}^r\mathbf{p}$. On the other hand, the best we can do with *men* is to analyze it as Plur *man*, the plural of *man*, which suggests the inflector Plur has type $\mathbf{pc}^\ell$. In a production grammar we would postulate

$$\text{Plur } pig \geq pig +s \geq pigs,$$

but it seems difficult to incorporate such rules into a type grammar.

The contrast between mass nouns and count nouns reflects an early dispute in Greek philosophy, concerning substance versus discrete entitites, and in Greek mathematics, concerning measuring versus counting. The dispute in mathematics was resolved by Eudoxus, who essentially invented what we now call Dedekind cuts; the dispute in philosophy was resolved by Aristotle, who suggested that to measure water is to count *cups of water*. Linguistically, we could type the expression Plur *cup of water* as:

$$(\mathbf{pc}^\ell)\mathbf{c}(\mathbf{c}^r\,\mathbf{cm}^\ell)\mathbf{m} \le \mathbf{p}.$$

4.2 Propositional noun phrases

Behaving much like noun phrases are indirect sentences, namely indirect statements of type $\bar{\mathbf{s}}$ and indirect questions of type $\bar{\mathbf{q}}$. (I suppose this use of the bar bears some correlation to that in the literature.) For example:

that he goes has type $\bar{\mathbf{s}}$,
whether he went has type $\bar{\mathbf{q}}$.

We are led to assign types $\bar{\mathbf{s}}\mathbf{s}^\ell$ and $\bar{\mathbf{q}}\mathbf{s}^\ell$ to the so-called complementizers *that* and *whether* respectively.

Indirect sentences can appear both in subject and in object position. To take care of the former, we postulate $\bar{\mathbf{s}} \le \mathbf{n}$ and $\bar{\mathbf{q}} \le \mathbf{n}$, so that $\bar{\mathbf{s}} \le \pi_3$ and $\bar{\mathbf{q}} \le \pi_3$. To take care of the latter, we assign types $\mathbf{i}\bar{\mathbf{s}}^\ell$ and $\mathbf{i}\bar{\mathbf{q}}^\ell$ to certain verbs such as *say* and *know*.

Thus we can account for

whether he went does not concern me

of type $\bar{\mathbf{q}}(\pi_3^r \mathbf{s}_1) \le \mathbf{s}_1$ and

I did not say that he is going

of type

$$(\mathbf{s}_2\mathbf{i}^\ell)(\mathbf{i}\bar{\mathbf{s}}^\ell)\bar{\mathbf{s}} \le \mathbf{s}_2.$$

Thus, we must allow *say* to have not only type $\mathbf{i}\mathbf{s}^\ell$ as before, but also type $\mathbf{i}\bar{\mathbf{s}}^\ell$ and $\mathbf{i}\bar{\mathbf{q}}^\ell$. Presumably, this multiplicity of type assignments calls for some unification. In object position, $\bar{\mathbf{s}}$ can usually be replaced by $\mathbf{s}$, but in subject position the complementizer *that* is obligatory. It remains to be explained why this complementizer cannot occur before a trace.

4.3   Indirect Wh-questions

There are also indirect Wh-questions which can be assigned type $\overline{\mathbf{q}}$, for example in:

I don't know whom he saw –

of type

$$(\mathbf{s}_1\overline{\mathbf{q}}^\ell)(\overline{\mathbf{q}}\mathbf{o}^{\ell\ell}\mathbf{s}^\ell)(\mathbf{s}_3\mathbf{o}^\ell) \leq \mathbf{s}_1,$$

provided we assign yet another type $\overline{\mathbf{q}}\mathbf{o}^{\ell\ell}\mathbf{s}^\ell$ to *whom* in this context. The same assignment will work in:

I don't know whom she says he saw –.

Of course, to account for indirect questions of type $\overline{\mathbf{q}}$ such as

whom he saw – yesterday,   whom you taught – English

we require modified or additional types for *whom*, as we did for direct questions. The easiest way to accomplish this is with the help of a metarule:

if *whom* has type $\mathbf{q}' \cdots \mathbf{q}^\ell$ in a direct question, then it has type $\overline{\mathbf{q}} \cdots \mathbf{s}^\ell$ in an indirect one.

This metarule will yield types $\overline{\mathbf{q}}\mathbf{i}^\ell\mathbf{io}^{\ell\ell}\mathbf{s}^\ell$ and $\overline{\mathbf{q}}x\mathbf{o}'^{\ell\ell}x^{\ell\ell}\mathbf{s}^\ell$, with $x = \mathbf{o}, \overline{\mathbf{q}}$ or $\overline{\mathbf{i}}$, for *whom*.

As in direct questions, we seem to require two types for *who*, $\overline{\mathbf{q}}\mathbf{s}^\ell\pi_3$ and $\overline{\mathbf{q}}\mathbf{s}^\ell\pi_3\mathbf{s}^{\ell\ell}\mathbf{s}^\ell$, to account for *who is going* of type

$$(\overline{\mathbf{q}}\mathbf{s}^\ell\pi_3)(\pi_3^\ell\mathbf{s}_1) \leq \overline{\mathbf{q}}$$

and *who she said – is going* of type

$$(\overline{\mathbf{q}}\mathbf{s}^\ell\pi_3\mathbf{s}^{\ell\ell}\mathbf{s}^\ell)(\mathbf{s}_2\mathbf{s}^\ell)(\pi_3^r\mathbf{s}_1) \leq \overline{\mathbf{q}}.$$

Note that $\mathbf{s}^{\ell\ell}\mathbf{s}^\ell \leq 1$, so $\overline{\mathbf{q}}\mathbf{s}^\ell\pi_3\mathbf{s}^{\ell\ell}\mathbf{s}^\ell \leq \overline{\mathbf{q}}\mathbf{s}^\ell\pi_3$, hence the second type would do for both examples. However, it would be a mistake to contract $\mathbf{s}^{\ell\ell}\mathbf{s}^\ell$ to 1 when interpreting *who she said – is going*.

4.4   Infinitival noun phrases and gerunds

There are other expressions that should be assigned type $\overline{\mathbf{q}}$, e.g.

whether to go, whom to see –

Let us provisionally assign type $\overline{\mathbf{i}}$ to *to go*, hence $\overline{\mathbf{i}}\mathbf{o}^\ell$ to *to see*, then we are led to supply *to*, *whether* and *whom* in this context with types $\overline{\mathbf{i}}\mathbf{j}^\ell, \overline{\mathbf{q}}\overline{\mathbf{i}}^\ell$ and $\overline{\mathbf{q}}\mathbf{o}^{\ell\ell}\overline{\mathbf{i}}^\ell$ respectively.

If we now look at

I may wish to go, you may want to go

we are led to say that *wish* and *want* have type $\mathbf{ii}^{\vec{-}\ell}$. However, we shall here refrain from typing the more elaborate sentences

I may wish for him to go, you may want her to go,

where *for* seems to be another kind of complementizer. These expressions correspond to the Latin "accusative with infinitive".

We shall also here refrain from typing gerunds such as

him seeing her, his seeing her,

which form some kind of noun phrases, the second construction being obligatory in subject position. But we will point out that participles of transitive verbs can also be used to form mass nouns, such as: *killing of pigs*. On the other hand, the similar construction *killer of pigs* must be treated as a count noun.

One is tempted to assign the types $\mathbf{oi}^r\mathbf{c}$ and $\mathbf{oi}^r\mathbf{m}$ to the morphemes $+ing$ and $+er$ respectively. However, it is not clear how to establish a systematic link between the inflector Part of type $\mathbf{p}_1\mathbf{i}^\ell$ and the morpheme $+ing$ for transitive verbs. In a production grammar one can state a rule:

$$V + ing \leq \text{Part } V$$

for any infinitivial verb form V, but how can such a rule be incorporated into a type grammar?

4.5 Relative clauses

The words *who* and *whom* also appear in relative clauses, of which there are two kinds: the nonrestrictive ones which modify a name or noun phrase and the restrictive ones which modify a noun.

The nonrestrictive relative clauses should have type $\mathbf{n}^r\mathbf{n}$, so in *John, who left* we assign to *who* the type $\mathbf{n}^r\mathbf{ns}^\ell\mathbf{n}$. Here we have exploited the facts that $\mathbf{n} \leq \pi_3$ and $\mathbf{s}_2 \leq \mathbf{s}$. On the other hand, in *John, whom I saw -*, we assign to *whom* the type $\mathbf{n}^r\mathbf{no}^{\ell\ell}\mathbf{s}^\ell$. Like the interrogative pronoun *whom*, this should be modified to account for such clauses as

whom I saw – yesterday, whom I saw – leave.

Incidentally, it is not a good idea to treat the relative and interrogative pronouns in common, since they have different inanimate versions *which* and *what* respectively.

The restrictive relative clause should have type $x^r x$, where $x = \mathbf{c}, \mathbf{m}$ or $\mathbf{p}$. The most economic way to handle the restrictive relative pronouns *who* and *whom* is to assign to them the types $x^r x s^\ell \mathbf{n}$ and $x^r x o^{\ell\ell} s^\ell$ respectively. Both *who* and *whom*, when occurring restrictively, can be replaced by *that*, so this should be assigned the same types. However, the restrictive *whom* can be left out altogether, as in

$$\textit{the man I saw - , people I know -.}$$

This causes a problem: should the type of *whom* be attached to a zero morpheme, advocated e.g. by Moortgat? At one time I thought of assigning a new type to the article *the* in *the man I saw -*, namely $\mathbf{no}^{\ell\ell} s^\ell c^\ell$, but this would not help with *people I know-*.

If we don't like naked types or zero morphemes, there is another way: we could adopt the rule

$$x s o^\ell \leq x.$$

In either case, we must abandon the attempt to push all the grammar into the dictionary. If the second remedy is adopted, as I prefer, this means that there are grammatical rules in addition to the type assignments, hence our protogroup is no longer free. Having accepted this, we can also explain *the man that I saw - by the rule

$$x \bar{s} o^\ell \leq x,$$

rather than assign a new type to *that*.

4.6 Adjectives

Once we have decided to abolish freeness, we can also attack other problems, for example, how to handle adjectives. While adjectives modifying nouns could be assigned types $x x^\ell$, with $x = \mathbf{c}, \mathbf{m}$ or $\mathbf{p}$, as in *the good old man*, this won't work for adjectives in predicative position, as in **the man is good old*. I think it is best to adopt a new basic type $\mathbf{a}$ for all adjectives and account for their attributive function by the rule

$$\mathbf{a} x \to x.$$

Their predicative function can be handled by assigning an appropriate type to the copula *be*. Thus, in *John may be old*, *be old* should have type $\mathbf{j}$, hence *be* the type $\mathbf{j a}^\ell$. To account for *John is old*, we recognize *is* as the third person present tense of *be*, that is, we decompose it as $C_{13} be$ of type

$$(\pi_3^r \mathbf{s}_1 \mathbf{j}^\ell)(\mathbf{j a}^\ell) \leq \pi_3^r \mathbf{s}_1 \mathbf{a}^\ell.$$

Occasionally adjectives can also modify names, as in *poor John*, but not other noun phrases, thus supporting the remark near the end of Section 4.1 that $\mathbf{n}$ should be split into two types.

Among adjectives we should also count present participles of intransitive verbs and past participles of transitive verbs as in

$$\textit{the bird flying past , the kettle watched by him,}$$
$$\textit{water boiling , a woman scorned.}$$

Thus, we should adopt the rules

$$x\mathbf{p}_1 \leq x \quad , \quad x\mathbf{p}_2\mathbf{o}^\ell \leq x,$$

where $x = \mathbf{c}, \mathbf{m}$ or $\mathbf{p}$.

4.7   Historical digression

My early work on what I called the "syntactic calculus" was inspired by ideas from logic (type theory) and homological algebra. As it turned out, it had been partly anticipated by Ajdukiewicz and Bar-Hillel, and similar ideas were being pursued independently by Curry on what, in retrospect, should be called "semantic types", later to give rise to Montague semantics.

Ajdukiewicz, influenced by Husserl, had explored the rule $(c/b)b \leq c$, and Bar-Hillel distinguished this from the rule $a(a\backslash c) \leq c$ (in my notation). In my own work, I explored a more general setup:

$$ab \leq c \Leftrightarrow a \leq c/b \Leftrightarrow b \leq a\backslash c.$$

After assigning types $\mathbf{n}$, $\mathbf{n}\backslash\mathbf{s}$ and $\mathbf{s}/(\mathbf{n}\backslash\mathbf{s})$ to *John, goes* and *he* respectively, one could then prove not only that *John goes* has type $\mathbf{n}(\mathbf{n}\backslash\mathbf{s}) \leq \mathbf{s}$, and *he goes* has type $(\mathbf{s}/(\mathbf{n}\backslash\mathbf{s}))(\mathbf{n}\backslash\mathbf{s}) \leq \mathbf{s}$, but also that $\mathbf{n} \leq \mathbf{s}/(\mathbf{n}\backslash\mathbf{s})$, which may be interpreted as saying that every name also has the type of a pronoun.

Over time, I have vacillated between the associative and the non-associative syntactic calculus. Although the latter has recently gained popularity, e.g. in the work of Moortgat and Oehrle, who introduce special modality operators for licensing associativity, I shall here stick to the associative calculus. I have also vacillated between the syntactic calculus with 1 and that without 1, 1 being the type of the empty string. I may take this opportunity to point out that the latter is not a conservative extension of the former, since, in the presence of 1, we have

$$a = a1 \leq a(b/b),$$

but $a \leq a(b/b)$ does not hold in the original syntactic calculus, unless we give it a Gentzen style presentation allowing empty strings of types on the left of a sequent.

Poset models of the syntactic calculus are known as "residuated semigroups" or "residuated monoids", the latter if the unity element 1 of the semigroup is admitted. One may think of 1 as the type of the empty string. By an "AB-monoid" I shall understand a poset model of the original system of Ajdukiewicz as modified by Bar- Hillel, provided the type 1 is incorporated.

The protogroups we have studied here are special cases of AB-monoids, as in an AB- monoid one can define

$$a^r = a\backslash 1, \quad a^\ell = 1/a.$$

But also, conversely, in a protogroup one can define

$$c/b = cb^\ell, \quad a\backslash c = a^r c.$$

although these two definitions are not inverse to one another.

My early work on the syntactic calculus was largely ignored by the linguistic community and I myself became converted to the generative-transformational grammars pioneered by Chomsky. However, in recent years there has been a revival of interest in categorial grammars based on the syntactic calculus, largely initiated by van Benthem. Far reaching applications to natural languages were made by Casadio, Moortgat, Morrill and Oehrle among others. Much important work was done in resolving theoretical questions associated with the syntactic calculus viewed as a formal system, for example by Buszkowski, Došen, Kanazawa, Kandulski, Mikulás and Pentus. There were also a number of excellent doctoral dissertations written in the Netherlands, mostly directed by van Benthem. For detailed references see Moortgat [1997].

A new impetus was given to this revival of interest after the influential introduction of (classical commutative) linear logic into computer science by Girard, when it was realized that the syntactic calculus was just the multiplicative fragment of intuitionistic non-commutative linear logic, or "bilinear logic", as I prefer to call it. It was the brilliant insight by Claudia Casadio that classical bilinear logic could also be used in linguistics which prompted me to take another look at type grammars.

It so happens that the multiplicative fragment of classical bilinear logic had been studied by Grishin [1983] even before the advent of linear logic. Unfortunately, his article was published in Russian. I have called poset models of this logic "Grishin monoids". They are residuated monoids with a dualizing object 0 satisfying

$$0/(a\backslash 0) = a = (0/a)\backslash 0.$$

It will be convenient to write

$$a\backslash 0 = a^r, \quad 0/a = a^\ell,$$

so that $a^{r\ell} = a = a^{\ell r}$. It is easily shown that

$$(b^\ell a^\ell)^r = (b^r a^r)^\ell,$$

for which I have written $a + b$, although Girard in his commutative version has used an upside-down ampersand in place of $+$. We may think of $a + b$ as the De Morgan dual of $a \cdot b$.

We now have

$$aa^r \leq 0, \quad 1 \leq a^r + a; \quad a^\ell a \leq 0, \quad 1 \leq a + a^\ell,$$

and we may introduce

$$c/b = c + b^\ell, \quad a\backslash c = a^r + c.$$

To show the first of these, for example, one proceeds thus:

$$(c/b)b = (c + b^\ell)b \leq c + (b^\ell b) \leq c + 0 = c,$$

making use of one of what Grishin calls "mixed associative laws" (and what Cockett and Seely at one time called "weak distributive laws"), which are easily proved:

$$(a + b)c \leq a + (bc), \quad c(a + b) \leq (ca) + b.$$

Classical bilinear logic, or rather its multiplicative fragment, is known to be a conservative extension of the syntactic calculus, as follows e.g. from the work of Abrusci.

After listening to Claudia's exposition of her ideas, I felt that there were too many operations and that it might be reasonable to require that

$$a + b = a \cdot b, \quad 0 = 1,$$

rendering the Grishin monoid "compact". (This word, attributed to Max Kelly, had been used by Barr in a similar context, namely that of star-autonomous categories.)

One reason for proposing compactness has to do with Gentzen style deductions for bilinear logic. These have the form $\alpha \to \beta$, when α and β are strings of formulas, here types. According to Gentzen, juxtaposition on the left of an arrow should stand for the tensor product, here represented by a dot (usually omitted), a kind of non-commutative conjunction, and juxtaposition on the right should stand for its De Morgan dual, here denoted by $+$. However, we know that one way to describe the grammar of a natural language is with the help of rewrite rules, or productions, $\alpha \to \beta$, where juxtaposition on the two sides of the arrow (corresponding to our $\geq$) has exactly the same interpretation.

I should say a word about the proofnets proposed by Girard for checking proofs in linear logic geometrically. Many people have been enthusiastic about this method, even in linguistic applications. Although, following Descartes, I personally have held the opposing view that one should use algebra to explicate geometry and not vice versa, in the present context even I must admit the advantage of the geometric method. To verify that a string α of types ultimately contracts to the single type b it is necessary and sufficient that one can draw non-crossing linkages for all generalized contractions. I had planned to illustrate this method by a single example:

whom did Jane say she saw –?

$$(q'o^{\ell\ell}q^\ell) \; (q_2 i^\ell \pi_3^\ell) \; \mathbf{n} \; (is^\ell) \; \pi_3 \; (\pi^\ell s_2 o^\ell)$$

Unfortunately the typist has difficulty drawing the linkages; but the reader can easily supply them by linking corresponding left and right parentheses in the following:

$$\mathbf{q}'(\mathbf{o}^{\ell\ell}(\mathbf{q}^\ell \mathbf{q}_2)(\mathbf{i}^\ell(\pi_3^\ell \mathbf{n})\mathbf{i})(\mathbf{s}^\ell(\pi_3 \pi^\ell)\mathbf{s}_2)\mathbf{o}^\ell).$$

5 Pregroups

From now on, I shall call a compact Grishin monoid a "pregroup". A *pregroup* is just an ordered monoid in which each element a has both a left adjoint a^ℓ and a right adjoint a^r such that

$$a^\ell a \leq 1 \leq aa^\ell, \quad aa^r \leq 1 \leq a^r a.$$

These adjoints can be defined in terms of residual quotients:

$$a^\ell = 1/a, \quad a^r = a\backslash 1.$$

Conversely, one may recover the residual quotients from the adjoints:

$$a/b = ab^\ell, \quad b\backslash a = b^r a.$$

Again, these two definitions are not inverse to one another, see the argument at the end of this section.

Pregroups are easily seen to be the same as protogroups which satisfy the equations (E) and the implications (I) of Section 1. For example, under these conditions we have

$$a^r a = a^r a^{\ell r} = (a^\ell a)^r \geq 1^r = 1.$$

If we stipulate $a^r = a^\ell$ (the so-called "cyclic" case), the pregroup becomes an ordered group. One advantage of pregroups over protogroups is this: the dual of a pregroup, replacing $\leq$ by $\geq$ and interchanging r and ℓ, is also a pregroup.

At the time of writing this, I know of only one example of a non-cyclic pregroup, aside from the free pregroups to be considered presently. This is the ordered monoid of unbounded order preserving mappings $\mathbb{Z} \to \mathbb{Z}$. To see that this is not cyclic, take $f(n) = 2n$ and calculate

$$f^r(n) = [n/2], \quad f^\ell(n) = [(n+1)/2].$$

where $[x]$ denotes the greatest integer $\leq x$.

The *free pregroup* $F(A)$ generated by a poset A is defined like the free protogroup of Section 1, only now there is an additional case in the definition of $\alpha \leq \beta$, to be called an *expansion*:

Case 3. $\qquad\qquad \alpha_i = \gamma\delta, \alpha_{i+1} = \gamma a^{(n)} a^{(n-1)}\delta.$

It is easily verified that $F(A)$ is a pregroup with the expected universal property.

A *generalized expansion* has the form

$$\gamma\delta \leq \gamma a^{(n)} b^{(n-1)}\delta,$$

where n is odd and $a \leq b$ in A or n is even and $b \leq a$ in A.

The following proposition will yield an effective procedure for deciding when $\alpha \leq \beta$, for elements α, β of $F(A)$. While the corresponding problem for free residuated monoids was solved with the help of a technique borrowed from logic, namely Gentzen's method of cut elimination, the present decision procedure (like that for protogroups) is borrowed from highschool algebra, where one simplifies each side of a potential equation as much as possible, expecting to arrive at a common answer.

Proposition 2. *If $\alpha \leq \beta$ in a free pregroup, then there exist strings α' and β' such that $\alpha \leq \alpha' \leq \beta' \leq \beta$, where $\alpha \leq \alpha'$ by generalized contractions only, $\alpha' \leq \beta'$ by induced steps only and $\beta' \leq \beta$ by generalized expansions only.*

Proof. Consider a sequence

$$\alpha \leq \alpha_1 \leq \alpha_2 \leq \cdots \leq \alpha_n = \beta$$

in $F(A)$, where each step is induced from A or is a generalized contraction or expansion. We claim that all generalized expansions can be postponed to the end, after which the proof of Proposition 1 takes over.

Indeed, suppose a generalized expansion, say

$$\gamma\delta \leq \gamma a^{(n+1)} b^{(n)} \delta,$$

with n odd and $a \leq b$ in A, immediately precedes an induced step, say

$$\gamma a^{(n+1)} b^{(n)} \delta \leq \gamma a^{(n+1)} c^{(n)} \delta,$$

where $b \leq c$ in A, then we may combine these two steps into a single generalized expansion with $a \leq c$. (Other subcases of this situation are left to the reader.)

Suppose a generalized expansion is immediately followed by a generalized contraction, then we have essentially two cases:

Case A. Say m odd, $a \leq b$, n even and $c \leq d$, so that

$$\gamma\lambda b^{(m)} a^{(m+1)} \delta \leq \gamma c^{(n)} d^{(n-1)} \lambda b^{(m)} a^{(m+1)} \delta \leq \gamma c^{(n)} d^{(n-1)} \lambda \delta.$$

This can be replaced by

$$\gamma\lambda b^{(m)} a^{(m+1)} \delta \leq \gamma\lambda\delta \leq \gamma c^{(n)} d^{(n-1)} \lambda \delta.$$

(Other subcases are treated similarly.)

Case B. Say n odd and $a \leq b \leq c$, then

$$\gamma a^{(n)} \delta \leq \gamma a^{(n)} b^{(n-1)} c^{(n)} \delta \leq \gamma c^{(n)} \delta.$$

This can be replaced by a single induced step. (Other subcases are treated similarly.)

Corollary 1. *If $\alpha \leq \beta$ and β has length 1, one can go from α to β by contractions and induced steps only.*

Can we use pregroups in place of protogroups when looking at English grammar? Whereas a pregroup may be viewed as a residuated monoid satisfying

$$1 \leq (a\backslash 1)a, \quad 1 \leq a(1/a),$$

these inequalities are not justified by the usual models of the syntactic calculus, e.g. the monoid of subsets of the free monoid generated by the English vocabulary. Fortunately, they play no role in checking the sentencehood of a string of words. For, in view of the above corollary, to verify $\alpha \leq \mathbf{s}$ requires contractions and induced steps only, just as though we were operating in a free protogroup instead of a free pregroup.

While pregroups may be more interesting mathematically than protogroups, what can they do for linguistics that protogroups can't? We shall look at a few potential applications.

The phrase *does not*, often contracted to *doesn't*, has type

$$(\pi_3^r \mathbf{s}_1 \mathbf{i}^\ell)(\mathbf{i}\mathbf{i}^\ell) \leq \pi_3^r \mathbf{s}_1 \mathbf{i}^\ell.$$

However, using the expansion $1 \leq \mathbf{i}\mathbf{i}^\ell$, we can reverse the inequality, hence obtain equality. Perhaps this observation lends some weight to the suggestion in Section 3.2 that *doesn't* should be regarded as a verb form.

We have analyzed *he goes* and *John goes* as $\pi_3(\pi_3^r \mathbf{s}_1)$ and $\mathbf{n}(\pi_3^r \mathbf{s}_1)$ respectively and justified $\mathbf{n}(\pi_3^r \mathbf{s}_1) \leq \mathbf{s}_1$ by postulating $\mathbf{n} \leq \pi_3$. An alternative approach, in the spirit of my older work, would be to give to *goes* the type $\mathbf{n}^r \mathbf{s}_1$ and to define π_3 as $\mathbf{s}_1 \mathbf{s}_1^\ell \mathbf{n}$. Then $\mathbf{n} \leq \pi_3$ could be proved as a consequence of $1 \leq \mathbf{s}_1 \mathbf{s}_1^\ell$ and need not be postulated. The only problem with this approach is that it won't account for *he went*, which would require that *he* has two types: not only $\mathbf{s}_1 \mathbf{s}_1^\ell \mathbf{n}$, but also $\mathbf{s}_2 \mathbf{s}_2^\ell \mathbf{n}$. Since π_3 cannot be defined to be equal to both of them, we would have to dispense with π_3 altogether.

This problem would not arise with *him*, which pronoun could be assigned the single type $\mathbf{n}\mathbf{i}^r \mathbf{i}$. In a similar fashion we can treat *it* and *so* in

you may be saying so, you may have said it.

I would assign to *so* the type $\mathbf{s}\mathbf{i}^r \mathbf{i}$ and to *it* the type $\bar{\mathbf{s}}\mathbf{i}^r \mathbf{i}$, assuming that *saying* and *said* here have types $(\mathbf{p}_1 \mathbf{i}^r)(\mathbf{i}\mathbf{s}^\ell)$ and $(\mathbf{p}_2 \mathbf{i}^r)(\mathbf{i}^r \bar{\mathbf{s}}^\ell)$ respectively.

Of course the extension of a free residuated monoid into a pregroup is not conservative, since $(1/a)\backslash 1 = a$ holds in the latter but not in the former. Unfortunately, the same objection applies to the extension of a free residuated semigroup, since after the extension we obtain the equation

$$a(b/c) = abc^\ell = (ab)/c,$$

which does not hold originally. This objection already applies to embedding a free AB-semigroup into a protogroup.

6 Concluding remarks

This article advocates a number of ideas, which are essentially independent of one another:

(1) to use classical bilinear logic in place of the syntactic calculus, as had been suggested by Claudia Casadio;
(2) to allow the set of basic types to be partially ordered;
(3) to require ordered models of the resulting calculus to be freely generated by the poset of basic types, thus ensuring that all grammatical information is found in the dictionary;
(4) to simplify the algebra by identifying multiplication with addition, its De Morgan dual, hence the unit 1 with the dualizing object 0 (since $1 = 1 + 0 = 1 \cdot 0 = 0$).

Of these ideas, I share Casadio's confidence in (1). (2) is quite useful, though not essential, as it can be circumvented by multiple type assignments. (3) proved useful as a starting point, but ultimately had to be abandoned when confronted with typed zero morphemes, as in

$$people \quad \emptyset \quad I \ know \ -$$

$$\mathbf{p} \ (\mathbf{p}^r \mathbf{p} \mathbf{o}^{\ell\ell} \mathbf{s}^\ell) \pi_1 (\pi_1^r \mathbf{s}_1 \mathbf{o}^\ell)$$

or with the equivalent postulate

$$\mathbf{pso}^\ell \leq \mathbf{p}.$$

It would appear that a speaker of English can avoid such constructions, in this example by replacing the zero morpheme by *that.* Anyway, there is no problem with generating *people I know* -; all one has to do is to suppress the complementizer *that.* The difficulty arises with recognition, as illustrated by the well-known example:

$$the \ horse \ raced \ - \ past \ the \ barn \ fell,$$

where recognition depends on the postulate

$$\mathbf{cp}_2 \mathbf{o}^\ell \mathbf{i}^r \mathbf{i} \leq \mathbf{c}.$$

Finally, (4) causes serious problems when we want the grammar to account for semantics in the spirit of Curry and Montague. The syntactic calculus carries with it an implicit semantics: by introducing Gentzen's three structural rules, interchange, contraction and thinning, one essentially turns it into Curry's semantic calculus. On the level of proofs rather than provability, the syntactic calculus may be viewed as a biclosed monoidal category and the semantic calculus as a cartesian closed category. Since cartesian closed categories are known to be equivalent to lambda calculi, Montague semantics arises naturally.

Unfortunately, the compact bilinear logic advocated in (4) is not a conservative extension of the syntactic calculus, hence its relationship with semantics is less evident. Perhaps we should retreat and abandon compactness, thus returning to Casadio's original suggestion?

Indeed, many of the linguistic examples studied here can also be handled without compactness. All one has to do is to replace multiplication of types inside a word by addition, but to allow multiplication between words to stand.

Consider, for instance, the example:

I may be going.

$$\pi_1(\pi^r + s_1 + j^\ell)(j + p_1^\ell)p_1$$

We calculate successive initial segments of the associated string of types, making use of the mixed associative laws:

$$\pi_1(\pi^r + s_1 + j^\ell) \leq (\pi_1\pi^r) + s_1 + j^\ell \leq 0 + s_1 + j^\ell = s_1 + j^\ell;$$

$$(s_1 + j^\ell)(j + p_1^\ell) \leq s_1 + j^\ell(j + p_1^\ell) \leq s_1 + (j^\ell j) + p_1^\ell \leq s_1 + 0 + p_1^\ell = s_1 + p_1^\ell;$$

$$(s_1 + p_1^\ell)p_1 \leq s_1 + (p_1^\ell p_1) \leq s_1 + 0 = s_1.$$

Similarly, looking at

did he see her?

$$(q_2 + i^\ell + \pi^\ell)\pi_3(i + o^\ell)o$$

we calculate successive initial segments, making implicit use of mixed associativity:

$$q_2 + i^\ell, \quad q_2 + o^\ell, \quad q_2.$$

A problem arises with examples involving double negation such as $o^{\ell\ell}$, indicative of a Chomskian trace. Consider

I may be seen –

$$\pi_1(\pi^r + s_1 + j^\ell)(j + o^{\ell\ell} + p_2^\ell)(p_2 + o^\ell)$$

The initial segments here are:

$$s_1 + j^\ell, \quad s_1 + o^{\ell\ell} + p_2^\ell, \quad s_1 + o^{\ell\ell} + o^\ell.$$

Unfortunately, the last does not contract to s_1, unless $o^{\ell\ell} + o^\ell \leq 0$. This would however follow from $o^{\ell\ell}o^\ell \leq 1$ by compactness.

Similar, consider:

whom did you see –?

$$(q' + o^{\ell\ell} + q^\ell)(q_2 + i^\ell + \pi^\ell)\pi_2(i + o^\ell)$$

The initial segments are:

$$q' + o^{\ell\ell} + i^\ell + \pi^\ell, \quad q' + o^{\ell\ell} + i^\ell, \quad q' + o^{\ell\ell} + o^\ell.$$

Again, compactness is required to ensure that this contracts to q'.

However, according to Claudia Casadio, there is no reason why the types inside a word should be linked only by addition. Indeed, the last two examples will work out if we assign to the passive auxiliary *be* the type $j + o^{\ell\ell}p_2^\ell$ and to the question word *whom* the type $q' + o^{\ell\ell}q^\ell$.

References

V.M. Abrusci, Sequent calculus and phase semantics for pure noncommutative classical propositional linear logic, Journal of Symbolic Logic 56 (1991), 1403–1451.

....., Lambek calculus, cyclic multiplicative - additive linear logic, non- commutative multiplicative - additive linear logic: language and sequent calculus; in: V.M. Abrusci and C. Casadio (eds), Proofs and linguistic categories, Proceedings 1996 Roma Workshop, Cooperativa Libraria Universitaria Editrice Bolognia (1996), 21–48.

K. Ajdukiewicz, Die syntaktische Konnexität, Studia Philosophica 1 (1937), 1–27. Translated in: S. McCall, Polish Logic 1920-1939, Claredon Press, Oxford 1967.

Y. Bar-Hillel, A quasiarithmetical notation for syntactic description, Language 29 (1953), 47–58.

M. Barr, *-Autonomous categories, Springer LNM 752 (1979).

M. Brame and Youn Gon Kim, Directed types: an algebraic theory of production and recognition, Preprint 1997.

W. Buszkowski, W. Marciszewski and J. van Benthem, Categorial grammar, John Benjamins Publ. Co., Amsterdam 1988.

C. Casadio, A categorical approach to cliticization and agreement in Italian, Editrice Bologna 1993.

....., Unbounded dependencies in noncommutative linear logic, Proceedings of the conference: Formal grammar, ESSLLI 1997, Aix en Provence.

....., Noncommutative linear logic in linguistics, Preprint 1997.

N. Chomsky, Syntactic structures, Mouton, The Hague 1957.

....., Lectures on government and binding, Foris Publications, Dordrecht 1982.

J.R.B. Cockett and R.A.G. Seely, Weakly distributive categories, J. Pure and Applied Algebra 114 (1997), 133–173.

H.B. Curry, Some logical aspects of grammatical structure, in: R. Jacobson (editor), Structure of language and its mathematical aspects, AMS Proc. Symposia Applied Mathematics 12 (1961), 56–67.

C. Dexter, The second Inspector Morse omnibus, Pan Books, London 1994.

K. Došen and P. Schroeder-Heister (eds), Substructural logics, Oxford University Press, Oxford 1993.

G. Gazdar, E. Klein, G. Pullum and I. Sag, Generalized phrase structure grammar, Harvard University Press, Cambridge Mass. 1985.

J.-Y. Girard, Linear Logic, J. Theoretical Computer Science 50 (1987), 1–102.

V.N. Grishin, On a generalization of the Ajdukiewicz-Lambek system, in: Studies in nonclassical logics and formal systems, Nauka, Moscow 1983, 315-343.

R. Jackendoff, $\overline{X}$ Syntax, a study of phrase structure, The MIT Press, Cambridge Mass. 1977.

M. Kanazawa, The Lambek calculus enriched with additional connectives, J. Logic, Language & Information 1 (1992), 141–171.

J. Lambek, The mathematics of sentence structure, Amer. Math. Monthly 65 (1958), 154-169.

....., Contribution to a mathematical analysis of the English verb-phrase, J. Canadian Linguistic Assoc. 5 (1959), 83–89.

....., On the calculus of syntactic types, AMS Proc. Symposia Applied Mathematics 12 (1961), 166–178.

....., On a connection between algebra, logic and linguistics, Diagrammes 22 (1989), 59–75.

....., Grammar as mathematics, Can. Math. Bull. 32 (1989), 257–273.

....., Production grammars revisited, Linguistic Analysis 23 (1993), 205–225.

....., From categorial grammar to bilinear logic, in: K. Došen et al. (eds) (1993), 207–237.

....., Some lattice models of bilinear logic, Algebra Universalis 34 (1995), 541–550.

....., On the nominalistic interpretation of natural languages, in: M. Marion et al. (eds), Québec Studies in Philosophy of Science I, 69-74, Kluwer, Dordrecht 1995.

....., Bilinear logic and Grishin algebras in: E. Orlowska (editor), Logic at work, Essays dedicated to the memory of Helena Rasiowa, Kluwer, Dordrecht, to appear.

S. Mikulás, The completeness of the Lambek calculus with respect to relational semantics, ITLT Prepublications for Logic, Semantics and Philosophy of Language, Amsterdam 1992.

M. Moortgat, Categorial investigations, Foris Publications, Dordrecht 1988.

......, Categorial type logic, in: J. van Benthem et al. 1997, 93–177.

G. Morrill, Type logical grammar, Kluwer, Dordrecht 1994.

R.T. Oehrle, Substructural logic and linguistic inference, Preprint 1997.

R.T. Oehrle, E. Bach and D. Wheeler (eds), Categorial grammar and natural language structures, D. Reidel Publishing Co., Dordrecht 1988.

M. Pentus, Lambek grammars are context free, Proc. 8th LICS conference (1993), 429–433.

M. Pentus, Models for the Lambek calculus, Annals Pure & Applied Logic 75 (1995), 179–213.

J. van Benthem, Language in action, Elsevier, Amsterdam 1991.

J. van Benthem and A. ter Meulen (eds), Handbook of Logic and Language, Elsevier, Amsterdam 1997.

Acknowledgements

This project was supported in part by a shared FCAR grant from the Province of Quebec. I would like to thank the audiences at 1997 conferences in Nancy and Rome for asking pertinent questions, in particular, François Lamarche for his encouragement and support and Michael Moortgat for challenging me to face some important issues. I am grateful to Claudia Casadio, not only for re-awakening my interest in this topic in the first place, but also for her constructive criticism of a preliminary manuscript. I have been encouraged by Michael Brame, who has arrived at rather similar linguistic applications, while relying on a quite different algebraic machinery. Finally, I am endebted to Michael Barr for a number of helpful comments.

Optimal Parameters

Denis Bouchard

Université du Québec à Montréal[*]

1. Parameters and Minimalism

Generative grammar has been concerned with two central questions from its outset: (i) how to characterize the linguistic knowledge of a speaker (descriptive adequacy) and (ii) explain how language is learned (explanatory adequacy). In the current stage of the framework (the Principles & Parameters approach as for example in Chomsky 1995), the answers are based on the hypothesis that UG is rich, constraining, so that acquisition reduces to narrowly defined parametric choices and the linguist must determine how the correct values can be established by experience. Variation among languages is described in terms of tightly knitted parameters, with a minor change in one setting potentially having multiple effects on the surface.

The main shift in the *minimalist* approach is that there is an increased insistance on the methodological value of the notions of simplicity and economy. There are two ways in which this is put to work in the framework, and these should not be confused. An *external* use of simplicity evaluates the parsimony of the theory, relying on conceptual necessity as is generally the case in science. By reducing the vocabulary of the theory, simplicity constrains rule formulation: it limits what processes can be formulated. For instance, following a long tradition going back at least to Aristotle, linguistic models take language to be a relation between form and meaning. Thus, Chomsky (1995) assumes that UG has only three basic components: the two levels of representation PF and LF which interact with two "external" systems — the articulatory-perceptual system (A-P) and the conceptual-intentional system (C-I) —, and a computational system that relates PF and LF.

Virtual conceptual necessity requires that the three components C_{HL}, A-P and C-I be present. Thus, one may imagine, in some mental game, that a language has no physical realizations (if humans could communicate by telepathy for example), but one cannot imagine a language with no contentful elements and no means to interpret them: so C-I is conceptually necessary. Moreover, in the absence of telepathy, information must be conveyed between humans via their sensory and motor apparatus: hence a "form" component interfacing with A-P is a virtual necessity. Given these two components of a different nature, a system is required to mediate between them. One general property of language is that the mediation between meaning and form is computational: complex meanings are expressed by small units of meaning that are combined to create larger ones. This may be instantiated by an operation like Chomsky's (1995) Select, which takes a lexical item and introduces it in the derivation, and a second procedure,the operation Merge, that combines objects, with a licensing procedure based on semantic selectional properties. Though not absolutely logically necessary—a string of lexical items could be interpreted piecemeal, in an ultratelegraphic way—, a merging operation seems to be a defining property of natural language: it is empirically unescapable, hence a virtual necessity.

In this vein, Frege's *principle of compositionality* is implicitly part of most current models of linguistic analysis. It states that "[t]he meaning of a complex expression is a function of the meaning of its parts and of their syntactic mode of combination... [This assumption is] essential to any account of the ability to understand the meaning of novel utterances on first hearing" (Kamp & Partee 1995: 135). Compositionality guides the elaboration of the C_{HL}.

There are some aspects of the minimalist program's discussion of the relation between form and meaning that appeal to *external* simplicity. However, the vast majority of appeals to external simplicity in this framework deal with one of its secondary implementations: reduction of redundancy. Eliminating redundancy is secondary in the sense that it does not really constrain rule formulation: it just removes one formulation of equal power with another that is maintained. Less redundancy may help state some generalizations in a simpler way or make them more transparent because their effects are not spread over two components, but it does not have the impact of constraining rule formulation by considerations of necessity.

For instance, Chomsky (1995) argues that the level of D-Structure should be eliminated because the information it provides for interpretation is recoverable from LF. D-Structure presents an array of items from the lexicon in an X-bar format from which the computation proceeds. It is indeed possible to have this technical work done at a level other than D-structure. But the main reason to have it done on a separate level in earlier proposals remains: LF, by means of movement operations and traces, provides a level of representation in which some elements are interpreted in positions other than the surface positions in which they appear, which was the main reason to separate D-structure from SS. If anything, this shift brings about an increase in the power of rule formulation: *covert* movement rules can be formulated in addition to the overt movements of the D-structure model. Moreover, traces are now part of the tools of the model in addition to transformations. If the conditions on these elements (and on empty categories in general) are reducible to independently motivated conditions for lexical items, then this may contribute to the solution of the induction problem for language acquisition (see Bouchard (1984), Koster (1978) for efforts in that direction[1]). If conditions specific to empty categories must be added to UG, they will require very strong empirical motivation.

Another appeal to a secondary implementation of *external* simplicity is found in the elimination of the categories AGRS and AGRO (Chomsky 1995, section 4.10). These seem to be irrelevant at both interface levels A-P and C-I, so should be eliminated according to Chomsky. However, what he analysed as movements of the object and subject triggered by AGRO and AGRS is now analysed as a movement triggered by a [+strong] feature of a v in the larsonian VP shell, and a [+strong] feature of T, respectively. He also introduces semantically and phonologically empty verbal heads under the main v of the VP shell to allow for the generation of multiple adverbs. To assume "lexical" categories like these or second order features like [-interpretable] and [+strong], all of which are not manifested at the interface levels, is just as inconsistent with an optimal minimalist approach as assuming functional categories that are not manifested at the interface levels.

Let us now turn to the *internal* use of simplicity. Economy then functions as a mechanism internal to the theory to insure that particular analytical tools — in most proposals, movement transformations — are limited in their application. For example, the shortest move condition incorporated in the definition of Attract and the principle of Last Resort have for effect that shortest derivations and those with the least steps block less optimal derivations.

(1) K attracts F if F is the closest feature that can enter into a checking relation with a sublabel of K.

(2) Last Resort*:*
Move F raises F to target K only if F enters into a checking relation with a sublabel of K.

Propositions like these reduce the options of rule application. Fewer derivations need to be considered by a learner, thus potentially contributing to the primary goal of explanatory adequacy. However, this is only a potential contribution towards that goal: constraining rule application effectively reduces options only if the system as a whole reduces the choices available to the learner, and if the reduction is significant (i.e., the reduction is such that choices are actually quantitatively or qualitatively reduced in a way that has an impact on learnability; this is a difficult question which I cannot address here). It is of little use to have a highly restricted component of Grammar if those effects are canceled out by other aspects of the system. For example, the notion of *closeness* in the definition of *Attract* in (84) is defined in terms of c-command:

(3)   Closeness (Chomsky 1995: 358)
      β is closer to the target K than α if β c-commands α.

Since c-command is itself dependent on the categories present and projecting in the structure, it is crucial to have a precise formulation of what counts as a category and when it can be introduced in a structure, in particular elusive functional categories that have little substantive content. In the absence of constraints on the formulation of what are possible categories, it is always possible to void the effects of a constraint on rule application such as closeness. Thus, any structure arrived at by an analysis can always be conveniently modified by adding a blocking functional category to account for the absence of movement, or conversely, the absence of such a category or a non-blocking structure (such as adjunction) can be assumed if ever it turns out that movement is possible where it was predicted not to be.

The same holds for Last Resort. Checking is defined on features, and their presence should be determinable on grounds other than whether movement is triggered; without a precise formulation of features that potentially trigger movement and where they may appear, a constraint on rule application such as Last Resort is easy to circumvent.

On the whole, systemic restrictiveness is extremely low if free insertion of functional categories or second order features is admitted. The construction specific rules of the early days of transformational grammar are replaced by construction specific functional categories or features that trigger movement. An unconstrained use of covert, contentless functional categories and second order features essentially amounts to a listing of properties, with no accountability to the articulatory-perceptual component or the conceptual-intentional component.

There are two avenues that one can pursue in order to reconcile functional categories and movement transformations with the fundamental assumptions of conceptual necessity and of accountability to the articulary-perceptual or the conceptual-intentional. First, one may look for some independent motivation for functional categories and provide an explanation why features of these categories trigger the movements that they do.

A second avenue to explore is to dismiss the notions of movement transformation and of contentless functional category, and to look for some other, more restrictive form of analysis, in the spirit of a minimalist approach that values conceptual necessity and accountability to the articulary-perceptual and the conceptual-intentional. Rather than trying to constrain rule application, we could try to constrain rule formulation.

As Goldsmith (1989) points out, only constraints on formulation actively reduce the class of possible grammars, not those on application. Since Principles and Parameters play a central role in current theorizing, it is important to constrain their formulation, to acertain what is an optimal principle and an optimal parameter on general grounds of parsimony. In short, the task is to try to formulate the basic notions in terms of the ultimate necessities: there must be a meaning interface and a form interface to express this meaning.

There have been considerable efforts to formulate various components of UG in terms of notions drawn strictly from the domain of conceptual necessity, the ideal goal being "a theory of language that takes a linguistic expression to be nothing other than a formal object that satisfies interface conditions in the optimal way" (Chomsky 1995: 171). However, *parameters* are an exception to this rigour. They have generally been introduced in the spirit of constraints on application. i.e., of internal economy: typically, a value setting for a feature (such as [+strong] triggers some process (most often, a movement transformation). In this way, parameters have an effect on the steps in a derivation. Moreover, the restrictions imposed on parameters are also in terms of internal economy: they would be restricted to formal features of functional categories. This limitation on what must be checked may constrain derivations. However, as indicated above, the learners choices are effectively reduced only if functional categories and second order features are properly limited. In terms of external economy, an appeal to formal features of functional categories raises several questions. What are possible functional categories and formal features? What is their necessity besides theory-internal motivation? Why must these features be checked? Why and how do options arise about them?

In sum, there is no direct link with conceptually necessary properties of interfaces in this type of parameterization, since parameters are encoded deeply into the C_{HL} as second order features on functional categories. Therefore, the relation that parameters have with external economy, with conceptual necessity, is very tenuous in the minimalist program. Chomsky (1995: 8) states that variation among languages should be "the result of interaction of fixed principles under slightly varying conditions." At first glance, it seems paradoxical that optimal satisfaction allows variation at all. However, if parameterization is made dependent on conceptually necessary properties of interfaces, the paradox can be resolved and the varying conditions that give rise to the options can be identified on principled grounds.

From the perspective of external minimalism, of restrictions on formulations, the key task is to determine what is a possible parameter in language, what may be parameterized. The optimal kind of parameterization (and so, ideally, the only one we should appeal to) arises from the interaction of necessity and constraints on usability. The situation should be such that (i) some element is required by conceptual necessity, is expected to be part of the human language faculty, and (ii) there is more than one way to satisfy this requirement, given the nature of the interfaces, i.e., given bare output conditions imposed from outside. The parametric situation arises because, for reasons of parsimony, it is less costly to leave all options free, than to add a statement in universal grammar restricting it to a particular choice. Value setting derives from considerations of usability, which force a particular language to make a particular choice.

Moreover, the properties involved are salient features of the two "external" systems — the articulatory-perceptual system (A-P) and the conceptual-intentional system (C-I) which are readily accessible at the PF and LF interfaces. Therefore, very limited experience should suffice to set the values of the parametric settings since data are readily available to determine particular choices.

To illustrate this way of involving necessity in parametric choices, I will discuss parametric effects in adjectival modification in French and English. It will be argued that minimal assumptions about phrase structure and two parameters based on salient, necessary properties of the interfaces derive a host of properties of adjectival modification inside the Noun phrase.

2. Minimal Assumptions

Any language must have meaning-bearing elements — lexical items. In a phrasal-structural language like French and English, relations between linguistic elements are mainly encoded by having them share a temporal edge. A minimal operation Merge is therefore required to put two elements together. The resulting complex element can in turn be combined with another element. This hierarchical organization may be represented in terms of a phrase structure.[2] Imposing even more stringent conditions of necessity on proposals by Bouchard (1979, 1984, 1991, 1995) and Chomsky (1994, 1995), I assume the bare phrase structure theory in (8):

(4) Basic assumptions of Integral Minimalism:
  i. *The only structural primitives are lexical items and an associative function Merge that combines them together.*
  ii. *It follows from the underspecification of the operation Merge that the merger of α and β is licensed by selectional properties: if the complex expression resulting from the combination of α and β cannot be interpreted by the rules of the language, the result is gibberish (i.e., human languages combine meaningful elements into larger ones). Typically, one of α or β is a functor category which the other one saturates or modifies by assigning a property to it.*
  iii. *Since the only primitives available are those taken from the lexicon, the result of Merging α and β is labelled α or β, not some additional label (I use labels like N, A, P only for convenience; they have no status in the theory, and are just abbreviations).*
  iv. *The functor category is the one that projects (Flynn 1983, Speas 1986): the idea is that, even though a category X is slightly changed since it is saturated or modified by its sister category, it remains essentially an X.*

With these minimal assumptions in mind, let us now turn to the data:

(5) Basic phenomena that any analysis must account for:
Semantics

i. compositionality of ADJ and N meanings
ii meaning differences between ADJ-N and N-ADJ combinations in French
iii. the "scope" of ADJs in the sequences ADJ-ADJ-N and N-ADJ-ADJ
iv. the "scope" of the ADJs in the sequence ADJ-N-ADJ
v. the mirror order of French post-N ADJs and English pre-N ADJs
Phonology
i. liaison in ADJ-N sequences, but not in N-ADJ sequences
Syntax
i. the structure of ADJ-N and N-ADJ sequences in French
ii. the fact that N-ADJ sequences are possible in French but not in English
iii. the No Complement restriction on pre-N ADJs
iv. Noun Ellipsis is less restricted in French than English
v. Determiner Ellipsis is less restricted in English than French

The data concerning semantics will be discussed in section 3, those about phonology in section 4, and syntactic aspects of adjectival modification will be presented in section 5.

3. The Semantics of Adjectival Modification

3.1. Compositionality of ADJ and N Meanings

In a syntactic theory in which the only combinatorial process is the pared down operation Merge, semantic-selection is a crucial notion for licensing (Grimshaw 1979, Pesetsky 1982, Rochette 1988). Merge cannot operate without selection licensing it, they are inseparably linked. So when we indicate that an element α combines with β by Merge, we must also indicate *how* α combines with β according to selection: which of α or β acts as a functor category, and whether the relation is one of complementation or modification.[3]

Given the crucial role of lexical semantics in the licensing of the syntactic operation Merge, it is important to look into the nature and organization of semantic components of lexical items, in order to determine at least in broad outlines how these components operate in the licensing of syntactic combination. For example, the semantic part of the entry of a N is a network of interacting elements that determine its extension. Simplifying, the lexical entry of a N like *senator* contains elements such as a characteristic function c providing the property that interprets the N ("a measure of the degree to which an object falls in the extension of a given concept" (Kamp & Partee 1995: 131)), an indication of the certain time interval i at which c holds, an indication of the possible world w at which c holds. This determines the set of things that have the property of being a senator in w at i, i.e., the extension of *senator*. Given that this network of interacting elements is unified into a lexical item, it generally functions as a whole with respect to selection and the licensing of Merge. In other words, when a lexical item α acts as a functor category and merges syntactically with some β, it does so as a fully specified set of descriptive features which is closed off, and this functor category gets saturated or modified as a whole. This seems to be the general case.

This general case works fine for the broad class of intersective ADJs. The syntactic combination of an intersective ADJ and N translates into predicate conjunction (set intersection) in semantics: the N acts as a functor category and the whole network of components relevant for selection is involved. Thus, the set of things that have the property of being a N in *w* at *i* intersects with the set determined by the ADJ:

(6) ‖mammal‖ ∩ ‖carnivorous‖

However, a simple rule of intersection with the functor category —with the selectional network as a whole—does not seem to hold for all ADJs. There are at least two classes of ADJs that cannot directly be treated in a comparable way. Subsective ADJs such as *skillful* are non-intersective: they obey the rule in (7):

(7) Subsective: ‖skillful N‖ ⊆ ‖N‖

"Intensional" ADJs like *future, former, alleged, false* are neither intersective nor subsective:

(8) ‖*alleged communist*‖ ≠ ‖*alleged*‖ ∩ ‖*communist*‖
    ‖alleged communist‖ ⊄ ‖communist‖

It is possible that part of the problem is only apparent. Kamp & Partee (1995) argue that a substantial proportion of subsective ADJs may be brought under the rules governing intersective ADJs by taking into account contextual recalibration: subsective ADJs like those in (9) would actually be intersective, but context-dependent.

(9) *a*   Sam is a giant and a midget.
    b   Sam is a giant midget.
    c   Sam is a midget giant.

With overt conjunction as in (9a), the sentence is interpreted as contradictory (unless different respects are introduced, such as a mental giant and a physical midget). In (9b) and (9c), the predicate serving as head N is interpreted relative to the external context, and the predicate functioning as a modifier is recalibrated to make distinctions within the class of possible referents of the N: the interpretation of the modifier is adjusted according to the context created by the head N (Kamp & Partee 1995).

In fact, intersective ADJs are probably all contextually calibrated. As indicated in Bouchard (to appear), even typical intersective ADJs such as color ADJs are contextually calibrated. For instance, a sheet of paper of the same color as a white person is not considered white. In a row of white houses, one with 2% of red trim will be referred to as the red house, but as the white house in a context of multi-colored houses. A purple finch or a pink frog may show very tenuous shades of those colors. There may therefore be a vast class of ADJs for which the simple hypothesis of intersection holds, taking into account the modular effects of contextual calibration.

There still remain some subsective ADJs such as *skillful* and the whole class of ADJs like *former, alleged, future*, which apparently do not fall under a simple isomorphic compositional analysis based on intersectivity. This lead formal semanticists to propose that these ADJs are not functions that map sets with sets, but properties with properties, that is, that they are intensional rather than extensional. The property that a predicate stands for determines not only its actual extension, but also the extensions which it would have in other possible circumstances (i.e., by varying the values of i, w, and other such elements). This spectrum of actual and potential extensions presents an intensional view of the predicate. It is this aspect of the N that would be affected by ADJs such as *former, alleged, future*.

Note that these ADJs do not affect the intension of the N by targeting the whole complex of interacting elements internal to N that allow it to range over extensions, but only one of those elements in particular, depending on the meaning of the ADJ. For instance, in *alleged Communist*, *alleged* is not a function mapping the properties of *Communist* with the properties of the ADJ-N combination: rather, *alleged* affects more precisely something like the characteristic function that provides the property that interprets the N. So *alleged Communist* conveys something like "it is claimed that there is some degree to which an object falls in the extension of the concept *communist*," the implication being that this property may be wrongly attributed to some individual, without however negating the ontology of such an individual. The ADJs *former* and *future* in *former/future president* also affect something internal to N: they say something about the interval of time i at which the property *president* holds for some individual. In *fake pianos,* the pianos have some pianoness about them, some of the characteristic properties of a piano; but something is not true about the assignment of values to the variables in the relevant possible world$w$, i.e., in the real worl. These are pianos, but not "real ones", they cannot do all that real pianos do. So the ADJ *fake* modifies yet another component internal to N, the possible world$w$.

Given that the semantic part of the entry of a lexical item is a network of interacting elements (such as a characteristic function c , a time interval i, a possible world w, etc.), this is expected: nothing rules out the possibility that Merge be licensed by a subpart of this network in some cases. This different kind of selectional licensing should then have structural effects of its own. The generalization that emerges is that all ADJs are intersective. Standard intersective ADJs are "extensional" in the sense that they affect the set defined by the whole complex of interacting elements internal to N (c, i, w...): modification of the N as a functor category licenses Merge. "Intensional" ADJs like *former, alleged, future, fake* are also intersective, but they affect sets defined by a subpart of this network of the N: modification of a subcomponent of N licenses Merge. Thus, *former* and *future* affect the set of time intervals defined by i, and so on. This unification of adjectival types solves the problem for compositionality raised by an apparent discrepancy between semantic and syntactic combination. It appeared as if different types of semantic combination corresponded to a single type of syntactic combination between an ADJ and a noun. Given the effects of selectional licensing on how one "reads" a structure resulting from Merge, the two types of selectional licensing—as a functor category or as a subcomponent of it—should each induce structural effects of their own. The syntax of French adjectival modification indicates that this is precisely what takes place. Intensional ADJs that assign properties to sets of elements determined by subcomponents of N must appear in pre-N position:

(10) a	ce supposé communiste	*that alleged Communist*
b	le futur président	*the future president*
c	l'ancien président	*the former president*
d	de faux pianos	*false (fake) pianos*

On the other hand, all ADJs that modify the N as a whole are post-N. Thus, ADJs that assign concrete properties, such as specifications of shape, color, taste (12), and ADJs that express the relation of an object with another (13), overwhelmingly appear in post-N position:

(11) shape*:* une table ronde *a round table,* un chapeau plat *a flat hat*
     color*:* un arbre vert *a green tree,* du vin rouge *some red wine*
     taste*:* un vin rance *a rancid wine*
(12) a le fils aîné   *the eldest son*
    b un fait anachronique   *an anachronistic fact*
    c un oiseau captif   *a captive bird*
    d un homme marié/célibataire/veuf *a married/single/widowed man*

This kind of concrete property can only be assigned to sets of individuals determined by the whole network of interacting elements in the entry of N: they are not attributable to subcomponents of N.

In sum, all combinations of ADJ and N are intersective, including intensional ADJs: their Merging is licensed by modification of a subcomponent of the entry of N rather than by the whole N acting as a functor category.

3.2. Meaning Differences Between ADJ-N and N-ADJ in French

Compositionality faces a second important problem: many combinations of ADJ and N result in more than one meaning.

(13) a poor man = not rich man
        poor man = pitiful man
    b It's a perfect lie = it's a total, complete lie, it's all lies
       It's a perfect lie = it's a lie that is constructed perfectly, with no flaws
in it

So the same parts, apparently combined in the same way, result in a complex expression with different meanings, in contradiction with the principle of compositionality. This lead semanticists to propose adjustment devices, such as type shifting rules (Siegel 1980, Kamp & Partee 1995), category changing rules (Flynn 1983), or multiple rules potentially governing the relation between ADJ and N (Higginbotham 1985). But all these proposals go against the spirit of compositionality, since they explicitly break the homomorphism between semantic representation and syntactic representation.

French also provides a key to solve this problem for compositionality. As we can see in (14), the French equivalents of the English examples in (13), the differences in meaning when the same ADJ and N combine seem to come from a different syntactic combination: as the order in French indicates, the differences in meaning correlate with different positions.

(14) a pauvre homme = *pitiful man*
        homme pauvre = *not rich man*

    b   C'est un parfait mensonge!
             It's a perfect/total/complete lie! (It's all lies!)
             C'est un mensonge parfait.
             It's a perfect lie, constructed perfectly, with no flaws in it

In the post-N construction *un mensonge parfait* in (14b), a property is assigned to the set of individuals determined by the whole semantic network of *mensonge*: the N is modified as a whole. But when *parfait* appears in pre-N position, its modification is restricted to the characteristic function of *mensonge*: *parfait* in pre-N position indicates that the degree to which an object falls in the extension of the concept *mensonge* is at its utmost (which explains why pre-N *parfait* is often translated in English as "complete", "total" or "thorough").
    A similar effect arises in (15):

(15) a   une femme seule *a woman who is alone*
    b   une seule femme *a sole woman, only one woman*
    c   La seule femme seule s'est isolée dans un coin.
           The only woman who was alone isolated herself in a corner.

In its post-N use, *seule* "sole, single" indicates that, in the relevant context, there is only one referent, one individual in the set determined by the whole semantic network of *femme*. In its pre-N use of the ADJ, yet another subcomponent of N is affected, namely, the variable assignment function *g* associated with N: *seule* indicates that a single value may be attributed to the variable of N, or in other words, that only one individual has the characteristic properties of a woman in the model (a man could be present in (b), but not in (a)). Moreover, (15c) provides direct evidence that pre-N and post-N ADJs do not modify the same element: the same ADJ appears twice without a feeling of redundancy.
    Subsective ADJs may also appear on either side of the N, with a meaning difference between the two combinations.

(16) a   Enfin un habile chirurgien   *Finally a skillful surgeon (as a surgeon)*
*   b*   Enfin un chirurgien habile   *Finally a skillful surgeon (for a surgeon)*

In pre-N position, *habile* affects the property interpreting the N *chirurgien*, hence the 'as a' interpretation. In post-N position, *habile* gets a 'for a' interpretation because it modifies something different, namely the whole set of components of the N. This goes contra Siegel (1980), who says that subsective ADJs like *skillful* occur with *as*-phrases, whereas it is context-dependent intersective ADJs that occur with *for*-phrases to indicate a comparison class. The difference between pre-N and post-N *habile* is very subtle: since the most salient, discriminating element among the semantic components of N is the property interpreting the N, this is very close to the interpretation in which the ADJ affects only the property interpreting the N. The difference is nonetheless real and can be teased out in appropriate contexts. For instance, if a group of friends at a hospital regularly get together to play hockey, and surgeons who have showed up in the past have all been poor players, but tonight surgeon Richard is burning the ice, then it is appropriate for someone to shout (16b), but not (16a). In this context, Dr Richard is not skillful as a surgeon (he may in fact not be that sharp a surgeon), but the fact that he is a surgeon is relevant: he is skillful for a surgeon, i.e., among the set of individuals determined by the whole semantic network of *chirurgien*, its extension.

It is also very revealing that even typical intersective ADJs assigning concrete properties, which tend to be post-N, may appear in pre-N position:

(17) a   tes lisses cheveux *your sleek hair*
  b   ce plat pays *that flat country*
  c   ma verte prairie *my green prairie*
  d   ce rance vin *that rancid wine*

In all the examples in (17), placing the ADJ in pre-N position induces a "poetic" effect which the English translations do not convey. For instance, in *tes lisses cheveux*, the hair is not merely *described* as sleek, it is *defined* as sleek, as if it could not be otherwise. The same holds for the other examples, where the property of the ADJ is asserted to be part of the defining features of the object in question. The poetic effect arises from an interaction of grammatical and pragmatic factors. Because these ADJs assign concrete properties, they normally modify the referents, the individuals determined by the interaction of all the components of N (the denotation assignment function, at interval i, in possible world w, etc.). As we saw, this kind of modification takes place in the post-N position. But in pre-N position, the property of the ADJ is added to a subcomponent of N—its denotation assignment function. The poetic effect in *tes lisses cheveux* comes from this inherent attribution to a person of a concrete property: the person is not presented as merely having sleek hair, but as a person with another type of object, SLEEK-HAIR, hair that would be sleek in all worlds, not conceivable as different. In short, the intension of the expression is changed by having the ADJ intersect with the denotation assignment of the N.

The theory arrived at is compositional: it offers an explanation of the meaning of complex expressions in terms of properties of constituent expressions. Thus, the combination N+ADJ in French is a straightforward case of intersection between the set of things that have the property of being a N in w at i and the set determined by the ADJ. The combination ADJ+N occurs when the intended interpretation requires a modification of a subcomponent of N: the set determined by the ADJ intersects with the set determined by this component. The combination does not result in a saturated or modified functor category, since the combination is not with the N as a functor category: rather, it results in a complex functor category. Given the basic assumptions of Integral Minimalism in (4), the N in the N+ADJ combination projects since it is a functor category; in the ADJ+N combination however, it is the complex functor category that projects. Accordingly, the structure that Integral Minimalism derives for a simple NP containing a pre-N and a post-N ADJ projection is as in (18), where AN is an abbreviation for the complex functor category *bon père*:

(18)

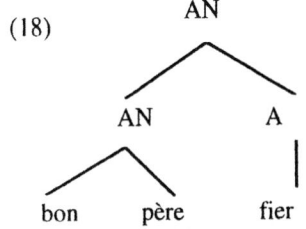

bon   père   fier

We are thus driven on principled grounds to the conclusion that pre-N ADJs are closer to N than post-N ADJs, since pre-N ADJs project with the N. It is interesting to note that the idea that pre-N ADJs are closer to the head N than post-N ADJs has been proposed on empirical grounds by several authors in the past. Waugh (1977) notes that the lexicographer Pierre Joseph André Roubaud made the observation in 1785 in his *Nouveaux synonymes françois*. She provides several examples of the observation being repeated in various forms by almost all the numerous authors who have studied French ADJs since then.

3.3. The Scope of ADJs in the Sequences ADJ-ADJ-N and N-ADJ-ADJ

It has often been observed by linguists of a wide variety of allegiances, that when there are two (or more) ADJs on the same side of N, one of the two ADJs determines not the substantive, but the constituent formed by the substantive and the other ADJ (Blinkenberg 1933, Dixon 1982, Sproat & Shih 1990, and many others cited in Waugh 1977). For example, if I ask someone to show me *les lignes parallèles colorées* (19a), the task is presented as a search among parallel lines for the colored ones. On the other hand, if the order of the ADJs is inverted, and I ask for *les lignes colorées parallèles*, then we have a different task—a search among colored lines for the parallel ones (19b). Similar mirror effects hold for the pre-N ADJs in (19c-d).

(19) a	les lignes **parallèles colorées**	*(the colored parallel lines)*
b	les lignes **colorées parallèles**	*(the parallel colored lines)*
c	le *futur faux* président	*(the futur false president)*
d	le *faux futur* président	*(the false futur president)*

This is exactly as expected in the Integral Minimalist account: the relative distance of an ADJ from N is determined by selectional factors, the ADJ closest to N forming a constituent with it which is modified by the furthest ADJ. Thus, the structure for (19a) is (20), in which *parallèles* combines first with *les lignes*, and then *colorées* combines with this constituent. As expected, the furthest ADJ from the N also takes scope over the inner phrase made up the ADJ+N in (19c), which has the structure in (20'):

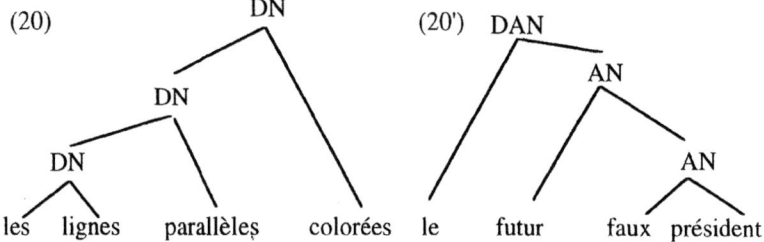

(20) DN ... les lignes parallèles colorées

(20') DAN ... le futur faux président

3.4. The Scope of the ADJs in the Sequence ADJ-N-ADJ

The "scope" of two ADJs relative to one another gets more complicated if they are not both on the same side of the N:

(21) une nouvelle proposition intéressante
    a   new   proposition   interesting
    "a new interesting proposition" OR "an interesting new proposition"

As we see in (21), the scope of a pre-N and a post-N ADJ relative to one another is fairly free: intonation and pragmatic factors determine which reading is the most salient. Given the structure in (18) above, the post-N ADJ is expected to have scope over the pre-N ADJ, since it c-commands it. However, isomorphy between syntactic and semantic composition seems to be lost in the interpretation with the pre-N ADJ having scope over the post-N ADJ. But in fact, we can reconcile the syntax and the semantics if we analyze the pre-N ADJ and head N as a complex functor head that behaves like a portmanteau, as in French *du* "of"-MASC-SING-DEF, *des* "of"-PLUR-DEF, *au* "to"-MASC-SING-DEF and *aux* "to"-PLUR-DEF. These words have features of both a preposition and a determiner, and yet the sets of features appear to interact with other constituents independently from one another. Thus, in *aux enfants* "to the children", *aux* expresses both the features of a preposition that has a DP argument and the features of the Det. So for example, the pre-N ADJ *nouvelle* in (21), being part of the complex head, could have "scope" over the post-N ADJ just like the prepositional features of *au* x"to"-MASC-PLUR-DEF can have "scope" over its argumental complement.

3.5. The Mirror Order of French Post-N ADJs and English Pre-N ADJs

The order of post-N ADJs in French is a mirror image of the same ADJs in pre-N position in English:

(22) a   les lignes **parallèles colorées**
   b   *the **colored parallel** lines*

Since the relative distance of an ADJ from N depends on semantic factors, this predicts that the same relative distance should be observed to the right or left of N. If the two ADJs are forced to appear to the left of N in the English equivalent of (22a) for reasons given below, the analysis predicts that the order should be reversed if we intend to preserve the composition of the ADJs, as is indeed the case:

(23)

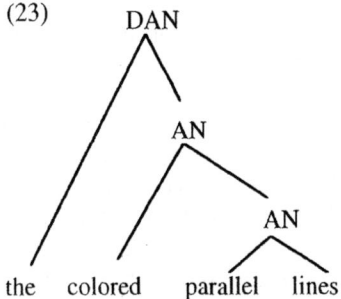

DAN

AN

AN

the   colored   parallel   lines

4. Phonological Effects: Liaison in ADJ-N Sequences

In recent studies, the idea that pre-N ADJs are closer to the head N than post-N ADJs is proposed on phonological grounds in Delattre (1966), Schane (1968), Selkirk (1972), (1986), Encrevé (1988), Miller (1991), Valois (1990, 1991), Lamarche (1990), (1991). The tendency for liaison is much stronger in for ADJ+N than for N+ADJ. Given that liaison is not purely phonological, but is also restricted by a certain condition of proximity, a pre-N ADJ seems to be closer to N.

(24) a   les__amis   *(Det-N: obligatory liaison for all registers)*
            the friends

b   les__énormes arbres   *(Det-ADJ: obligatory liaison for all registers)*

            the enormous trees

c   mauvais__amis   *(ADJ-N: very strong tendency for liaison)*
            bad friends

d   #amis__anglais   *(N-ADJ: weak tendency, only plural -s)*
            English friends

e   #Les enfants__ont un chat.   *(Spec-Head: very weak tendency for liaison)*

            The children have a cat.

f   #J'ai pris__une pomme.   *(Head-Cpl: very weak tendency for liaison)*
            I have taken an apple

In bare phrase structure, the "proximity" requirement for liaison cannot be expressed in terms of bar levels and the like, since they have no theoretical status. A natural way to express it in my analysis is in terms of complex functor domain: a relation between α and β counts as closer when they form a complex functor than when α is a functor category taking β as a complement or modifier.[4]

5. The Syntax of Adjectival Modification

5.1. The Structure of ADJ-N and N-ADJ Sequences in French

There remains to explain the order of the elements in a structure like (18), namely, the fact that it is the post-N ADJ that holds the "normal" saturator or modifier relation with the functor category N, and the pre-N ADJ that has access to components internal to N. The combination relation established between two elements α and β by the operation Merge is licensed by selectional properties (4iii): so there must be some indication whether α or β acts as a functor category with respect to the other. The operation Merge derives from the linearization that results from having two elements share a temporal edge: at the PF interface, α either precedes or follows β. In other words, the operation Merge expresses the fact that a semantic combination of α and β is encoded by a temporal linearization of α and β. Since it reveals the existence of the combination, linearization is a natural means to indicate which of α or β is the functor category in this semantic combination. Therefore, I assume that the central linearization parameter is defined on the functor relation established between two nodes as in (25):

(25) Linearization Parameter:
   The functor category precedes its saturator or modifier in French.
   (i.e, the head precedes its complement or adjunct in French)

This is an optimal parameter since it arises from the interaction of necessity and constraints on usability: when Merge operates, the output must be ordered. This kind of linearization parameter is implicit in most analyses, including that of Kayne (1994), where the notion of complement plays a key role in the Linear Correspondence Axiom: the notion of complement, which is defined by a functor relation, determines whether branching will be nonsegmented (for complements) or segmented (for non-complements).[5] The parameter in (25) directly determines the order between a N and an intersective ADJ as in (11)-(12): the ADJ modifies the closed off functor category determined by the N as a whole, so the ADJ must follow the N. When the ADJ is intensional as in (10) and relates only to an internal component of N, not to the whole N as a full closed off functor category, N may not precede the ADJ according to (25): an Elsewhere application of (25) derives the order ADJ-N. The order of the elements in a structure like (18) is explained.

The Elsewhere application of (25) extends to three well known exceptions to the No Complement restriction on left branch projections: Spec of IP (subject), Spec of CP (WH), Spec of DP (Genitive NP). In all three cases, the phrasal element is actually engaged in two relations, one "thematic" and one functional. A subject relates thematically to VP and functionally to Tense; a sentence-initial Wh-phrase relates thematically to a sentence-internal element and functionally to C; a Genitive NP relates semantically to N and functionally to Case features of Det. In all three cases, the phrasal specifier does not establish a "whole-to-whole" relation with the head that follows it, since it is split between two relations. Therefore, the functor-head parameter setting for English, which is the same as in French, does not apply directly to these Phrase+Head combinations, but in an Elsewhere fashion because the Phrase does not hold an exclusive relation with one head.

5.2. N-ADJ Sequences in French but not in English

If French and English have the same setting for parameter (25), we must explain why bare ADJs must overwhelmingly appear pre-N in English, whereas many bare ADJs may appear post-N in French. Lamarche (1990, 1991) observes that the difference in ADJ placement between French and English correlates with a difference in the position where semantically relevant Number is realized:

(26) French: Number is on Det[6]
    English: Number is on N

If we further assume that a bare ADJ must be in the scope of Number, the possibility for ADJs to appear post-N may be attributed to the wider scope of Number in French than in English. I will now show that there is a natural explanation for Lamarche's insight.

First, let's take a step back and ask what kind of information a nominal expression must provide in a sentence, and how it could do it. I have to restrict myself to a broad outline, but it will suffice for our present purposes. Whenever we have a nominal expression, what is required is something that can function as an expression that has the semantic properties of a kind. A kind can be modelled as a set. A primary necessity for a nominal expression is therefore to define a set to satisfy this semantic requirement. A set may be defined on the basis of a property shared by its members, or on the basis of the totality of its instances. So a parametric choice arises from this contingency. French and English opt for the definition based on instances, Chinese for the one based on properties (see Chierchia (1996)). A secondary necessity arises from choosing to define the set by instances: Number must be expressed in the nominal expression. This necessity derives from the fact that the potential reference of a nominal expression is, roughly, the extension of the natural kind designated by the head N (along the lines of Carlson (1980), Milner (1989), Longobardi (1994)). This referential potential is steered to a particular possibility by the addition of features indicating Number, definiteness, specificity, demonstrativity, etc. The particular possibility thus determined constitutes the *extensity* of the nominal expression, a certain quantity of objects to which the expression is being applied (Wilmet 1986). Of these features, Number seems to be the minimum required for a nominal expression to actually receive some extensity.

Number may be realized on the core element of the nominal expression bearing the characteristic function (N) or on the periphery (the Det system). This option derives from the fact that semantic-selection is the relevant notion for grammar, constituent-selection being only derivative (Grimshaw 1979, Pesetsky 1982, Rochette 1988). If a nominal expression must fulfill the s-selection requirement of bearing Number, it makes no difference whether Number is realized on N or Det, since, as far as selection of the nominal is concerned, the phrase as a whole satisfies the requirement. I am following here an idea that has occasionally been put forward in syntax for WH-constructions with percolation of the WH-feature, and frequently advanced in morphology for some time (see for instance Bloomfield (1933),

Chomsky (1965)). In essence, Number inflection is treated in a way similar to the portmanteau cases discussed above.[7]

We now have an explanation for Lamarche's observation about the parameterized realization of Number in (26): it arises from the necessity to have Number if a set is defined on instances, as in French and English, and the contingency that Number may be satisfactorily coded on either Det or N. Usability forces each language to make a particular choice. There are numerous indications that French opts to code Number on Det, whereas English codes it on N. I will discuss two with regards to ellipsis below. Lamarche (1990, 1991) and Bouchard (to appear) present several other correlations with the position of Number.

There remains to explain why a bare ADJ must be in the scope of Number. Given the relation between Number and extensity, it is natural to assume that what determines the extensity of a nominal expression falls under the scope of Number, as indicated in (27):

(27) The Number Scope Condition:
   The realization of Number in a nominal expression must have scope over the elements that determine the extensity of the expression.

The distribution of ADJs is affected by this condition because complementless ADJs are part of what determines the extensity of a nominal expression, ADJs with complements are not. Therefore, bare ADJs must be under the scope of Number. Since Number is not coded in the same position in French and in English, its scopal domain is different, hence the difference in the distribution of bare ADJs. We thus derive Lamarche's insight.

An indication that ADJs differ in their involment in the determination of extensity depending on whether or not they have a complement comes from their interaction with an element that has its extensity fully determined, such as the pronouns *celui, ceux,* "the one, the ones/those" (FEM: *celle, celles*). As shown by Rothenberg (1985) and Miller (1991), these pronouns may be followed by various types of phrases. However, when the demonstrative is followed by an adjectival expression, there is a sharp contrast depending on whether or not the ADJ has a complement.

(28) a   *Celu fier regardait Paul.
      The one proud looked at Paul.*
   b   Celui fier de son fils regardait Paul.
      The one proud of his son looked at Paul.

This indicates that complementless ADJs participate in the determination of the extensity of a N, so that they are not compatible with an element that has its extensity fully determined, whereas ADJs with complements do not participate in the determination of the extensity of a N.[8]

5.3. The No Complement Restriction on Pre-N ADJs

There is also syntactic evidence that pre-N ADJs are closer to the head N than post-N ADJs. As is well known, an ADJ taking a complement may not appear in a pre-N position:

(29) a   *une fière de sa fille mère *a proud of her daughter mother*
     b   une mère fière de sa fille   *a mother proud of her daughter*

If we make the natural assumption that only lexical items may be internal to a functor category, then pre-N adjectival modifiers, being internal to a complex functor category N, may not be phrasal. Moreover, it is natural to assume that elements which are part of a complex functor participate in the determination of its extensity; but as we just saw, ADJs with complements cannot do so, hence the ungrammaticality of (29a). The No Complement restriction for left branch ADJs follows directly. (An NP like *un très gros chat* "a very big cat" is not a counterexample, but a case of iteration of complex functor category formation: *très* and *gros* form a complex ADJ head, which in turn forms a complex N head with *chat.*). Weinreich (1966: 82-89) and Stowell (1981) propose a similar account, except that they both consider that these complex forms are morphological words.[9]

5.4. Noun Ellipsis Less Restricted in French than English

In English, noun ellipsis occurs quite freely if the nominal contains a numeral, an ordinal, a demonstrative, or a possessive (Sleeman 1996):

(30) a   *I read two of his books. Bill also read two.*   numeral
     b   *He prefers the third.*   ordinal
     c   *Do you like this?*   demonstrative
     d   *He read John's.*   possessive

The minimal indication of Number required for extensivity is not on Det in English, but a numeral provides it directly. An ordinal provides Number indirectly: it has a partitive meaning, which indicates the one (or ones) having a certain ranking in a particular set. Demonstratives used pronominally as in (30c) provide Number directly by deixis (a gesture typically indicates what is the relevant set of individuals). A possessive has a partitive meaning similar to that of ordinals: it picks out the object belonging to a certain individual in a particular reference set established in discourse. As expected, this way of getting the minimal Number specification by "partitivity" through a set established in the domain of discourse (see Sleeman 1996) also arises when some kind of comparison takes place, since a reference set is established:

(31) a   *She married the eldest.*
     b   *Take this end. I'll take the other.*
     c   *Examples like the following are not as good.*

If an ADJ does not have some kind of comparative meaning that introduces a reference set, it is not possible to have a nominal expression consisting of only a DET and this ADJ: the Number feature minimally required for extensity would be missing, since Number is not realized on the DET in English. So the combination Det+ADJ must be completed by a N (*one*) to realize Number.[10]

(32) the big *(one), the blue *(ones), the interesting *(one)

There are some exceptions: a few ADJs do not require the N *one*:

(33) the rich; the poor; the lonely; the good, the bad and the ugly

But notice that in this use, reference is limited by convention to human beings. This convention provides a reference set in the domain of discourse through which the minimal Number specification may be obtained by partitivity.

Noun ellipsis is possible in most of the French nominals equivalent to the English ones in (30) and (31), presumably for the same reasons as in English:[11]

(34) a   J'ai lu deux de ses livres.
        I have read two of his books.
    b   Il préfère le troisième.
        He prefers the third.
    c   Aimes-tu ça?
        Do you like this?
    d   *Il a lu sa.
        He read hers.

(35) a   Elle a épousé le plus âgé.
        She married the eldest.
    b   Prend ce bout-là. Je vais prendre l'autre.
        Take this end. I'll take the other.
    c   Des exemples comme les suivants ne sont pas aussi bons.
        Examples like the following are not as good.

If Number is realized on Det in French, we expect that noun ellipsis should be freer than in English. This is indeed the case. The most obvious case is when nothing but the Det is present: being a weak morphological form and having no head to cliticize to in the nominal, its morphological nature forces it to appear on another host, the inflected verb:

(36) Jean **les** voit.
    John THEM sees
    John sees them.

In addition, the Number in the French Det provides a reference set through which the minimal Number specification may be obtained by partitivity for a whole set of "classifying" ADJs (see Barbaud 1976, Ronat 1977, Sleeman 1996 for a discussion of the properties of these ADJs). So contrary to English, a combination of a DET and a classifying ADJ is possible without a dummy N like *one*:

(37) les bleus *'the blue ones',* le gros *'the big one',* la rouillée *'the rusted one'*

This greater productivity of noun ellipsis is another indication that the DET realizes Number in French, whereas N does in English.

5.5. Determiner Ellipsis Less Restricted in English than French

Another striking difference is that English allows bare plurals, whereas French does not.

(38) a   Beavers build dams everywhere.
    b   I hate beavers.
(39) a   *Castors construisent barrages.
    a'   Les castors construisent des barrages.
    b   *Je déteste castors.
    b'   Je déteste les castors.

I cannot go into the details of this highly complex topic here: the theoretical issues are vast (see Chierchia (1996) and Dobrovie-Sorin (1996) for recent reappraisals), and so are the facts, with variations across Romance languages, as well as apparently very different strategies in languages like Chinese and Persian (Gomeshi 1997). However, it may be useful to give some brief indications of the general direction of inquiry suggested by the present approach. Assuming that Number is the minimum needed for an expression to have some extensity (at least in French and English), as discussed above, a nominal expression marked only for Number could have extensity, but with "no frills", i.e., with no indications of definiteness, specificity, demonstrativity, etc. Since Number is realized on the N in English (the DET supplying the other sorts of features), it is possible for a N with a Number feature but none of the other features restricting the potential reference, i.e., a bare plural, to refer in this basic way as in (38). The determinerless nominal is then simply the name of a kind. Carlson (1980) shows that such a name of a kind functions as an individual, and furthermore, that the kind denoted by the nominal may be realized by objects or by stages. We may assume that a plural marking on the N indicates countability of the realizing objects or stages.

In short, the fact that Number appears on the N in English explains why a determinerless N may refer in this pared down way. On the other hand, this is impossible in French (39), since Number is not realized on the N, but on the DET; so even to have a minimal extensity, the presence of DET is required in French.

As expected, the contrast is not restricted to plural Number marking: singular Number also allows a minimal sort of extensity in English, but not in French.

(40) a   Lion tastes awful.
    b   I ate lion yesterday.
(41) a   Le/*Ø lion, ça goûte très mauvais.
    b   J'ai mangé du/*Ø lion hier.

The singular marking on the N seems to indicate something logically complementary to what the plural marking indicates -- noncountable objects or stages realizing the kind.

6. Conclusion

I have proposed to restrict assumptions about structure to the minimal ones deriving from conceptual necessity in (4), and to restrict parameters to those based on the interaction of necessity and usability at the interfaces. Thus, the ordering parameter (25) arises from the necessary temporal linearization at the PF interface. The Number parameter (26) arises from the necessity for a nominal expression to function as an expression that has the semantic properties of a kind, hence to define a set, French and English opting for a definition based on instances, which introduces the secondary necessity that Number must be expressed, and the contingent property that Number may be realized on the core N or on the peripheral Det. This kind of optimal parameter was shown to give a principled solution for the longstanding problem of compositionality of ADJs and Ns, and to provide an efficient account of variation in French and English.

This discussion is a sample of an integrally minimalist method that I think might be fruitfully exploited in constructing a more comprehensive theory of syntactic and semantic combination. The coverage is far from exhaustive, but the fragments studied should give an idea of the potential insights that may be achieved.

---

[*] I have benefitted greatly from the comments of members of the audience to which I presented this material in Nancy, Ottawa and Utrecht. This work was supported by grant # 410-95-1177 from the Social Sciences and Humanities Research Council of Canada.

[1] Strangely, the tendency in mainstrem generative grammar is currently to go the other way. For example, Chomsky (1995) adopts Lebeaux's (1988) proposal to have lexical anaphors raise at LF in order to create traces that have the proper locality relations: so it is lexical anaphors that must now exhibit properties of covert elements.

[2] See Kayne (1994) who explicitly links temporal linearization and phrasal structure by his Linear Correspondence Axiom. Kayne assumes that all natural languages are subject to the LCA. As is implicit in the formulation in the text, I do not assume that temporal linearization and the phrasal structure that arises from it are universal. Rather, as argued in detail in Bouchard (1996), I assume that it is one form among a few possible forms allowed by the sensorimotor apparatus of humans which may be used to encoded semantic and grammatical information. Therefore, temporal linearization should not have a special status among these possible forms: it is part of a parameterization on encoding of information with the other forms. This accounts in particular for functional covariation among languages, such as relative free word order when information is encoded by rich morphology (Meillet 1949, 1950; Keenan 1978).

[3] In some current theories, this distinction is encoded structurally: a complement is attached to an unsegmented node, whereas a modifier is an adjunct attached to a segmented node. However, this is a diacritic means to reindicate what type of semantic relation holds between two elements and should have no theoretical status, since it is redundant. For instance, an adjunction structure is used to distinguish the non-argument *like a pig* from the argument *two bananas* in sentences like (i) and (ii):

(i)   John ate all the time.
(ii)   John ate all the bananas.

The verb *ate* and the phrase *all the bananas* do not combine semantically in the same way as *ate* and *lall the time* But there is no reason to distinguish these cases structurally: these could be two instances of the same sisterhood relation. The fact that the semantic combination is different independently comes from the fact that the nature of the elements being combined is different. Making a structural distinction is redundant since different structures are proposed on the basis of how the daughters differ semantically. Moreover, a posteriori justification of a different structure to account structurally for extraction differences between adjuncts and complements is circular. Even more so given that the notion of barrier node is defined in terms of a selectional relation in Chomsky (1986): a node is not a barrier if it is theta-marked. In addition, there are semantic conditions on extraction which do not reduce to structural properties, as shown in Ertechik-Shir (1973, 1981), and Ertechik-Shir & Lappin (1979). The distinction between the two types of relations being semantic, a semantic account of extractability differences is the optimal hypothesis, as argued in Bouchard (1995).

[4] Liaison facts are more complicated than this simplified presentation indicates. See Bouchard (to appear) for further discussion.

[5] In a typical derivational account, a single, universal "basic order" results from the interaction of Merge, Select and the Linear Correspondence Axiom (with specific assumptions about c-command, complement relations, etc.). Having a single "basic" order such as Spec-head-complement may seem to be a good result, since no options at all would be available in the ordering of the base (such as head parameters). But in fact, it is more costly than the ordering choice arising from necessity and usability, since it requires an additional stipulation to restrict the base to a single order. For instance, in Kayne's proposal, which order is singled out depends on the crucial placement of an abstract segment A at the beginning of all strings (rather than at the end, for example): this segment has no other function, so is equivalent to an ordering setting. Moreover, UG must be rich enough to account for the data, and not all languages are overtly SVO. So additional tools are required to derive other orders, such as a movement operation and features that trigger it idiosyncratically across languages. Each new order requires different feature settings. Additionally, the features must be placed in a way to attract phrases in the appropriate positions: the hierarchy of functional categories would crucially derive the order of the ADJs. But without an indication of the selectional properties of these categories that determine this hierarchy, the structure is stipulated: this is equivalent to introducing a component as overly powerful as rewriting rules. (This proliferation of stipulations is a property of the approach in general: for instance, a close study of the empirical results that Kayne (1994) presents in support for his analysis shows that the theory requires additional disconnected stipulations for each set of evidence.) So if the whole system is taken into consideration, an approach based on functional features scattered in a structure and checking theory requires more idiosyncratic statements about ordering than one based on a linearization parameter such as (25).

[6] In many instances, Number is visible on more than one element in the nominal expression in French. The minimal assumption is that Number is coded for semantic

interpretation only once, the other elements getting superficial markings of Number by agreement. In fact, multiple semantic encoding of Number for the same expression could lead to incoherence.

[7] The idea that selectional requirements imposed on a nominal expression may be realized in different components of this expression is somewhat implicit in the proposal by Abney (1987) that N is the semantic head of a nominal expression, and Det its structural head; this is even more directly expressed in Grimshaw (1991), who assumes that the N-D system is a multi-headed extended projection, and that N and D belong to the same category [-V, +N], the difference being that N is lexical, whereas D is functional. My view is not as structural as what these authors propose. I see the central characteristic of meaning relations not as relations holding between positions, but between elements that possess certain properties, however these are structurally or otherwise expressed.

[8] There is a class of ADJs that may appear with these pronouns: *ceux présents, coupables, prêts, responsables* "those present, guilty, ready, responsible". This class of ADJs is also special in English: they are the only bare ADJs that may follow a head N.

(i)   a   Who are the people guilty?

        b   The materials ready will be shipped.

        c   The students present (in class today)...

        d   The man responsible (for the crime)...

As noted by Bolinger (1967), post-N bare ADJs become possible if they receive a particular interpretation, as transitory, stage-level ADJs. So they do not seem to participate in the determination of the extensity of the N.

Italian differs from French in that demonstratives may be followed by bare ADJs other than those of the restricted class in (i):

(ii) Preferisco quello alto.

      I prefer the high one.

However, as the translation indicates, in this use, *quello* does not have the deictic force of an element with its extensity fully determined. See Rizzi (1979), Sleeman (1996: 56-58).

[9] A morphological account runs into the problem since it predicts that ADJ and N combinations should be opaque. Yet, the N can be modified by a relative clause alone, not with the ADJ, as in (i), and the ADJ can be a Negative Polarity Item, as in (ii):

(i)   *La première étudiante qui répond correctement recevra un prix spécial.*

     The first student that answer correctly will receive a special prize.

(ii) *Je n'ai vu aucun étudiant.*

     I haven't seen any student.

[10] In other Germanic languages (German, Dutch and the Scandinavian languages), the N can be left out more easily. All inflected ADJs allow noun ellipsis, while the non-inflected ones do not (Sleeman (1996) and references therein), as illustrated in the following Dutch example:

(i)   *Zij heeft een zwarte auto, maar ik heb een groene/*groen.*

     She has a black car, but I have a green (one)

Assuming that these languages are like English and do not realize Number on the Det, the nominal satisfies the Number requirement only if something else provides the feature, such as an inflected ADJ.

[11] There is a notable exception: the genitive in (34d) is ill-formed. This is due to an independent property of French genitives: they are clitics (Miller 1991, among others).

References

Abney, Steven. 1987. *The English Noun Phrase in its Sentential Aspect.* Ph.D. dissertation, Massachusetts Institute of Technology, Cambridge.

Barbaud, Philippe. 1976. Constructions superlatives et structures apparentées. *Linguistic Analysis* 2.2, 125-174.

Blinkenberg, Andreas. 1933. *L'ordre des mots en français moderne: Deuxième partie.* Copenhagen: Levin & Munksgaard.

Bloomfield, Leonard. 1933. *Language.* London: G. Allen and Unwin.

Bolinger, Dwight. 1967. Adjectives in English: Attribution and Predication. *Lingua* 18, 1-34.

Bouchard, Denis (to appear). The Distribution and Interpretation of Adjectives in French: A consequence of Bare Phrase Structure. *Probus.*

Bouchard, Denis (1996). Sign Languages and Language Universals: The Status of Order and Position in Grammar. *Sign Language Studies* 91, 101-160.

Bouchard, Denis. 1979. *Conjectures sur une grammaire indépendante du contexte pour les langues naturelles.* M.A. dissertation, Université de Montréal.

Bouchard, Denis. 1984. *On the Content of Empty Categories.* Dordrecht: Foris Publications.

Bouchard, Denis. 1991. From Conceptual Structure to Syntactic Structure. *Views on Phrase Structure*, ed. by Katherine Leffel and Denis Bouchard, 21-35. Dordrecht: Kluwer Academics.

Bouchard, Denis. 1995. *The Semantics of Syntax.* Chicago: The University of Chicago Press.

Carlson, Gregory. 1980. *Reference to Kinds in English.* New York: Garland Publishing Inc.

Chierchia, Gennaro. 1996. *Reference to Kinds iAcross Languages.* Ms. University of Milan.

Chomsky, Noam. 1965. A*spects of the Theory of Syntax.* Cambridge: MIT Press.

Chomsky, Noam. 1994. *Bare Phrase Structure, MIT Occasional Papers in Linguistics 5.* Cambridge.

Chomsky, Noam. 1995. *The Minimalist Program.* Cambridge: MIT Press.

Delattre, Pierre. 1966. *Studies in French and Comparative Phonetics.* Mouton: The Hague.

Dixon, Robert. 1982. *Where Have All the Adjectives Gone?* The Hague: Mouton.

Dobrovie-Sorin, Carmen. 1996. Types of Predicates and the Representation of Existential Readings. Ms., CNRS-URA 1028, Université Paris 7.

Encrevé, Pierre. 1988. *La liaison avec et sans enchaînement.* Paris: Editions du Seuil.

Ertechik-Shir, Nomi & Shalom Lappin. 1979. Dominance and the Functional Explanation of Island Phenomena. *Theoretical Linguistics* 6: 41-86.

Ertechik-Shir, Nomi. 1973. *On the Nature of Island Constraints*. Ph.D. dissertation, Massachusetts Institute of Technology.

Ertechik-Shir, Nomi. 1981. More on Extractability from Quasi-NPs. *Linguistic Inquiry* 12: 665-670.

Flynn, Michael. 1983. A categorical theory of structure building. *Order, Concord and Constituency*, ed. by Gerald Gazdar, Ewan Klein and Geoffrey Pullum, 139-174. Dordrecht: Foris Publications.

Ghomeshi, Jila. 1997. Bare Singulars, Bare Plurals and Functional Structure. Ms., Université du Québec à Montréal.

Goldsmith, John. 1989. Review of van Riemsdijk & Williams: Introduction to the theory of grammar. *Language* 65, 150-159.

Grimshaw, Jane. 1979. Complement Selection and the Lexicon. *Linguistic Inquiry* 10: 279-326.

Grimshaw, Jane. 1991. *Extended Projection*. Ms. Brandeis University.

Higginbotham, James. 1985. On Semantics. *Linguistic Inquiry* 16: 547-593.

Kamp, Hans and Barbara Partee. 1995. Prototype theory and compositionality. *Cognition* 57, 129-191.

Kayne, Richard. 1994. *The Antisymmetry of Syntax*. Cambridge: MIT Press.

Keenan, Edward. 1978. Language variation and the logical structure of universal grammar. *Language Universals*, ed. by Hansjacob Seiler, 89-123. Tübingen: Gunter Narr Verlag.

Koster, Jan. 1978. *Locality Principles in Syntax*. Dordrecht: Foris.

Lamarche, Jacques. 1990. *Tête-à-tête et autres relations: La position et l'interprétation des ADs*. M.A. thesis, Université du Québec à Montréal.

Lamarche, Jacques. 1991. Problems for N^0-movement to Num-P. *Probus* 3: 215-236.

Lebeaux, David. 1988. Language acquisition and the form of grammar. Ph. D. Dissertation, University of Massachusetts, Amherst.

Longobardi, Giuseppe. 1994. Reference and Proper Names. *Linguistic Inquiry* 25: 609-665.

Meillet, Antoine 1949. Caractères généraux des langues germaniques. Paris: Hachette.

Meillet, Antoine 1950. Les dialectes indo-européens. Paris: Champion.

Miller, Philip. 1991. *Clitics and Constituents in Phrase Structure Grammar*. Ph.D. dissertation, University of Utrecht.

Milner, Jean-Claude. 1989. *Introduction à une science du langage*. Paris: Editions du Seuil.

Pesetsky, David. 1982. *Paths and Categories*. Ph.D. dissertation, Massachusetts Institute of Technology.

Rizzi, Luigi. 1979. Teoria della traccia e processi fonosintattici. *Rivista di Grammatica Generativa* 4, 165-181.

Rochette, Anne. 1988. *Semantic and Syntactic Aspects of Romance Sentential Complementation*. Ph.D. dissertation, Massachusetts Institute of Technology.

Ronat, Mitsou. 1977. Une contrainte sur l'effacement du nom. *Langue*, ed. by Mitsou Ronat, 153-169. Paris: Hermann.

Rothenberg, Mira. 1985. Le pronom démonstratif et ses déterminants en français. *Bulletin de la Société de Linguistique de Paris* 80.1: 165-200.

Schane, Sanford. 1968. *French Phonology and Morphology*. Cambridge: The MIT Press.

Selkirk, Elisabeth. 1972. *The Phrase Phonology of English and French*. Ph. D. dissertation, Massachusetts Institute of Technology.

Selkirk, Elisabeth. 1986. On derived domains in sentence phonology. *Phonology Yearbook* 3, 371-405.

Siegel, Muffy. 1980. *Capturing the Adjective*. New York: Garland Publishing Inc.

Sleeman, Petra. 1996. *Licensing Empty Nouns in French*. The Hague: Holland Academic Graphics.

Speas, Margaret. 1986. *Adjunctions and Projections in Syntax*. Ph. D. dissertation, Massachusetts Institute of Technology.

Sproat, Richard and Chilin Shih. 1990. The Cross-linguistic Distribution of Adjective Ordering Restrictions. *Interdisciplinary Approaches to Language. Essays in Honor of S. Y. Kuroda*, ed. by Carol Georgopoulos and Roberta Ishihara, 565-593. Dordrecht: Kluwer.

Stowell, Timothy. 1981. *Origins of Phrase Structure*. Ph. D. dissertation, Massachusetts Institute of Technology.

Valois, Daniel. 1990. The internal syntax of DP and adjective placement in English and French. *Proceedings of NELS 21*, 367-381. Graduate Linguistic Student Association, Amherst.

Valois, Daniel. 1991. *The Internal Syntax of DP*. Ph. D. Dissertation, UCLA.

Waugh, Linda. 1977. *A Semantic Analysis of Word Order*. Leiden: E.J. Brill.

Weinreich, Uriel. 1966. Explorations in semantic theory. *Current Trends in Linguistics* Vol. III, ed. by Thomas A. Sebeok, 395-417. The Hague: Mouton.

Wilmet, Marc. 1986. *La détermination nominale*. Paris: Presses Universitaires de France.

Strong Equivalence of Generalized Ajdukiewicz and Lambek Grammars

Maciej Kandulski

Faculty of Mathematics and Computer Science
Adam Mickiewicz University, Poznań, Poland
mkandu@math.amu.edu.pl

Abstract. We consider Ajdukiewicz and Lambek syntactic calculi based on an algebra of arbitrary syntactic operations and prove that categorial grammars employing both of those calculi as type reduction systems generate the same class of phrase languages.

1 Introduction

Concatenation was initially the only syntactic operation on words considered in the categorial description of languages. Consequently, calculi of syntactic types initially admitted this operation as the only mode of combining types on the left-hand side of reduction formulas. Later on other modes of combining types such as nonassociative concatenation or commutative concatenation were considered but attempts undertaken to capture significant syntactic phenomena within categorial systems equipped with a single syntactic operation on types usually resulted in failure. On the other hand numerous examples indicated that the coexistence of different modes of putting types together serves much better to make categorial description of languages flexible than keeping the system unimodal, see for example [11], where a linguistic application of a Lambek system with two products is presented. Additionally, in order to gain a better conformity of categorial grammars with linguistic reality, multimodal systems can contain structural rule packages and interaction postulates. In this paper we will consider Ajdukiewicz and Lambek calculi based on an algebra of arbitrary syntactic operations and their residuals. Such systems, called here the generalized calculi, were introduced by Buszkowski, see [2], [4], and also [1], and independently, with slightly another motivation, by Moortgat, see the survey [10]. Kołowska-Gawiejnowicz in [9] has recently proved the completeness of the generalized Lambek calculus with respect to powerset residuated algebras.

It is well known that unimodal categorial grammars based on the associative Ajdukiewicz or Lambek calculi are equivalent to CF-grammars in the scope of string languages. Similar equivalences hold for grammars based on the nonassociative versions of those calculi. Nonassociative categorial grammars can also be viewed as generators of phrase languages. As a result there arises the problem of strong generative power of those grammars, i.e. the problem of their ability in generating phrase languages, as opposed to their weak generative power in the scope of string languages. It has been proved that nonassociative Ajdukiewicz grammars are strongly equivalent to nonassociative Lambek grammars. However, contrary to weak equivalence, strong equivalence of both of those categorial systems to CF-grammars does not hold, see [3] and [6].

The calculi we are concerned with can be viewed as extensions of nonassociative Ajdukiewicz and Lambek systems. In our setting a pair of indexed brackets is associated with each syntactic operation. Consequently, grammars based on the examined calculi generate languages which can be viewed as generalizations of phrase languages in the sense that each pair of brackets is marked by the symbol of an applied operation. We prove that Ajdukiewicz and Lambek categorial grammars employing arbitrary syntactic operations are equivalent in the scope of such generalized phrase languages. Weak generative capacity of those systems will naturally vary according to the nature of the particular operations admitted. Our argument makes use of some results and methods established earlier. In particular, we use characterizations of languages generated by generalized product-free classical categorial grammars given in [2], and adopt ideas from [6], where the strong equivalence of nonassociative Ajdukiewicz and Lambek grammars with product was established.

The paper is organized as follows. Preliminary notions are described in section 2. Classical categorial grammars and degrees of complexity are defined in section 3. In section 4 a characterization of b-languages generated by product-free classical categorial grammars is given. This characterization is used in section 5 to prove that phrase languages generated by classical categorial grammars with product can also be generated by product-free grammars. In section 6 the main result of the paper is given.

2 Preliminaries

We fix a countable set $\mathcal{F}$ of (at least binary) operation symbols. A symbol $f \in \mathcal{F}$ will be referred to as an *f-product symbol*. The arity of f will be denoted $\varrho(f)$. For each product symbol and each i such that $1 \leq i \leq \varrho(f)$ we introduce a new operation symbol f/i called an *i-th f-functor symbol*. We assume that for all $1 \leq i \leq \varrho(f)$ the arity of f/i is the same as that of f. Let $\mathcal{F}^0 = \{f/i : f \in \mathcal{F}, 1 \leq i \leq \varrho(f)\}$, and $\overline{\mathcal{F}} = \mathcal{F} \cup \mathcal{F}^0$. The absolutely free algebra of signature $\overline{\mathcal{F}}$ (resp. $\mathcal{F}$, $\mathcal{F}^0$) over a set of atoms V will be denoted $\mathrm{PF}(V)$ (resp. $\mathrm{B}(V)$, $\mathrm{F}(V)$). We identify the algebras with their universes and call elements of $\mathrm{PF}(V)$ (resp. $\mathrm{B}(V)$, $\mathrm{F}(V)$) *product-functorial structures* or in short *pf-structures* (resp. *phrase structures, product-free pf-structures*). A *product* (resp. *functorial*) *pf-structure* is a structure from $\mathrm{PF}(V)$ in which the outermost symbol is a certain f-product (resp. *i*-th f-functor). Atoms from V will be treated both as functorial and product pf-structures. Throughout the paper we adopt a vector-style notation for structures writing $p(\mathbf{A}_n)$ instead of $p(A_1, \ldots, A_n)$, and $p(\mathbf{A}_n|i : B)$ instead of $p(A_1, \ldots, A_{i-1}, B, A_{i+1}, \ldots, A_n)$ for p being a product or functor symbol.

Given a countable set Pr of *primitive types* the set $\mathrm{PF}(\mathrm{Pr})$ (resp. $\mathrm{F}(\mathrm{Pr})$) will be referred to as the set of *types* (resp. *product-free types*) and denoted T (resp.

T^0). The *generalized Lambek calculus of syntactic types* GL is a formal system defined in the following way: formulas of GL have the shape $x \to y$, where $x, y \in$ T, the system admits one axiom scheme

(A0) $x \to x$, for all $x \in$ T.

and three rules of inference:

(R1) $$\frac{f(\mathbf{x}_n) \to y}{x_i \to f/i(\mathbf{x}_n|i : y)}$$

(R2) $$\frac{x_i \to f/i(\mathbf{x}_n|i : y)}{f(\mathbf{x}_n) \to y}$$

(cut) $$\frac{x \to y \quad y \to z}{x \to z} \,,$$

in which $f \in \mathcal{F}$ and $1 \leq i \leq \varrho(f) = n$. The reader is encouraged to compare this axiomatization with that of the nonassociative Lambek calculus as presented in [8] and [5].

In order to employ GL as a type reduction system underlying categorial grammars we will present it in a different yet equivalent form. By the set BS(V) of *bracketed strings of types* we understand the smallest set fulfilling the following conditions: (i) $V \subset$ BS(V), (ii) if $X_1, \ldots, X_n \in$ BS(V), $f \in \mathcal{F}$ and $\varrho(f) = n$, then ${}^f(X_1, \ldots, X_n)^f \in$ BS(V). The alternative axiomatization of GL will employ formulas from an auxiliary set of formulas Ax defined as follows: (i) formulas

(A1) $f(\mathbf{x}_n|i : f/i(\mathbf{x}_n)) \to x_i$

(A2) $x_i \to f/i(\mathbf{x}_n|i : f(\mathbf{x}_n))$,

where $f \in \mathcal{F}$, $1 \leq i \leq \varrho(f) = n$, and the axiom (A0) are in Ax, (ii) Ax is closed with respect to the rules

(P1) $$\frac{x \to y}{f/i(\mathbf{x}_n|i : x) \to f/i(\mathbf{x}_n|i : y)}$$

(P2) $$\frac{x \to y}{f/i(\mathbf{x}_n|j : y) \to f/i(\mathbf{x}_n|j : x)} \,, \quad \text{where } i \neq j$$

(P3) $$\frac{x \to y}{f(\mathbf{x}_n|i : x) \to f(\mathbf{x}_n|i : y)} \,.$$

Let GLC be a system whose formulas have the shape $X \to x$, for $X \in$ BS(T) and $x \in$ T, formalized by the axiom (A0) (observe that x in (A0) can be treated both as an element of T and as a bracketed string from BS(T)) and three rules of inference:

(A) $$\frac{X_i \to f/i(\mathbf{x}_n) \quad \{X_j \to x_j\}_{1 \leq j \leq n,\, j \neq i}}{{}^f(X_1, \ldots, X_n)^f \to x_i}$$

(P) $$\frac{\{X_j \to x_j\}_{1 \leq j \leq n}}{{}^f(X_1, \ldots, X_n)^f \to f(\mathbf{x}_n)}$$

(C) $\qquad \dfrac{X \to x}{X \to y}$ if $x \neq y$ and $x \to y \in \mathrm{Ax}$.

For any $X \in \mathrm{BS}(V)$ let $[X]$ be an element of $\mathrm{PF}(V)$ defined inductively as follows: (i) $[X] = X$ for $X \in V$, (ii) if $X = {}^{f}(X_1, \dots, X_n)^{f}$, then $[X] = f([X_1], \dots, [X_n])$. (In fact, $[X]$ is an element of $B(V)$, as it contains no functorial symbols.)

The following theorem establishes the equivalence of GL and GLC, cf. [7]:

Theorem 1. $\vdash_{\mathrm{GLC}} X \to x$ *if and only if* $\vdash_{\mathrm{GL}} [X] \to x$.

Proof. ($\Rightarrow$). Induction on the length of derivation.

($\Leftarrow$). It can be shown that if $\vdash_{\mathrm{GL}} [X] \to x$, then there exists a sequence $x_1 \to x_2, \dots, x_{n-1} \to x_n$ of formulas from Ax such that $x_1 = [X]$ and $x_n = x$. Moreover, one also proves that the formula $X \to [X]$ is derivable in GLC. Thus the derivation D of $X \to [X]$ in GLC can be extended by $n-1$ instances of (C) employing the aforementioned formulas $x_1 \to x_2, \dots, x_{n-1} \to x_n$ from Ax. This extension gives a derivation of $X \to x$ in GLC. $\qquad \square$

The system formalized by (A0), (A) and (P) will be called the *generalized Ajdukiewicz calculus of syntactic types* and denoted GAC. The product-free version of GAC, which employs only product-free types from T^0 and makes use of (A0) and the rule (A), will be denoted GAC^0.

All calculi mentioned above can serve as type reduction systems in categorial grammars. A *categorial grammar based on a syntactic calculus* C (in short a *C-grammar*) is an ordered quadruple $G = \langle V_G, I_G, s_G, \mathrm{C} \rangle$ whose components fulfill the following conditions: V_G is a nonempty, finite *vocabulary*, I_G is a finite relation on $V_G \times \mathrm{T}$ called the *initial type assignment of* G, and s_G is a distinguished primitive type. In a natural way one can extend I_G to the relation $F_G \subset \mathrm{BS}(V_G) \times \mathrm{BS}(\mathrm{T})$ such that: (i) $I_G \subset F_G$, (ii) if $(A_i, X_i) \in F_G$, for all $1 \leq i \leq \varrho(f) = n$, then $({}^{f}(A_1, \dots, A_n)^{f}, {}^{f}(X_1, \dots, X_n)^{f}) \in F_G$. The set $\{A \in \mathrm{BS}(V_G) : (\exists X \in \mathrm{BS}(\mathrm{T}))(A, X) \in F_G \ \& \vdash_{\mathrm{C}} X \to s_G\}$ will be called the *phrase language generated by* G and denoted $\mathrm{BL}(G)$.

3 Classical categorial grammars

Let $A = p(A_1, \dots, A_n)$, $p = f/i$ or $p = f$ for some $f \in \mathcal{F}$, be a pf-structure. pf-structures $A_1, \dots, A_n$ will be referred to as the *direct substructures of* A. In particular, if $p = f/i$, then A_i (resp. A_j, $j \neq i$) will be called the *functor* (resp. *arguments*) *of* A. If $p = f$ then each direct substructure of A will also be called an *element of* A. The set $\mathrm{sub}(A)$ of *substructures of* A is defined by the following induction: (i) $A \in \mathrm{sub}(A)$, (ii) if $B \in \mathrm{sub}(A)$ and C is a direct substructure of B then $C \in \mathrm{sub}(A)$. The *size of* A, to be denoted $\mathrm{s}(A)$, is the set consisting of all $f \in \mathcal{F}$ such that f or f/i occurs in A, and the *complexity* $\mathrm{c}(A)$ *of* A is the total number of all those occurrences. The notions of the set of substructures and of size can be extended to sets of pf-structures by putting $\mathrm{sub}(U) = \bigcup\{\mathrm{sub}(A) : A \in U\}$ and $\mathrm{s}(U) = \bigcup\{\mathrm{s}(A) : A \in U\}$ for any $U \subset \mathrm{PF}(V)$. By a *product-functorial language* (in short *pf-language*) we mean a set $L \subset \mathrm{PF}(V)$ fulfilling the conditions:

(PFL1)   if $A \in L$, then A is a functorial structure,

(PFL2)   if $f/i(A_1, \ldots, A_n) \in \mathrm{sub}(L)$, then A_i is a functorial structure.

The notions defined above for pf-structures have their natural counterparts in the case of bracketed strings of types. In particular, we can consider the set $\mathrm{sub}(A)$ of *bracketed substrings of $A \in \mathrm{BS}(V)$* and properly define the set $\mathrm{s}(A)$ (resp. $\mathrm{s}(U)$) as well as the number $\mathrm{c}(A)$ for A being a bracketed string of types (resp. $U \subset \mathrm{BS}(V)$). Any subset of $\mathrm{BS}(V)$ will be called a *b-language*. It is easily observed that elements of $\mathrm{B}(V)$ stay in one-to-one correspondence with elements of $\mathrm{BS}(V)$. For $A \in \mathrm{PF}(V)$ a bracketed string $\mathrm{bs}(A)$ is defined by the following induction: (i) $\mathrm{bs}(A) = A$ for $A \in V$, (ii) $\mathrm{bs}(f/i(\mathbf{A}_n)) = \mathrm{bs}(f(\mathbf{A}_n)) = {}^f(\mathrm{bs}(A_1), \ldots, \mathrm{bs}(A_n))^f$, and for $L \subset \mathrm{PF}(V)$ we refer to the set $\mathrm{bs}(L) = \{\mathrm{bs}(A) : A \in L\}$ as the *b-language determined by L*.

In what follows we will use the notion of classical categorial grammar, cf. [2]. As far as the ability to generate languages is concerned, classical categorial grammars are equivalent with GAC-grammars, see lemma 4. They are, however, a formalism which is more convenient for presentation of properties of pf- and b-languages.

A *classical categorial grammar* (CCG) is an ordered triple $G = \langle V_G, I_G, s_G \rangle$ in which V_G is a nonempty *vocabulary*, $I_G \subset V_G \times \mathrm{T}$ and $s_G \in \mathrm{Pr}$. As in the case of categorial grammars defined in the previous section, I_G will be called the *initial type assignment of G* but no finiteness of I_G in CCG is required. By the *terminal type assignment in G* we understand the minimal relation T_G on $\mathrm{PF}(V_G) \times \mathrm{T}$ which includes I_G and satisfies the following two conditions:

(GF)   if $f/i(\mathbf{x}_n) \in T_G(A_i)$, where $1 \leq i \leq n = \varrho(f)$ and $x_j \in T_G(A_j)$ for all $j \neq i$, then $x_i \in T_G(f/i(\mathbf{A}_n))$,

(GP)   if $x_i \in T_G(A_i)$, $1 \leq i \leq n = \varrho(f)$, then $f(\mathbf{x}_n) \in T_G(f(\mathbf{A}_n))$.

Lemma 2. *(i) The terminal type assignment T of a CCG satisfies the conditions:*

(NF) $x_i \in T(f/i(\mathbf{A}_n))$, $1 \leq i \leq n = \varrho(f)$ *if and only if there exist $x_j \in T(A_j)$, $1 \leq j \leq n$, $i \neq j$, such that $f/i(\mathbf{x}_n) \in T(A_i)$,*

(NP) $x \in T(f(\mathbf{A}_n))$ *if and only if there exist $x_i \in T(A_i)$, $1 \leq i \leq n = \varrho(f)$, such that $x = f(\mathbf{x}_n)$.*

(ii) If a relation $T \subset \mathrm{PF}(V) \times \mathrm{T}$ satisfies the conditions (NF) and (NP), then $T = T_G$ for a certain CCG G.

Proof. (i) The 'if' parts of (NF) and (NP) follow from the fact that T satisfies the conditions (GF) and (GP). In order to prove the 'only if' part it suffices to make use of the minimality of T.

(ii) We put $G = \langle V, I_G, s \rangle$, where s is any primitive type and $I_G = T \cap (V \times \mathrm{T})$. As T_G is the minimal relation satisfying (GF) and (GP) and T fulfills those conditions we get immediately the inclusion $T_G \subset T$. The opposite inclusion can be proved by induction on the complexity of $A \in \mathrm{FS}(V)$. $\qquad\qquad\square$

A *product-free classical categorial grammar* CCG^0 is a CCG in which only product-free structures and types are considered. For any relation $T \subset \mathrm{PF}(V) \times \mathrm{T}$ we put $\mathrm{TYP}(T) = \{x \in \mathrm{T} : (A,x) \in T \text{ for some } A \in \mathrm{PF}(v)\}$ and call a CCG (CCG^0) *finite* if the set $\mathrm{TYP}(I_G)$ is so.

Let G be a CCG (resp. CCG^0). By the *pf-language* (resp. *f-language*) generated by G we mean the set $\mathrm{L}(G) = \{A \in \mathrm{PF}(V_G) : s_G \in T_G(A)\}$. The set $\mathrm{BL}(G) = \mathrm{bs}(\mathrm{L}(G))$ will be referred to as the *b-language generated by* G.

Lemma 3. *If G is a CCG then $\mathrm{L}(G)$ satisfies (PFL1) and (PFL2).*

Proof. According to lemma 2(i) T_G satisfies (NF) and (NP). If $A \in \mathrm{L}(G)$ then either it is an atom from V_G, thus a functorial structure by definition, or it is a complex structure, but then, by (NF), it must be a functorial structure as well. If a functor A_i of a functorial structure $f/i(\mathbf{A}_n)$ were not a functorial structure, then it would be of the shape $a_i = g(\mathbf{B}_m)$, for some natural $m \geq 2$ and $g \in \mathcal{F}$. But then T_G would assign to A_i a type of the form $g(\mathbf{x}_m)$, which would contradict (NF). $\qquad\qquad\square$

Lemma 4. *(i) For every finite CCG G there exists a GAC-grammar G' such that $\mathrm{BL}(G) = \mathrm{BL}(G')$.*

(ii) For every GAC-grammar G' there exists a finite CCG G such that $\mathrm{BL}(G') = \mathrm{BL}(G)$.

Proof. (i) Given $G = \langle V_G, I_G, s_G \rangle$ we put $G' = \langle V_G, I_G, s_G, \mathrm{GAC} \rangle$. By induction on $c(A)$ and $c(B)$ one can prove the following facts:

Fact 1. If $(A, x) \in T_G$, then there exists $X \in \mathrm{BS}(\mathrm{T})$ such that $(\mathrm{bs}(A), X) \in F_G$ and $\vdash_{\mathrm{GAC}} X \to x$.

Fact 2. If $(B, X) \in F_G$ and $\vdash_{\mathrm{GAC}} X \to x$ for some $X \in \mathrm{BS}(\mathrm{T})$, $B \in \mathrm{BS}(V_G)$. and $x \in \mathrm{T}$, then there exists $A \in \mathrm{PF}(V_G)$ such that $B = \mathrm{bs}(A)$ and $(A, x) \in T_G$.

In order to show that $\mathrm{BL}(G) \subset \mathrm{BL}(G')$ let us assume that $B \in \mathrm{BL}(G)$. Thus there exists $A \in \mathrm{L}(G)$ such that $B = \mathrm{bs}(A)$ and $(A, s_G) \in T_G$. According to fact 1, for some $X \in \mathrm{BS}(\mathrm{T})$ we have $(B, X) \in F_G$ and $\vdash_{\mathrm{GAC}} X \to s_G$, which means that $B \in \mathrm{BL}(G)$. Conversely, if $B \in \mathrm{BL}(G')$, then there is $X \in \mathrm{BS}(\mathrm{T})$ such that $(B, X) \in F_G$ and $\vdash_{\mathrm{GAC}} X \to s_G$. Thus, by fact 2, for some $A \in \mathrm{PF}(V_G)$ we have $(A, s_g) \in T_G$ and $B = \mathrm{bs}(A)$. Consequently, $B \in \mathrm{bs}(\mathrm{L}(G)) = \mathrm{BL}(G)$.

(ii) If $G' = \langle V_{G'}, I_{G'}, s_{G'}, \mathrm{GAC} \rangle$, then we put $G = \langle V_{G'}, I_{G'}, s_{G'} \rangle$ and proceed exactly in the same way as in (i). $\qquad\qquad\square$

In a similar way we prove the product-free version of lemma 4:

Lemma 5. *For every finite product-free CCG G there exists an GAC-grammar G' such that $\mathrm{BL}(G) = \mathrm{BL}(G')$, and conversely.*

By a *congruence in* PF(V) we understand an equivalence relation $\sim$ on PF(V) such that for all $p \in \overline{\mathcal{F}}$ the following condition holds:

if for all $1 \leq i \leq n = \varrho(p)$ $A_i \sim B_i$ then $p(\mathbf{A}_n) \sim p(\mathbf{B}_n)$.

A congruence $\sim$ in PF(V) is called a *congruence on* $U \subset$ PF(V) if it satisfies the condition:

if $A \sim B$, then $A \in U$ if and only if $B \in U$.

It is clear that in order to prove that $\sim$ is a congruence on U it suffices to show that from $A \sim B$ and $A \in U$ follows $B \in U$.

Given a pf-language $L \subset$ PF(V) the largest congruence on L with respect to inclusion will be called the *intersubstitutability relation for* L and denoted INT$_L$. From the set-theoretical point of view INT$_L$ amounts to the least transitive relation which contains all congruences on L. One can easily show that INT$_L$ is also a congruence on sub(L) and consequently elements of PF(V)\ sub(L), if there are any, form a unique class of equivalence. By int$_L(A)$ we will denote the equivalence class of INT$_L$ determined by A, by L^{int} the set of all such equivalence classes, and by ind(L) the cardinality of L^{int}, to be called the *index of* L. The set L^{int} can be treated as (the universe of) a quotient algebra with induced operations introduced in a standard way (we use the same symbols to denote operations in PF(V) and in L^{int}):

$$p(\mathrm{int}_L(A_1), \ldots, \mathrm{int}_L(A_n)) = \mathrm{int}_L(p(A_1, \ldots, A_n)).$$

Naturally, the notions described above are applicable to the algebras F(V) and B(V), see [2] and [4]. In particular, due to the one-to-one correspondence between elements of B(V) and BS(V), we can introduce the relation INT$_L$ and the number ind(L) for any b-language $L \subset$ BS(V).

The internal structure of elements of PF(V) can be characterized by means of paths and their lengths. A *path in* $A \in$ PF(V) is a sequence $A_0, A_1, \ldots, A_n$ such that $A_0 \in$ sub(A) and for all $1 \leq i \leq n$ A_i is a direct substructure of A_{i-1}. The number n is called the *length* of this path. A sequence $A_0, A_1, \ldots, A_n$ is referred to as a *functorial path* or shortly *f-path* (resp. *product path*, *p-path*) if A_i is a functor (resp. an element) of A_{i-1}, $1 \leq i \leq n$. A path $A_0, A_1, \ldots, A_n$ such that A_0 is a product structure and for some $1 \leq k < n$ $A_0, A_1, \ldots, A_k$ is a p-path in A_0 and $A_k, \ldots, A_n$ is a f-path in A_k (resp. A_0 is a functorial structure and for some $1 \leq k < n$ $A_0, A_1, \ldots, A_k$ is an f-path in A_0, A_{k+1} is an argument of A_k and $A_{k+1}, \ldots, A_n$ is a p-path in A_{k+1}) is called a *product-functorial path* or *pf-path* (resp. *functorial-product path*, *fp-path*).

By the *external degree of* $A \in$ PF(V), to be denoted $\deg^{\mathrm{e}}(A)$, we mean the minimal length of paths in A whose initial term is A and whose terminal term is an atom from V. If $A \in$ PF(V) is a product (resp. functorial) structure then the maximal length of p-paths (resp. f-paths) in A whose initial term is A is called the *external product* (resp. *functorial*) *degree* of A and denoted $\deg_{\mathrm{p}}^{\mathrm{e}}(A)$ (resp. $\deg_{\mathrm{f}}^{\mathrm{e}}(A)$). The maximal length of p- or pf-paths (resp. f- or fp-paths) in a product (resp. functorial) structure A whose initial term is A is called the *external compound degree of* A and denoted $\deg_{\mathrm{cc}}^{\mathrm{e}}(A)$.

For $A \in \mathrm{PF}(V)$ the numbers

$$\deg(A) = \max\{\deg^e(B) : B \in \mathrm{sub}(A)\}$$
$$\deg_p(A) = \max\{\deg_p^e(B) : B \in \mathrm{sub}(A)\}$$
$$\deg_f(A) = \max\{\deg_f^e(B) : B \in \mathrm{sub}(A)\}$$
$$\deg_c(A) = \max\{\deg_c^e(B) : B \in \mathrm{sub}(A)\}$$

are called the *degree* and the *product, functorial* and *compound degree of A*. For $L \subset \mathrm{PF}(V)$ the numbers

$$\deg(L) = \sup\{\deg(A) : A \in L\}$$
$$\deg_p(L) = \sup\{\deg_p(A) : A \in L\}$$
$$\deg_f(L) = \sup\{\deg_f(A) : A \in L\}$$
$$\deg_{pf}(L) = \deg_p(L) + \deg_f(L)$$
$$\deg_c(L) = \sup\{\deg_c(A) : A \in L\}$$

are referred to as the *degree* and the *product, functorial, product-functorial* and *compound degree of L* respectively. Observe that the definition of a path can be formulated for phrase structures and for bracketed strings of types. Consequently, one can introduce the notion of $\deg(L)$ for any b-language. In addition, product-free structures admit characterization in terms of degree and functorial degree.

4 A characterization of b-languages generated by product-free classical categorial grammars

Let x be a product-free type. The *order of x* is a natural number $o(x)$ such that: (i) for $x \in \mathrm{Pr}\ o(x) = 0$, (ii) $o(f/i(x_1,\ldots,x_n)) = \max\{o(x_i), \max\{o(x_j) + 1 : j \neq i\}\}$. The number $\sup\{o(x) : x \in \mathrm{TYP}(I_G)\}$, for I_G being the initial type assignment of a CCG^0 or a GAC^0-grammar G will be called the *order* of G and denoted $o(G)$.

The following two theorems were proved in [2]:

Theorem 6. *If $L = \mathrm{L}(G)$ for a finite product-free CCG G, then $L = L(G')$ for some finite product-free CCG G' such that $o(G') \leq 1$.*

Theorem 7. *$L = \mathrm{L}(G)$ for a finite product-free CCG G if and only if the numbers $\deg_f(L)$, $\mathrm{ind}(L)$ and $\mathrm{s}(L)$ are finite.*

The next theorem is an analogue of a result given in [3], see also [4], where the operation considered was nonassociative concatenation.

Theorem 8. *$L = \mathrm{BL}(G)$ for a certain finite product-free CCG G if and only if the numbers $\deg(L)$, $\mathrm{ind}(L)$ and $\mathrm{s}(L)$ are finite.*

Proof. We adopt the idea of the proof from [3]. As all pf-structures which appear in our proof are product-free, they are in fact elements of $\mathrm{F}(V_G)$ and we will call them simply structures.

($\Rightarrow$). Let $G = \langle V_G, I_G, s_G \rangle$. If $L = \mathrm{BL}(G)$, then $L = \mathrm{bs}(\mathrm{L}(G))$ and by theorem 7 the numbers $\deg_f(\mathrm{L}(G))$, $\mathrm{ind}(\mathrm{L}(G))$ and $\mathrm{s}(\mathrm{L}(G))$ are finite. Each functorial path in a (product-free) structure $A \in \mathrm{F}(V_G)$ yields a path in $\mathrm{bs}(A)$, thus we have $\deg(L) \leq \deg_f(\mathrm{L}(G))$. We have also $\mathrm{s}(\mathrm{L}(G)) = \mathrm{s}(L)$, which means that $\deg(L)$ and $\mathrm{s}(L)$ are finite.

For $B \in \mathrm{BS}(V_G)$ let us define

$$\mathbf{F}(B) = \{\mathrm{int}_{\mathrm{L}(G)}(A) \colon A \in \mathrm{F}(V_G) \text{ and } \mathrm{bs}(A) = B\},$$

and put $B \sim C$ if and only if $\mathbf{F}(B) = \mathbf{F}(C)$. We are going to show that the relation $\sim \subset [\mathrm{BS}(V_G)]^2$ is a congruence on $\mathrm{BL}(G)$. Obviously $\sim$ is an equivalence relation. Let us assume that for some $f \in \mathcal{F}$ and for all $1 \leq j \leq n = \varrho(F)$ we have $A_j, B_j \in \mathrm{BS}(V_G)$ and $A_j \sim B_j$. There hold the following equalities:

$\mathbf{F}({}^f(A_1, \ldots, A_n)^f) = \{\mathrm{int}_{\mathrm{L}(G)}(C) : C \in \mathrm{F}(V_G), \mathrm{bs}(C) = {}^f(A_1, \ldots, A_n)^f\} =$
$\{\mathrm{int}_{\mathrm{L}(G)}(f/i(C_1, \ldots, C_n)) : 1 \leq i \leq n, C_j \in \mathrm{F}(V_G), \mathrm{BS}(C_j) = A_j$
for all $1 \leq j \leq n\} =$
$\{f/i(\mathrm{int}_{\mathrm{L}(G)}(C_1), \ldots, \mathrm{int}_{\mathrm{L}(G)}(C_1)) : 1 \leq i \leq n, C_j \in \mathrm{F}(V_G), \mathrm{BS}(C_j) = A_j$
for all $1 \leq j \leq n\} =$
$\{f/i(\mathrm{int}_{\mathrm{L}(G)}(C_1), \ldots, \mathrm{int}_{\mathrm{L}(G)}(C_1)) : 1 \leq i \leq n, C_j \in \mathrm{F}(V_G), \mathrm{BS}(C_j) = B_j$
for all $1 \leq j \leq n\} =$
$\{\mathrm{int}_{\mathrm{L}(G)}(f/i(C_1, \ldots, C_n)) : 1 \leq i \leq n, C_j \in \mathrm{F}(V_G), \mathrm{BS}(C_j) = B_j$
for all $1 \leq j \leq n\} =$
$\{\mathrm{int}_{\mathrm{L}(G)}(C) : C \in \mathrm{F}(V_G), \mathrm{bs}(C) = {}^f(A_1, \ldots, A_n)^f\} = \mathbf{F}({}^f(B_1, \ldots, B_n)^f),$

which means that ${}^f(A_1, \ldots, A_n)^f \sim {}^f(B_1, \ldots, B_n)^f$. Consequently, $\sim$ is a congruence.

In order to show that $\sim$ is a congruence on $\mathrm{BL}(G)$ let us take $A, B \in \mathrm{BS}(V_G)$ and assume that $A \sim B$ and $A \in \mathrm{BL}(G)$. Thus there exists $C \in \mathrm{L}(G)$ such that $A = \mathrm{bs}(C)$ and $\mathrm{int}_{\mathrm{L}(G)}(C) \in \mathbf{F}(A)$. As $\mathbf{F}(A) = \mathbf{F}(B)$, we get $\mathrm{int}_{\mathrm{L}(G)}(C) \in \mathbf{F}(B)$. As a consequence we find such $C' \in \mathrm{F}(V_G)$ that $\mathrm{bs}(C') = B$ and $C' \in \mathrm{int}_{\mathrm{L}(G)}(C)$. Thus $\mathrm{int}_{\mathrm{L}(G)}(C) = \mathrm{int}_{\mathrm{L}(G)}(C')$, and $C\mathrm{INT}_{\mathrm{L}(G)}C'$. As $C \in \mathrm{L}(G)$ we get $C' \in \mathrm{L}(G)$ and, as $B = \mathrm{bs}(C')$, we have $B \in \mathrm{BL}(G)$.

We can easily evaluate the index of the relation $\sim$: there will be no more equivalence classes of $\sim$ as there are different sets consisting of equivalence classes of the relation $\mathrm{INT}_{\mathrm{L}(G)}$. Thus $\mathrm{ind}(\sim) \leq 2^{\mathrm{ind}(\mathrm{L}(G))}$, and the latter number is finite. We proved that $\sim$ is a congruence on $L = \mathrm{BL}(G)$. Obviously, as INT_L is the largest congruence on L we get $\sim \subset \mathrm{INT}_L$. Consequently, $\mathrm{ind}(L) \leq \mathrm{ind}(\sim)$, which yields the finiteness of $\mathrm{ind}(L)$.

($\Leftarrow$). Let us assume that for a set $L \subset \mathrm{BS}(V)$ the numbers $\deg(L)$, $\mathrm{ind}(L)$ and $\mathrm{s}(L)$ are finite. We will construct a CCG^0 G such that $L = \mathrm{BL}(G)$. Let $L' = \{A \in \mathrm{FS}(V) : \mathrm{bs}(A) \in L \ \& \ \deg_f(A) \leq \deg(A)\}$. L' is not empty as in each substructure of $B \in L$ we can mark as a functorial path a path leading from this substructure to the nearest atom from V. The length of such an f-path will always be shorter than $\deg(L)$. It is easily seen that $\mathrm{s}(L') = \mathrm{s}(L)$ and $\deg_f(L') \leq \deg(L)$, thus the numbers $\mathrm{s}(L')$ and $\deg_f(L')$ are finite. We want to show that the number $\mathrm{ind}(L')$ is finite as well.

Let a relation $\sim \subset [\mathrm{BS}(V_G)]^2$ be defined as follows: $A \sim B$ if and only if

either $\deg_f(A) > \deg(L)$ and $\deg_f(B) > \deg(L)$, or
$\mathrm{bs}(A)\mathrm{INT}_L\mathrm{bs}(B)$, $\deg_f^e(A) = \deg_f^e(B)$ and $\deg_f(A) = \deg_f(B)$.

We will make use of the equalities which hold true for functorial degrees:

$\deg_f^e(v) = \deg_f(v) = 0$ for $v \in V$,
$\deg_f^e(g/i(\mathbf{A}_n)) = \deg_f^e(A_i) + 1$,
$\deg_f(g/i(\mathbf{A}_n)) = \max\{\deg_f^e(g/i(\mathbf{A}_n)), \max\{\deg_f(A_j) : 1 \le j \le n\}\}$.

It is clear that $\sim$ is an equivalence relation. We will show that it is a congruence on L'. Assume that $g/i \in \mathcal{F}^0$ and let for all $1 \le j \le n = \varrho(g)$ we have $A_J \sim B_j$. We must prove that $g/i(\mathbf{A}_n) \sim g/i(\mathbf{B}_n)$. There are two cases to consider:

1. For some $1 \le j \le n$ the relation $A_j \sim B_j$ holds because of the fact that $\deg_f(A_j) > \deg(L)$ and $\deg_f(B_j) > \deg(L)$. Thus

$\deg_f(g/i(\mathbf{A}_n)) \ge \deg_f(A_j) > \deg(L)$ and
$\deg_f(g/i(\mathbf{B}_n)) \ge \deg_f(B_j) > \deg(L)$,

consequently, $g/i(\mathbf{A}_n) \sim g/i(\mathbf{B}_n)$ in this case.

2. For all $1 \le j \le n$ we have $\mathrm{bs}(A_j)\mathrm{INT}_L\mathrm{bs}(B_j)$, $\deg_f^e(A_j) = \deg_f^e(B_j)$ and $\deg_f(A_j) = \deg_f(B_j)$. We show that those three conditions are also fulfilled by the structures $g/i(\mathbf{A}_n)$ and $g/i(\mathbf{B}_n)$.

(i) If for all $1 \le j \le n$ $\mathrm{bs}(A_j)\mathrm{INT}_L\mathrm{bs}(B_j)$ hold, then, as INT_L is a congruence in $\mathrm{BS}(V)$, we have ${}^g(\mathrm{bs}(A_1), \ldots, \mathrm{bs}(A_n))^g \mathrm{INT}_L \, {}^g(\mathrm{bs}(B_1), \ldots, \mathrm{bs}(B_n))^g$. But ${}^g(\mathrm{bs}(A_1), \ldots, \mathrm{bs}(A_n))^g = \mathrm{bs}(g/i(\mathbf{A}_n))$ and ${}^g(\mathrm{bs}(B_1), \ldots, \mathrm{bs}(B_n))^g = \mathrm{bs}(g/i(\mathbf{B}_n))$, thus $\mathrm{bs}(g/i(\mathbf{A}_n))\mathrm{INT}_L\mathrm{bs}(g/i(\mathbf{B}_n))$.

(ii) If for all $1 \le j \le n$ $\deg_f^e(A_j) = \deg_f^e(B_j)$, then $\deg_f^e(g/i(\mathbf{A}_n)) = \deg_f^e(A_i) + 1 = \deg_f^e(B_i) + 1 = \deg_f^e(g/i(\mathbf{A}_n))$.

(iii) If for all $1 \le j \le n$ we have $\deg_f(A_j) = \deg_f(B_j)$ then $\deg_f(g/i(\mathbf{A}_n)) = \max\{\deg_f^e(g/i(\mathbf{A}_n)), \max\{\deg_f(A_j) : 1 \le j \le n\}\} = \max\{\deg_f^e(g/i(\mathbf{B}_n)), \max\{\deg_f(B_j) : 1 \le j \le n\}\} = \deg_f(g/i(\mathbf{B}_n))$.

In order to prove that $\sim$ is a congruence on L' let us assume that $A \sim B$ and $A \in L'$. Consequently, $\deg_f(A) \le \deg_f(L') \le \deg(L)$, thus we must have $\mathrm{bs}(A)\mathrm{INT}_L\mathrm{bs}(B)$, $\deg_f^e(A) = \deg_f^e(B)$ and $\deg_f(A) = \deg_f(B)$. If $A \in L'$ then $\mathrm{bs}(A) \in L$, hence $\mathrm{bs}(B) \in L$. But we also have $\deg_f(B) = \deg_f(A) \le \deg(L)$, consequently by the definition of L' we have $B \in L'$.

The definition of $\sim$ gives rise to the following estimation of its index:

$$\mathrm{ind}(\sim) \le 1 + \mathrm{ind}(L) \cdot \deg(L) \cdot \deg(L).$$

As a consequence, the number $\deg(\sim)$ is finite. Moreover, as $\mathrm{INT}_{L'}$ is the largest congruence on L' we have $\sim \subset \mathrm{INT}_{L'}$ and $\mathrm{ind}(L') \le \mathrm{ind}(\sim)$, which means that $\mathrm{ind}(L')$ is a finite number. According to theorem 7 $L' = \mathrm{L}(G)$ for some CCG^0 G and for this grammar we have $L = \mathrm{BL}(G)$. $\qquad\square$

5   b-languages generated by classical categorial grammars with product

Lemma 9. *If L is a pf-language, then* $\deg(\mathrm{bs}(L)) = \deg(L) \leq \deg_c(L)$.

Proof. The equality follows from the fact that the definitions of the degree of a pf-structure and of a bracketed string take into consideration paths which are descending sequences of direct substructures and substrings. Obviously, the lengths of those paths are equal. It is easily seen that for any $A \in \mathrm{sub}(L)$ we have $\deg^e(A) \leq \deg_c^e(A)$. Thus in order to prove the inequality it suffices to employ this fact in the definitions of $\deg(L)$ and $\deg_c(L)$. $\qquad\square$

Let G be a CCG. We put

$$\mathrm{TYP}_{\mathrm{sub}}(I_G) = \{x \in \mathrm{T} : (\exists A \in \mathrm{sub}(\mathrm{L}(G)))(x \in I_G(A))\},$$
$$\mathrm{TYP}_{\mathrm{sub}}(T_G) = \{x \in \mathrm{T} : (\exists A \in \mathrm{sub}(\mathrm{L}(G)))(x \in T_G(A))\},$$
$$\mathrm{r}_{\mathrm{sub}}(G) = \mathrm{card}(\mathrm{TYP}_{\mathrm{sub}}(T_G)).$$

Lemma 10. *(i)* $\mathrm{TYP}_{\mathrm{sub}}(I_G) \subset \mathrm{TYP}(I_G)$, $\mathrm{TYP}_{\mathrm{sub}}(T_G) \subset \mathrm{TYP}(T_G)$.

(ii) Let L be a pf-language. Each non-atomic product structure $A \in \mathrm{sub}(L)$ is either an argumant of some functorial structure from $\mathrm{sub}(L)$ or an element of some product structure from $\mathrm{sub}(L)$.

(iii) Let L be a pf-language and assume that $A \in \mathrm{sub}(L)$ is a non-atomic product structure which is an argument of no functorial structure from $\mathrm{sub}(L)$. There exist $n \geq 1$ and a p-path $A_0, A_1, \ldots, A_n$ such that $A_n = A$ and A_0 is an argument of some functorial structure from $\mathrm{sub}(L)$.

Proof. (i) is an immediate consequence of the definitions of $\mathrm{TYP}_{\mathrm{sub}}(I_G)$ and $\mathrm{TYP}_{\mathrm{sub}}(T_G)$. (ii) as well as (iii) are consequences of the conditions (PFL1) and (PFL2). $\qquad\square$

Lemma 11. *Let G be a CCG. If $A \in \mathrm{sub}(\mathrm{L}(G))$ is a product structure and $x \in T_G(A)$, then there exists a functorial structure $B \in \mathrm{sub}(\mathrm{L}(G))$, its argument C and some $y \in T_G(C)$ such that $x \in \mathrm{sub}(y)$.*

Proof. We make use of lemma 10(iii) and conditions (NF) and (NP). $\qquad\square$

The necessity for introducing the sets $\mathrm{TYP}_{\mathrm{sub}}(I_G)$ and $\mathrm{TYP}_{\mathrm{sub}}(T_G)$ follows from the fact that conditions (NF) and (NP) ascribe types to structures which does not necessarily belong to $\mathrm{sub}(\mathrm{L}(G))$.

Lemma 12. *For a CCG G the following inclusions are true:*

$$\mathrm{TYP}_{\mathrm{sub}}(I_G) \subset \mathrm{TYP}_{\mathrm{sub}}(T_G) \subset \mathrm{sub}(\mathrm{TYP}_{\mathrm{sub}}(I_G)).$$

Proof. We have $I_G \subset T_G$, thus the first inclusion is obvious. As for the second one, it is sufficient to show that if $A \in \mathrm{sub}(\mathrm{L}(G))$ then $\{x \in \mathrm{T} : x \in T_G(A)\} \subset \mathrm{sub}(\mathrm{TYP}_{\mathrm{sub}}(I_G))$. Moreover, by lemma 11 we can restrict our considerations only to functorial structures.

Induction on $c(A)$.

(i) Let $A = v \in V_G \cap \text{sub}(\text{L}(G))$ and $x \in T_G(v)$. We have $T_G(v) = I_G(v) \subset \text{TYP}_{\text{sub}}(I_G) \subset \text{sub}(\text{TYP}_{\text{sub}}(I_G))$, thus $x \in \text{sub}(\text{TYP}_{\text{sub}}(I_G))$.

(ii) Let $A = f/i(\mathbf{A}_n)$, $1 \le i \le n = \varrho(f)$, and $x \in T_G(A)$. By (PFL1) A_i is a functorial structure, and by (NF) there exist types $x_j \in T_G(A_j)$, $j \ne i$, such that $f/i(\mathbf{x}_n|i : x) \in T_G(A_i)$. But by the inductive assumption $f/i(\mathbf{x}_n|i : x) \in \text{sub}(\text{TYP}_{\text{sub}}(I_G))$, consequently we have also $x \in \text{sub}(\text{TYP}_{\text{sub}}(I_G))$. $\quad\square$

Inclusions established in the previous lemma immediately yield

Lemma 13. *If G is a finite CCG, then the sets $\text{TYP}_{\text{sub}}(I_G)$ and $\text{TYP}_{\text{sub}}(T_G)$ are finite.*

We say that structures $A, B \in \text{PF}(V_G)$ are *equivalent* in a CCG G and write $A\text{EQ}_G B$ if and only if $T_G(A) = T_G(B)$.

Lemma 14. EQ_G *is a congruence on* $\text{L}(G)$ *and* $\text{EQ}_G \subset \text{INT}_{\text{L}(G)}$.

Lemma 15. *Let G be a CCG. If $A \in \text{sub}(\text{L}(G))$, then $T_G(A) \ne \emptyset$.*

Theorem 16. *If G is a CCG, then the following estimations are true:*

(i) $\text{ind}(\text{L}(G)) \le \min(\aleph_0, 2^{r_{\text{sub}}(G)} + 1)$,

(ii) $\text{s}(\text{L}(G)) \subset \text{s}(\text{TYP}_{\text{sub}}(I_G)) = \text{s}(\text{TYP}_{\text{sub}}(T_G))$,

(iii) $\deg_{\text{c}}(\text{L}(G)) \le \deg_{\text{pf}}(\text{TYP}_{\text{sub}}(I_G)) = \deg_{\text{pf}}(\text{TYP}_{\text{sub}}(T_G))$.

Proof. (i) The set L^{int} of the equivalence classes of $\text{INT}_{\text{L}(G)}$ consists of the class $\text{PF}(V_G)\backslash\text{sub}(L(\text{G}))$ and of classes included in $\text{sub}(\text{L}(G))$. By lemma 14 each equivalence class of $\text{INT}_{\text{L}(G)}$ is a union of some equivalence classes of EQ_G. Let the symbol $R \downarrow A$ denote the restriction of a relation R to a set A. We have $\text{INT}_{\text{L}(G)} \downarrow \text{sub}(\text{L}(G)) \supset \text{EQ}_G \downarrow \text{sub}(\text{L}(G))$ and the index of $\text{EQ}_G \downarrow \text{sub}(\text{L}(G))$ does not exceed $2^{r_{\text{sub}}(G)}$. Consequently,

$$\text{ind}(\text{L}(G)) = 1 + \text{ind}(\text{INT}_{\text{L}(G)} \downarrow \text{sub}(\text{L}(G))) \le$$
$$1 + \text{ind}(\text{EQ}_G \downarrow \text{sub}(\text{L}(G))) \le \min(\aleph_0, 2^{r_{\text{sub}}(G)} + 1).$$

(ii) The equality is a consequence of lemma 12. We use induction on the complexity $c(A)$ of a pf-structure $A \in \text{sub}(\text{L}(G))$ and show that $\text{s}(\text{sub}(\text{L}(G)) \subset \text{s}(\text{TYP}_{\text{sub}}(T_G))$.

If $A \in V_G$, then $\text{s}(A) = \emptyset \subset \text{s}(\text{TYP}_{\text{sub}}(T_G))$. Let $A = f/i(\mathbf{A}_n) \in \text{sub}(\text{L}(G))$. Then by lemma 15 there is a type x such that $x \in T_G(A)$, and by (NF) there exist $x_j \in T_G(A_j)$, $i \ne j$, such that $f/i(\mathbf{x}_n|i : x) \in T_G(A_i)$. By the inductive assumption $\text{s}(A_j) \subset \text{s}(\text{TYP}_{\text{sub}}(T_G))$, $1 \le j \le n$, thus $\bigcup\{\text{s}(A_j) : 1 \le j \le n\} \subset \text{s}(\text{TYP}_{\text{sub}}(T_G))$. We have $\bigcup\{\text{s}(A_j) : 1 \le j \le n\} \subset \text{s}(A)$, and f may be the only functor symbol which is in $\text{s}(A)$ but not in $\bigcup\{\text{s}(A_j) : 1 \le j \le n\}$. But $f/i(\mathbf{x}_n|i : x) \in T_g(A_i)$, thus $f \in \text{s}(\text{TYP}_{\text{sub}}(T_G))$. As a consequence $\text{s}(A) \subset \text{s}(\text{TYP}_{\text{sub}}(T_G))$. In a similar way we treat product structures. Now, as $\text{L}(G) \subset \text{sub}(\text{L}(G))$, we obtain the inclusion $\text{s}(\text{L}(G)) \subset \text{s}(\text{TYP}_{\text{sub}}(T_G))$.

(iii) As in (ii) the equality follows from lemma 12. In order to prove the inequality it suffices to show that if $A \in \text{sub}(L(G))$, then the length of any p-, f-, fp- or pf-path in A is not greater than $\deg_{\text{pf}}(\text{TYP}_{\text{sub}}(T_G))$. We do it employing the conditions (NP), (NF) and definitions of paths, cf. [6]. $\square$

Lemma 17. *If $L = \text{BL}(G)$ for a finite CCG G, then $\text{ind}(L) \leq 2^{\text{ind}(L(G))}$.*

Proof. We modify a part of the proof of theorem 8 for the case of a grammar with product. For $B \in \text{BS}(V_G)$ let $\mathbf{F}(B) = \{\text{int}_{\text{L}(G)}(A): A \in \text{PF}(V_G) \text{ and } \text{bs}(A) = B\}$. The relation $\sim \subset [\text{BS}(V_G)]^2$ is defined as follows: $B \sim C$ if and only if $\mathbf{F}(B) = \mathbf{F}(C)$. $\sim$ is a congruence on $\text{BL}(G)$, thus $\text{ind}(L) \leq \text{ind}(\sim) \leq 2^{\text{ind}(L(G))}$. $\square$

Theorem 18. *If $L = \text{BL}(G)$ for a finite CCG G, then there exists a finite product-free CCG G' such that $L = \text{BL}(G')$.*

Proof. As G is a finite CCG, the sets $\text{TYP}(I_G)\}$ and $\text{TYP}_{\text{sub}}(I_G)$ are finite as well. By lemma 12 $r_{\text{sub}}(G) = \text{card}(\text{TYP}_{\text{sub}}(T_G)) < \aleph_0$. Consequently, by theorem 16 the numbers $\text{ind}(L(G))$, $\text{s}(L(G))$ and $\deg_{\text{c}}(L(G))$ are finite. As $\text{s}(\text{BL}(G)) = \text{s}(L(G))$, we have also $\text{s}(L) < \aleph_0$. By lemmas 9 and 17 the numbers $\deg(L)$ and $\text{ind}(L)$ are finite, thus, according to theorem 8, we have $L = \text{BL}(G')$ for a finite CCG^0 G'. $\square$

6 Strong equivalence of GAC- and GLC-grammars

In this section we present the main result of the paper establishing the equality of classes of languages $\mathcal{L}(\text{GAC})$ and $\mathcal{L}(\text{GLC})$. The inclusion $\mathcal{L}(\text{GLC}) \subset \mathcal{L}(\text{GAC})$ was proved in [7], but in order to make our presentation self-contained we briefly sketch the main idea of the proof and encourage the reader to consult the mentioned paper to get to know the details of the argument.

Lemma 19. *The formula*

$\quad$(A3)$\qquad x_j \to f/j(\mathbf{x}_n|i : f/i(\mathbf{x}_n), j : x_i)$

where $j \neq i$, $1 \leq j, i \leq n = \varrho(f)$, is derivable in GL.

Let $\overline{\text{Ax}}$ denote the smallest set of formulas containing (A0), (A1), (A2), (A3) and closed with respect to the rules (P1), (P2) and (P3). By $\overline{\text{GLC}}$ we denote the system formalized in a similar way as GLC except for the rule (C), which is replaced by $(\overline{\text{C}})$ of the form:

$\quad(\overline{\text{C}})\qquad \dfrac{X \to x}{X \to y} \quad$ if $x \neq y$ and $x \to y \in \overline{\text{Ax}}$

Lemma 20. *$\vdash_{\text{GLC}} X \to x$ if and only if $\vdash_{\overline{\text{GLC}}} X \to x$.*

Each formula derivable in $\overline{\text{GLC}}$ possesses a derivation from which one can separate a pure GAC-subderivation such that the remaining part consists only of instances of $(\overline{\text{C}})$-rule. It is easily observed that for each formula $x \to y$ in

$\overline{\text{Ax}}$ which is not an instance of (A0) we have either $c(x) > c(y)$ or $c(x) < c(y)$. An instance of $(\overline{\text{C}})$ employing a formula $x \to y$ from $\overline{\text{Ax}}$ such that $c(x) < c(y)$ (resp. $c(x) > c(y)$) will be called an *E-instance* (resp. *R-instance*) of the rule. Moreover, a derivation D of $X \to x$ in $\overline{\text{GLC}}$ is called *normal* if all E-instances of $(\overline{\text{C}})$ follow all instances of (A) and (P), and all R-instances of $(\overline{\text{C}})$ precede them. The following theorem is valid, see [7]:

Theorem 21. *Each derivation* D *of a formula* $X \to x$ *in* $\overline{\text{GLC}}$ *can be transformed to a normal derivation.*

Theorem 22. *For every* $\overline{\text{GLC}}$*-grammar* G *one can find a* $\overline{\text{GAC}}$*-grammar* G' *such that* $\text{BL}(G) = \text{BL}(G')$.

Proof. Let $G = \langle V_G, I_G, s_G, \overline{\text{GLC}} \rangle$. We construct G' in the following way: $V_{G'} = V_G$, $s_{G'} = s_G$ and for $x \in \text{T}$, $v \in V_{G'}$ we put $(v, x) \in I_{G'}$ if and only if there are types $x_1, \ldots, x_n$ such that $(v, x_1) \in I_G$, $x_n = x$ and $x_1 \to x_2$, $x_2 \to x_3, \ldots, x_{n-1} \to x_n$ is a sequence of formulas from $\overline{\text{Ax}}$ such that for all $1 \le i < n$ we have $c(x_i) > c(x_{i+1})$. Now, let $A \in \text{BS}(G)$. Consequently, for some $X \in \text{BS}(\text{T})$ we have $(A, X) \in F_G$ and $\vdash_{\overline{\text{GLC}}} X \to s_G$. According to theorem 21 there exists a normal derivation D of $X \to s_G$ in $\overline{\text{GLC}}$. This derivation contains no E-instances of $(\overline{\text{C}})$ as s_G is a primitive type. In return to the change of the initial type assignment from I_G to $I_{G'}$ we can cut off all branches of D employing R-instances of $(\overline{\text{C}})$ and get from X a bracketed string Y such that $(A, Y) \in F_{G'}$ and $\vdash_{\text{GAC}} Y \to s_{G'}$. Thus $A \in \text{BL}(G')$. The proof of the converse inclusion $\text{BL}(G') \subset \text{BL}(G)$ is similar. □

Immediately we get

Theorem 23. $\mathcal{L}(\text{GLC}) \subset \mathcal{L}(\text{GAC})$.

Proof. By lemma 20 the systems GLC and $\overline{\text{GLC}}$ are equivalent in the scope of derivable formulas. Thus the thesis of our theorem follows from theorem 22. □

Theorem 24. *For each* GAC*-grammar* G *there exists a* GLC*-grammar* G' *such that* $\text{BL}(G) = \text{BL}(G')$.

Proof. Let $G = \langle V_G, I_G, s_G, \text{GAC} \rangle$. By lemma 4 the grammar $G_1 = \langle V_G, I_G, s_G, \rangle$ is a finite CCG such that $\text{BL}(G) = \text{BL}(G_1)$. According to theorem 18 there exists a finite CCG^0 G_2 such that $\text{BL}(G_1) = \text{BL}(G_2)$. In the light of theorem 6 for the grammar G_2 one can find a finite CCG^0 G_3 such that $L(G_2) = L(G_3)$, thus $\text{BL}(G_2) = \text{BL}(G_3)$, and $o(G_3) \le 1$. We apply lemma 4 to G_3 and get a GAC^0-grammar G_4 of order ≤ 1 such that $\text{BL}(G_3) = \text{BL}(G_4)$. Consequently, the language $\text{BL}(G)$ is generated by a GAC^0-grammar G_4 such that $o(G_4) \le 1$. Let us transform G_4 into a GLC-grammar G' replacing the system GAC^0 by GLC and leaving all other components untouched. We claim that $\text{BL}(G) = \text{BL}(G')$. The inclusion $\text{BL}(G) \subset \text{BL}(G')$ holds as each formula derivable in GAC^0 is derivable in GLC as well. To prove the opposite inclusion it suffices to show that if X is a bracketed string of product-free types of order ≤ 1, then from $\vdash_{\text{GLC}} X \to s_{G'}$ follows $\vdash_{\text{GAC}^0} X \to s_{G'}$. By theorem 21 the formula $X \to s_{G'}$ possesses a normal derivation D in $\overline{\text{GLC}}$. D employs no E-instances of $(\overline{C})$ as $s_{G'}$ is a primitive type. We show that R-instances of $(\overline{C})$ does not occur in D as well. Assume that such an instance exists in D. Thus there must be the first instance of $(\overline{C})$ applied to a (product-free) type x from X, which employs such a formula $x \to y$ from $\overline{\text{Ax}}$ that $c(x) > c(y)$. The formula $x \to y$ can be neither an instance of (A1) (x is froduct-free) nor an instance of (A2) or (A3) (because the complexity of the type on the left-hand side of (A2) and (A3) is smaller than the complexity of the type on the right-hand side). Obviously, $x \to y$ can not be a result of an application of the rule (P3) which introduces a product symbol. As for the rules (P1) and (P2) we must consider two subcases. If one consecutively applies (P1) or (P2) to (A1) or (A2), then it is easily observed that the side of the resulting formula which is of greater complexity contains also a product symbol. Consequently, such a formula can not be employed in the first instance of $(\overline{C})$. On the other hand, if (P1) or (P2) were applied to (A3), then in the resulting formula the side of greater complexity would be of order > 1, which again disqualifies such a formula. As a result, no R-instances of $(\overline{C})$ are employed in D, thus D is a derivation in GAC. Now it suffices to observe that the rule (P) can not be used in D: the product type it creates would have to be a subtype of a type from X, which contradicts the fact that all types in X are product-free. Finally, D is a derivation of $X \to s_{G'}$ in GAC^0. □

From theorem 24 we get

Theorem 25. $\mathcal{L}(\text{GAC}) \subset \mathcal{L}(\text{GLC})$.

Theorems 23 and 25 give

Theorem 26. $\mathcal{L}(\text{GAC}) = \mathcal{L}(\text{GLC})$.

References

1. BUSZKOWSKI, W., Fregean grammar and residuated semigroup. In: Frege Conference 1984, (G. WECHSUNG, ed.). Akademie-Verlag, Berlin 1984, 57–62.
2. BUSZKOWSKI, W., Typed functorial languages. Bulletin of the Polish Academy of Sciences: Mathematics **34** (1986), 495–505.
3. BUSZKOWSKI, W., Generative capacity of nonassociative Lambek calculus. Bulletin of the Polish Academy of Sciences: Mathematics **34** (1986), 507–516.
4. BUSZKOWSKI, W., Logical Foundations of Ajdukiewicz-Lambek Categorial Grammars. Polish Scientific Publishers, Warszawa 1989 (in Polish).
5. KANDULSKI, M., The non–associative Lambek calculus. In: Categorial Grammar, (W. BUSZKOWSKI, W. MARCISZEWSKI, J. VAN BENTHEM, eds.). J. Benjamins, Amsterdam 1988, 141–151.
6. KANDULSKI, M., Phrase structure languages generated by categorial grammars with product. Zeitschrift für mathematische Logik und Grundlagen der Mathematik **34** (1988), 373–383.

7. KANDULSKI, M., On generalized Ajdukiewicz and Lambek calculi and grammars. Fundamenta Informaticae **30** (1997), 169–181.

8. LAMBEK, J., On the calculus of syntactic types. In: Structure of Language and Its Mathematical Aspects (JACOBSON, R., ed.). Amer. Math. Soc., Providence, R.I., 1961, 166–178.

9. KOŁOWSKA-GAWIEJNOWICZ, M., Powerset residuated algebras and generalized Lambek calculus. Mathematical Logic Quarterly **43** (1997), 60–72.

10. MOORTGAT, M., Categorial type logics. In: Handbook of Logic and Language (J. VAN BENTHEM and A. TER MEULEN, eds.). Elsevier and The MIT Press, 1997.

11. OEHRLE, R., ZHANG, S., Lambek calculus and extractions of subjects. In: Proceedings of the 25th Meeting of the Chicago Linguistic Society. University of Chicago, Department of Linguistics, 1989.

Linguistic, Philosophical, and Pragmatic Aspects of Type-Directed Natural Language Parsing

Sebastian Shaumyan[1] and Paul Hudak[2]

[1] Yale University, Department of Linguistics, New Haven CT 06520, USA
[2] Yale University, Department of Computer Science, New Haven CT 06520, USA

Abstract. We describe how type information can be used to infer grammatical structure. This is in contrast to conventional type inference in programming languages where the roles are reversed, structure determining type. Our work is based on *Applicative Universal Grammar* (AUG), a linguistic theory that views the formation of phrase in a form that is analogous to function application in a programming language. We descibe our overall methodology including its linguistic and philosophical underpinnings.

The natural language parser that we have constructed should be interesting to computer scientists in the way in which AUG relates to types and combinatory calculus, and to linguists in the way in which a very simple, brute force parsing strategy performs surprisingly well in both performance and accuracy. Both computer scientists and linguists should also be interested in the convergence of the theory of functional programming languages and AUG with regard to their conceptual bases. Both have been motivated by entirely different goals and have developed independently, but they are rooted in a common conceptual system of an applicative calculus.

1 Functional Programming Languages and Applicative Universal Grammar: a Common Paradigm

The central goal of a *theoretical* study of linguistics is to reveal how a human being uses languages to express and communicate thought. The *philosophy* of language is concerned with evaluating how particular theories of language succeed in attaining this central goal. Finally, the *pragmatics* of language concerns itself with the ability to implement a theory, for example in the form of a natural language processing system. Linguists and computer scientists benefit from exchanges concerning theory, philosophy, and pragmatics.

In this paper we touch on all three of these issues. We first argue that the theories of *functional languages* and *Applicative Universal Grammar* (AUG) share a common underlying paradigm. By paradigm we mean a pattern of thought, a system of concepts and assumptions underlying a group of theories, regardless of how they differ from one another in detail. Some of the fundamental ideas of this common paradigm can be traced to the works of Haskell B. Curry on combinatory logic and its philosophical and linguistic implications. Indeed, our argument leads to the realization of a natural language parser written in the functional language Haskell, and based on the theory of AUG.

The first complete description of AUG was published in 1965 [16], unifying the categorical calculus of Lesniewski [12] with the combinatory calculus of Curry and Feys [5]. The semantic theory of AUG was presented in [17], and its use in the translation of natural languages is given in [19]. A full description of the current state of AUG is given in [18].

A description of the feasibility of natural language parsing using AUG was first given in [11] as a literate Haskell [10] program. The functional language Haskell is named in the memory of Haskell B. Curry, the logician whose work on combinatory logic provides much of the foundation for both functional programming languages and AUG. Indeed, Curry himself was interested in the study of natural language and grammatical structure [4]. Related work on using a functional language for NLP may be found in [6], which differs from ours by being based on principles proposed by Montague [15].

2   The Rise of Functional Programming Languages

The earliest programming languages were developed with one goal in mind: to provide a vehicle through which one could control the behavior of computers. This goal seemed reasonable, but quickly ran into two problems: first, it became obvious that what was easy for a machine was not necessarily easy for a human being; and second, as the number of different kinds of machines increased, the need arose for a common language with which to program them all.

Thus from raw object code and primitive assembly languages, a large number of *high-level* programming languages emerged, beginning with FORTRAN in the 1950's. High-level languages are generally divided into two classes: *imperative* languages and *declarative* languages. Imperative languages are lower level—they say a lot about *how* to compute a result—whereas declarative languages are at a higher level—they say most about *what* should be computed, rather than how. *Functional* programming languages are declarative languages whose underlying model of computation is the function (in contrast to the relation that forms the basis for logic programming languages). (See [8] for a more thorough discussion of these issues.)

The key point here is that higher-level languages are less dependent on the details of the underlying hardware. The earliest programming languages depended on the hardware completely, reflecting fairly accurately the structure of the underlying machine. The emergence of high-level imperative languages was a considerable step forward; still, it was only a partial liberation from the machine. Only through the emergence of declarative languages, in particular pure functional languages, did a fairly complete liberation take place.

Indeed, in studying any language—a programming language, a language of mathematics or logic, or a natural language such as English or Russian—we must distinguish two very different kinds of structure: the *physical* structure and the *functional* structure of language. The physical structure of programming languages is a reflection of the physical structure of the computer. The physical structure of natural language is so-called *phrase-structure*, which reflects the action of the human machine; i.e. the organs of speech. Because of the dependence on the human organs of speech, natural language has a *linear* phrase-structure. However, the essential structure of natural language, its functional structure, is independent of the linear phrase-structure.

The parallel between programming languages and natural languages with respect to the distinction of the physical structure and functional structure is clear. Does this distinction apply to the languages of mathematics and logic? We find a partial answer to this question in the illuminating studies of Haskell B. Curry, who distinguished two kinds of structure: the structure of *concatenative* systems in standard formalizations of logic and the *applicative* structure of *ob-systems* in combinatory logic. In Curry's terminology, a concatenative system is a concrete system depending on physical properties of signs; that is, on their properties represented as linear strings. The concatenation operation is an operation of combining signs in their linear order. Here's how Curry contrasts the concatenative structure and the applicative structure:

> "In the first place, combinatory logic was formulated as a system in which the formal objects were rather differently conceived than was the case in the standard formalization of logic. The standard procedure at that time was to demand that the formal objects be expressions of some "object language;" this means that they be strings formed from the symbols of that object language by concatenation. In combinatory logic these formal objects, called obs, were wholly unspecified. It was merely postulated that there was a binary operation of application among them, that the obs be constructed from the primitive objects, called atoms, by these operations, and that the construction of an ob be unique. This means that the obs were thought of not as strings of atoms, but as structures like a genealogical tree." [4, pp. 64–65]

From this discussion we adopt the premise that the applicative structure is the essential structure of any language—a programming language, a language of mathematics or logic, or a natural language.

3 The Rise of Applicative Universal Grammar

Applicative Universal Grammar (AUG) develops the ideas of Ferdinand de Saussure about language as a system of signs. It is based on the observation that some fundamental ideas of linguistics and combinatory logic converge. Thus AUG consists of a formal model of natural languages, called *genotype*, that is based on combinatory logic.

The basic concept of AUG is the *applicative structure*, which contrasts sharply with the concept of *phrase structure*, the standard formal system in many linguistic theories. The essential properties of the applicative structure of AUG are characterized by the following principles:

Principle 1 The Transfer Principle.

A grammatical structure or class is independent of its symbolic representation, and so may be transferred from one symbolic device into another without changing its meaning.

For example, subject-object relations can be represented by case markers as in Russian or Latin or by word order as in English. In a Russian sentence consisting of three words—subject, predicate, and direct object—the words can be permuted in six different ways without changing the meaning of the sentence. Grammatical relations are invariant of their symbolic representations.

Principle 2 The Genotype-Phenotype Principle.

Grammatical structures and classes, independent of their symbolic representation, form a universal system of grammatical categories of natural languages, called a genotype. *Symbolic representations of grammatical structures and classes of specific natural languages form concrete systems called* phenotypes.

This principle is a corollary of the Transfer Principle, and further constrains grammar by imposing the genotype and phenotype levels on it. It calls for a revision of linguistic theories which confound these levels.

In accordance with the Genotype-Phenotype Principle, we must clearly distinguish *rules of grammar* from *laws of grammar*. Rules of grammar are language-specific; they are part of phenotypes. Laws of grammar are universals underlying rules of grammar; they are part of the genotype. A law of grammar is an invariant over a class of particular rules of grammar.

As an example, consider the active/passive distinction in English:

Columbus discovered America.
America was discovered by Columbus.

Various formulations of the rule of passivization in English greatly differ in detail, but it is generally agreed that (1) passive in English applies to strings in which two noun phrases and a verb occur in this order: First Noun Phrase—Active Verb—Second Noun Phrase; and (2) passivization involves the postponing of the preverbal noun phrase and presposing of the postverbal noun phrase: Second Noun Phrase—Passive Verb—First Noun Phrase. In other words, the standard rule of passivization in English is stated in terms of the word order.

A rule of passivization such as this is clearly language specific. Since different languages have different word order—for example, in Malagasy, the direct object precedes the verb and the subject follows the verb—there must be distinct language-specific rules of passivization for these other languages. Furthermore, in languages such as Russian or Latin where word order does not have grammatical meaning, the rule of passivization is stated in terms of case endings.

From the perspective of the Transfer Principle, we face an empirical question: is there an invariant of the particular rules of passivization in particular languages? We believe that there is: a universal law that we call the *Law of Passivization*. This law is roughly characterized by two invariant processes: (1)

a conversion of the predicate relation, and (2) a superposition of the second term of the converted predicate with an oblique term. This law will become clearer later, although its complete formulation is beyond the scope of this paper, and may be found in [18].

We claim that the Law of Passivization—and other laws as well—are *universal*. But in fact, in some cases a law is simply not applicable to certain languages, and the Law of Passivization is no exception: the active/passive correspondance does not exist in some languages. Our use of the term "universal" is from the perspective of treating the theory of grammar as a highly abstract branch of linguistics whose goal is to establish a single hypothetical grammatical system from which all possible structures and entities may be deduced. Universal laws hold for this abstract system, but concrete languages are in many cases subsets of the whole system, and thus certain laws may not be applicable.

This should not deter us from seeking universal laws, for two important reasons. First, the universal laws allow us to recognize common characteristics of otherwise very different languages. Second, they allow us to imagine, theoretically at least, what the instantiation of particular laws might look like in languages for which they are currently not applicable.

Principle 3 The Principle of Semiotic Relevance.

The only distinctions that are semiotically relevant are those that correlate with the distinctions between their signs, and, vice versa, the only distinctions between signs that are relevant are those that correlate with the distinctions between their meanings.

One can never overstate the significance of the Principle of Semiotic Relevance. If one wants to present de Saussure's doctrine in a single theoretical statement, the Principle of Semiotic Relevance is it. This principle defines the essence of linguistic reality, and is a keystone of the semiotic study of language.

The Principle of Semiotic Relevance is a powerful constraint on the theory of grammar, and not all linguistic theories conform well with this principle. For example, *generative phonology* [13, 3, 7] considers only the sound patterns of morphemes, completely disregarding their meanings. As a result, it wrongly identifies certain morphemes by posting fictitious relationships between them. The fundamental error of generative phonology is that is generates away cognate forms based entirely on formal criteria without regard to the meanings of the forms. For example, disregard of the meanings of the forms of morphemes leads to a confusion between synchrony and diachrony [18].

The opposite error is encountered in *generative semantics*, which fails to support distinctions in meanings with concomitant distinctions in phonic expressions. Consider, for instance, the famous McCawley's analysis of 'kill' as a causative verb in English. In a bracketed notation this analysis reads: *(cause (become (minus alive)))*; that is, "cause becomes minus alive," which is meant to be a semantic componential analysis of the verb 'kill'. This analysis is weak because it is based on the idea that given a possible paraphrase of the verb 'kill', it must therefore *ipso facto* be considered a causative verb. In accordance with the Principle of Semiotic Relevance, any difference between linguistic meanings must be correlated with differences between phonic expressions. Real causative verbs are characterized by appropriate phonic markers as in the forms *sit : set* (I *sit* by the table, I *set* the table,) and *fall : fell* (the tree *falls*, the lumberjack *fells* the tree). The verb "kill" has none of these signs of the causative meaning.

Linguistic meaning is vital for communication, and is an essential aspect of every use of language; but the linguistic meaning does not constitute the total meaning of a sentence or word. Consider the sentence 'Garry Kasparov and I.B.M.'s computer Deep Blue came to draw in the fourth game yesterday.' The linguistic meaning of the sentence is determined by the dictionary and the rules of the grammar of English. But the sentence means more than that. A man who knows chess can infer from the context of the word 'game' that it was the game of chess. He may also infer that Kasparov and Deep Blue had played three games before the game yesterday. He may infer further that Deep Blue is a superstrong chess program because Kasparov is the world champion of chess. A man who does not know chess cannot infer from the meaning of the word 'game' that it was a chess game. From the sentence 'John killed a bear' we infer that John caused a bear not to be alive, but causation is an inferential meaning that is parasitic on the linguistic meaning of kill.

The total meaning of a sentence or word is a compound containing the linguistic meaning combined with other kinds of meaning just as a chemical compound contains a certain substance combined with other substances. To isolate a certain substance from other substances, one uses chemical reagents. The analysis of meaning is mental chemistry. The chemical reagent of the linguist is the Principle of Semiotic Relevance. Using it, the linguist isolates the linguistic meaning in its pure form.

Principle 4 The Unity of Syntactic and Semantic Representation.
Syntactic and Semantic representation cannot be separated from each other; they constitute a unique representation, called contensive representation.

This principle is a corollary of the Principle of Semiotic Relevance. It follows from this principle that any distinction in semantic representation must correlate with a distinction in syntactic representation, and vice versa: any distinction in syntactic representation must correlate with a distinction in semantic representation. A system of contensive representation is called *contensive syntax*.

Contensive syntax is a new concept which should not be confused with semantics. The existence of semantic rules presupposes the existence of syntactic rules. In contrast, contensive syntax is a unitary system of rules which is, so to speak, a chemical bond of structure and meaning. Just as water is a completely new substance in comparison with hydrogen and oxygen taken separately, so contensive syntax is a completely new entity in comparison with structure and meaning, which taken separately are not part of linguistics; they are part of logic.

The fundamental constraint on the combination of signs is the Sign Combination Principle.

Principle 5 The Sign Combination Principle.

A sign, called an operator, *combines with one or more signs, called its* operands, *to form a new sign, called its* resultant, *on condition that its meaning is incomplete and needs to be supplemented by meanings of other signs.*

The term "sign" in the statement of this principle covers words and other units. For example, verbs and adjectives are operators with respect to nouns because meanings of verbs and adjectives are incomplete and are in need of supplementation by meanings of nouns. Consider 'boy' or 'paper.' The meanings of these nouns are complete. Take now 'writes' and 'white.' We ask: Who writes? What is white? The meanings of the words are incomplete. They need to be supplemented by meanings of nouns such as 'boy' or 'paper'. In 'the boy writes' the verb 'writes' is an operator and 'the boy' is its operand; in 'white paper' the adjective 'white' is an operator and 'paper' is its operand. Similarly, the meaning of prepositions is incomplete without supplementation by meaning of nouns; therefore prepositions are operators with respect to nouns. In 'on the table,' 'on' is an operator and 'the table,' its operand. Furthermore, the meaning of a conjunction is incomplete, and needs to be supplemented by the meaning of words belonging to basic word categories—nouns, adjectives, verbs, adverbs, or complete sentences. Therefore a conjunction is an operator with respect to expressions of all these categories: in 'black and white,' 'and' is an operator with respect to 'black' and 'white.'

In a later section we will see more elaborate examples of the Sign Combination Principle, including chains and hierarchies of meaning supplementations.

Principle 6 The Principle of Monotonic Constructions.

Any combination of linguistic units has a unique construction; in algebraic terms, any combination of linguistic units is non-associative.

Being a corollary of the Sign Combination Principle, the Principle of Monotonic Constructions is of paramount importance for linguistics. It excludes systems such as *generalized categorial grammar* [14], whose associativity means that a sentence can be bracketed in every possible way. Moorgat motivates the use of the associative calculus as follows:

> The application analysis for 'John loves Mary' is strongly equivalent to the conventional phrase-structure representation for a sequence subject—transitive verb—direct object, with the transitive verb and the direct object grouped into a VP constituent. Suppose now that we are not so much interested in constituent structure, as commonly understood, but rather in the notion of derivability, that is, in the question: Given a sequence of input types (viewed as sets of expressions), what type(s) can be derived from the concatenation of the input sentences? It will be clear that the result type S would also be derivable in the transitive verb had been assigned the type $NP \setminus (S/NP)$ instead of $(NP \setminus S)/NP$ [14, p. 148].

Associativity considerably simplifies the construction of mathematical models of language, but it distorts linguistic reality. Associativity is motivated primarily by convenience: an associative calculus is much more convenient for parsing a string of words in a purely mechanical fashion. The trouble is, as follows from the Sign Combination Principle, the sentences of a natural language have a non-associative structure. Thus if we want to understand their structure, we have no choice but to construct a non-associate calculus.

In defense of the associative calculus, one might argue that associativity allows one to forget about spurious ambiguity (parse of verbal phrases with multiple complements). But this argument is irrelevant here, since Principle 6 in conjunction with the other principles of AUG precludes spurious ambiguity.

Principle 7 The Principle of Type Assignment.

Every sign of the applicative system is assigned a type which defines its syntactic function.

The Principle of Type Assignment is subject to the following conditions:

1. *Inclusion.* Every atomic sign is assigned a characteristic type.
2. *Exclusion.* No sign belongs to more than one characteristic type.
3. *Superposition.* Every sign can be assigned a complementary type superposed on its characteristic type.
4. *Polymorphism.* Some signs can be assigned variable types. The range of a variable type includes concrete types having related functions.

Principle 8 The Superposition Principle.

Any unit has one characteristic function, which is context independent, and a series of complementary functions, defined by different contexts. If in a given context C a unit A takes on the function of the unit B as its complementary function, a syncretic unit $\langle A/B \rangle$ is formed. We say that A and B are superposed in the syncretic unit $\langle A/B \rangle$, and we call the operation of forming $\langle A/B \rangle$ the superposition of A with B. Given $\langle A/B \rangle$, A is called the basis, and B the overlay.

Superposed types are governed by the following principles:

1. *Existence.* The unit $\langle x/y \rangle$ exists in a given context C if the unit x is superposed with the unit y.
2. *Identity.* A superposed unit is distinct from its basis. Two superposed types are the same only if their bases and overlays are the same.
3. *Inheritance.* In any context C in which a superposed unit exists, it has those normal properties possessed by its basis.

Let us turn to examples of superposition. Consider the word 'lion'. The characteristic meaning of 'lion' is the name of an animal. But in combination with some words it takes on the meaning 'a famous and important person,' as in a 'literary lion'. The characteristic meaning of black is 'of the darkest color,' but the word may take on the meaning 'very bad,' as in 'black despair'. These are examples of the action of modifying contexts. A modifying context changes the meaning of the word with which it comes: the word becomes synonymous with some other word or expression. In our examples, the word 'lion' is synonymous with 'a famous and important person' in the context of literary; and the word 'black' is synonymous with 'very bad' in the context of despair. Due to the action of its modifying context the meaning of a word becomes figurative, representing a syncretism of two meanings: the initial meaning of the word and the meaning of the expression with which the word is synonymous. This is a case of polysemy. Due to the action of the modifying context the word becomes polysemous.

Nouns and adjectives seem to behave in a similar way: in some contexts they fulfill the role of the argument of a predicate, in other contexts, the role of an attribute of a noun. If we classify nouns and adjectives as polymorphic, then we must admit that their polymorphism is identical and that nouns and adjectives are identical at the level of their phrasal projection. But the resulting type ambiguity of lexical classes would then conflict with the generally accepted notion of lexical classes as morphologically and syntactically distinct entities. In search of a plausible explanation, we arrive at the hypothesis of a hierarchy of syntactic types assigned to each lexical class. It is this hierarchy that is explained by the Superposition Principle.

This analysis reveals the opposition between the noun and the adjective: the characteristic type of the noun is the complementary type of the adjective, and, conversely, the characteristic type of the adjective is the complementary type of the noun. A sign with a complementary type superposed on its characteristic type displays duality: it takes on the properties of the complementary type superposed on its characteristic type but retains at least part of properties of its characteristic type.

4   Parsing Natural Language Based on AUG

To understand the way in which parsing using AUG works, it is useful to think of words and phrases as atoms and expressions, respectively, in a typed language of combinators. For our simplified version of AUG, there are just two primitive types: T representing terms (for example, nouns such as 'friend' and noun phrases such as 'my friend'), and S representing complete sentences (such as 'my friend runs'). The only non-primitive type is of the form Oxy, denoting phrases that transform phrases of type x to modified phrases of type y; this is the most important concept behind the AUG formalism.

For example, the word 'my' is treated as having type OTT since it is applied to a term of type T to obtain a modified term, also of type T (every word is pre-assigned one or more types in this way). Thus the construction of the noun phrase 'my friend' can be described by an inference:

$$\frac{\text{'my'} :: OTT \quad \text{'friend'} :: T}{\text{'my friend'} :: T}$$

More generally, we can use the following rule to describe the application of one phrase, p of type Oxy, to another, q of type x:

$$\frac{p :: \mathsf{O}xy \quad q :: x}{pq :: y}$$

Clearly, types of the form $\mathsf{O}xy$ correspond to function types, written as $(x \to y)$ in more conventional notation, while the typing rule above is the standard method for typing the application of a function p to an argument value q. The O for function types is used in the descriptions of AUG cited above, and for the most part we will continue to use the same notation here to avoid any confusion with type expressions in Haskell; in our program, the types of natural language phrases are represented by data values, not by Haskell types. Another advantage of the prefix O notation is that it avoids the need for parentheses and allows a more compact notation for types.

The results of parsing a complete sentence can be described by a tree structure labelled with the types of the words and phrases that are used in its construction. The following example is produced directly by the program described later from the input string "my friend lives in Boston".

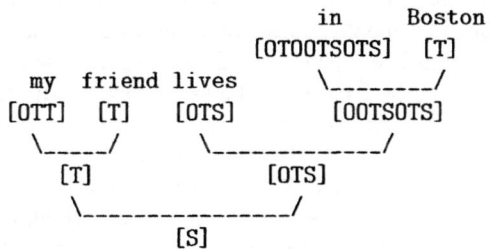

Notice that, to maintain the original word order, we have allowed both forward and backward application of functions to arguments. The first of these was described by the rule above, while the second is just:

$$\frac{q :: x \quad p :: \mathsf{O}xy}{qp :: y}$$

For example, in the tree above, we have used this rule to apply the phrase in Boston to the intransitive verb lives; the function acts as a modifier, turning the action of 'living' into the more specific action of 'living in Boston'.

It is sometimes useful to rearrange the trees produced by parsing a phrase so that functions are always written to the left of the arguments to which they are applied. This reveals the *applicative* structure of a particular phrase and helps us to concentrate on underlying grammatical structure without being distracted by concerns about word order — which vary considerably from one language to another. Rewriting the parse tree above in this way we obtain:

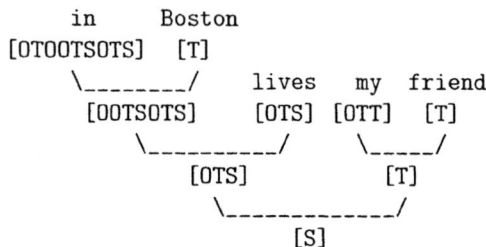

```
              in       Boston
        [OTOOTSOTS]    [T]
            _____/    lives   my  friend
            [OOTSOTS]    [OTS] [OTT]  [T]
               _____/     \_____/
                  [OTS]           [T]
                   _____/
                        [S]
```

In situations where the types of subphrases are not required, we can use a flattened, curried form of these trees, such as in Boston lives (my friend), to describe the result of parsing a phrase. The two different ways of arranging a parse tree shown here correspond to the concepts of *phenotype* and *genotype* grammar described earlier.

One of the most important tasks in an application of AUG is to assign suitable types to each word in some given lexicon or dictionary. The type T is an obvious choice for simple nouns like 'friend' and 'Boston' in the example above. Possessive pronouns like 'my' can be treated in the same way as adjectives using the type OTT. In a similar way, intransitive verbs, like 'lives', can be described by the type OTS transforming a subject term of type T into a sentence phrase of type S. The word 'in', with type OTOOTSOTS, in the example above deserves special attention. Motivated by the diagram above, we can think of 'in' as a function that combines a place of type T (where?), an action of type OTS (what?), and a subject of type T (who?) to obtain a sentence phrase of type S.

One additional complication we will need to deal with is that, in the general case, a single word may be used in several different ways, with a different type for each. In this paper we adopt a simple solution to this problem by storing a list of types for each word in the lexicon. We will see later how we can take advantage of this, including the possibility of a word having several roles (and types) *simultaneously* in the same sentence.

5   An NLP Prototype Written in Haskell

Our NLP prototype was written in Haskell [10], a standard for non-strict purely functional programming languages. Tutorial information on Haskell may be found elsewhere [1, 9]; in the following discussion we assume basic familiarity with the language. Our use of Haskell is fitting since the language is, in fact, named for the logician Haskell B. Curry whose work on combinatory logic cited above provides much of the foundation for both functional programming and AUG. As mentioned earlier, Curry himself was interested in the study of linguistics [4].

5.1 Types, Trees and Sentences

Our first task in the implementation of the parser is to choose a representation for types. Motivated by the description above, we define:

```
> data Type = T | S | O Type Type    deriving Eq
```

The specification `deriving Eq` declares that the new datatype `Type` is a member of Haskell's pre-defined class `Eq`, and that the system should therefore derive a definition of equality on values of type `Type`. This is needed so that we can test that the argument type of a function is equal to the type of value that it is applied to.

The result of parsing a string will be a tree structure with each node annotated with a list of types (each type corresponding to one possible parse).

```
> type TTree = (Tree,[Type])
> data Tree = Atom String | FAp TTree TTree | BAp TTree TTree
```

Applications of one tree structure to another are represented using the `FAp` (forward application) and `BAp` (backward application) constructors.

We will also need a way to display typed tree structures, and so we define a function:

```
> drawTTree :: TTree -> String
```

to display a typed tree in the form shown earlier.

The first step in the parser is to convert an input string into a list of words, each annotated with a list of types. For simplicity, we use the `Atom` constructor so that input sentences can be treated directly as lists of typed trees:

```
> type Sentence = [TTree]

> sentence :: String -> Sentence
> sentence = map wordToTTree . words
>   where wordToTTree w = (Atom w, wordTypes w)
```

The function `wordTypes` used here maps individual words to the corresponding list of types. For example, `wordTypes "friend" = [T]`. This function can be implemented in several different ways, for example, using an association list or, for faster lookup, a binary search tree. For all of the examples in this paper, we used a simple (unbalanced) binary search tree containing 62 words. However, we will not concern ourselves with any further details of the implementation of `wordTypes` here.

The following text strings will be used to illustrate the use of the parser in later sections:

```
> myfriend  = "my friend lives in Boston"
> oldfriend = "my old friend who comes from Moscow"
> long      = "my old friend who comes from Moscow thinks that\
>              \ the film which he saw today was very interesting"
```

For example, the first stage in parsing the `myfriend` string is to split it into the following list of typed tree values:

```
? sentence myfriend
[(Atom "my",[OTT]),
 (Atom "friend",[T]),
 (Atom "lives",[OTS]),
 (Atom "in",[OTOOTSOTS]),
 (Atom "Boston",[T])]
```

5.2 From Sentences to Trees

We have already described how individual words, or more generally, phrases can be combined by applying one to another. Now consider the task of parsing a sentence consisting of a list of words $[w_1, \ldots, w_n]$. One way to proceed would be to choose a pair of adjacent words, w_i and w_{i+1}, and replace them with the single compound phrase formed by applying one to the other, assuming, of course, that the types are compatible. Repeating this process a total of $n - 1$ times reduces the original list to a singleton containing a parse of the given sentence.

The most important aspect of this process is not the order in which pairs of phrases are combined, but rather the tree structure of the final parsed terms. In this sense, the goal of the parser is to find all well-typed tree structures that can be formed by combining adjacent phrases taken from a given list of words.

5.3 Enumerating Types/Trees

We wish to define the following function to enumerate all of the typed trees that can be obtained from a given sentence:

```
> ttrees :: Sentence -> [TTree]
```

The simplest case is when the list has just one element, and hence there is just one possible type:

```
> ttrees [t] = [t]
```

For the remaining case, suppose that we split the input list `ts` into two non-empty lists `ls`, `rs` such that `ts = ls ++ rs`. Using recursion, we can find all the trees `l` than can be obtained from `ls` and all the trees `r` that can be obtained from `rs`. We then wish to consider all pairs of these that can be combined properly to form a well-typed phrase. This yields the final line in the definition of `ttrees`:

```
> ttrees ts  = [ t | (ls,rs) <- splits ts, l <- ttrees ls,
>                                           r <- ttrees rs,
>                                           t <- combine l r ]
```

The function `splits` is used here to generate all pairs of non-empty lists `(ls,rs)` such that `ls ++ rs = ts`. It can be defined using:

```
> splits        :: [a] -> [([a],[a])]
> splits ts      = zip (inits ts) (tails ts)

> inits, tails :: [a] -> [[a]]
> inits [x]      = []
> inits (x:xs)  = map (x:) ([]:inits xs)

> tails [x]      = []
> tails (x:xs)  = xs : tails xs
```

For example:

```
? inits "abcde"
["a", "ab", "abc", "abcd"]
? tails "abcdef"
["bcde", "cde", "de", "e"]
? splits "abcdef"
[("a","bcde"), ("ab","cde"), ("abc","de"), ("abcd","e")]
```

The function combine is used in ttrees to generate all possible typed trees, if any, that can be obtained by combining two given typed trees. For the framework used in this paper, the only way that we can combine these terms is to apply one to the other.[3] To allow for variations in word order, we consider both the possibility that l is applied to r, and also that r is applied to l:

```
> combine     :: TTree -> TTree -> [TTree]
> combine l r = app FAp l r ++ app BAp r l
```

The rule for application of one term to another is encoded as follows:

```
> app :: (TTree -> TTree -> Tree) -> TTree -> TTree -> [TTree]
> app op (a,ts) (b,ss)
>   = [ (op (a,[O x y]) (b,[x]), [y]) | (O x y)<-ts, z<-ss, x==z ]
```

The expression (op (a,[O x y]) (b,[x]), [y]) here corresponds to the rule that, if a has type O x y and b has type x, then the application of a to b has type y. The use of singleton lists signals that the type of an application is uniquely determined by the type of its arguments. Clearly, we could extend the definition of combine to deal with other methods of combining terms in extended AUG frameworks.

The fact that we allow two different ways of combining a pair of terms by applying either one to the other, causes an exponential increase in the number of possible parse trees that might, in theory, need to be considered. For example, we can show that there are 8,448 different ways to construct a parse tree for a

---

[3] This limitation is not as severe as it might sound, linguistically, since *currying* permits application to several arguments. The parse described earlier involving the word 'in', with type OTOOTSOTS, is an example of this, as are transitive and ditransitive verbs, having types OTOTS and OTOTOTS, respectively.

sentence like `oldfriend` in Section 5.1 with only 7 words! Fortunately, the use of types eliminates almost all of these. Using the Gofer interpreter, we obtain just three parses for this sentence with no noticeable delay:

```
? (map show . ttrees . sentence) oldfriend
["(my (old (who friend (from Moscow comes))),[T])",
 "(my (who (old friend) (from Moscow comes)),[T])",
 "(who (my (old friend)) (from Moscow comes),[T])"]
(8302 reductions, 23220 cells)
```

We comment on these parses in more detail in Section 6.

For larger sentences, however, the definition of `ttrees` is not efficient enough. Fortunately, there is a much more efficient algorithm (described in [11]) based on *tabulation* [2]. With this change, our Haskell interpreter takes just a second to determine that there are 60 different parses of the 19 word sentence `long` given earlier, and this result would be at least an order of magnitude faster if it were compiled. (The original program took over 8 hours to achieve the same task!)

6   A Simple Example

For the purposes of simple experiments, we combine the components of the parser described above by defining the function:

```
> explain :: String -> String
> explain = unlines . map drawTTree . fastTtrees . sentence
```

For example, consider the phrase 'my old friend who comes from Moscow'. The result of parsing this phrase using our program are shown in Figure 1. As the figure shows, there are three different ways to parse this phrase, each of which produces a term phrase of type T. Without a deeper underlying semantics for the language, it is difficult to justify any formal statement about these three parses. However, from an informal standpoint, for example by observing the grouping of words, we can argue that all three of these parses are valid interpretations of the original phrase, each with slightly different meaning and emphasis:

- `my (old (who friend (from Moscow comes)))`: The words 'friend who comes from Moscow' are grouped together; of all my friends who come from Moscow, this phrase refers to the one that is old.
- `my (who (old friend) (from Moscow comes))`: In this case, the emphasis is on the word 'my'; perhaps you also have an old friend who comes from Moscow, but in this phrase, I am referring specifically to my old friend from Moscow.
- `who (my (old friend)) (from Moscow comes)`: A reference to 'my old friend' who comes from Moscow (but doesn't necessarily live there now).

When we started work on the program described in this paper, we were concerned that the rules for constructing parses of sentences were too liberal and that, even

85

? explain "my old friend who comes from Moscow"

my (old (who friend (from Moscow comes))):

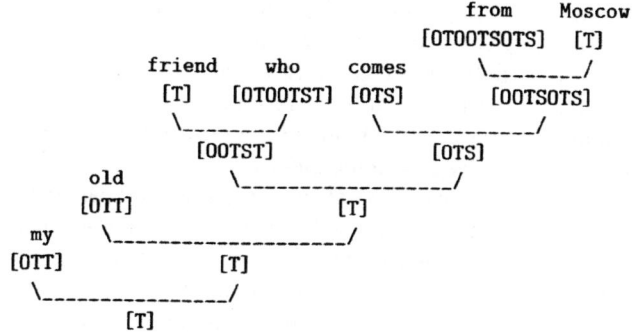

my (who (old friend) (from Moscow comes)):

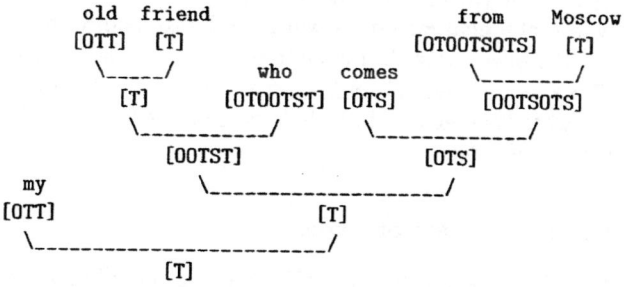

who (my (old friend)) (from Moscow comes):

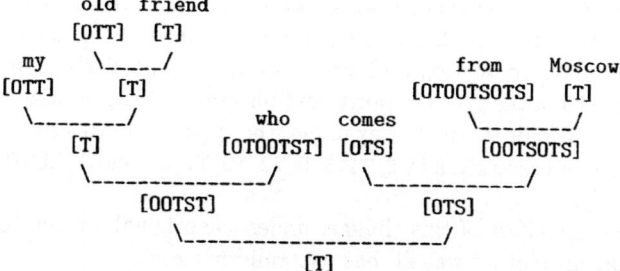

Fig. 1. Parsing the phrase 'my old friend who comes from Moscow'.

for small sentences, we would obtain many different parses, perhaps including some that did not make any sense. From this perspective, it is encouraging to see that there are only three possible parses of the example sentence used here and that all of them have reasonable interpretations. Of course, it is possible that there may be ways of interpreting this phrase that are not included in the list above; these might be dealt with by adding new types for some of the words involved to reflect different usage or meaning. Another possibility is that we might find a phrase with different interpretations that cannot be distinguished by their grammatical structure alone, in which case some form of semantic analysis may be needed to resolve any ambiguities.

While it seems reasonable to allow three different parses for the sentence above, we may be a little concerned about the 60 different parses mentioned above for the 19 word sentence that was used as a test in the previous sections. However, it turns out that half of these parse trees include one of the three different trees for 'my old friend who comes from Moscow' as a proper subphrase; this immediately introduces a factor of three into the number of parses that are generated. Similar multiplying factors of two and five can be observed in other parts of the output. Once we have identified these common elements, the results of the parser are much easier to understand.

Clearly, a useful goal for future work will be to modify the parser to detect and localize the effect of such ambiguities. For example, it might be useful to redefine `TTree` as `([Tree],[Type])` and store lists of subphrase parse trees at each node, rather than generating whole parse trees for each different combination subphrase parse trees.

6.1   A Refined Domain of Types

The datatype `Type` used to capture AUG types is actually a simplifed version of that used in AUG. Thus we have extended it to the following:

```
data Type = T | S | T1 | T2 | T3 | O Type Type | Sup Type Type
```

The new constructor `Sup` is for superposition, and will be explained later. The new constructors `T1`, `T2`, and `T3` capture a refined viewpoint of noun phrases called *primary*, *secondary*, and *tertiary* terms, respectively. This refinement is then reflected in the types of words and phrases that expect arguments or return results in this refined set. For example, the types of intransitive, transitive, and ditransitive verbs are given by `O T1 S`, `O T2 (O T1 S)`, and `O T3 (O T2 (O T1 S))`, respectively.

To see the effect of this change, under the original scheme the sentence 'he knew that his mother was ill' has two valid parses:

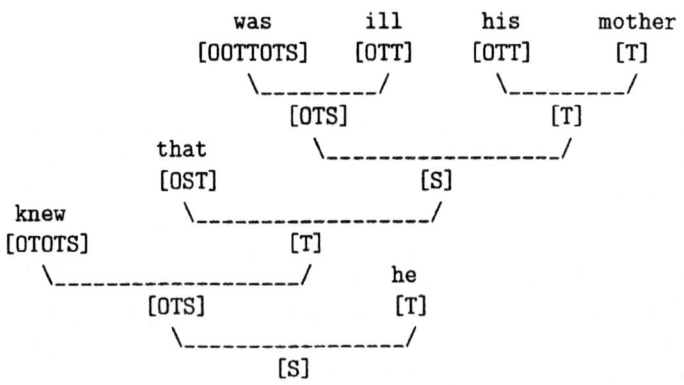

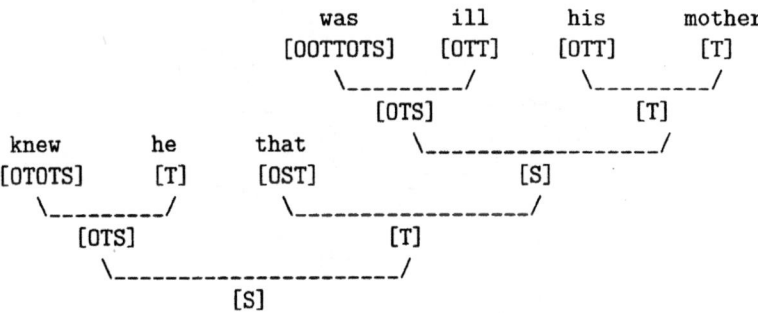

But the second of these is nonsense, since it reverses the roles of the noun phrases 'he' and 'that his mother was ill' with respect to the verb 'knew'. However, by declaring 'he' as T1, 'that' as OST2, and 'knew' as OT2OT1S, we arrive at the single sensible parse:

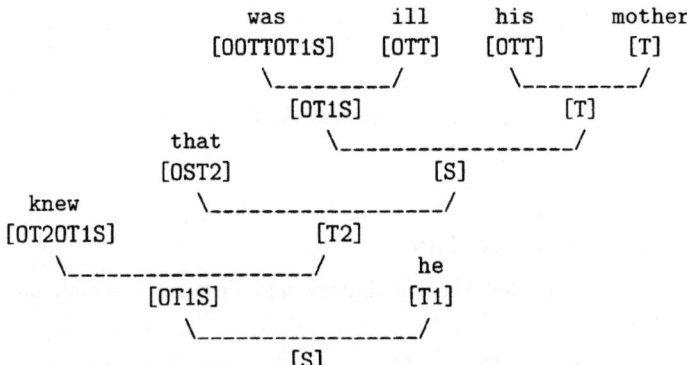

6.2 Superposition

An important aspect of AUG is its ability to deal with a word or phrase serving several simultaneous grammatical roles in a single sentence. The best example of this is the *gerund*, and we have implemented the rules to make this work. As an example, consider the sentence 'I see her coming home'. Here the word 'coming' serves both as an object (action) that is being seen, and as a verb applied to a secondary term 'home'. To represent phrases having more than one meaning, AUG uses the notation $\langle t_1/t_2 \rangle$ which is read: "the type t_1 *superposed* on type t_2." The typing rules for superposition are given in Figure 2.

We have implemented these rules, using the constructor Sup in the revised Type datatype to represent superposed types. As an example of the new parser in action, the parse of the sentence given above is:

```
                        coming          home
                      [T/OT2OT1S]        [T]
              her          _____/
             [OTT]              [T/OT1S]
      see        _____/
    [OT2OT1S]          [T]
        _____/          I
            [OT1S]            [T1]
              _____/
                    [S]
```

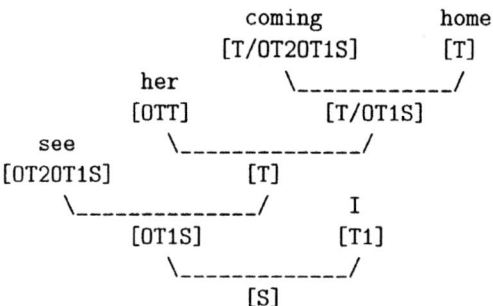

$$\frac{p :: 0x\langle y/x \rangle \quad q :: x}{pq :: \langle y/x \rangle}$$

$$\frac{p :: 0xy \quad q :: \langle x/z \rangle}{pq :: y}$$

$$\frac{p :: 0xy \quad q :: \langle z/x \rangle}{pq :: \langle z/y \rangle}$$

$$\frac{p :: \langle 0xy/z \rangle \quad q :: x}{pq :: y}$$

$$\frac{p :: \langle z/0xy \rangle \quad q :: x}{pq :: \langle z/y \rangle}$$

$$\frac{p :: \langle 0xy/z \rangle \quad q :: \langle x/u \rangle}{pq :: y}$$

Fig. 2. Typing Rules for Superposition

6.3 Expanded Vocabulary

We have also expanded the vocabulary and dictionary search mechanism in several ways:

1. We have increased the number of words considerably; currently the vocabulary contains over 2000 words.
2. Many of these words have multiple types. For example, 'branch' has both types T and OT1S.
3. We have implemented a simple form of singular/plural word inference.

6.4 Passivization

As a final extension of our basic scheme, we have added the notion of *passivization* to our parser. With this extension, we have defined a function `passive` that first parses a source string, passivizes the abstract parse, then regenerates the string in passive form. For example:

```
? passive "my friend will bring hats home"
"hats will be brought home by my friend"
```

Note that this also required dealing with verb tenses, which we implemented at least to a limited extent. Note also the introduction of the word 'by' when moving to the passive form. Overall this is not a trivial transformation, and is a promising indication of the viability of our approach.

7 Conclusion

The history of computer science, mathematical logic, and linguistics presents a striking parallel with respect to their approach to language. Computer science constructs programming languages. Metamathematics is concerned with a critique of existing languages of mathematics and with constructing better languages. Linguistics is concerned with developing formal structures modeling natural languages.

Every language–a programming language, a language of logic or mathematics, or a natural language—depends on a physical substratum, which makes the existence of the language possible. The physical structure of programming languages is a reflection of the physical structure of the computer. The physical structure of natural language is so-called phrase structure which reflects the action of the human machine: the organs of speech. Thus natural language has a linear phrase-structure. The essential structure of natural language, its functional structure, is independent of the linear phrase-structure, because the raison d'etre of language, the sole reason for the existence of language, is to be a tool for the expression of thought and communication. Hence the need for a functional structure of language.

In computer science, mathematical logic, and linguistics we observe a consistent trend towards liberation from dependence on the physical structure of languages towards the representation of its pure functional structure. In computer science we observe three stages: (1) languages reflecting physical structure of computers; (2) imperative languages: a mixture of physical and functional structure; and (3) functional (applicative) languages: pure functional structure. In mathematical logic we observe two stages: (1) concatenative languages, tied to the linear representation of abstract systems; and (2) applicative languages, independent of the linear representation of abstract systems. Finally, in linguistics we observe two stages: (1) phrase-structure grammar, a mixed system tied to the linear representation/physical system; and (2) applicative grammar, a pure functional system. We also observe a strong correspondence between the functional structure of new functional programming languages such as Haskell and the functional structure of genotype, the underlying language of AUG.

8 Acknowledgements

We would like to thank Mark Jones, now at Nottingham University, for doing much of the initial Haskell programming on this project when he was at Yale, and who should probably be a co-author if time constraints had permitted it for him. Also thanks to the second author's funding agencies, DARPA under grant number F30602-96-2-0232, and NSF under grant number CCR-9633390.

References

1. R. Bird and P. Wadler. *Introduction to Functional Programming*. Prentice Hall, New York, 1988.
2. R.S. Bird and O. de Moor. Relational program derivation and context-free language recognition. In A.W. Roscoe, editor, *A Classical Mind: Essays in Honour of C.A.R. Hoare*, pages 17–35. Prentice-Hall International Series in Computer Science, 1994.
3. Noam Chomsky. On the notion 'rule of grammar'. In *Proceedings of Symposium in Applied Mathematics*, volume 12 (Structure of Language and Its Mathematical Aspects). 1961.
4. H.B. Curry. Some logical aspects of grammatical structure. In *Structure of language and its mathematical aspects*. American Mathematical Society, Providence, 1961.
5. H.B. Curry and R. Feys. *Combinatory Logic, Vol. 1*. North-Holland, Amsterdam, 1958.
6. R. Frost and J. Launchbury. Constructing natural language interpreters in a lazy functional language. *The Computer Journal*, 32(2):108–121, April 1989.
7. Morris Halle. *The Sound Pattern of Russian*. Mouton, The Hague, 1959.
8. P. Hudak. Conception, evolution, and application of functional programming languages. *ACM Computing Surveys*, 21(3):359–411, 1989.
9. P. Hudak and J. Fasel. A gentle introduction to Haskell. *ACM SIGPLAN Notices*, 27(5), May 1992.
10. P. Hudak, S. Peyton Jones, and P. Wadler (editors). Report on the Programming Language Haskell, A Non-strict Purely Functional Language (Version 1.2). *ACM SIGPLAN Notices*, 27(5), May 1992.
11. M.P. Jones, P. Hudak, and S. Shaumyan. Using types to parse natural language. In *Proceedings of Glasgow Functional Programming Workshop*. IFIP, Springer Verlag, 1995.
12. Stanislaw Lesniewski. Grundzuge eines neuen Systems der Grundlagen der Mathematik. *Fundamenta Mathematicae*, 14:1–81, 1929.
13. Theodore M. Lightner. Generative phonology. In William Orr Dingwall, editor, *Survey of Linguistic Science*, pages 489–574. Linguistics Program, University of Maryland, 1971.

14. M. Moortgat. The generalized categorial grammar. In Flip G. Droste and John E. Joseph, editors, *Linguistic Theory and Grammatical Description*, pages 489–574. John Benjamins Publishing, Amsterdam/Philadelphia, 1991.
15. Richard Montague. Formal philosophy. In R.H. Thomason, editor, *Selected writings of Richard Montague*. Yale University Press, New Haven, CT, 1974.
16. Sebastian Shaumyan. Strukturnaja lingvistika, 1965.
17. Sebastian Shaumyan. *Applicative grammar as a semantic theory of natural language*. University of Chicago Press, 1977.
18. Sebastian Shaumyan. *A Semiotic Theory of Language*. Indiana University Press, 1987.
19. Sebastian Shaumyan. Applicative universal grammar as a linguistic framework of the translation model. In *Proceedings of the Fifth International Conference on Symbolic and Logical Computing*. Dakota State University, Madison, Dakota, 1991.

Derivational and Representational Views of Minimalist Transformational Grammar

Thomas Cornell

University of Tübingen, Seminar für Sprachwissenschaft, Kleine Wilhelmstrasse 113,
D-72074 Tübingen, Germany
cornell@sfs.nphil.uni-tuebingen.de

Abstract. In this paper we cast the long-standing debate in transformational grammar over movement derivations vs. well-formedness conditions on chains in a new light. We claim that the argument itself is misguided: a transformational grammar should have *both* a derivational and representational interpretation, connected by soundness and completeness results. Second, we argue that the proper form of the representational interpretation is as an axiomatization of T-markers rather than P-markers (e.g., LF structures). Little of significance in representationalist approaches is lost by this move, however. Antecedent goverment conditions on chains, for example, can still be easily stated in terms of the kinds of T-markers that we propose. Many well-known problems for representational approaches are avoided, however. In addition, from a derivational perspective, global constraints on derivations become simple structural well-formedness conditions on T-markers. We offer a rigorous formalization of a simple system of T-markers and show its equivalence to a simple minimalist derivation system.

1 Introduction

The recent swing in modern transformational generative grammar from the focus on essentially axiomatic definitions of well-formed structures back to more derivational methods (e.g., Chomsky 4) has added fuel to an old debate over the proper place of derivational and representational methods in transformational grammar, that is, whether it is better to account for extraction constructions by building them up with a series of movement transformations or by appeal to well-formedness conditions on chains (see, e.g., Brody 1). In this paper we investigate the possibility of "having one's cake and eating it too," that is, the possibility of dealing with modern-day transformational grammar in a framework which provides both derivational and representational interpretations and where furthermore these interpretations are provably equivalent. For our approach to derivations we will mainly rely on formalizations of "minimalist" derivations offered by Stabler (see, especially, Stabler 7), and we will focus here on presenting an equivalent representational system.

Let us define a representation system for a transformational grammar as an axiomatic definition of a set of well-formed structures which we will call *T-markers*. The term is adapted from Chomsky (2), and is meant to be understood by analogy to P-markers (phrase structure trees), which are structures which record the history of a derivation from a phrase structure grammar, and serve simultaneously as a static, declarative analysis of the constituent structure of a sentence.

There are a number of reasons to want a declarative picture of "structure at the level of transformations" beyond the desire to clarify debates about Universal Grammar and how to describe it. Maybe most importantly, in a setting in which economy conditions on derivations play such a large role, it is crucial to have a good static picture of a derivation. Constraints that hold on entire derivations (e.g., that all features be checked, or that Spell Out occur as soon as all strong features have been checked) then become simple structural well-formedness conditions, for example. Beyond this, addressing more global "economy" conditions, we can expect to use techniques from model theory or denotational semantics to order and structure sets of T-markers in ways which support a clear mathematical understanding of which derivations should be taken to be "less than" which others. Simply put, if one wants to compare derivations, then being able to treat derivations as objects is going to be necessary.

Other motivations come from concerns of computational linguistics. Suppose that we want to actually compute syntactic structures, and we are given only a derivation system. This is already a procedural system but not necessarily a computationally efficient one, and we are somewhat limited as to the ways in which we can construct equivalent but more efficient procedural interpretations of grammar. Equivalent in what sense, we might ask, to start with. A representation system can help here, in that it offers a notion of equivalence among derivations (namely: two derivations are equivalent if they have the same representation) which is independent of the chosen order of processing steps.

Finally, we know already from logic and computer science that the more ways one has of looking at a problem the better, in particular if those ways are equivalent. A classic example comes from the formally very distinct approaches to the tricky notion of logical consequence offered by proof theory and model theory, which are (in almost all popular logics) equivalent in the sense made precise in theorems of soundness and completeness. Apart from its practical usefulness this equivalence gives us some confidence that we have actually got a handle on what Consequence is. Similarly, the many different equivalent characterizations of computation give us confidence in the Church-Turing hypothesis that we have at least got the idea of Computation surrounded, if not captured. The fact that we can entertain such formally different approaches to Universal Grammar as those employed in Government Binding theory and in the Minimalist Program already suggests that Grammar, even assuming that the transformational generative grammar tradition is basically correct about it, is another one of these slippery notions, which must be approached cautiously and from a number of angles.

The simplest and most uncontroversial notion of T-marker which fits the Minimalist Program is just a term in an algebra with operations Merge and Move (or "Attract") with sets or sequences of features as its constants. Such a term is much like a P-marker in that it represents not a single unique derivation but rather an equivalence class of derivations, in that distinct subtrees can be constructed in any order, but the operations used and the arguments they are used upon are fixed. Unlike a P-marker, however, such T-markers have never seemed to offer much insight as static representations of the syntactic structure of a sentence.

The least obvious and most controversial notion of a T-marker comes from a tradition of proposing representational versions of transformational grammar with its roots in trace theory. The central proposal there, most obvious in recent work of Michael Brody (e.g., Brody 1), but phrased here in our own terms, is that the final P-marker in a transformational derivation—i.e., LF—is also a T-marker. In this case the proposed representation is very revealing of syntactic structure, but it is not at all clear that it is adequate as the representation of the history of a transformational derivation. This proposal is controversial mainly as a result of the fact that the proposed representation system is not constructed so as to match any derivation system. There are really two claims rolled into one here: that LFs capture all the information necessary to reconstruct their derivation and that the set of well-formed LFs can be defined independently of any derivation system. The first point is the starting point that motivates representationalist syntax, but it is the second that is really the focus of empirical and formal research. Things are complicated by the fact that (a) claims about Universal Grammar may differ even when the assumed derivation and representation systems are equivalent and (b) neither side of the debate develops adequate versions of the other side's formal foundations. So claims tend to take the form: derivations are unnecessary because representations are empirically adequate, and counter claims take the form: representations are not empirically adequate. (The reader may freely substitute "derivation" for "representation" and vice versa in the preceding sentence.) One goal of the research reported on here is to try to tease apart substantive claims about Universal Grammar on which Brody and Chomsky, for instance, certainly disagree, from formal claims about the properties of derivations and representations.

Our own proposal is intermediate between these two poles. It takes considerable inspiration from Brody's work, in particular his focus on chains. On the other hand our representation system is developed with the specific intention of being equivalent to a derivation system. The fact that we even use the term "T-markers" is a symptom of this focus. The term is not used in derivational approaches, since something like a derivation term is only interesting as a summary of a derivation, and does not offer particular insights into the structure of sentences. Nor is it used in pure representational approaches, which, as noted, focus instead on an empirically adequate axiomatization of LF structures (or (DS,SS,PF,LF) quadruples, in older GB era proposals).

The organization of this paper is in three main parts. In the remainder of this introduction we present our ideas informally, motivated as a solution to some problems for the LF-as-T-marker proposals. There follows a section in which we develop these ideas rigorously. Finally, we consider the kinds of derivation systems that Stabler (7) has proposed, and sketch the proof of a sort of soundness and completeness result for our representation system and a Stabler-style derivation system. We have attempted to make the presentation as self-contained as possible in such a limited space. However, as far as our motivations and design decisions go, we must here and there assume some familiarity with the Minimalist Program, as it is presented in Chomsky (4), though for the most part some familiarity with Government-Binding theory will suffice. Also we will at various points lean rather heavily on Stabler (7); indeed in many respects this paper is a response to the line of research reported there.

1.1 Two Puzzles for the geometry of chains

In this section we present two famous problems for the geometry of chains which make it difficult to formulate the notion of "well-formed chain" at the level of LF and without reference to any derivation of that chain. In Fig. 1(a), a head a moves to incorporate into another head b which locally governs it, and then the complex $[a\ b]$ head moves to incorporate into yet another head c which locally governs it in turn.[1] Each movement step is extremely local. The whole procedure can clearly be iterated at will to allow the formation of arbitrarily complex word-level structures from a sequence of extremely simple movement operations. Even after two such movements, however, the chain link—depicted as a dotted line in the figure—which connects the head we moved first (here a) to its trace (written here t_a) is no longer local, at least not in the same simple sense as in the movement derivation. It becomes quite challenging to state general well-formedness conditions on chains that will allow structures such as those in Fig. 1(a), while ruling out all the unacceptable structures, such as that shown in Fig. 1(b). This structure is derived by moving a across b, which is generally barred. However, the relevant chain link is superficially rather similar to the acceptable case. In particular, a governs its trace and—since b later also moves to c—only a trace intervenes, just as in the good example.

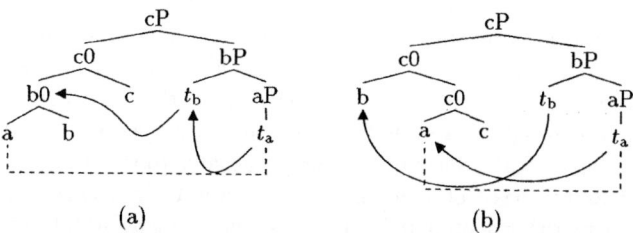

(a)   (b)

Fig. 1. (a) A complex but well-formed head-movement construction. (b) A similar but ill-formed head-movement construction.

---

[1] We use a two valued X-bar notation here, distinguishing only word internal or "0 level" nodes from word external or "phrase level" nodes.

At least the antecedent *a* in Fig. 1(a) still governs its trace. In Fig. 2 we present, schematically, a structure in which this keystone of the traditional theory of chains is violated. In this example, a phrase aP first moves out of bP to attach to a specifier position in cP. Subsequently, bP itself moves to some higher position, "abducting" the trace of aP. (We have represented the target of movement as a higher specifier or adjunct in cP to keep the tree small.) In the resulting structure aP no longer governs its trace.[2]

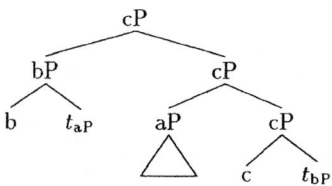

Fig. 2. An apparent violation of the antecedent government condition.

1.2 T-Markers: Informal Presentation

We first lay out our solutions to the foregoing puzzles informally. The intuitions involved are rather easy to grasp, though the execution is rather tricky in detail. Traditionally, two types of solutions have been offered for puzzles such as those in Sect. 1.1: Reconstruction and the Copy Theory of movement. Reconstruction allows for a moved expression to be "reconstructed" in the position of one of its traces, and is independently motivated by such constructions as backwards anaphora: *Pictures of himself always amuse John.* It can be used in our problem cases to reconstruct the derivation stages at which head chain links were local and an antecedent did indeed govern its trace. The copy theory of movement just proposes that "traces" are in fact copies of the moved expression, so, for example, the locality of head *a* to its trace can be determined by examining the copy of the complex head [*a b*] that *b* leaves behind when it moves to *c*. Both of these solutions are based on the same essential idea: that the internal structure of a phrase is potentially accessible from any one of the chain of positions through which that phrase has been moved. Our proposal is to isolate this essential idea and use it as the basis of structures which capture in a single representation all (and only) the essential information about a transformational derivation.

---

[2] Such a construction may arguably be exemplified by the case of Remnant Topicalization in German (Müller 6 and refs.). For example:

$[_{VP}$ Gelesen t_2 $]_1$ hat [das Buch]$_2$ keiner t_1.
    read   has the book$_{acc}$ no-one$_{nom}$

Adopting the terminology of Chomsky (2), we refer to these structures as *T-markers*.

Consider first the case of "trace abduction" illustrated in Fig. 2. This example is more exotic and controversial than the head movement example, but the structures involved are simpler, as it involves no head movement or head adjunction structures. This tree contains three phrases, projected from the three heads a, b and c, and two chains $\langle aP, t_a \rangle$ and $\langle bP, t_b \rangle$. Let us think of the nodes in a tree as positions that expressions can occupy. Then we have two main types of position: phrasal positions, i.e., positions to which an expression can be attached, and chain positions, i.e., positions through which or to which an expression moves. From this perspective, all non-terminal nodes in the tree are phrasal positions, but some are also at the same time chain positions. In fact, if we adopt the standard assumption that all potentially movable expressions form chains, then we have also to include the trivial XP chain $\langle cP \rangle$. In Fig. 3(a) we see the tree from Fig. 2, with the nodes relabeled to indicate their distinct functions as both phrasal and chain positions. Here chain positions are indicated with an asterisk, e.g., aP_0^* is the root position in the chain of aP, i.e., the trace of aP.

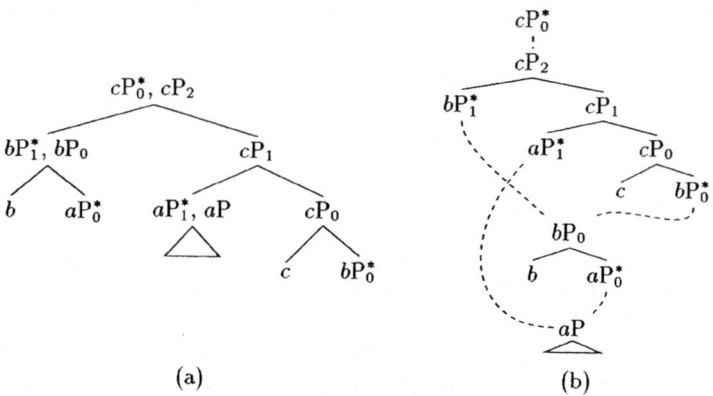

Fig. 3. Analyzing Fig. 2: (a) with phrase and chain positions; (b) an "exploded view" of (a).

Our rather simple proposal is just this. We propose to separate chains from phrases in a rather radical sense: chain positions and phrase positions will be treated as completely separate objects. Chain positions represent the *external* syntax of a construction, that is, the way it takes part in larger constructions, and phrase positions represent the *internal* syntax of a construction, that is, the way in which smaller constructions are combined to form it. Observe that this description of chains and phrases makes no reference to movement transformations; in particular, there is no sense in which chains are essentially conceptually just the vapor trails of moving phrases.

The structure displayed in Fig. 3(b) presents a sort of "exploded view" of the structure in Fig. 3(a), which splits the nodes which are both phrasal and chain positions into two separate nodes. We also add arcs back from each chain position to the maximal element of the corresponding phrase, indicating that the target phrase may potentially be spelled out in any one of its chain positions. In this way the single graph structure of Fig. 3(b) can be used to represent any stage of the corresponding transformational derivation, basically by choosing one of the chain-to-phrase arcs from each chain as the "spell-out position" for that stage. For example, the tree in Fig. 3(a) arises from choosing the highest-numbered element of each chain as its spell-out position.

Note that in Fig. 3(b), all chain positions of one head are attached to phrasal positions of some other head. All interaction between heads thus depends on these chain position-phrase position links. This composition of structures out of nodes of opposite polarities rather directly reflects the theory of feature checking in the minimalist program, according to which derivations are driven by the attraction between oppositely charged features.

This T-marker, ignoring for now the different kinds of arcs that are drawn here, is a rooted directed acyclic graph (RDAG), a structure with many properties in common with trees. In particular, it is still possible to define a dominance partial order, and therefore also the c-command relation, which is the keystone of the government relation. Let us ask, then, whether or not the chain position aP_1^* c-commands its trace, the chain position aP_0^*. Since aP_1^* is immediately dominated by cP_1, the question reduces to the question of whether cP_1 is an ancestor of aP_0^*. It is, as witnessed by the path:

$$cP_1 \rightarrow cP_0 \rightarrow bP_0^* \dashrightarrow bP_0 \rightarrow aP_0^*$$

The "trace abduction" problem simply disappears. More precisely, the chain position bP_1^* at which bP is spelled out in Fig. 2 simply plays no role in the computation of the c-command relation between aP_1^* and aP_0^*. Unlike a P-marker with indexed traces, the crucial structural properties of the T-marker in Fig. 3 are invariant under the movement transformation that "abducts" the trace of aP in Fig. 2. Put another way, since aP_1^* c-commands aP_0^*, there must exist a corresponding derivation in which, at some stage, aP could have moved to position aP_1^* from position aP_0^*.[3]

What we have done, by separating chain positions from phrasal positions, is to separate the problems of chain geometry (government and locality) from the problems of spell-out. Spell-out, in a very general sense which includes both surface and LF interpretation, can be defined very simply by selecting from every chain one position as its spell-out position. Then the spell-out function, applied to a spell-out position in a chain, is defined as having the same value as that

---

[3] This could be a problem, in fact. While Remnant Topicalization is attested and must be accounted for, most languages disallow trace-abduction structures. Note that disallowing such movements is a matter of placing a condition on the chain of b, not a: bP, containing a trace, should be frozen in place.

function applied to the maximal phrasal position; at all other chain positions its value is nil.

In this way a single T-marker can stand for the entire sequence of (forests of) P-markers that define a derivation. A derivation necessarily involves much needless copying of unaffected structure from one stage to the next. The T-markers that we propose collect just what is essential from the derivation in a single structure. This in turn allows us to consider how to construct a Government-Binding style, purely declarative, axiomatic definition of transformational syntactic structures, that is, to pursue model theoretic syntax despite the resolutely proof theoretic character of most current theorizing within the minimalist program.

Consider now what we would do with the head movement examples. The "exploded view" of the tree in Fig. 1(a) is shown in Fig. 4. The solution to that puzzle will be seen to follow essentially the same lines as the trace abduction example, that is, we find that the crucial structural properties of our T-markers are invariant under movement transformations owing to the separation of structural conditions on chains from the theory of spell out. Note however that our structures become somewhat more complex here, owing to the presence of both XP and X0 chains.

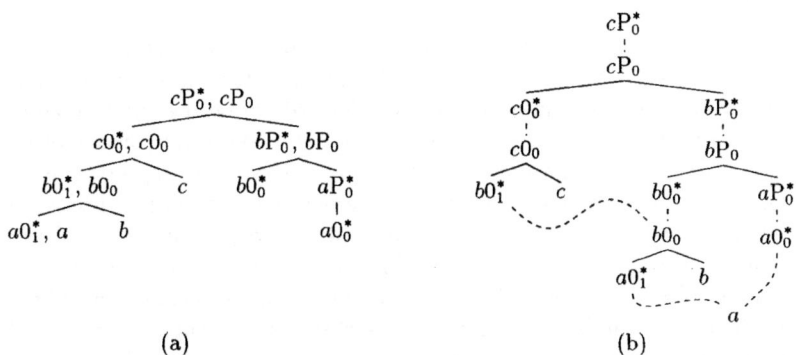

(a)   (b)

Fig. 4. Complex head movement: (a) phrase and chain positions; (b) exploded view.

Consider again the paths that witness the c-command relation between the two moved heads b and a and their traces. In the case of $b0_1^*$, the first category that completely dominates it is cP_0, and in the case of $a0_1^*$ it is bP_0.[4] Then the

---

[4] The relevant notion of "dominance" here is in terms of "categories" rather than "segments of categories". See Chomsky (3) for details. However, below we will observe that in the Minimalist Program a stronger condition than c-command holds, for which a proper understanding of the category/segment distinction is unnecessary.

paths down to the traces $b0_0^*$ and $a0_0^*$ are as follows.

$$b0_1^* : \ cP_0 \to bP_0^* \dashrightarrow bP_0 \to b0_0^*$$
$$a0_1^* : \ bP_0 \to aP_0^* \dashrightarrow aP_0 \to a0_0^*$$

Again, the structural deformation of the chain link (a, t_a) (here $(a0_1^*, a0_0^*)$) plainly visible in Fig. 1(a) is simply absent here, because we have separated the problem of how the structure should be spelled out from the problem of the well-formedness of its chains. In a real structure the paths would not be quite so isomorphic of course, since one XP might have a different number of specifiers from the other, for example. Nonetheless, the same conditions that govern locality in a movement transformation hold here of the corresponding chain links, which is the crucial point. For reasons of space we do not illustrate the (ill-formed) T-marker for the (underivable) structure in Fig. 1(b). It is left as a simple exercise for the reader to verify that in this case the higher chain position of a will be found to c-command a chain position of b and that chain position of b to c-command the trace of a yielding the same violation of the Head Movement Condition as would the corresponding derivation.

2 The Formalism

2.1 Structures

The syntactic framework we are developing here is lexicalist in nature, that is, the material for building well-formed syntactic structures, or, equivalently, the constraints which isolate just the well-formed structures, all originate with lexical items. We will have more to say about the syntactic content of lexical items in Sect. 2.2. For the moment we simply observe that any given syntactic structure will be the extension in syntax of a particular multiset of lexical items, called in Chomsky (4) the *numeration*. In what follows we will reserve the (often overloaded) term *head* for lexical item instances from the numeration.

The simplest definition of T-markers adopts the informal notation of Sect. 1.2 fairly directly. That is, we think of T-markers as structures over a set $\mathcal{U}$ of abstract positions, some of which are head positions. The rest of $\mathcal{U}$ is partitioned into phrases and chains, which are sequences of positions (which we will assume to be finite). We say of a phrase or chain position x such that $\text{head}(x) = y$ that "x extends y." Phrases may be empty, but chains will always be considered to contain at least one element, mainly for ease of presentation.

Definition 1 (Extended Numeration). *An* extended numeration *is a structure* $\mathcal{A} = \langle A, \text{head}, 0, \text{P}, 0^*, \text{P}^*, \leq \rangle$, *with unary operations* head, $0, \text{P}, 0^*, \text{P}^*$ *and binary relation* $\leq$. head *maps positions to their head positions (and is the identity on head positions).* $0, \text{P}, 0^*, \text{P}^*$ *(written postfix) map positions to subsets of* A, *called* phrases *and* chains. *For all phrases and chains* C, $\leq$ *restricted to* C *is required to be a total order. That is, phrases and chains are required to be sequences of positions. In addition they are required to be disjoint from each other.*

We will often use subscripts to indicate relative position in the $\leq$ order. The direction of the $\leq$ ordering reflects distance from the head position, so that, for instance, $x\mathrm{P}_0$ is the structurally lowest position in $x\mathrm{P}$ and $x\mathrm{P}_0^*$ is the derivationally initial position of $x\mathrm{P}$.

The following convention simply makes the notation a little easier to use.

Convention 1.

$$(\forall x, y)[y = \mathsf{head}(x) \Rightarrow (x\mathrm{P}^* = y\mathrm{P}^* \wedge x\mathrm{P} = y\mathrm{P} \wedge x0^* = y0^* \wedge x0 = y0)]$$

This condition makes it possible to refer to $x\mathrm{P}_i$, for instance, without restricting x to head positions. Note that $x \in x\mathrm{P}$ now implies that x is a position in a word external phrasal extension. Informally, we will write "x is an XP position" for $x \in x\mathrm{P}$, and analogously for the other extensions.

Unlabelled T-markers, that is, T-markers without any concern for the distribution of lexical features, are got from extended numerations by attaching chain positions of one head to phrase positions of a distinct head. We call the attachment relation T.

Definition 2 (Unlabelled T-Marker). $\mathcal{T} = \langle \mathcal{A}, T \rangle$, *with $\mathcal{A}$ an extended numeration, T a binary attachment relation on $\mathcal{A}$, such that*

$$(\forall x, y : T(x, y))[(x \in x\mathrm{P}^* \wedge y \in y\mathrm{P}) \vee (x \in x0^* \wedge y \in y0)] \tag{1}$$

$$(\forall x, y : T(x, y))[\mathsf{head}(x) \neq \mathsf{head}(y)] \tag{2}$$

$$(\forall x, y, z)[T(y, x) \wedge T(z, x) \Rightarrow y = z] \tag{3}$$

$$(\forall x)\big[(x \in x\mathrm{P} \vee x \in x0) \Rightarrow (\exists y)[T(y, x)]\big] \tag{4}$$

$$(\forall x)\neg(\exists y)[T(x0_0^*, y)] \tag{5}$$

T attaches chain positions to phrase positions (1) of distinct heads (2). Every phrasal position has a unique dependent attached to it by T (3,4). Movement of any structure smaller than the entire phrase must necessarily leave a trace within the phrase. Therefore, the minimal position of every X0 chain must be found at the base of its head's XP. Therefore it must not be attached anywhere else, so we must exclude it from the domain of T (5).

The following convention makes some definitions easier.

Convention 2. *For all head positions x, we assume that $x0_0^*$ always exists.*

Elements of an extended numeration, and the T-markers we get by attaching them together, form rather dense and complex graphs. The following definition is helpful in getting useful pictures of the essential structure of T-markers.

Definition 3 (Immediate Dominance). *We write $x \triangleleft y$ for "x immediately dominates y," and $x \triangleleft^* y$ and $x \triangleleft^+ y$ for the reflexive and irreflexive transitive closures of $\triangleleft$. Then $\triangleleft$ is the smallest relation such that, for all positions z:*

$$(\forall x \in z\mathrm{P}^*)(\forall y \in z\mathrm{P})[x \triangleleft^+ y] \wedge (\forall x \in z0^*)(\forall y \in z0)[x \triangleleft^+ y] \tag{6}$$

$$(\forall x, y \in z\mathrm{P})[x \leq y \Rightarrow y \triangleleft^* x] \wedge (\forall x, y \in z0)[x \leq y \Rightarrow y \triangleleft^* x] \tag{7}$$

$$(\forall x)(\forall y)[T(x, y) \Rightarrow y \triangleleft x] \tag{8}$$

$$(\forall x \in z\mathrm{P}^* \cup z\mathrm{P})[x \triangleleft^+ z0_0^*] \wedge (\forall x \in z0^* \cup z0)[x \triangleleft^+ \mathsf{head}(z)] \tag{9}$$

The $\lhd$ relation is built up from $\leq$ restricted to phrases plus the attachment relation T; the $\leq$ relation on chains is replaced by links connecting chain positions directly to their maximal phrasal position (if it exists) or to the minimal $X0^*$ position otherwise. It is the $\lhd$ relation which is actually pictured in the figures in Secs. 1.1 & 1.2. The dotted lines connecting chain positions to (maximal) phrasal positions in those figures correspond to $\lhd$ links contributed by (6).

Condition 1 (RDAG Condition). *For all T-markers $\mathcal{T}$, the graph of the $\lhd$ relation on $\mathcal{T}$ is required to be a rooted directed acyclic graph (RDAG).*

Proposition 1.

1. *With respect to $\lhd$, phrasal positions are binary branching and endocentric: one of the two daughters has the same head as the mother while the other is attached via T.*
2. *For all heads x except the head of the root, $xP^* \neq \emptyset$.*

We derive (2) by noting that by the RDAG Condition every head x must be connected into the $\lhd$ graph. Only via chain positions can it be connected outside its own extension. If $x0^*$ is nonempty then $x0_0^*$ exists, and the parent of $x0_0^*$, by the definition of T and $\lhd$, cannot fall outside of the extension of x, so only via an XP chain position can $x0_0^*$ be connected outside its own extension. So xP^* must be nonempty, so as to connect either x or $x0_0^*$ to the rest of the graph.

We lose a global notion of precedence in these structures, in the sense that the order of sisters does not give rise to a partial order over the whole structure. Precedence order in illustrations of T-markers is conventional and reflects the sisterhood relationships of the corresponding phrase structure trees.

We present now some definitions and conditions of a more linguistic nature. Intuitively, a head connects its specifiers and word internal adjuncts to its complement in a way analogous to the way in which operators take scope in logic. Note that in these definitions no attempt is made to include a theory of locality.

Definition 4 (Domain). *The domain of a head x is the set of positions y such that $T(y, w) \land head(w) = x$.*

Definition 5 (Scope). *Suppose we are given a head x and a position z such that $xP_0 \lhd z$. The scope of x is the subgraph of $\lhd$ rooted at z. That is, it consists of the $\lhd$ relation restricted to the set of positions y such that $z \lhd^* y$.*

Definition 6 ((Trace) Binding). *A non-minimal chain position x binds its predecessor y just in case x is in the domain of a head z and y is in the scope of z. That is, there is a w such that $T(x, w)$ and $wP_0 \lhd^+ y$.*

Condition 2 (Trace Binding Condition). *All non-minimal chain positions must bind their predecessors.*

Note that our definition of domain has left open the possibility that an element in complement position can bind a trace. This is ruled out by the RDAG Condition, however.

Proposition 2. *Only minimal* XP* *positions can attach to minimal* XP *positions:* $(\forall x = x\mathrm{P}_0)(\forall y)[T(y,x) \Rightarrow y = y\mathrm{P}_0^*]$.

Proof. Suppose that we attach $y\mathrm{P}_{i>0}^*$ to $x\mathrm{P}_0$. $y\mathrm{P}_i^*$ must bind its trace. It follows that $x\mathrm{P}_0 \lhd^+ y\mathrm{P}_{i-1}^*$ and so $y\mathrm{P}_i^* \lhd^* y\mathrm{P}_{i-1}^*$ and so $y\mathrm{P}_{max} \lhd^* y\mathrm{P}_{i-1}^*$. But we have by the definition of $\lhd$ (Def'n 3) that $y\mathrm{P}_{i-1}^* \lhd^+ y\mathrm{P}_{max}$. This introduces a loop into the graph of $\lhd$, violating the RDAG Condition (Cond. 1). $\qquad\square$

Proposition 3. *The trace binding relation is transitive and irreflexive and a total order for any particular chain.*

In light of this we could redefine our T-markers with $\lhd$ and trace binding as primitives and derive the $\leq$ ordering instead. The $\leq$ ordering is convenient to our purposes here because it very closely reflects the order of derivation.

2.2 Features

The ideas about syntactic structures presented in Sect. 2.1 are actually substantially independent of the main proposals of the minimalist program. They are in many ways suitable for use in more classical Government Binding (GB) theory, in fact. The Minimalist Program is concerned mainly with issues of *economy*; the most basic level at which these issues play a role is in the adherence of the Minimalist Program to an essentially *resource conscious* approach to derivation and representation, with features as the resources in question. Adding a step to a derivation is only possible if the lexical features exist to license it, and executing that step consumes some of those features, so that they cannot be used again by that derivation. Our approach to features here follows very closely the formalism of Stabler (7).

Definition 7. *We assume a basic set of* feature labels, *partitioned into* attraction features *(Chomsky's "formal features") and* selection features. *All feature labels can appear in one of two polarities. We refer to negatively charged selection feature labels as* category features, *written* x, *positively charged selection feature labels as* selector features, *written* =x, *negatively charged attraction feature labels as* licensee features, *written* -x, *and positively charged attraction feature labels as* licensor features, *written* +x. *Among attractor features we distinguish* strong *and* weak *occurrences; this distinction plays a role in defining the surface order of constituents. We write* +X *for the strong version of a licensor feature. We assume here that all selectors are strong.*

For example, an interrogative determiner like English *which*, as in *which children*, selects a nominal argument and requires Case and Wh licensing. Such a lexical item could be given the features d, =n, -case, -wh. A relative clause complementizer might be given the features c, =i, +wh. In the Minimalist Program, movement of a determiner phrase like *which children* into the domain of the complementizer is driven by the need to check the -wh licensee against the +wh licensor. A strong +Wh licensor will cause overt movement; a weak +wh licensor will allow covert, "inaudible" movement.

As far as the syntax is concerned:

Definition 8. *A* lexical item *is a sequence of features.*

Definition 9 (Labelled T-Marker). *In a* labelled *T-marker, we associate each head position with a lexical item (instance), and we associate with the T-marker a map ϕ from features in the lexical item of a head x to positions extending x such that the following hold.*

1. *ϕ maps negative features to chain positions and positive features to phrasal positions.*
2. *ϕ maps all and only licensee features to nonminimal chain positions.*
3. *ϕ respects the sequential ordering of features in a lexical item. That is, Given two extensions x and y of a head z, and two features f_1 and f_2 mapped to x and y respectively and such that f_1 precedes f_2 in the lexical item, $\neg y \leq x$.*

Condition (2) reflects the division in the theory according to which Selection is a theory about minimal chain positions (e.g., the "Generalized Projection Principle" of Brody 1) while Attraction is about movement, i.e., nonminimal chain positions. Condition (1) is motivated by the observation that, for example, a -wh determiner phrase will move to attach in the domain of a +wh complementizer, not vice versa.

Definition 10 (Feature Checking). *A pair of features of similar type (Attraction or Selection) and clashing polarity* check *each other if they are assigned to positions x and y such that $T(x, y)$. A position x in which a feature f could possibly be checked is called a* checking position *for f.*

Condition 3 (Representational Economy).

1. *All features associated with all head positions must be checked, except for the category feature of the root.*
2. *All arcs in T must check at least one pair of features.*

Condition (1) corresponds to (part of) the definition of a convergent derivation and condition (2) implements Chomsky's principle of Last Resort. Observe how these two conditions on derivations appear here as structural well-formedness conditions.

Proposition 4.

1. *Category features can only be checked in positions $x\mathrm{P}_0^*$. It follows that, since for all x, $x\mathrm{P}^* \neq \emptyset$, every head has a (unique) category feature.[5]*
2. *Complement position is never a checking position for attraction features. Therefore it must be a checking position for selection features.*
3. *If a head has any positive features, one of them must be a selector feature.*
4. *Positions $x0_0^*$ and head positions are never checking positions for any feature.*
5. *X0 internal positions are never checking positions for selection features.*

---

[5] I owe this observation to the anonymous reviewer.

(1) follows the fact that minimal XP chain positions can only be licensed by negative selection features, i.e., categories, and selection features can only be mapped to minimal chain positions. (2) is really a corollary of Prop. 2, given the definition of ϕ. (3) then follows from the Trace Binding Condition: without a selector feature no head would be able to attach to a scope, so it could not cancel any attractor features. (4) follows from the definition of feature checking and the definition of T. (5) is a direct corollary of (4) and the definition of ϕ: X0 internal positions are only checking positions for features which can be associated with nonminimal chain positions.

2.3 Spell-Out

Transformational generative grammar falls in the classical Saussurean tradition, taking the objects of interest to the theory of grammar to be sound-meaning pairs of some sort. In principle, in the Minimalist Program, the members of such pairs are instructions which can be interpreted by the articulatory-perceptual system, on the one hand, and the conceptual-intentional system on the other. In practice, it is usually taken to be sufficient to define a pair of P-markers which occur at some designated point in the derivation and which take the place of whatever programs the syntax should deliver from its lexical ingredients. We will here refer to these P-markers as PF and LF, though Chomsky himself may intend to reserve "PF" for the output of the phonological component and not as a strictly syntactic object. A little more formally, we take our T-markers to be such that we can define a pair of projection functions which will act to compute PF and LF P-markers from the overall T-marker.

Definition 11. *A* prominence function *is a choice function on chains, i.e., a function that maps a chain to a member of that chain.*

We will actually identify the levels of PF and LF with particular prominence functions, which select which chain position will be "spelled out" at the relevant interface level.

Definition 12. *We assume now that our basic feature labels include some which are interpretable. These are not polarized and play no (direct) role in feature checking. For any prominence function F we assume that some of these interpretable features are interpretable at the level of representation associated with F (e.g., PF or LF). We call these features F-interpretable. Given a head x, we write the F-interpretable features of x as $[x]_F$.*

Definition 13 (P-Markers). *P-markers are terms in an algebra of headed concatenation where we also distinguish between words and phrases, i.e., between X0's and XP's. We will use $>$ to indicate right-headed concatenation (specifier attachment) and $<$ to indicate left-headed concatenation (complement attachment) at the XP level, and $\blacktriangleright$ to indicate the corresponding concatenations at the X0 level (head adjunction). 0-ary elements (constants) are sequences of features or else the symbol λ.*

Definition 14 (Spell-Out Functions). *Given a prominence function F, we define the action of the spell-out projection function π_F from T-markers to P-markers as follows.*

1. On chains: *Given a chain position x in chain C, such that x immediately dominates (phrasal position) y,*

$$\pi_F(x) = \begin{cases} \pi_F(y) & , \text{ if } x = F(C); \\ \lambda & , \text{ otherwise.} \end{cases}$$

2. On phrases: *Recall that all phrasal positions are binary branching and endocentric, that is, exactly one daughter shares the same head. So, for phrasal node x such that $x \lhd y \wedge x \lhd z \wedge \mathsf{head}(x) = \mathsf{head}(y)$, we have the following.*

$$\pi_F(x) = \begin{cases} \overbrace{\pi_F(y) \quad \pi_F(z)}^{<} & , \text{ if } x \text{ is } x\mathrm{P}_0 \ , \\[2ex] \overbrace{\pi_F(z) \quad \pi_F(y)}^{>} & , \text{ if } x \text{ is } x\mathrm{P}_{i>0} \ , \\[2ex] \overbrace{\pi_F(z) \quad \pi_F(y)}^{\blacktriangleright} & , \text{ if } x \text{ is in } x0 \ . \end{cases}$$

3. On heads: $\pi_F(x) = [x]_F$.

Proposition 5. *The possible prominence functions over a given T-marker form a partial order, defined pointwise based on the linear order of chain elements: $F \sqsubseteq F'$ iff for all chains $C \in \mathrm{X0}^* \cup \mathrm{XP}^*$, $F(C) \leq F'(C)$ in the $\leq$ order on positions. (In fact the prominence functions form a lattice.) We can extend this ordering even further, to the trees generated by the projection functions π_F and $\pi_{F'}$.*

Given this fact, we can state the *Strong Feature Condition*, which relates strong features to the surface order of constituents, as a definition of the PF prominence function.

Definition 15. *A chain position x is* strongly attached *to phrasal position y if a strong feature is checked by $T(x, y)$, or if x is minimal in its chain. A prominence function is* strong *if it selects only strongly attached positions.*

Condition 4 (Strong Feature Condition). *PF is the greatest strong prominence function.*

Note that this gets around so called Procrastinate Violations, constructions in which an expression must move to a weakly attached position before it can move to a strongly attached position. An account of such constructions has been rather awkward to state in derivational terms, since movement is supposed to carry along PF-interpretable material only if it is to check a strong feature.

We have no equivalent defining condition on LF. In general, we want LF to select the maximal position of every XP chain and the minimal position of every X0 chain, but reconstruction effects are often exceptions to this generalization. Lacking the space to present a comprehensive theory of reconstruction, we will sweep the problem under the rug.

3 On the Relation of T-Markers to Derivations

In the main we follow Stabler (7) in our characterization of minimalist derivations. We depart from that treatment in one significant respect, namely that Stabler treats "head movement" as part of the theory of the Merge transformation rather than the Move transformation, making it a consequence of Selection rather than Attraction. Less significantly, the results of head movement are interpreted directly via concatenation of interpretable features, so no X0 internal structure is ever built in the syntax. Here we have taken pains to indicate X0 internal structure, introducing an explicit ▶ operator for the purpose.

Definition 16. *The* head *of a P-marker is the terminal found by recursively selecting the head subterm of a concatenation. We write $t^{\max}$ for the largest subexpression of a P-marker whose head is the same as the head of t and $t^{0\,\max}$ for the largest ▶-subexpression with the same head as t. We refer to the sister of $t^{0\,\max}$ as the* attraction domain *of the head of t.*

We will make use of the following rather informal notation. Given a P-marker t and a feature f, we write $t[f]$ for the result of adding f as the initial feature in the head of t.

Definition 17 (Merge).

$$
\mathrm{Merge}(t[\texttt{=f}], s[\texttt{f}]) =
\begin{cases}
\overset{<}{\overbrace{\quad}} \atop {t \quad s} & ,\ \textit{if } t \textit{ is } t^{0\,\max}, \\[2em]
\overset{>}{\overbrace{\quad}} \atop {s \quad t} & ,\ \textit{otherwise.}
\end{cases}
$$

For discussing movement we assume that we have as terminal elements not only lexical items but also variables $v_0, v_1, \ldots$. Then given P-markers $t, u_0, \ldots, u_k$, the expression $t(u_0, \ldots, u_k)$ will be taken to mean the substitution in t of u_i for v_i. We assume further that each v_i occurs at most once in t.

Definition 18 (Move). *Given a P-marker t containing two variables v_0 and v_1, such that v_0 is $t^{0\,\max}$ and v_1 occurs somewhere in the attraction domain of the head of t.*

$$
\mathrm{Move}(t[\texttt{+f}](t_1, t_2[\texttt{-f}])) =
\begin{cases}
\overset{>}{\overbrace{\quad}} \atop {t_2 \quad t(t_1, \lambda)} & ,\ \textit{if } t_2 \textit{ is } t_2^{\max}, \\[2em]
t(\overset{\blacktriangleright}{\overbrace{\quad}} \atop {t_2 \quad t_1}, \lambda) & ,\ \textit{if } t_2 \textit{ is } t_2^{0\,\max},
\end{cases}
$$

We assume without further comment that the choice between whether to execute XP movement or head movement is determined by **+f**.

Definition 19. *A derivation state is a multiset of P-markers. A derivation is a sequence of derivation states such that each successive state S_{i+1} is the result of applying either* Merge *or* Move *to P-markers in S_i and replacing them with the result of the operation. A numeration is a derivation state containing only trivial P-markers. A derivation converges if its final state contains only a single P-marker, containing only a single category feature in its head. All other terminals must be λ.*

Definition 20. *We say that a T-marker $\mathcal{A}$ corresponds to a derivation Δ just in case there is a bijection between edges in $T^{\mathcal{A}}$ and transformations in Δ such that:*

1. *$Merge(t, u)$ corresponds to $T(uP_0^*, tP_j)$ for some j;*
2. *Moving an XP u in t corresponds to $T(uP_{i>0}^*, tP_{j>0})$;*
3. *Moving an X^0 u in t corresponds to $T(u0_{i>0}^*, t0_j)$.*

Observe that every edge in T will be of exactly one of these three forms.

Definition 21. *An ordering on T is* admissible *iff it meets the following conditions.*

1. *It obeys the internal ordering of phrase and chain positions: for all positions x and y, if $x \leq y$ then x appears no later than y in the ordering.*
2. *Given a head x, all phrase positions of x appear before all chain positions of x in the ordering.*
3. *Given a head x, xP_0 appears before any position of $x0$ in the ordering and xP_0^* appears before any position of $x0^*$.*

Lemma 1. *For any T-marker $\mathcal{A}$, there exists an admissible ordering on its T relation.*

The derivation system we have presented includes no facilities for handling phonologically or semantically interpretable features, so we offer here only a relatively weak equivalence theorem. A stronger result, that the systems yield the same (PF,LF) pairs from the same numerations, is possible with only a little more work, however.

Theorem 1. *For every convergent derivation Δ there is a corresponding T-marker $\mathcal{A}$, and for every T-marker $\mathcal{A}$ there is a corresponding convergent derivation Δ.*

Proof. (Sketch) The first direction is easiest. Given an operation we just construct two new positions, assign them the correct heads and structural levels and add an appropriate edge to T, following Def'n 20. Since all operations extend the structure they affect, and since derivations are already linearly ordered, we can deduce the correct $\leq$ ordering on constructed positions from the order of operations in the derivation.

For the other direction, first assume an admissible ordering of T in $\mathcal{A}$ given to us by Lemma 1. The proof is an induction on T, so ordered. In the inductive step, we assume that we have processed a certain prefix of T, and constructed a corresponding derivation state. We now consider the next edge in T and construct a new derivation state. There are three kinds of edge to consider, as given by Def'n 20. The only bit of reasoning that does not come directly from the definition of admissible order involves Move operations. In these cases, we must assure that the attracting head actually has an attraction domain, and that the attraction domain includes the subtree we are instructed to move. That is, given an edge in T $(y\mathrm{P}^*_{i>0}, x\mathrm{P}_{j>0})$, we must be able to construct a Move operation moving $y\mathrm{P}$ from within the attraction domain of x.

By the well-formedness of $\mathcal{A}$, we know that $y\mathrm{P}^*_i$ antecedent governs $y\mathrm{P}^*_{i-1}$ in $\mathcal{A}$, that is, $x\mathrm{P}_0$ dominates $y\mathrm{P}^*_{i-1}$. By the inductive hypothesis and the definition of admissible order, we have already processed the T-edge connected to $x\mathrm{P}_0$; it connects some $z\mathrm{P}^*_0$ to $x\mathrm{P}_0$. Then by clause (2) of Def'n 21 we know that we must have processed all of the nodes of $z\mathrm{P}$ already, and all of the edges leading into them, and so also all of the phrases below those chain positions, and so forth. So we must have constructed already the entire attraction domain of x, including $y\mathrm{P}^*_{i-1}$, where $y\mathrm{P}$ is currently attached. So the application of Move is well-defined. The reasoning for head movement is the same, except that we must rely on clause (3) of Def'n 21 to assure that the attraction domain has already been constructed. $\square$

Consider now an example, given in Fig. 5, on page 20. This is a T-marker for the sentence *Some linguist speaks every language*. Features of lexical items are given under every head position, and again in the positions to which they are mapped by ϕ. There is no head movement or head internal structure in this example, so we do not illustrate $x0^*_0$ positions. All positions, other than head positions and the minimal $X0^*$ positions that we have suppressed, are associated with some feature that is checked in that position. Order of features is respected; category features are always associated with minimal XP^* positions; the licensee feature $-\mathbf{k}$ (for $-\mathtt{case}$) is associated with the nonminimal XP^* positions of the two DPs.

An admissible ordering of the T-edges is provided, with position in the order written next to the phrasal end of the edge. We also indicate which transformation that edge corresponds to (Mg for Merge, Mv for Move). This ordering corresponds to a convergent derivation for this sentence, in particular, the derivation presented in Sect. 2.1 of Stabler (7).

Of the edges in T, only $(\mathrm{smP}^*_1, \mathrm{tP}_1)$ checks a strong feature, so PF will be the prominence function selecting the minimal position of every chain except for smP^*, in which it selects smP^*_1. LF is the prominence function which selects the highest position of every chain. If $\pi_{pf}(c\mathrm{P}^*_0)$ and $\pi_{lf}(c\mathrm{P}^*_0)$ are superimposed, then together they yield the output of the derivation presented in Stabler (7), except that the surviving category feature c is not output by either spell-out function but is retained by the derivation.

Such a structure could be computed from a numeration of lexical items by executing a convergent derivation and adding pieces to the T-marker at each derivation step, along the lines suggested in the proof of Th'm 1. Other ways readily suggest themselves, however. For example, we could first form the extended numeration by considering the features in each lexical item and constructing the positions to which they would have to be mapped. Within the formalism presented here, this is deterministic, and could even be done off line for an entire lexicon. We could then proceed to construct the T relation. Finally, we would have to check the $\lhd$ graph for loops, and verify that the antecedent government condition was satisfied. Observe that this algorithm is very similar to the construction of a Proof Net (cf. Lecomte 5): unfold lexical type formulas (sequences of positive and negative types), attach them together with axiom links, which "check" them in the same way that T-edges check features here, and then check the resulting network for structural well-formedness. Here there are significant differences, since our chosen well-formedness conditions have a strictly linguistic rather than mathematical pedigree. The main point to observe, in any case, is the following: we can approach computational problems for transformational grammars from a much wider variety of perspectives than we might have imagined if we considered only the derivations themselves and not their underlying structure.

4 Conclusions

In this limited space we have only been able to present the foundations of an approach to transformational grammar which emphasizes the "soundness and completeness" of a derivation system with respect to a representation system. We have not dealt with successive cyclic movement, nor with issues of locality conditions on movements or chain links, nor have we dealt with economy conditions which force the consideration of multiple distinct derivations. Successive cyclic movement requires the ability to map a feature to multiple positions, but seems restricted to licensee features; the positive features then remain a fixed limit on the consumption of resources. As far as locality conditions go, one observes easily enough that they must be stated over single P-markers, since that is the domain over which the Move operation is defined, so they typically have a rather representational flavor to begin with. As far as economy conditions go, if one must compare derivations, then it seems essential to be able to treat derivations as objects. Some form of T-marker seems inevitable, then, in getting a decent mathematical grip on the economy of derivations. So none of these limitations seem insurmountable.

Finally, we have restricted ourselves here to addressing challenges to representational approaches. There are also a number of challenges to derivational approaches from the representationalist side (see, in particular, Brody 1), and the adequacy of our two-sided system must be assessed from that direction as

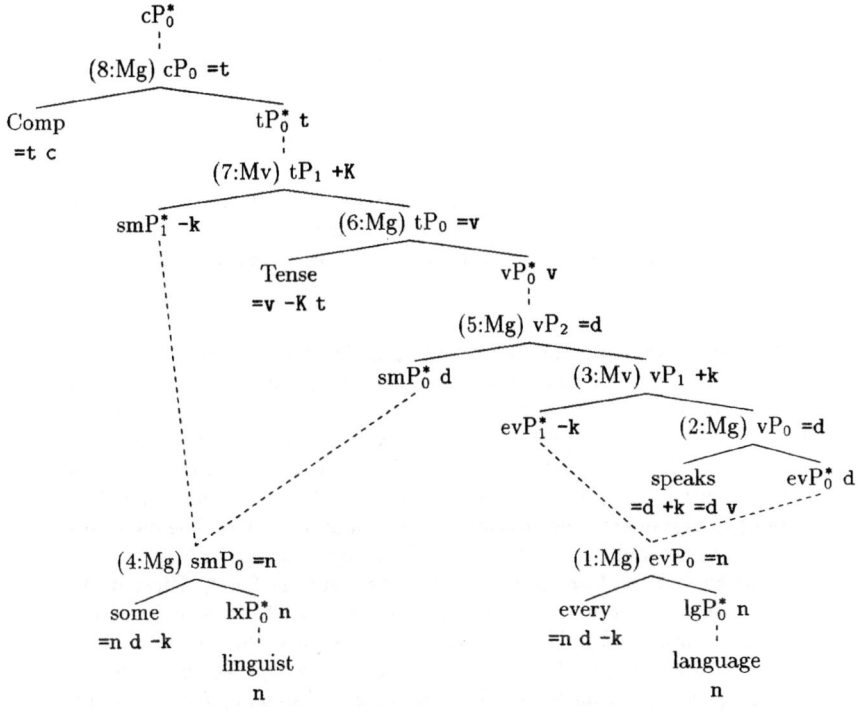

Fig. 5. T-marker for *Some linguist speaks every language.*

well. These approaches typically offer an enriched notion of chain, which is what makes them challenging to derivational approaches, and so addressing the challenges they pose will require changes to the representation system as well.

References

Michael Brody. *Lexico-Logical Form: A Radically Minimalist Theory.* MIT Press, Cambridge, MA, 1995.

Noam Chomsky. *The Logical Structure of Linguistic Theory.* University of Chicago Press, Chicago, 1975/1955.

Noam Chomsky. *Barriers.* MIT Press, Cambridge, MA, 1986.

Noam Chomsky. *The Minimalist Program.* MIT Press, Cambridge, MA, 1995.

Alain Lecomte. POM-nets and minimalism. In Claudia Casadio, editor, *Proceedings of the IV Roma Workshop: Dynamic Perspectives in Logic and Linguistics.* SILPS Group in Logic and Natural Languages, 1997.

Gereon Müller. *Incomplete Category Fronting: A Derivational Approach to Remnant Movement in German.* Kluwer Academic Publishers, Dordrecht, 1998.

Edward Stabler. Derivational minimalism. In Christian Retoré, editor, *Logical Aspects of Computational Linguistics*, pages 68–95, Berlin, 1997. Springer. LNAI 1328.

The MSO Logic–Automaton Connection in Linguistics

Frank Morawietz and Tom Cornell

Universität Tübingen, Seminar für Sprachwissenschaft, Kleine Wilhelmstraße 113,
72074 Tübingen, Germany
Email: {frank,cornell}@sfs.nphil.uni-tuebingen.de

Abstract. In this paper we discuss possible applications of a system which uses automata-based theorem-proving techniques drawing on the decidability proof for weak monadic second-order (MSO) logic on trees to implement linguistic processing and theory verification. Despite a staggering complexity bound, the success of and the continuing work on these techniques in computer science promises a usable tool to test formalizations of grammars. The advantages are readily apparent. The direct use of a succinct and flexible description language together with an environment to test the formalizations with the resulting finite, deterministic tree automata offers a way of combining the needs of both formalization and processing. The aim of this paper is threefold. Firstly we show how to use this technique for the verification of separate modules of a Principles-and-Parameters (P&P) grammar and secondly for the approximation of an entire P&P theory. And thirdly, we extend the language of the MSO tree logic to overcome remaining engineering problems.

1 Introduction

There is continuing interest in computational linguistics in both model-theoretic syntax and finite-state techniques. The decidability proof for the (weak) monadic second-order logic (MSO) of two successor functions (WS2S) furnishes a technique for deriving (bottom-up) tree automata for recognizable relations from the MSO constraints effectively (Thatcher and Wright 1968, Doner 1970).[1] The connection between MSO constraints and tree automata is based on techniques for coding variable-assignment functions as labeled trees; then tree automata can be "compiled" from the source formula in such a way that they accept exactly the trees which represent satisfying assignments to the source formula. While these results have been known for some time, the suitability of this formalism as a description language for Principles-and-Parameters (P&P) based linguistic theories has only recently been shown by Rogers (To appear) in a large scale formalization of most of the ideas from Rizzi (1990).

In general, on an abstract level, we address two issues in this paper: firstly, how we can use this technique in (computational) linguistics and secondly how

---

[1] Generalizing a similar result by Büchi (1960) from S1S and finite state automata to WS2S and tree automata.

useful it is. Naturally the first issue is more theoretically and the second one is more practically oriented. The paper proceeds by sketching the technique we want to make use of by presenting a short introduction into its background and an example of an MSO constraint and the correspondingly generated tree automaton. The following sections deal with possible applications of the technique to natural language processing (NLP). In particular, we discuss the separate compilation and verification of modules of a P&P theory and how to approximate P&P grammars within MSO tree logic despite its limited generative capacity. We illustrate the usefulness of the technique with a section on our experiences with a software tool. We conclude by applying a constraint logic programming (CLP) extension—resulting from the embedding of the compiler as its constraint solver—to remaining engineering problems.

We assume some basic familiarity with both the decidability proof for WS2S (an introductory presentation is in Gurevich 1985) and tree automata (an introduction can be found in Gécseg and Steinby 1997).

2   From Logic to Automata

MSO logic is a straightforward extension of first-order logic to include variables that range over sets (i.e., monadic predicates) and quantifiers over these variables. Let $\mathcal{N}_n$ denote the structure of $1 \leq n \leq \omega$ successor functions. $\mathcal{N}_n$ is the infinite, uniformly n-branching tree with the ith successor function leading to the ith daughter of a node. By SnS we denote the MSO theory of n successor functions, and by WSnS we denote the *weak* MSO theory of n successor functions, meaning that set variables are constrained to range only over *finite* sets. We will overload the term WSnS in the sense that we use it also to denote the MSO language over (W)SnS. In this paper we will focus in particular on WS2S: the weak monadic second-order theory of $\mathcal{N}_2$, the structure of two successor functions.

A (maximally) binary branching tree is a rooted, dominance connected subset T of the domain of $\mathcal{N}_2$. A labeled tree is a tuple $\langle T, F_1, \ldots, F_k \rangle$ of subsets of this domain, with the sets F_i being the features labeling the nodes of tree T. A grammar is an axiomatic definition of a $k + 1$-ary relation in $\mathcal{N}_2$ picking out all and only the well-formed labeled trees.

There is a close correspondence between formulas in WSnS and finite automata. More precisely, any relation definable in WS2S can also be defined by a tree automaton, which encodes the satisfying assignments to the formula in the labels on the nodes of the trees that it accepts. The coding is simple: assignment functions map first-order variables to nodes in $\mathcal{N}_2$ and second-order variables to sets of nodes in $\mathcal{N}_2$. The labeling functions on the trees the automaton accepts do the converse: they map nodes to the set of variables to which that node is assigned. Concretely, we can think of nodes as being labeled with bit-strings such that bit i is on at node n if and only if n is to be assigned to variable X_i. Because all sets are required to be finite, we can restrict our attention to automata over finite trees. This makes the development of software tools possible, since an efficient minimization algorithm exists for automata over finite sets.[2]

The proof of the logic-automaton correspondence is by induction. In the base step one need only exhibit automata recognizing the atomic formulas of the logic, given the coding of assignment functions sketched above. In the inductive step one need only show that that operators in the logic correspond to constructions on automata: conjunction corresponds to a cross-product construction on automata, negation to the inversion of final states of the automaton and existential quantification to a projection construction which converts an automaton over a k bit alphabet to a (nondeterministic) automaton over a $k - 1$ bit alphabet. It follows that a sentence in the language of WSnS which is not in the theory of $\mathcal{N}_n$, having no satisfying assignments, will correspond to an automaton which accepts no trees. Since the emptiness problem for tree automata is decidable, so is WSnS. For the special case of S1S this was shown in Büchi (1960), for WSnS in Thatcher and Wright (1968) and independently in Doner (1970) and finally for SnS in Rabin (1969).

There are, however, some very daunting engineering problems which have prevented the implementation of these results in practical theorem provers. In particular, the negation construction on automata only works for deterministic automata, and the projection construction, which implements quantification, outputs nondeterministic automata. It is always possible to determinize a (bottom-up) tree automaton, using essentially the same subset construction as is used for finite-state automata. Using the subset construction can in the worst case exponentially increase the number of states in the input automaton. Since the subset construction must be used every time a negation has an existential quantifier in its scope, the number of states can grow according to a function with a stack of exponents whose height is determined by the number of ∀–∃ quantifier alternations. In spite of this, some very encouraging recent results from the areas of computer hardware and system verification (e.g., Kelb et al. 1997; Basin and Klarlund (To Appear); Møller and Klarlund 1998) suggest that these techniques are in fact efficient; it is the problem space expressible in MSO tree logics that is hard.

Since the decidability proof for WS2S is inductive on the structure of MSO formulas, we can choose our particular tree description language rather freely, knowing that the resulting logic will be decidable and that the translation to automata will go through as long as the atomic formulas of the language represent relations which can be translated (by hand if necessary) to tree automata.[3] For example, Niehren and Podelski (1992) and Ayari et al. (1998) have investigated the usefulness of these techniques in dealing with feature trees which unfold feature structures; there the attributes of an attribute-value term are translated to distinct successor functions. On the other hand, Rogers (To appear) has de-

---

[2] There exists a class of automata working on infinite sets. But for these so called Büchi or Rabin automata there is no efficient minimization routine, which prevents a reasonable implementation of a tool for (strong) SnS.

[3] It requires further proof that such a language has the full power of WS2S, though.

veloped a language with long-distance relations (dominance and precedence) which is more appropriate for work in Government-Binding (GB) theory. One can imagine other possibilities as well: the automaton for Kayne-style asymmetric, precedence-restricted c-command (Kayne 1994) is very compact, and makes a suitable primitive for a description language along the lines suggested by Frank and Vijay-Shanker (1998).

We will illustrate these techniques with a simple example. We define a property Path which holds of a dominance-connected set P just in case for every pair of nodes in P one dominates the other.[4] For this and all other formulas in the paper, we use the language of Rogers (To appear), which is interdefinable with (W)S2S. Notational conventions will be the following: Uppercase letters denote second-order variables, lowercase letters denote first-order ones. The binary relation symbol $\lhd$ denotes parenthood, i.e., immediate dominance, $\lhd^*$ and $\lhd^+$ denote reflexive and proper domination, respectively, and $\prec$ denotes the precedence relation. Sans-serif labels stand for defined predicates (with their arguments). We include comments in the formulas for better understanding.

(1)

$$\mathsf{Connected}(P) \stackrel{def}{\Longleftrightarrow}$$

% If an element falls between any two other elements
% wrt domination it has to be in P.

$$(\forall x, y, z)[(x \in P \wedge y \in P \wedge x \lhd^* z \wedge z \lhd^* y) \Rightarrow z \in P]$$

(2)

$$\mathsf{Path}(P) \stackrel{def}{\Longleftrightarrow}$$

% P is connected and linearly ordered.

$$\mathsf{Connected}(P) \wedge (\forall x, y \in P)[x \lhd^* y \vee y \lhd^* x]$$

The tree automaton corresponding to the formula for Path in (2) resulting from the compilation procedure is shown in Fig. 1. For readability, we denote the alphabet of node labels as tuples indicating for each free variable whether a node is assigned to it or not. In this case we have only one free variable, P, so the alphabet just consists of the tuples $\langle P \rangle$ and $\langle \neg P \rangle$.

The initial state is a_0. We remain in the initial state until we encounter a node labeled for membership in P, at which point we transit to state a_1. As long as we are in a_1 on exactly one daughter and the mother node is also assigned to P, we remain in a_1. Note that if we find ourselves in a_1 on *both* daughters, then we enter a_3, the sink state. If we are in a_1 on one daughter and the mother is not in P, then we enter state a_2, indicating that we have completed our search for the path P. Any further P-nodes force us into state a_3: this tree cannot represent an assignment function satisfying the constraints on Path-hood. All of

---

[4] Observe that this is a property of sets, and so, apparently, a third-order variable. However, we can freely use any relations which are over sets or non-monadic provided that we explicitly define them in MSO—as we do here in (1) and (2)—such that they are reducible via syntactic substitution to an MSO signature, i.e., $r(X) \stackrel{def}{\Longleftrightarrow} \phi(X)$. We cannot quantify over them, of course.

$$\mathfrak{A} = \langle A, \Sigma, a_0, F, \alpha \rangle$$
$$A = \{a_0, a_1, a_2, a_3\}$$
$$\Sigma = \{\langle \neg P \rangle, \langle P \rangle\}$$
$$F = \{a_0, a_1, a_2\},$$

$$\alpha(a_0, a_0, \langle \neg P \rangle) = a_0 \quad \alpha(a_0, a_0, \langle\ P \rangle) = a_1$$
$$\alpha(a_0, a_1, \langle \neg P \rangle) = a_2 \quad \alpha(a_0, a_1, \langle\ P \rangle) = a_1$$
$$\alpha(a_1, a_0, \langle \neg P \rangle) = a_2 \quad \alpha(a_1, a_0, \langle\ P \rangle) = a_1$$
$$\alpha(a_0, a_2, \langle \neg P \rangle) = a_2 \quad \alpha(a_2, a_0, \langle \neg P \rangle) = a_2$$

all other transitions are to a_3

Fig. 1. The tree automaton for Path(P)

states a_0, a_1 and a_2 are final states: P may be the empty set (a_0), it may include the root (a_1) or not (a_2).

Obviously, there are many other ways one can define Path. However, any other equivalent definition would still yield an automaton isomorphic to the one in Fig. 1. That is, minimized automata are normal forms. Since they allow for the direct and efficient recovery of particular solutions, they make appropriate solved forms for use in constraint programming, a point we will take up and develop in Sect. 6.

There are two perspectives one can take on the equivalence of MSO logic to tree automata as ways of defining sets of syntax trees. First, one can think of the decidability proof as suggesting a way of doing (MSO) theorem proving. This is the way things are done in computer science applications such as hardware and system verification. However, one can also think of things the other way around, and take MSO logic as a specification language for automata. Tree automata have the advantages of finite-state machines presented in Roche and Schabes (1997): They provide a compact and uniform framework, i.e., they are space and time efficient and suitable for many aspects of NLP such as morphology, lexicon, syntax and input descriptions and they provide decidable tests for a number of important questions.[5] So we can make use of the logic-automaton correspondence either as a way of proving theorems using automata or as a way of manufacturing automata to MSO specifications.

Furthermore, we have a descriptive complexity result for MSO logic on trees. Since tree automata accept *recognizable* sets of trees, which are sets of trees which yield (all and only) the context-free languages, we have that we can only define in MSO logic principle-based grammars which are weakly context-free. The extensive formalizations of GB theories in MSO logic presented in Rogers represent the first descriptive complexity results of this kind for principle-based

---

[5] For example: $w \in \mathcal{L}$, $\mathcal{L} = \emptyset$, $\mathcal{L} = \Sigma^*$, $\mathcal{L}_1 \subset \mathcal{L}_2$, $\mathcal{L}_1 = \mathcal{L}_2$.

grammars, which had been thought to have considerably more expressive power and to be in a format for which any kind of descriptive complexity analysis would be impossible.

Consider, from these perspectives, the parsing problem and the recognition problem for a principle-based grammar. If the grammar (a collection of "principles" and "parameters") can be formalized in MSO logic, then it is logically possible to compile it into a single (huge) tree automaton, which accepts all and only the well-formed parse trees strongly generated by the grammar. In this setting, the parsing problem is—as standardly for satisfiability based grammars—the conjunction of a formula characterizing the input (as the set of all trees yielding the input string proper) with a grammar formula. In automata theoretic terms, we are considering two tree automata, and the parsing problem reduces to the problem of forming the cross-product automaton recognizing the intersection of the two input tree sets, i.e., the parse forest for the input. The recognition problem just reduces to the problem of determining the emptiness of this intersection. These are both decidable, in fact polynomial problems. Technically they are polynomial in the size of the input, since the grammar is a constant. Practically speaking, however, this "grammar constant" can be overwhelming, since the compilation from a formula to an automaton can be so explosive. Note that using minimal automata offers the easiest way of deciding emptiness. The language recognized by a minimal automaton is empty iff it has only one state which is initial but not final.

This problem of explosiveness is a problem in practice, but there is also a problem in principle, namely that the recognizable forests only yield context free string languages. It is generally believed that at least some languages (e.g., Swiss German) are not even weakly context-free, and the theoretical analysis in the P&P framework of some constructions like complex verb cluster formation in Dutch definitely define unrecognizable forests of syntax trees. In the remainder of this paper we consider three ways to deal with these limitations in practice and in principle.

First one can entertain more modest goals than the compilation of a complete grammar: there certainly are many grammatical properties besides the property of global well-formedness that can be fully formalized in MSO logic, and if such properties can be compiled on the computers of the present day then we have at once computationally efficient, automata-based implementations of those properties and also a means to perform extensive verification and debugging of the underlying theory of that module.

The second approach actually follows from the first. If one looks for modules of the grammar that drive it beyond the context free boundary, it appears that there may in fact be a single culprit. Rogers shows that the notion of Free Indexing, that is, that constituents can be assigned numerical indices freely, with the distribution later constrained by the grammar, is inexpressible in MSO logic.[6]

---

[6] More formally, he shows that the addition of co-indexation to the logic makes it undecidable and, since SnS is decidable, there cannot possibly be any definition of co-indexation in SnS.

Simplifying a good deal, indices are features, and features must be implemented as free set variables; obviously, there can only be a bounded number of variables appearing in a formula. From the automaton perspective, indices must be encoded in the alphabet, and the alphabet must be fixed before an automaton can be generated, so an automaton can be defined only given a bounded number of indices. We address the problem of working with a bounded number of indices in Sect. 4.

The third approach is based on the observation that minimal automata are normal forms for formulas and that concrete solutions, i.e., acceptable trees, can be extracted very efficiently. Therefore minimal automata make appropriate solved forms for a constraint solver. In Sect. 6 we consider embedding an MSO-compiler in a CLP scheme. This extends the power of the formalism (indeed, we lose decidability), and also adds a degree of control to the compilation process by using constraint logic programs.

3 Compiling Grammatical Principles to Tree Automata

In this section, we consider our most modest proposal, namely to do automaton construction and theory verification on subparts of the grammar. The question of which grammatical properties can be compiled in a reasonable time is largely empirical. The high-quality software tool MONA for the compilation of MSO formulas into both FSAs and tree automata has been made available recently (Klarlund and Møller 1998, URL: .http://www.brics..dk/~mona/), so we can now investigate this question.[7]

As an example of the application of this tool, we compiled an automaton from the X-Bar Theory presented in Rogers monograph. Note that this is a non-trivial part of the overall P&P theory formalized there.

In many variants of P&P theories this module of the grammar is essentially a set of simple phrase structure rules defining possible d-structures, over which transformations will later operate. Rogers' formalization is of a monostratal theory, however, in which well-formedness conditions on chains take the place of movement transformations. As a result, the X-Bar theory Rogers presents is far from trivial, since it must describe the kinds of structures that arise after transformations have applied. As a result it amounts to some five pages of MSO formulas which serve as input to MONA, and we cannot hope to present it in detail here.

Additional complications arise in the MSO specification of X-Bar theory because, in the underlying grammatical theory, there are three layers of structure: nodes of the tree are "segments" which are grouped into "categories" (here referring to a purely structural notion having little or nothing to do with morphosyntactic categories like noun, verb, preposition, etc.). Then categories are assigned "bar-level" features. So bar-levels, being features, are sets of categories, which

---

[7] An older version of MONA (Henriksen et al. 1995), restricted to strings and finite state automata, has been in use for some time in hardware and system verification, see references above.

in turn are sets of segments. However, it is easy to avoid this third-order notion by associating features with the segments in such a way as to assure that every segment of a category has features identical to those which, in the grammatical theory, are to be assigned to the category. Furthermore we have to keep track of which nodes are *trace* positions in their chains, which nodes by contrast are still in their *base* positions, and which phrases are *adjuncts*, i.e., attached to a segment of a non-trivial category.

The main content of X-Bar theory is a set of conditions on the distribution of the bar-level features, and a principle which states that every category has a "head", another category immediately below it with which it shares essential features like grammatical category (noun, verb, etc.). A node is allowed to be labeled with *Bar0* if it has exactly one lexical child category whose features it inherits. It is labeled *Bar1* if its category immediately dominates a node (its head) which is labeled *Bar0* and all its other (non-head) children are labeled *Bar2*. Finally, a node is labeled *Bar2* if it is a trace (i.e., is assigned to the set *Trace*) or its category immediately dominates some corresponding category belonging to *Bar1* and all its non-head children are in *Bar2*. The X-Bar module encodes these three definitions and principles limiting the distribution of adjuncts (i.e., of the *Adj* feature) such that no node is marked as adjoined unless it is the immediate child of a non-minimal node of a non-trivial category and that we cannot adjoin to any arbitrary node, e.g., not to traces.

One sees immediately that such an X-Bar theory becomes quite complicated indeed, and its correctness correspondingly hard to verify by hand! In fact, we did discover a minor bug in Rogers' formalization. We attempted to prove the assertion that Rogers' X-Bar theory implies the disjointness of the three bar-levels, i.e., that no node can belong to more than one bar-level. That is, we coded the implication as an MSO formula, and attempted to prove it in MONA. The attempt failed, with MONA reporting a counterexample.[8] In particular, Rogers' X-Bar theory does not imply that the *Bar0*-feature is disjoint from the *Bar1* and *Bar2* features.

The problem arises because of the fact that the distribution of features is such that they can appear anywhere they are not explicitly forbidden. In our case this means that the constraints allow for example a unary branching subtree with two nodes; a node which is labeled with both *Bar0* and *Bar1* and whose (unique) daughter is at the same time lexical and *Bar0*. In such a tree all constraints are satisfied. The mother node fulfills the *Bar1* constraint since it has a *Bar0* daughter and no other children and the *Bar0* constraint since it has a unique daughter which is lexical. This second node is allowed since Rogers does not place a constraint on the sets denoting lexical elements. Positively expressed this means that they are allowed to appear on internal nodes of a parse tree. To avoid this we have to add conditions forcing the lexical variables to only

---

[8] Without reference to special properties of a particular software tool, in general if $P \Rightarrow Q$ is unsatisfiable then any MSO logic-to-automaton compiler will construct the empty automaton. In that case $P \wedge \neg Q$ will be satisfiable and the resulting automaton can be used to generate counterexamples to the original query.

appear on the frontier of our parse tree. Furthermore, both to avoid errors of this type and to improve efficiency, we added a constraint which makes all our features appear only on nodes in the parse tree, i.e., we ensured that all our features are subsets of the set encoding our parse tree. The variable we use to denote the parse tree is initialized as a connected, rooted set for convenience. That constraint is not necessary, but makes the results much more readable.

The resulting corrected XBar-predicate has 11 free variables and its description consists of the aforementioned five pages of MONA formulas. We only assumed absolutely necessary features and a minimum of lexical entries (in fact only two lexical entries and 8 features).[9] Nevertheless it represents a full module of a large scale formalization of a P&P theory, it could be compiled in less than 5 min, see Table 1, and it could be used in further verification tasks. This shows that—while we still do not know whether it is feasible to compile a grammar automaton—we can indeed handle interesting linguistic properties with these techniques. And, as a further advantage of the presented technique, we can verify even immensely complicated theories automatically and generate counterexamples which help in debugging.

4 Approximating P&P Grammars

As stated, the set of well-formed trees defined by a P&P grammar is not in general recognizable. Therefore we cannot hope in principle to construct a grammar formula which defines exactly the well-formed parse trees strongly generated by a P&P grammar using just the MSO logic–tree automaton correspondence. One question which arises immediately in a more practical and less theoretical setting is how well we can approximate a strictly context sensitive language with a context free grammar. There are two features of P&P grammars which help us here. First, P&P grammars are *principle-based*, so they are readily formalized in logic. The logic of WS2S is insufficient, but it should be easy to embed it in a more powerful logic which is sufficient. Then the techniques of general model theory become available to address the question of how good an approximation we can achieve. Secondly, P&P grammars are *modular*, so it may be possible to isolate those parts of the grammar which exceed the expressive capacity of WS2S. In that case we can observe quite directly the compromises that would have to be made to stay within an MSO logic for natural language. This is indeed the case here: the power of a P&P grammar seems to come rather directly from the assumption of an unbounded supply of referential indices, which can be used to keep track of arbitrarily many simultaneously occurring long-distance dependencies. Tree automata, on the other hand, can only keep track of a bounded number of distinct objects via their (finite) set of states. Hence, no formalization of a grammar in MSO logic is possible without the assumption of a bounded number of indices.

So the problem of approximating a full P&P grammar becomes the problem of estimating in advance how many indices will be enough. Clearly, any given

---

[9] We come back to the problem of lexical entries in Sect. 6.

sentence will require a bounded number of indices, but we cannot realistically expect to recompile our entire grammar automaton for each input sentence.[10] We can, however, precompile a number of different versions of a grammar offline, each with an index theory of a different size, and then select which grammar automaton to use given the input sentence. So it makes sense to consider how one could formalize the parts of the grammar that rely on indices in such a way that they can be parameterized with the number of indices and compiled in a variety of sizes.

Furthermore there are a number of ways in which one can "engineer" a theory so that it uses a minimal number of indices. For example, any one index can be used to keep track of any number of distinct chains, as long as those chains do not overlap. Also, there is no need to make each notionally distinct index correspond to a single feature: if we have n "index variables" I_i then we can use them as bits of a complex index, meaning that we have in fact 2^n possible distinct indices. We can extend this idea by making use of other features besides special purpose index (or index-bit) features: using bar-level features for example we can distinguish between the twelfth *Bar2* chain and the twelfth *Bar0* chain. Pursuing this strategy we end up with the approach Rogers actually employs. He uses no special purpose index variables but rather only combinations of those features which are independently required in the grammar. This reduces the number of possible alphabet symbols that an automaton must deal with.

Given such a bounded set of indices which we can use on a particular parse, we proceed to formalize the necessary conditions in our MSO tree logic. As noted above, what we use for our "indices" is formally relatively unimportant. What matters is what it means for two nodes to be co-indexed, see (3). That is the definition which gives the theory its "memory resources". Note that in MSO logic free variables must be represented in both the head of the formula and the resulting automaton to preserve their satisfying assignments.[11] Where readability is more of an issue, one can leave these "global" variables out under the assumption that they are implicit. However, since they cannot be ignored in the alphabet of the automata, we try to be more exact. Therefore, I_n stands for the n indices we have to create depending on the input, and the "definitions" we now present are really definition schemata.

(3)
$$\text{Co\_Idx}(x, y, I_n) \overset{def}{\Longleftrightarrow}$$
$$(x \in I_1 \Leftrightarrow y \in I_1) \land \ldots \land (x \in I_n \Leftrightarrow y \in I_n)$$

After the instantiation of the schematic representation, we can compile an automaton for the corresponding memory limited grammar formula. All the predicates which depend on any predicate scheme at any point will themselves

---

[10] Note that the problem of estimating the number of indices a sentence will require is considerably simpler than the problem of estimating the number of traces it may contain. Roughly, every movable expression (overt or covert) is either headed by an overt lexical item or else licensed by an overt lexical item's selectional properties.

[11] If one is not interested in the information provided by a particular variable, it can be bound existentially at the top level of the formula.

have to be schematized, of course, and realized as families of definitions which vary in the number of their arguments. As an example of these we present a formula scheme encoding a simple version of a "trace binding condition" (a simplified version of the empty category principle which uses c-command instead of local government), which simply requires that all traces have a c-commanding antecedent with which they are co-indexed. TBind will have $n + 2$ arguments; n depending on the number of indices currently allowed and the chosen coding. The needed c-command definition simply says that all nodes z which properly dominate x also have to dominate y and that x must not reflexively dominate y.

(4)
$$C\text{-}Com(x,y) \stackrel{def}{\Longleftrightarrow}$$
$$(\forall z)[z \lhd^+ x \Rightarrow z \lhd^+ y] \land \neg(x \lhd^* y)$$

$$TBind(P, Trace, \boldsymbol{I_n}) \stackrel{def}{\Longleftrightarrow}$$
% for all traces in the parse tree
(5)
$$(\forall x \in P)[x \in Trace \Rightarrow$$
% there exists a proper antecedent.
$$(\exists y \in P)[C\text{-}Com(y,x) \land Co\_Idx(x,y,\boldsymbol{I_n})]]$$

In this definition scheme we use a set called *Trace* to identify traces. Naturally this presupposes that we formulate more appropriate constraints on the distribution of this label in the resulting parse tree in our grammar.

In conclusion, we note that the logic-automaton connection may be fruitful for doing principle-based parsing, even in spite of the principled limitation to weakly context-free languages. In particular, it seems unlikely that in any given corpus of input sentences there are any which require large numbers of overlapping chains: the same drain on memory which this causes for tree automata seems to affect human language users as well (Stabler 1994). The fact that we can adjust to such memory limitations without substantially affecting the underlying grammar—all we require is a special definition of what it means to be co-indexed—is especially welcome. However, for doing theory verification these limitations remain serious: given n indices, the claim that there are only n indices is a theorem, but not a theorem of the underlying grammar. On the other hand, if there is a sentence in the language which actually does have $n + 1$ overlapping chains it will be rejected by a limited grammar. So we have neither soundness nor completeness for doing theorem proving.

5 Some Experimental Results

Even supposing, as seems reasonable, that real world parsers can function with a limited supply of indices, we still have to face the extreme explosive potential of the formula-to-automaton compilation procedure. It is still an open question which formulas can be compiled on present day computers. We used MONA

Table 1. Statistics for various predicates

Predicate/N	Total Time	|A|	|α|	|BDD|
Connected	00:00:00.090	4	25	7
Path	00:00:00.130	4	21	9
C-Com	00:00:00.170	5	40	19
TBind/2	00:00:00.230	12	832	52
TBind/4	00:00:01.610	80	76288	422
TBind/8	00:55:15.000	2304	–	13881
TBind/16	core dump after approx. 10 min			
TBind'/4	00:00:07.480	87	145963	759
TBind'/6	00:04:58.830	457	–	4901
TBind'/7	core dump after approx. 30 min			
XBar	00:04:51.080	66	18133	982

(Klarlund and Møller 1998) to provide some answers to the usability of these ideas in practice.

The main innovation in MONA, which seems indeed to be a real technical breakthrough, is the use of binary decision diagrams (BDDs) to compress the transition tables of the output automata.[12] Since an alphabet of k features contains 2^k symbols, alphabet size, and hence transition table size, is a problem which, while only elementarily complex, can actually dominate in practice the non-elementary complexity of the actual compilation procedure. The use of this technique significantly improves performance over our own prototype so that we can advance considerably further with compilations than what we reported in Morawietz and Cornell (1997). Now we can actually implement significant modules of a large scale P&P theory and verify them (recall the discussion of X-Bar theory in Sect. 3). But we also encountered limits on the number of indices in the compilation of various TBind predicates. In this section we summarize some of our results so far.

Timings where done on a SUN Sparc 20 with 225 MB of RAM using a beta release of version 1.2 of MONA. Our results are displayed in Table 1. The first column of the table contains the predicate identifier and the number of indices (not the index bits). The second column contains the time needed to compile the automaton without the printing of the actual output automaton. The third column contains the number of states in the output automaton, the fourth column the number of transitions. The number of transitions has been compacted in the

---

[12] An introduction to BDDs can for example be found in Bryant (1992).

sense that it uses a don't care symbol, i.e., if transitions on q_1 and q_2 and both $\langle x_1, \ldots, x_{i-1}, x_i, x_{i+1}, \ldots, x_n \rangle$ and $\langle x_1, \ldots, x_{i-1}, \neg x_i, x_{i+1}, \ldots, x_n \rangle$ lead to the same state q, we have only a single transition on $\langle x_1, \ldots, x_{i-1}, \bot, x_{i+1}, \ldots, x_n \rangle$. Also note that for very large automata we cannot present the exact number of transitions any more since printing the result takes too much time and space and unfortunately MONA does not have an option to display (only) the number of transitions without printing the full automaton. The last column contains the size of the BDD used to represent the transition table. One readily observes the enormous gains this compression scheme confers by comparing this to the transition table size.

Consider the tricky "grammar engineering" question of what kind of coding to use for indices, as discussed above. In TBind, we used features to encode index bits and in TBind' we naïvly used features to encode (disjoint) indices. The second approach turned out to consume considerable amounts of memory: we were only able to compile an automaton with six indices, though on a machine with 800 megabytes of RAM it is possible to compile TBind' with at least seven indices (Nils Klarlund, p.c.). Using the index-bit encoding we could compile a version of TBind with eight indices (i.e., three index bit features) on our own machines; however, adding another bit again ran us out of memory resources.[13] The steepness of the relevant curves leads us to suspect that no present day machine will be able to compile TBind/16. The use of index bits cannot in principle reduce the memory load which long distance dependencies place on automata. This shows that MSO logic is exponentially more compact in coding the facts than tree automata.

An interesting question is whether a large machine can compile TBind'/9. More generally, the discreet encoding allows one to better approximate the capacity of available machines. Adding a bit increases the number of chains that can be represented too greatly, even though in general this encoding leads to more compact automata. The compactness gain is more than offset by the memory requirements that even one more chain places on a tree automaton's state space.

Another interesting point to observe is that the memory demands in these compilations mainly came from intermediate automata. Considering Table 1, one notes that the BDD size and number of states in the automata which are actually output are not overwhelmingly large. So while it requires rather large and powerful computers to manufacture automata from MSO formulas, the resulting automata can potentially be put to use on much smaller machines.

6   MSO Logic and CLP

The automaton for a grammar formula is presumably quite a lot larger than a parse-forest automaton, that is, the automaton for the grammar conjoined with an input description. Considering the problems we might have in extending the

---

[13] This happened even on the machines of the MONA crew. (Nils Klarlund, p.c.).

compilation of separate modules to an entire grammar automaton it makes sense to search for ways to incrementally construct the parse-forest automaton for a particular input. For this, we propose the embedding of the MSO constraint language into a CLP scheme. Intuitively, the constraint base is an automaton which represents the incremental accumulation of knowledge about the possible valuations of variables constructed by applying and solving clauses with their associated constraints. We can start with a description of the input and add further constraints incrementally rather then having to represent all constraints at once and then limiting them to an input. That is, we actually use the compiler *on line* as the constraint solver. Some obvious advantages include that we can still use our succinct and flexible constraint language with negation and MSO quantification. In fact, we gain even more power, since we can include inductive definitions of relations and have a way of guiding the compilation process under the control of a program.

We define a relational extension $\mathcal{R}(\text{WS2S})$ of our constraint language following Höhfeld and Smolka (1988). Our constraint language WS2S is extended with a set of relations $\mathcal{R}$ such that we can formulate recursive definitions. From the scheme we get a sound and complete, but now only semi-decidable, operational interpretation of a definite clause based derivation process (for details see Morawietz (To appear)). The resulting structure of interpretation $\mathcal{R}(\text{WS2S})$ is an extension of the underlying constraint structure for WS2S with the interpretation of the new relations in $\mathcal{R}$ constructed via the least fixpoints of their defining clauses. For simplicity we assume a standard left-to-right, depth-first interpreter for the execution of the programs. The solution to a search branch of a program is a satisfiable constraint, represented in solved form as an automaton.

To demonstrate how we split the work between compiler and CLP interpreter, we present as a simple example the following naïve specification of a lexicon:

(6)
$$\text{Lexicon}(x, Sees, V, John, N, \dots) \stackrel{def}{\Longleftrightarrow}$$
$$(x \in Sees \land x \in V \land \dots)$$
$$\lor (x \in John \land x \in N \land \dots)$$
$$\lor \dots$$

Remember that, naïvely at least, every feature we use (e.g., *Sees*, *V*), has to be coded into the alphabet Σ of the automaton. So, $|\Sigma|$ with an encoding as bitstrings will be 2^n (n the number of free variables). It is immediately clear that the compilation of such an automaton—even if we use the discussed approach of using lexicon-bits—is extremely unattractive, if at all feasible.[14] We have several

---

[14] Lexical entries seem to be rather special variables. Usually each of them appears only once on the frontier labeling a single node. They are disjoint from each other (we do not want a node to be simultaneously *John* and *Bill*). Maybe this can be used to define a more efficient compilation process. But considering the number of lexical entries needed in an NLP application, it seems unlikely that even the representation using BDDs could be able to reduce the number of necessary alphabet symbols sufficiently.

choices here. Either we find some special higher-level language built on top of WS2S to enable more efficient compilation of the variables denoting the lexical items (e.g., LISA, Ayari et al. 1998), or one could separate the lexicon from the pure MSO specification. In fact this would mean that the MSO constraints apply only to the pre-terminals of which there are considerably less distinct ones. Alternatively, we propose to avoid having to compile the entire lexicon as one automaton by having the obvious clauses for each lexical entry in the CLP extension. Note that we write R(WS2S) clauses lowercase whereas MSO constraints are written uppercase.

$$\text{(7)} \quad \begin{aligned} &\text{lexicon}(x, Sees, V, \dots) \longleftarrow \\ &\qquad \{x \in Sees \wedge x \in V \wedge \dots\} \end{aligned}$$

$$\text{(8)} \quad \begin{aligned} &\text{lexicon}(x, John, N, \dots) \longleftarrow \\ &\qquad \{x \in John \wedge x \in N \wedge \dots\} \end{aligned}$$

$$\vdots$$

Clearly this shifts the burden of handling disjunctions to the interpreter. But it is no longer the case that every constraint in the grammar—and therefore every occuring free variable—has to be expressed in one single tree automaton. Constraint resolution will reject all clauses not bearing a satisfiable constraint on the node labelings such that we only compile those features/free variables from clauses into the constraint store whose lexical entries are given in the input description.

Another benefit of the CLP extension is that we can use offline compiled modules in a $\mathcal{R}$(WS2S) parsing program. As a source of examples we use the definition of P&P parsing from Johnson (1995), see (9)–(13). We have to define the subgoals in the body either via precompiled automata (so they are essentially treated as facts), or else with more standard definite clause definitions. In (9) and in the following clauses we simplify notation to achieve better readability. Instead of specifying all free variables which appear in the clauses explicitly, we focus on the relevant ones. We use V to stand for all free variables which are global but not relevant for the clause we are looking at. In practical terms this means that we have to use the automata theoretic operation of cylindrification whenever we have to add newly appearing variables to the constraint store, i.e., the tree automaton representing it.

$$\text{(9)} \quad \begin{aligned} &\text{parse}(Words, Parse, V) \longleftarrow \\ &\qquad \{\text{Tree}(Parse)\} \ \& \\ &\qquad \text{yield}(Words, Parse, V) \ \& \\ &\qquad \text{xbar}(Parse, V) \ \& \\ &\qquad \text{ecp}(Parse, V) \end{aligned}$$

We use two MSO variables to identify the input and the parse tree. *Words* denotes a set of nodes labeled according to the input description. Our initial con-

$\text{Tree}(P) \overset{def}{\Longleftrightarrow}$

    % A tree is a connected rooted set.

   $\text{Connected}(P) \wedge (\exists x \in P)[\text{Root}(P, x)]$

$\text{Root}(X, x) \overset{def}{\Longleftrightarrow}$

    % x dominates or equals all nodes in X.

   $x \in X \wedge (\forall y \in X)[x \vartriangleleft^* y]$

$\text{Yield}(W, P, Empty) \overset{def}{\Longleftrightarrow}$

    % All nodes of P which have no daughter

    % are either in W or phonologically empty

   $(\forall x \in P)[((\neg(\exists y \in P)[x \vartriangleleft y]) \Leftrightarrow (x \in W \vee x \in Empty)) \wedge$

    % but not both

     $\neg(x \in W \wedge x \in Empty)] \wedge$

    % and no other nodes are in W.

   $W \subseteq P$

Fig. 2. Some auxiliary formulas for the parse clause

straint base—which can be automatically generated from a list of input words—is the corresponding tree automaton. Its alphabet contains apart from the variables *Words* and *Parse* also the variables labeling the input string and the relevant precedence information. Now constraint solving and derivation refine information on variables which are already present, as is the case for the associated constraint Tree of the parse clause (for its full definition see Fig. 2). It is easily compilable and serves as the initialization for our parse tree. Or, in the case that we encounter new variables, the store is cylindrified accordingly. The Yield predicate serves as an example. It can be explicitly defined, compiled and treated as a fact (again, see Fig. 2), but it also introduces the additional MSO variable *Empty* into the constraint base which labels phonologically empty nodes. Naturally, we need more constraints to achieve a correct distribution of this feature.

Since the ecp is dependent upon the actual number of indices, it has to be schematically expressed. But it can be realized as either a fact as a variant of TBind in (5) or a number of recursive rules which traverse the structure of the parse tree as in Johnson's proposal (Chap. 3, pp 43–48). Rather than going into more detail here, we illustrate the rule-based approach to the definition of a relation with the xbar predicate in the next example. It is a disjunctive specification of licensing conditions depending on different configurations of the features in the trees, which can be more intuitively expressed as two separate rules as given in (10) and (11). In fact, since we want the lexicon to be represented as clauses (and xbar anchors the projections in the lexicon), we cannot have xbar as a pure MSO constraint.

$$\text{xbar}(X, V) \leftarrow$$

(10)
$$\{\text{Sing}(X)\} \, \&$$
$$\text{lexicon}(X, V)$$

$$\text{xbar}(X, V) \leftarrow$$

(11)
$$\{\text{Subtrees}(X, x, Y, y, Z, z)\} \, \&$$
$$\text{local\_xbar}(x, y, z, V) \, \&$$
$$\text{xbar}(Y, V) \, \&$$
$$\text{xbar}(Z, V)$$

The xbar clauses need some predicates defined in the associated constraints. They can be found in Fig. 3. The first xbar clause just licenses lexical elements. Note that this base case of xbar does not have a special clause for traces—we assume traces to be lexical entries. The second one allows binary forks in case there is a corresponding local rule and the subtrees obey the X-Bar theory. So we need further clauses specifying which local forks are valid. For examples of such clauses, see the following (12) and (13).

(12)
$$\text{local\_xbar}(x, y, z, V) \leftarrow$$
$$\{x \in CP \land y \in Wh \land z \in C1 \land y \prec z\}$$

(13)
$$\text{local\_xbar}(x, y, z, V) \leftarrow$$
$$\{x \in CP \land y \in C \land z \in IP \land y \prec z\}$$

$$\vdots$$

These clauses are taken straight out of Johnson's course notes. They do not represent a proper P&P account, but rather resemble phrase structure rules. Note that they are implemented simply by checking precedence constraints and membership in the right kind of feature set. For dominance we rely on the Subtrees constraint in the third clause of the X-Bar predicate.

For completeness, we also present a corresponding table of statistics for the auxiliary predicates we need for the clauses. But unfortunately we cannot present comparable timings for the CLP extension. So far, MONA cannot conveniently be used inside other programs. Therefore our very simple implementation of the basic interpreter has to use our own prototype of a compiler which is not sufficient for the compilation of (some of) the examples we give in the paper.[15] This is due to the two facts that we do not use BDDs to represent the transition tables such that the automata involved simply get too big for our constraint solver and that our implementation of the necessary cylindrification for simplicity uses assertion and retraction from files and databases which is too slow.

---

[15] For comparison, the compilation of Component which is a part of Roger' X-Bar theory takes on a comparable machine more than 330 seconds using our implementation, but less than 5 seconds using MONA.

$$\text{Sing}(X) \stackrel{def}{\Longleftrightarrow}$$

% All subsets of X are equal to X or the empty set

$$(\forall Y, Z)[Y \subseteq X \Rightarrow (X \subseteq Y \vee Y \subseteq Z)] \wedge$$

% and X is not the empty set.

$$(\exists Y)[X \not\subseteq Y]$$

$$\text{Dtrs}(x, y, z) \stackrel{def}{\Longleftrightarrow}$$

$$x \lhd y \wedge x \lhd z \wedge y \prec z$$

$$\text{Subtree}(X, y, Y) \stackrel{def}{\Longleftrightarrow}$$

% Y is the subtree of X rooted in y.

$$(\forall x \in X)[y \lhd^* x \Leftrightarrow x \in Y]$$

$$\text{Subtrees}(X, x, Y, y, Z, z) \stackrel{def}{\Longleftrightarrow}$$

% x is the root of X with daughters y and z

$$\text{Root}(X, x) \wedge \text{Dtrs}(x, y, z) \wedge$$

% with subtrees Y and Z.

$$\text{Subtree}(X, y, Y) \wedge \text{Subtree}(X, z, Z)$$

Fig. 3. Some auxiliary formulas for the xbar clauses

7 Summary

Summing up, we can say that while it is theoretically not possible to write a formula covering a non-context-free theory, we can still use the independent parts of the formalization and families of definitions with respect to a particular input to answer questions of grammaticality of sentences. On the practical side, the advent of MONA has enabled us to advance significantly with the experiments on the compilation of P&P based grammatical theories. Although a definitive answer on the question whether an entire grammatical theory can be compiled into one automaton is still not possible, we know that we can compile non-trivial modules. The CLP extension we propose would allow us to combine these modules in a principled way and interleaves the intersection of the grammar and the input automata so that only the minimal amount of information needed to determine the parse is incrementally stored in the constraint base. It offers an even more powerful language which allows a clear separation of processing and specification issues while retaining the flexibility of the original.

But there are still many problems left. The form of the formulas has a large effect on the time required by the compiler and it is important to figure out which sort of formulas can be compiled more efficiently than others. Furthermore, writing grammar formulas in WS2S is an experience akin to assembler programming, i.e., error prone and time consuming. Therefore it remains to be seen how much

Table 2. More statistics for predicates

Predicate	Total Time	|A|	|α|	|BDD|
Sing	00:00:00.050	3	12	5
Tree	00:00:00.130	4	23	8
Root	00:00:00.070	4	29	10
Yield	00:00:00.130	3	27	10
Dtrs	00:00:00.170	5	38	13
Subtree	00:00:00.340	5	67	19
Subtrees	00:00:00.290	7	168	49

impact higher-level languages such as FIDO (Klarlund and Schwartzbach 1997) and LISA have on the time required to formalize and compile P&P theories. The added power of the relational extension might also be seen as a source of problems. A closer investigation into which relations are definable inductively in MSO logic itself, into which stronger ones can be added without losing decidability and what effects are caused by them with respect to the generative capacity is necessary. Further work has to be done in the development of the CLP interpreter. Especially promising seems to be the incorporation of existential quantification into the relational extension which can be included into the Höhfeld and Smolka scheme. This theoretical background can be used to implement an explicit garbage collection procedure by marking certain variables for projection which are no longer needed thereby reducing the alphabet space of the constraint store, i.e., the size of the underlying automaton.

Acknowledgments. This work has been supported by the project A8 of the SFB 340 of the Deutsche Forschungsgemeinschaft. We wish especially to thank Uwe Mönnich and Jim Rogers for discussions and advice and three anonymous reviewers for comments on an abstract for this paper; Nils Klarlund and Anders Møller for valuable help with the installation and usage of MONA and Projects B4/B8 of the SFB 340 for letting us use their machine (especially Frank Richter). Needless to say, any errors and infelicities which remain are ours alone.

References

Ayari, A., Basin, D. and Podelski, A. (1998). LISA: A specification language based on WS2S, *in* M. Nielsen and W. Thomas (eds), *Computer Science Logic, 11th International Workshop, CSL'97*, LNCS 1414, Springer.

Basin, D. and Klarlund, N. (To Appear). Automata based symbolic reasoning in hardware verification, *The Journal of Formal Methods in Systems Design.*

Bryant, R. E. (1992). Symbolic boolean manipulation with ordered binary-decision diagrams, *ACM Computing Surveys* **24**(3): 293–318.

131

Büchi, J. R. (1960). Weak second-order arithmetic and finite automata, *Zeitschrift für mathematische Logik und Grundlagen der Mathematik* **6**: 66–92.

Doner, J. (1970). Tree acceptors and some of their applications, *Journal of Computer and System Sciences* **4**: 406–451.

Frank, R. and Vijay-Shanker, K. (1998). TAG Derivation as Monotonic C-Command, *Proceedings of the Fourth Workshop on Tree-Adjoining Grammars and Related Frameworks TAG+98*, Philadelphia, PA. (Extended abstract)

Gécseg, F. and Steinby, M. (1997). Tree languages, *in* G. Rozenberg and A. Salomaa (eds), *Handbook of Formal Languages: Beyond Words*, Vol. 3, Springer, Berlin.

Gurevich, Y. (1985). Monadic second-order theories, *in* J. Barwise and S. Feferman (eds), *Model-Theoretic Logics*, Springer, Heidelberg, pp. 479–506.

Henriksen, J. G., Jensen, J., Jørgensen, M., Klarlund, N., Paige, R., Rauhe, T. and Sandhol, A. (1995). MONA: Monadic second-order logic in practice, *in* Brinksma et al. (eds), *International Workshop TACAS '95*, LNCS 1019, Springer, pp. 89–110.

Höhfeld, M. and Smolka, G. (1988). Definite relations over constraint languages, *LILOG Report 53*, IBM Deutschland, Stuttgart, Germany.

Johnson, M. (1995). Constraint-based natural language parsing, European Summer School of Logic, Language and Information (ESSLLI '95), Barcelona, Course notes.

Kayne, R. S. (1994). *The Antisymmetry of Syntax*, Vol. 25 of *Linguistic Inquiry Monographs*, MIT Press, Cambridge, Mass. and London, England.

Kelb, P., Margaria, T., Mendler, M. and Gsottberger, C. (1997). MOSEL: A flexible toolset for monadic second-order logic, *in* E. Brinksma (ed), *International Workshop TACAS '97*, LNCS 1019, Springer, pp. 183–202.

Klarlund, N. and Møller, A. (1998). *MONA Version 1.2 User Manual*, BRICS Notes Series NS-98-3, Department of Computer Science, University of Aarhus.

Klarlund, N. and Schwartzbach, M. I. (1997). A domain-specific language for regular sets of strings and trees, *Proceedings of the Conference on Domain-Specific Languages*, USENIX, Santa Barbara, Ca.

Morawietz, F. (To appear). Monadic second order logic, tree automata and constraint logic programming, *in* H.-P. Kolb and U. Mönnich (eds), *The Mathematics of Syntactic Structure*, Mouton de Gruyter.

Morawietz, F. and Cornell, T. L. (1997). Representing constraints with automata, *Proceedings of the 35th Annual Meeting of the ACL and the 8th Conference of the EACL*, Madrid, Spain, pp. 468–475.

Niehren, J. and Podelski, A. (1992). Feature automata and recognizable sets of feature trees, *in* M.-C. Gaudel and J.-P. Jouannaud (eds), *Proceedings of the 4th International Joint Conference on Theory and Practice of Software Development*, Springer, LNCS 668, Orsay, France, pp. 356–375.

Rabin, M. O. (1969). Decidability of second-order theories and automata on infinite trees, *Transactions of the American Mathematical Society* **141**: 1–35.

Rizzi, L. (1990). *Relativized Minimality*, MIT Press.

Roche, E. and Schabes, Y. (1997). Introduction to finite-state devices in natural language processing, *in* E. Roche and Y. Schabes (eds), *Finite-State Language Processing*, Language, Speech, and Communication Series, MIT Press.

Rogers, J. (To appear). *A Descriptive Approach to Language-Theoretic Complexity*, Studies in Logic, Language and Information, CSLI Publications.

Stabler, E. (1994). The finite connectivity of linguistic structure, *in* C. Clifton et al. (eds), *Perspectives on Sentence Processing*, Lawrence Erlbaum, New Jersey.

Thatcher, J. W. and Wright, J. B. (1968). Generalized finite automata theory with an application to a decision problem of second-order logic, *Mathematical Systems Theory* **2**(1): 57–81.

The Logic of Tune
A Proof-Theoretic Analysis of Intonation

Herman Hendriks

Utrecht Institute of Linguistics OTS, Utrecht University, Trans 10, 3512 JK Utrecht,
The Netherlands
ILLC/Department of Philosophy, University of Amsterdam, Nieuwe Doelenstraat 15,
1012 CP Amsterdam, The Netherlands

Abstract. This paper presents a proof-theoretic sign-based grammar
founded on non-associative non-commutative linear logic which models
a compositional theory of the 'information packaging' meaning of intonational contours. Cross-language comparison reveals that in expressing information packaging, different languages exploit word order and
prosody in different ways: one single informational construct can be realized by drastically different structural means across languages. Thus
for languages such as English and Dutch it can be argued that, roughly
speaking, information packaging is structurally realized by means of alternative intonational contours of identical strings, while languages such
as Catalan and Turkish have a constant prosodic structure and realize information packaging by means of string order permutations. Such
cross-linguistic generalizations suggest that information packaging involves syntax as well as prosody, so that any attempt to reduce informational aspects to either syntax (for Catalan or Turkish) or prosody
(for English or Dutch) must be inadequate from a cross-linguistic point of
view. The present paper proposes to treat the different structural realizations of information packaging by means of a both intonationally/syn-
tactically and semantically/informationally interpreted sign-based version of the non-associative Lambek calculus, the 'pure logic of residuation'. The signs, the grammatical resources of this formalism, are form-
meaning units which reflect the fact that the dimensions of form and
meaning contribute to well-formedness in an essentially parallel way. The
proof-theoretic categorial engine of the formalism represents phonological head/non-head dependencies in terms of a doubling of the pure logic
of residuation which is enriched with unary modal operators, where the
unary brackets that come with these operators function as demarcations
of specific intonational domains.

1 Information Packaging

In Pierrehumbert and Hirschberg's paper 'The Meaning of Intonational Contours in the Interpretation of Discourse' (1990), it is proposed that speakers use
tune to specify a particular relationship between the propositional content of
the utterance and the mutual beliefs of the speaker S and the hearer H. As in
Pierrehumbert (1980), tune, or *intonational contour*, is taken to be a sequence

of low (L) and high (H) tones, made up from pitch accents, phrase accents and boundary tones. Pierrehumbert and Hirschberg follow Beckman and Pierrehumbert (1986) in distinguishing six pitch accents: two simple tones, H* and L*, and four complex ones, L*+H, L+H*, H*+L, H+L*, where the '*' indicates that the tone is aligned with a stressed syllable. Tune meaning is assumed to be built up compositionally, and 'intonational contour is used to convey information to H about how the propositional content of the [...] utterance is to be used to modify what H believes to be mutually believed' (Pierrehumbert and Hirschberg 1990: 289).

The present analysis pursues Pierrehumbert and Hirschberg's intonational-informational program and follows Hendriks (1997) in taking tune to be a structural realization of *information packaging*—the structuring by speakers of the propositional content of their utterances in function of their assumptions about the hearer's knowledge and attentional state. It focuses on the distribution of H* and L+H* pitch accents, since it is these accents that have been claimed to play a central role in information packaging.[1]

The basic idea of information packaging, a concept introduced in Chafe (1976) which accommodates traditional pragmatic notions such as focus, ground, topic and comment, is that speakers do not present information in an unstructured way, but that they provide a hearer with detailed instructions on how to manipulate and integrate this information according to their beliefs about the hearer's knowledge and attentional state. 'That is, information packaging in natural language reflects the sender's hypotheses about the receiver's assumptions and beliefs and strategies' (Prince 1981: 224).

For example, sentences such as (1) and (2) are truth-conditionally equivalent in that they express the same proposition, but each of them 'packages' this proposition in a prosodically different way:

$$\textit{The } \textbf{teacher } \textit{loves } \text{ICE CREAM} \qquad (1)$$

$$\textit{The } \textbf{teacher } \text{LOVES } \textit{ice cream} \qquad (2)$$

Typically, speakers will use (1) if the hearer at the time of utterance knows nothing about or is not attending to the teacher's relation to ice cream, while they will use (2) if the hearer at the time of utterance knows that there exists a relation between the teacher and ice cream, is attending to this relation, but does not know what it is. Apparently, speakers are sensitive to such differences in the hearer's knowledge and attentional state, and hearers rely on this: 'speakers not using this device systematically give their listeners a harder time' (Nooteboom

---

[1] We will use *italics* for unaccented expressions, SMALL CAPS for expressions that bear H* pitch accents, and **boldface** for expressions that bear L+H* pitch accents. (H* accent and L+H* accent are called A accent and B accent, respectively, in Jackendoff 1972.) As noted in Hendriks (1996a), a grammar that exhausts the full gamut of intonational contours studied in Pierrehumbert and Hirschberg (1990) may retain the elegance of the restricted system by actually *decomposing* Pierrehumbert and Hirschberg's grammar of intonation (something which is suggested in Hobbs 1990).

and Terken 1982: 317). Truth-conditionally equivalent sentences that encode different information packaging instructions are not mutually interchangeable *salva felicitate* in a given context of utterance: e.g., of the above sentences, only the first one is a felicitous answer to the questions *What about the teacher? What does he love?* It is this context-sensitivity that has traditionally placed information packaging within the realm of pragmatics, where two influential approaches can be distinguished, the focus/ground approach and the topic/comment approach.

According to the former approach, sentences consist of a focus and a ground.[2] The *focus* is the informative part of the sentence, the part that (the speaker believes) expresses 'new' information in that it makes some contribution to the hearer's mental state. The *ground* is the non-informative part of the sentence, the part that expresses 'old' information and anchors the sentence to what is already established or under discussion in (the speaker's picture of) the hearer's mental state. Although sentences may lack a ground altogether, sentences without focus do not exist.

The topic/comment (or theme/rheme) approach splits the set of subexpressions of a sentence into a *topic*, the—typically sentence-initial—part that expresses what the sentence is about, and a *comment*, the part that expresses what is said about the topic. Topics are points of departure for what the sentence conveys, they link it to previous discourse. Sentences may be topicless: so-called 'presentational' or 'news' sentences consist entirely of a comment.

In Reinhart (1982) it is argued that the dimension of 'old'/'new' information is completely orthogonal to (and hence irrelevant for) the analysis of sentence topics. Instead, a notion of 'pragmatic aboutness' is proposed, which involves the organization of information. The set $\text{PPA}_{(S)}$ of Possible Pragmatic Assertions that can be made with a sentence S expressing proposition φ is defined as follows:

$$\text{PPA}_{(S)} = \{\varphi\} \cup \{\langle a, \varphi \rangle \mid a \text{ is the interpretation of an NP in S}\} \qquad (3)$$

A pragmatic assertion $\langle a, \varphi \rangle$ is assumed to be 'about' the topic a. (The possibility for the interpretation a of an NP in S to serve as the topic of a pragmatic assertion $\langle a, \varphi \rangle$ is subject to further syntactic and semantic restrictions.)

Notice, by way of example (adopted from Dahl 1974), that the sentence *The* **teacher** *loves* ICE CREAM gives rise to the parallel topic/comment and ground/focus partitions indicated in (4) if it answers the questions *What about the teacher? What does he feel?*, whereas it induces the partitions specified by (5) in the interrogative context *What about the teacher? What does he love?*

topic	comment
The **teacher**	*loves* ICE CREAM
ground	focus

(4)

---

[2] The ground is also known as 'background', as 'presupposition' and as 'open proposition'. In phonology, the term 'focus' is often used for intonational prominence. That is, any constituent which bears pitch accent is said to be a focus. Although in general, (part of) the informational focus is marked by prosodic prominence, not every accented constituent is a focus in the informational sense. In particular, accented constituents may also be topics.

topic	comment
The **teacher** *loves* ICE CREAM	
ground	focus

(5)

The fact that the two informational articulations correspond to different partitions in (5) shows that neither the grond/focus partition nor the topic/comment partition is by itself capable of capturing all the informational distinctions that are present in the sentence.

Pace Reinhart (1982), the two traditional binomial focus/ground and topic/comment articulations are conflated into a single trinomial and hierarchical one in Vallduví's (1992, 1993, 1994) account of information packaging. The core distinction is the one between new information and anchoring, that is between focus and ground. In addition, the ground is further divided into the *link*, which corresponds approximately to the topic in the traditional topic/comment approach, and the *tail*.[3] In a picture:

$\gg$

topic	comment	'aboutness'
link	tail	focus
ground	focus	'old'/'new'

(6)

Given this articulation, the answer *The* **teacher** *loves* ICE CREAM to the questions *What about the teacher? What does he love?* will receive the following analysis:

The **teacher**	*loves*	ICE CREAM
link	tail	focus
ground		focus

(7)

The different parts—focus and ground, link and tail—of a sentence S have the following informational functions in Vallduví's theory. The focus encodes I_S, i.e., the *information* of S, which can be metaphorically described as: the proposition expressed by S minus the information (the speaker presumes) already present in the hearer's information state. The ground performs an *ushering* role—it specifies the way in which I_S fits in the hearer's information state: links indicate *where* I_S should go by denoting a location in the hearer's information state, and tails indicate *how* I_S fits there by signaling a certain mode of information update.

Of course, talking about ushering information to some location in the hearer's information state presupposes that this information state has some sort of internal structure. In this respect, Vallduví proposes to take the metaphor of Heim's (1982, 1983) file change semantics literally, in that he assumes that the information in the hearer's model is organized in files, i.e., collections of file cards, where

---

[3] The hierarchy does not imply constituency or (even) continuity. In particular, the two parts (link and tail) of the ground may not constitute a linear unit at the surface. Moreover, sentences may have more than one link, and more than one element may constitute the tail.

each file card represents a discourse entity: its attributes and its connections with other discourse entities are recorded on the card in the form of conditions. Links are associated with so-called GOTO instructions in file change semantics, where the target location of such an instruction is a file card, the 'locus of update'.[4]

To the extent that links correspond to the topic in the traditional topic/comment distinction, Vallduví's theory is quite similar to the analysis of sentence topics presented in Reinhart (1982), where a pragmatic assertion of φ about a is formalized as $\langle a, \varphi \rangle$, in that a functions as a kind of 'locus of update' for φ. Nonetheless, the two approaches differ in that Reinhart allows assertions without a 'locus of update' (since also $\varphi \in \text{PPA}_{(S)}$) and topics that express new information. Another 'locational' analysis of topics is the one presented in Erteschik-Shir (1996), where it is assumed that file cards are organized in stacks: the position of a card in the stack reflects the relative salience of the corresponding discourse entity.

We will not go into further semantic/informational details here, but merely mention that Vallduví's conclusion that 'the internal structure of information states which is, in fact, crucially exploited by the different information-packaging strategies used by speakers in pursuing communicative efficiency' (1994: 7) is at least a system of file cards is criticized in Hendriks and Dekker (1995), who argue that Ockham's razor can be applied to the concept of 'locations'. Accordingly, Hendriks (1996b) proposes a non-locational theory of aboutness as a special kind of anaphora, in which information states are modeled by means of the discourse representation structures of Discourse Representation Theory (DRT, see Kamp 1981, Kamp and Reyle 1993), which are ontologically less committed than the 'dimensionally richer' file card systems because they do not come with locations. This theory, which partly—viz., for L+H* pitch accent—executes the intonational-informational program outlined in Pierrehumbert and Hirschberg (1990) (see Hendriks 1997), resolves various problems that ensue from the use of locations and subsumes 'non-identity' anaphora, correctional and contrastive stress, pronoun referent resolution, and restrictiveness of relatives and adjectives. In addition, the non-locational perspective on information packaging affords an account of the cases of link-sensitive behaviour that are displayed by so-called 'focus-sensitive' operators (Hendriks 1998). Finally, it can be noted that this transition to a non-locational notion of information state means that on the semantic/informational side, the derivations of the proof-theoretic grammar can be assumed to be interpreted into a type-theoretical version of DRT along the lines of Muskens (1993), who shows that DRT can be reduced to type theory, and hence connected to categorial grammar in the same standard way as Montague semantics, viz., via the Curry-Howard isomorphism.

---

[4] A tail points at an information record—normally a (possibly underspecified) condition—on the file card fc that constitutes the locus of update, RECORD(fc), and indicates that it has to be *modified* (or further specified) by the focus information I_S of the sentence. The associated instruction type is called UPDATE-REPLACE. In the absence of a tail, the focus information I_S of a sentence is simply *added* at the current location. The associated instruction type is called UPDATE-ADD.

2 Word Order and Prosody

In expressing information packaging, different languages choose different structural means to spell out the same informational interpretations. Thus, roughly speaking, one can say that languages such as Catalan and Turkish have a constant prosodic structure and effectuate information packaging via word order permutations, whereas languages such as English and Dutch structurally realize information packaging by means of alternative intonational contours of identical strings.

In English, the focus is associated with an H* pitch accent, links are marked by an L+H* pitch accent, and tails are structurally characterized by being deaccented. One and the same string may be assigned different intonational phrasings in order to realize different informational interpretations. In particular, the focal pitch accent may be realized on different positions in the sentence. This is illustrated by the sentences (9), (11) and (13), construed as answers to the questions in (8), (10) and (12), respectively:

$$\textit{What about the company?} \qquad (8)$$
$$\textit{What did you find out about it?}$$

$$[_F \textit{The boss hates } \text{BROCCOLI}] \qquad (9)$$

$$\textit{What about the boss?} \qquad (10)$$
$$\textit{What did you find out about him?}$$

$$[_L \textit{The } \textbf{boss}][_F \textit{hates } \text{BROCCOLI}] \qquad (11)$$

$$\textit{What about the boss?} \qquad (12)$$
$$\textit{What does he feel about broccoli?}$$

$$[_L \textit{The } \textbf{boss}][_F \text{HATES}][_T \textit{broccoli}] \qquad (13)$$

In Catalan, the situation is quite different. Metaphorically speaking, one can say that Catalan focal elements remain within a so-called 'core clause', but that ground elements are 'detached' to a clause-peripheral position. In particular, links are detached to the left, and non-link ground elements undergo right-detachment. As a result of detaching both links and tails, the core clause (CC) is left containing only the focus of the sentence:

$$\text{LINKS } [_{CC} \text{ FOCUS }] \text{ TAILS} \qquad (14)$$

As a matter of fact, Vallduví argues that languages such as Catalan supply empirical support for a representation of information packaging along the lines sketched above, since these languages package their information in a much more salient way than, for example, English. Thus, while informational interpretations may be expressed exclusively by prosodic means in English, information packaging instructions in Catalan are straightforwardly reflected in syntax.

Consider the Catalan counterparts (15), (16) and (17) of (9), (11) and (13), respectively. The all-focus sentence (15) displays the basic verb-object-subject word order.[5] In (16) and (17), the link subject *l'amo* has been detached to the left. In (17), moreover, the tail direct object *el bròquil* has been detached to the right, leaving a clitic (*l'*) in the focal core clause. Note that intonational structure plays a part in Catalan too, albeit 'a rather lame one' (Vallduví 1993: 33): an H* pitch acent is invariably associated with the last item of the core clause.

$$[_F \textit{Odia el bròquil l'}\textsc{amo}] \tag{15}$$

$$[_L \textit{L'amo}][_F \textit{odia el} \textsc{bròquil}] \tag{16}$$

$$[_L \textit{L'amo}][\ _F \textit{l'}\textsc{odia}][_T \textit{el bróquil}] \tag{17}$$

The above observations provide confirmation that information packaging involves syntax as well as prosody, and suggest that any attempt to reduce information packaging either to syntax or to prosody will be inadequate from a cross-linguistic point of view.

Thus, noting that the notion of syntactic surface structure of Combinatorial Categorial Grammar (CCG) yields various alternative semantically equivalent proof unfoldings for identical strings of members of syntactic categories, Steedman (1991, 1992, 1993) hypothesizes that the notion of 'intonational structure' that has been postulated for assigning phrasal intonation to sentences can be subsumed under this notion of syntactic surface structure: in spoken utterances, intonation helps to determine which of the many possible syntactic derivations is intended. This subsumption of intonational structure under syntactic surface structure is formally enforced by imposing the *Prosodic Constituent Condition*: combination of members of two syntactic categories via a syntactic combinatory rule is allowed (if and) only if their prosodic categories can also combine via a prosodic combinatory rule. The condition admits only derivations consistent with both prosodic and syntactic information, so it 'has the sole effect of excluding certain derivations [and hence informational interpretations—HH] for spoken utterances that would be allowed for the equivalent written sentences' (Steedman 1992: 31). The latter points to a limitation inherent in Steedman's approach: it may adequately be applied to a language such as English, insofar as information packaging in English is structurally realized by means of alternative intonational contours of identical strings of members of syntactic categories, but

---

[5] Vallduví's (1992) assumption that Catalan is VOS is not uncontroversial (the onus of explanation seems to lie with those who say that Catalan is other than SVO), but makes for a highly elegant account of the facts of Catalan syntax. It can be noted, by the way, that there are Catalan speakers who say that the question (8) would be replied by (16), just as there are English speakers who say that it would be replied by (11). This reflects a problematic aspect of Vallduví's analysis of links which is remedied by the proposals of Hendriks (1996b).

it will by itself not be capable of providing an account of information packaging in Catalan or Turkish, 'where word order [...] serves to structure the information being conveyed to the hearer' (Hoffman 1995) and different informational interpretations are expressed by different strings of members of syntactic categories.

Accordingly, Hoffman (1995) formulates her treatment of information packaging in Turkish in terms of *Multiset Combinatory Categorial Grammar* (MCCG), where each verb is assigned a category in the lexicon which subcategorizes for a multiset of arguments, and 'each MCCG category encoding syntactic and semantic properties in Argument Structure is associated with an Ordering Category which encodes the ordering of Information Structure Components' (Hoffman 1995). Note, however, that there is also a limitation inherent in Hoffman's approach: it may adequately be applied to a language such as Turkish or Catalan, insofar as information packaging is structurally realized by means of different strings of members of syntactic categories, but it will by itself not be capable of providing an account of information packaging in English, where information packaging is structurally realized by means of alternative intonational contours of identical strings of members of syntactic categories.

The choice of different structural means to spell out informational interpretations apparently necessitates the application of drastically different types of Combinatory Categorial Grammars. It can be noted, however, that this is problematic—not only from a cross-linguistic point of view, but also because it can be argued that even within particular languages the structural realization of information packaging may involve both syntax and prosody.

For example, the Catalan sentences *Odia el bròquil* L'AMO and *Odia* EL BRÒQUIL *l'amo* have the non-equivalent informational interpretations suggested by (18) and (19), but differ only prosodically.

$$[_F \textit{Odia el bròquil } l\text{'AMO}] \tag{18}$$

$$[_F \textit{Odia el } \text{BRÒQUIL}] [_T l\text{'amo}] \tag{19}$$

The same holds for English, where the structural realization of information packaging can also be argued to involve syntax as well as prosody: Reinhart (1982: 63), for example, notes that in a sentence such as (20) the fronted NP must be interpreted as a topic (i.e., link).

$$\textit{Felix, it's been ages since I've seen him} \tag{20}$$

In view of the above phenomena, the present account of the range of variation in the structural realization of information packaging as displayed by Catalan and English will deal with intonation and word order at one and the same level. In order to be able to do so, it will make use of a sign-based categorial grammar formalism which takes its inspiration from Oehrle's (1988, 1994) work on generalized compositionality for multidimensional linguistic objects and shares characteristics with HPSG (Head-Driven Phrase Structure Grammar—see Pollard and Sag

1987, 1994). Basically, the—decidable—formalism is a both intonationally/syn-tactically and semantically/informationally interpreted version of an extension of the non-associative calculus of Lambek (1961). The signs, the grammatical resources of this formalism, are Saussurian form-meaning units which reflect the fact that the dimensions of linguistic form and meaning contribute to well-formedness in an essentially parallel way:

$$\text{intonational term} \triangleleft \text{type} \triangleright \text{informational term} \qquad (21)$$

The type calculus that functions as the proof-theoretic categorial engine of the grammar represents sequents as composed of such multidimensional signs. It instantiates a minimal 'base logic', which makes no assumptions at all about structural aspects of grammatical resource management, since the formalism is based on a doubling of the non-associative Lambek calculus, the 'pure logic of residuation'. In this system, the phonological head/non-head opposition is captured by decomposing the product into a left-dominant and a right-dominant variant and obtaining residuation duality for both variants. In order to account for more sophisticated, 'less lame' intonational facts such as English L+H* pitch accent, the calculus is enriched with the minimal logical rules for unary modal operators. These operators are used in a basic way as well: they do not figure in structural postulates, but are associated with unary brackets which serve to demarcate specific phonological domains.

The treatment of information packaging in this formalism differs from many of its predecessors (including categorial analyses of focus that employ extensions of the Lambek calculus such as Oehrle 1991, Van der Linden 1991, Moortgat 1997), in that it does not employ 'focusing' operators—functors that take the non-focused part of the sentence as their argument—but, instead, makes use of 'defocusing' operators. Analyses in terms of focusing operators have been in-spired by semantic studies of the phenomenon of 'association with focus' such as Jacobs (1983), Rooth (1985, 1992), Krifka (1991), among others, in which it is claimed that the quantificational structure of so-called focus-sensitive opera-tors is crucially determined by the traditional pragmatic focus-ground partition. However, Vallduví and Zacharski (1993) argue convincingly that 'association with pragmatic focus' is not an inherent semantic property of such operators, which may express their semantics on partitions other than the focus/ground one—witness observed cases of association with subsegments of the informa-tional focus, with links, and with other parts of the ground. The dissociation of the pragmatic focus/background distinction from issues of exhaustiveness and focus-sensitivity dispels the need to analyze focused constituents as operators that semantically take scope over the non-focused part of the sentence. This can be considered an advantage: as sentences may lack links and tails, such anal-yses do not immediately reflect the core status of the focus, which is the only non-optional part of a sentence. In some sense, all-focus sentences constitute the basic case, while the cases where there is a ground are derived from such basic all-focus structures.[6]

---

[6] For that matter, a closer look at Vallduví's various information packaging instruc-

Instead of focusing operators, then, the present treatment of information packaging employs 'defocusing' operators, higher-order functors that license the presence of links and tails. In the grammar of a language such as Catalan, such defocusing operators are realized as clitics and agreement morphology, whereas in English they are abstract items that merely have intonational repercussions.

3 Proof-Theoretic Grammar

In the Gentzen presentation of the associative Lambek calculus **L** (Lambek 1958), explicit application of the structural rule of Associativity is usually compiled away in the way in which the sequent language is defined. Thus, given some finite set ATOM of atomic categories (none of which coincides with a compound category (A/B), $(B\backslash A)$ or $(A \bullet B)$), the set CAT of categories based on ATOM is defined as the smallest set such that ATOM $\subseteq$ CAT, and if $A \in$ CAT and $B \in$ CAT, then $(B\backslash A) \in$ CAT, $(A/B) \in$ CAT and $(A \bullet B) \in$ CAT. (Outermost brackets of categories will be omitted.) On this basis, a sequent is then defined as an expression $T \Rightarrow C$, where T is a finite non-empty *sequence* of categories and $C \in$ CAT. So, $T = C_1, \ldots, C_n$, where $n > 0$ and $C_i \in$ CAT for all i such that $1 \leq i \leq n$. The sequence of left-hand side categories T is called the antecedent of the sequent $T \Rightarrow C$, and the single right-hand side category C is its consequent, or goal. In this set-up, the axioms and inference rules of the associative Lambek calculus **L** are as follows (where A, B, C denote arbitrary categories and S, T, U, V arbitrary finite sequences of categories, of which S and T are non-empty):

$$\frac{}{A \Rightarrow A} \ [Ax] \qquad \frac{T \Rightarrow A \quad U, A, V \Rightarrow C}{U, T, V \Rightarrow C} \ [Cut] \tag{22}$$

$$\frac{T \Rightarrow B \quad U, A, V \Rightarrow C}{U, T, B\backslash A, V \Rightarrow C} \ [\backslash L] \qquad \frac{B, T \Rightarrow A}{T \Rightarrow B\backslash A} \ [\backslash R] \tag{23}$$

$$\frac{T \Rightarrow B \quad U, A, V \Rightarrow C}{U, A/B, T, V \Rightarrow C} \ [/L] \qquad \frac{T, B \Rightarrow A}{T \Rightarrow A/B} \ [/R] \tag{24}$$

$$\frac{U, A, B, V \Rightarrow C}{U, A \bullet B, V \Rightarrow C} \ [\bullet L] \qquad \frac{S \Rightarrow A \quad T \Rightarrow B}{S, T \Rightarrow A \bullet B} \ [\bullet R] \tag{25}$$

It can be observed that reading antecedents of sequents as sequences involves an interpretation of the comma as a connective of variable arity, rather than as a binary one.

Alternatively, we can read antecedents of sequents as *structured terms*, where the set TERM of structured terms is the smallest set such that CAT $\subseteq$ TERM, and

---

tions corresponding to the four different sentence-types (focus, link-focus, focus-tail, link-focus-tail) also suggests a reverse approach, since it is the instructions induced by links and tails that invariably take scope over I_S, the information expressed by the focus of the sentence.

if $\Gamma \in$ TERM and $\Delta \in$ TERM, then $[\Gamma, \Delta] \in$ TERM. Under this approach, the associative Lambek calculus **L** can be formulated as follows. The axioms and inference rules in (22) through (25) get the respective counterparts in (26) through (29) below (where A, B, C denote categories, Γ and Δ (and $\Delta, \Delta', \Delta''$) structured terms, and $\Gamma\{\Delta\}$ represents a structured term Γ containing a distinguished occurrence of the structured subterm Δ):

$$\frac{}{A \Rightarrow A} \ [Ax] \qquad \frac{\Delta \Rightarrow A \quad \Gamma\{A\} \Rightarrow C}{\Gamma\{\Delta\} \Rightarrow C} \ [Cut] \tag{26}$$

$$\frac{\Delta \Rightarrow B \quad \Gamma\{A\} \Rightarrow C}{\Gamma\{[\Delta, B\backslash A]\} \Rightarrow C} \ [\backslash L] \qquad \frac{[B, \Gamma] \Rightarrow A}{\Gamma \Rightarrow B\backslash A} \ [\backslash R] \tag{27}$$

$$\frac{\Delta \Rightarrow B \quad \Gamma\{A\} \Rightarrow C}{\Gamma\{[A/B, \Delta]\} \Rightarrow C} \ [/L] \qquad \frac{[\Gamma, B] \Rightarrow A}{\Gamma \Rightarrow A/B} \ [/R] \tag{28}$$

$$\frac{\Gamma\{[A, B]\} \Rightarrow C}{\Gamma\{A \bullet B\} \Rightarrow C} \ [\bullet L] \qquad \frac{\Gamma \Rightarrow A \quad \Delta \Rightarrow B}{[\Gamma, \Delta] \Rightarrow A \bullet B} \ [\bullet R] \tag{29}$$

In addition, there are explicit structural rules AL and AR of Left and Right Associativity:

$$\frac{\Gamma\{[\Delta, [\Delta', \Delta'']]\} \Rightarrow C}{\Gamma\{[[\Delta, \Delta'], \Delta'']\} \Rightarrow C} \ [AL] \qquad \frac{\Gamma\{[[\Delta, \Delta'], \Delta'']\} \Rightarrow C}{\Gamma\{[\Delta, [\Delta', \Delta'']]\} \Rightarrow C} \ [AR] \tag{30}$$

The system that consists of the axioms and rules in (26) through (29) but *lacks* the structural rules in (30) is the Gentzen presentation of the *non*-associative Lambek calculus **NL** (Lambek 1961). The calculus **D** which is used in the present paper is essentially just a doubling of **NL**. It was introduced in Moorgat and Morrill (1991) in order to account for head/non-head dependency as an autonomous dimension of linguistic structure.[7] The head/non-head opposition is captured by decomposing the product into a left-dominant and a right-dominant variant and obtaining residuation duality for both variants. This means that the set CAT of categories based on ATOM is defined as the smallest set such that:

$$\text{ATOM} \subseteq \text{CAT}; \text{ and} \tag{31}$$
$$\text{if } A \in \text{CAT and } B \in \text{CAT, then } (B\backslash A) \in \text{CAT}, (A\mathbin{\overset{\cdot}{/}}B) \in \text{CAT},$$
$$(A\mathbin{\overset{\cdot}{\bullet}}B) \in \text{CAT}, (B\mathbin{\overset{\cdot}{\backslash}}A) \in \text{CAT}, (A\mathbin{\underset{\cdot}{/}}B) \in \text{CAT and } (A\bullet\mathbin{\cdot}B) \in \text{CAT}.$$

The set TERM of structured terms is defined as the smallest set such that:

$$\text{CAT} \subseteq \text{TERM}; \text{ and} \tag{32}$$
$$[\Gamma, \Delta] \in \text{TERM and } [\Gamma \,{}^\backprime \Delta] \in \text{TERM if } \Gamma \in \text{TERM and } \Delta \in \text{TERM}.$$

---

[7] Thus dependency structure may cross-cut semantic function/argument structure, since it is not defined in terms of it. (For that matter, the notation used here is quite different from the one employed in Moorgat and Morrill 1991).

The calculus **D** has the axioms and inference rules specified in (33) through (39) below (again, A, B, C denote categories, Γ and Δ structured terms, and $\Gamma\{\Delta\}$ represents a structured term Γ containing a distinguished occurrence of the structured subterm Δ):

$$\frac{}{A \Rightarrow A}\ [Ax] \qquad\qquad \frac{\Delta \Rightarrow A \quad \Gamma\{A\} \Rightarrow C}{\Gamma\{\Delta\} \Rightarrow C}\ [Cut] \tag{33}$$

$$\frac{\Delta \Rightarrow B \quad \Gamma\{A\} \Rightarrow C}{\Gamma\{[\Delta, B\backslash A]\} \Rightarrow C}\ [\backslash L] \qquad\qquad \frac{[B,\Gamma] \Rightarrow A}{\Gamma \Rightarrow B\backslash A}\ [\backslash R] \tag{34}$$

$$\frac{\Delta \Rightarrow B \quad \Gamma\{A\} \Rightarrow C}{\Gamma\{[\Delta{}^{\backprime} B\dot{\backslash}A]\} \Rightarrow C}\ [\dot\backslash L] \qquad\qquad \frac{[B{}^{\backprime}\Gamma] \Rightarrow A}{\Gamma \Rightarrow B\dot{\backslash}A}\ [\dot\backslash R] \tag{35}$$

$$\frac{\Delta \Rightarrow B \quad \Gamma\{A\} \Rightarrow C}{\Gamma\{[A/B, \Delta]\} \Rightarrow C}\ [/L] \qquad\qquad \frac{[\Gamma, B] \Rightarrow A}{\Gamma \Rightarrow A/B}\ [/R] \tag{36}$$

$$\frac{\Delta \Rightarrow B \quad \Gamma\{A\} \Rightarrow C}{\Gamma\{[A\dot{/}B{}^{\backprime}\Delta]\} \Rightarrow C}\ [\dot/L] \qquad\qquad \frac{[\Gamma{}^{\backprime}B] \Rightarrow A}{\Gamma \Rightarrow A\dot{/}B}\ [\dot/R] \tag{37}$$

$$\frac{\Gamma\{[A,B]\} \Rightarrow C}{\Gamma\{A\bullet B\} \Rightarrow C}\ [\bullet L] \qquad\qquad \frac{\Gamma \Rightarrow A \quad \Delta \Rightarrow B}{[\Gamma, \Delta] \Rightarrow A\bullet B}\ [\bullet R] \tag{38}$$

$$\frac{\Gamma\{[A{}^{\backprime}B]\} \Rightarrow C}{\Gamma\{A\dot\bullet B\} \Rightarrow C}\ [\dot\bullet L] \qquad\qquad \frac{\Gamma \Rightarrow A \quad \Delta \Rightarrow B}{[\Gamma{}^{\backprime}\Delta] \Rightarrow A\dot\bullet B}\ [\dot\bullet R] \tag{39}$$

Here, the calculus **D** is used in a so-called sign-based set-up. That is: the calculus functions as the proof-theoretic engine of a grammar that represents sequents as composed of multidimensional *signs*, i.e., objects of the following form:

$$\text{intonational term} \triangleleft \text{type} \triangleright \text{informational term} \tag{40}$$

As we said above, these signs, the grammatical resources of the formalism, are Saussurian form-meaning units which reflect the fact that the dimensions of linguistic form and meaning contribute to well-formedness in an essentially parallel way.

Interestingly, the calculus itself instantiates the minimal 'base logic' in that it makes no assumptions at all about structural aspects of grammatical resource management: the formalism is a both intonationally/syntactically and semantically/informationally interpreted version of a double, 'dependency' variant of the non-associative Lambek calculus, the pure logic of residuation. In order to account for the ('less lame') intonational facts of English, this pure logic of residuation will be enriched below with unary modal operators. However, it can be noted that these operators are used in a pure, basic way as well: they do not figure

in structural postulates, but merely serve to demarcate intonational domains—
something which is also suggested in Morrill (1994)—within which special pitch
accents are assigned in the process of prosodic substitution that will be defined
below.

More formally, SIGN, the set of signs, is the following set:

$$\{\varphi \triangleleft C \triangleright \gamma \mid \varphi \in \text{PROS and } C \in \text{CAT and } \gamma \in \text{SEM}\} \tag{41}$$

The sets PROS and CAT are defined in (45) below and (31) above, respectively,
and SEM is the set of simply-typed lambda terms built up from variables and
(possibly) constants using abstraction, application, projection and pairing. Given
SIGN, the set TERM of structured terms is defined as the smallest set such that:

$$\text{SIGN} \subseteq \text{TERM; and} \tag{42}$$
$$[\Gamma, \Delta] \in \text{TERM and } [\Gamma \, ` \Delta] \in \text{TERM if } \Gamma \in \text{TERM and } \Delta \in \text{TERM}.$$

For a structured term Γ, the sequence $s(\Gamma)$ of signs of Γ is defined as follows:

$$s(\alpha \triangleleft C \triangleright \tau) = \alpha \triangleleft C \triangleright \tau; \text{ and} \tag{43}$$
$$s([\Gamma, \Delta]) = s([\Gamma \, ` \Delta]) = s(\Gamma), s(\Delta).$$

The sign-based grammar derives sequents $\Gamma \Rightarrow S$, where Γ is a structured term
(as defined in (42)) and S is a sign (see (41)). Its axioms and rules are listed
in (46) through (59) below. Observe that apart from the respective assignments
$\varphi \triangleleft$ and $\triangleright \gamma$ of prosodic and semantic terms to categories, this system is identical
to the calculus **D** specified in (33) through (39) above. We will pay no attention
to the—standard—assignment of semantic terms. The assignment of prosodic
terms proceeds in an analogous—though type-free—fashion. First, the set of
simple prosodic terms is defined as the union of a (possibly empty) set CON of
prosodic constants, as well as an infinite set VAR of prosodic variables:

$$\text{VAR} = \{f_i \mid i \in \mathbb{N}\} \tag{44}$$

Next, the set PROS of prosodic terms is defined as the smallest set satisfying the
following:

$$\text{VAR} \cup \text{CON} \subseteq \text{PROS}; \tag{45}$$
$$\langle \phi, \psi \rangle \in \text{PROS if } \phi \in \text{PROS and } \psi \in \text{PROS } (\textit{head left}); \text{ and}$$
$$\langle \phi \, ` \psi \rangle \in \text{PROS if } \phi \in \text{PROS and } \psi \in \text{PROS } (\textit{head right}).$$

Furthermore, every category occurrence in a derivable sequent $\Gamma \Rightarrow S$ is assigned a prosodic term: the categories in the antecedent Γ are assigned distinct
prosodic variables, and the single category in the consequent S is assigned a possibly complex prosodic term. In (46) through (59) below, the expressions φ and
ψ denote arbitrary prosodic terms, and f, g and h represent prosodic variables.
In the prosodic domain, we let the expression $\varphi[\psi \rightarrow \chi]$ denote the result of replacing all occurrences of the subterm ψ in φ by occurrences of the term χ. This

may involve more than mere substitution for prosodic variables. Thus, prosodically, axioms amount to identity, the rules $Cut, \backslash L, \grave{\backslash} L, \acute{/} L, \underset{.}{/} L$ to substitution, the rules $\backslash R, \grave{\backslash} R, \acute{/} R, \underset{.}{/} R$ to taking a subterm, and the rules $\cdot\bullet R$ and $\bullet\cdot R$ to the construction of a head left and head right term, respectively, but the respective rules $\cdot\bullet L, \bullet\cdot L$ involve the replacement of the compound prosodic terms $\langle f, g \rangle$ and $\langle f \, ' \, g \rangle$ by a prosodic variable h.

In the context of a proof we will assume that all prosodic variables f, g and h that have been assigned to an axiom instance or that have been introduced in the conclusion of a $\backslash L, \grave{\backslash} L, \acute{/} L, \underset{.}{/} L, \cdot\bullet L, \bullet\cdot L$ inference are different. This has the same consequences as the parallel assumption concerning semantic variables: the prosodic variables $f_1, \ldots, f_n$ assigned to the antecedent categories of a sequent $\Gamma \Rightarrow S$ are all different, they make up the variables of the prosodic term φ assigned to the consequent category, and they occur exactly once in φ.

$$\frac{}{f \triangleleft A \triangleright u \Rightarrow f \triangleleft A \triangleright u} \; [Ax] \tag{46}$$

$$\frac{\Delta \Rightarrow \psi \triangleleft A \triangleright \alpha \quad \Gamma\{f \triangleleft A \triangleright u\} \Rightarrow \varphi \triangleleft C \triangleright \gamma}{\Gamma\{\Delta\} \Rightarrow \varphi[f \to \psi] \triangleleft C \triangleright \gamma[u \to \alpha]} \; [Cut] \tag{47}$$

$$\frac{\Delta \Rightarrow \psi \triangleleft B \triangleright \beta \quad \Gamma\{f \triangleleft A \triangleright u\} \Rightarrow \varphi \triangleleft C \triangleright \gamma}{\Gamma\{[\Delta, g \triangleleft B \backslash A \triangleright x]\} \Rightarrow \varphi[f \to \langle \psi, g \rangle] \triangleleft C \triangleright \gamma[u \to x(\beta)]} \; [\backslash L] \tag{48}$$

$$\frac{\Delta \Rightarrow \psi \triangleleft B \triangleright \beta \quad \Gamma\{f \triangleleft A \triangleright u\} \Rightarrow \varphi \triangleleft C \triangleright \gamma}{\Gamma\{[\Delta \, ' \, g \triangleleft B\grave{\backslash} A \triangleright x]\} \Rightarrow \varphi[f \to \langle \psi \, ' \, g \rangle] \triangleleft C \triangleright \gamma[u \to x(\beta)]} \; [\grave{\backslash} L] \tag{49}$$

$$\frac{\Delta \Rightarrow \psi \triangleleft B \triangleright \beta \quad \Gamma\{f \triangleleft A \triangleright u\} \Rightarrow \varphi \triangleleft C \triangleright \gamma}{\Gamma\{[g \triangleleft A \acute{/} B \triangleright x, \Delta]\} \Rightarrow \varphi[f \to \langle g, \psi \rangle] \triangleleft C \triangleright \gamma[u \to x(\beta)]} \; [\acute{/} L] \tag{50}$$

$$\frac{\Delta \Rightarrow \psi \triangleleft B \triangleright \beta \quad \Gamma\{f \triangleleft A \triangleright u\} \Rightarrow \varphi \triangleleft C \triangleright \gamma}{\Gamma\{[g \triangleleft A \underset{.}{/} B \triangleright x \, ' \, \Delta]\} \Rightarrow \varphi[f \to \langle g \, ' \, \psi \rangle] \triangleleft C \triangleright \gamma[u \to x(\beta)]} \; [\underset{.}{/} L] \tag{51}$$

$$\frac{[f \triangleleft B \triangleright v, \Gamma] \Rightarrow \langle f, \varphi \rangle \triangleleft A \triangleright \alpha}{\Gamma \Rightarrow \varphi \triangleleft B \backslash A \triangleright \lambda v.\alpha} \; [\backslash R] \tag{52}$$

$$\frac{[f \triangleleft B \triangleright v \, ' \, \Gamma] \Rightarrow \langle f \, ' \, \varphi \rangle \triangleleft A \triangleright \alpha}{\Gamma \Rightarrow \varphi \triangleleft B\grave{\backslash} A \triangleright \lambda v.\alpha} \; [\grave{\backslash} R] \tag{53}$$

$$\frac{[\Gamma, f \triangleleft B \triangleright v] \Rightarrow \langle \varphi, f \rangle \triangleleft A \triangleright \alpha}{\Gamma \Rightarrow \varphi \triangleleft A \acute{/} B \triangleright \lambda v.\alpha} \; [\acute{/} R] \tag{54}$$

$$\frac{[\Gamma \, ' \, f \triangleleft B \triangleright v] \Rightarrow \langle \varphi \, ' \, f \rangle \triangleleft A \triangleright \alpha}{\Gamma \Rightarrow \varphi \triangleleft A \underset{.}{/} B \triangleright \lambda v.\alpha} \; [\underset{.}{/} R] \tag{55}$$

$$\frac{\Gamma\{[f \lhd A \rhd u, g \lhd B \rhd v]\} \Rightarrow \varphi \lhd C \rhd \gamma}{\Gamma\{h \lhd A^\bullet{\bullet}B \rhd y\} \Rightarrow \varphi[\langle f, g\rangle \to h] \lhd C \rhd \gamma[u \to (y)_0, v \to (y)_1]} \; [^\bullet\!L] \tag{56}$$

$$\frac{\Gamma\{[f \lhd A \rhd u \, {}^\backprime g \lhd B \rhd v]\} \Rightarrow \varphi \lhd C \rhd \gamma}{\Gamma\{h \lhd A^\bullet{}^\bullet B \rhd y\} \Rightarrow \varphi[\langle f \, {}^\backprime g\rangle \to h] \lhd C \rhd \gamma[u \to (y)_0, v \to (y)_1]} \; [\bullet^\bullet\!L] \tag{57}$$

$$\frac{\Gamma \Rightarrow \varphi \lhd A \rhd \alpha \quad \Delta \Rightarrow \psi \lhd B \rhd \beta}{[\Gamma, \Delta] \Rightarrow \langle \varphi, \psi\rangle \lhd A^\bullet{\bullet}B \rhd \alpha \star \beta} \; [^\bullet\!R] \tag{58}$$

$$\frac{\Gamma \Rightarrow \varphi \lhd A \rhd \alpha \quad \Delta \Rightarrow \psi \lhd B \rhd \beta}{[\Gamma \, {}^\backprime \Delta] \Rightarrow \langle \varphi \, {}^\backprime \psi\rangle \lhd A^\bullet{}^\bullet B \rhd \alpha \star \beta} \; [\bullet^\bullet\!R] \tag{59}$$

Lambek's (1958) proof of *Cut* elimination and decidability for the associative calculus **L** is easily adapted to the non-associative calculi **NL** and **D**. A semantic version of the result holds as well: the result of applying Lambek's *Cut* elimination algorithm to a derivation is a *Cut*-free derivation which is semantically equivalent to the original derivation in that the semantic term assigned to the consequent of its conclusion sequent can be obtained from the semantic term assigned to the consequent of the conclusion of the original derivation via finitely many applications of β-conversion. It may be noted here that a prosodic version of the *Cut* elimination theorem can also be shown to hold, since application of the *Cut* elimination algorithm leads to a *Cut*-free derivation which is prosodically equivalent to the original derivation in that the prosodic term assigned to the consequent of its conclusion sequent is *identical* to the prosodic term assigned to the consequent of the conclusion of the original derivation. These results mean that we only have to consider the finite number of *Cut*-free derivations of a sequent in order to obtain all of its semantic and prosodic interpretations.

In keeping with the set-up outlined above, we will assume that the lexicon is a collection of lexical signs $\varphi \lhd C \rhd \gamma$, where φ is a prosodic term, C is a syntactic category, and γ is a semantic term of the type associated with C.

Given a lexicon L, we will say that a (possibly compound) sign $\varphi' \lhd C \rhd \gamma'$ is in the language of L iff for some derivable sequent $\Gamma \Rightarrow \varphi \lhd C \rhd \gamma$ with $s(\Gamma) = f_1 \lhd C_1 \rhd v_1, \ldots, f_n \lhd C_n \rhd v_n$, there are $\varphi_1 \lhd C_1 \rhd \gamma_1 \in L, \ldots, \varphi_n \lhd C_n \rhd \gamma_n \in L$ such that $\varphi\{ f_1 \to \varphi_1, \ldots, f_n \to \varphi_n \} = \varphi'$ and $\gamma[v_1 \to \gamma_1, \ldots, v_n \to \gamma_n] = \gamma'$.

Observe that the sequence $s(\Gamma)$ of signs of a structured term Γ has been defined in (43) above. The expression $\gamma[v_1 \to \gamma_1, \ldots, v_n \to \gamma_n]$ standardly denotes the result of simultaneously and respectively substituting $v_1, \ldots, v_n$ by $\gamma_1, \ldots, \gamma_n$ in γ. The expression $\varphi\{ f_1 \to \varphi_1, \ldots, f_n \to \varphi_n \}$ refers to the result of performing the following prosodic substitution:

$$\begin{aligned}
\langle \varphi, \psi\rangle\{ \mathbf{s} \} &= \varphi\{ \mathbf{s} \} \, \psi\{ \mathbf{s} \} \\
\langle \varphi \, {}^\backprime \psi\rangle\{ \mathbf{s} \} &= \varphi\{ \mathbf{s} \} \, \psi\{ \mathbf{s} \} \\
f\{ \mathbf{s}, f \to \mathrm{term}, \mathbf{s}' \} &= \mathrm{TERM} \\
\langle \varphi, \psi\rangle\{\!\{ \mathbf{s} \} &= \varphi\{\!\{ \mathbf{s} \} \, \psi\{\!\{ \mathbf{s} \} \\
\langle \varphi \, {}^\backprime \psi\rangle\{\!\{ \mathbf{s} \} &= \varphi\{\!\{ \mathbf{s} \} \, \psi\{\!\{ \mathbf{s} \} \\
f\{\!\{ \mathbf{s}, f \to \mathrm{term}, \mathbf{s}' \} &= term
\end{aligned} \tag{60}$$

The prosodic substitution defined in (60) is a forgetful mapping which takes care of the assignment of focal H* pitch accent to the prosodic terms that are substituted for the prosodic variables in the initial prosodic term. Note that this assignment of H* pitch accent proceeds in such a way that the accent is always aligned with the prosodically most prominent subexpression of a given structure, since it consistently follows its path down via prosodic heads.[8]

4 Catalan

We are now in a position to provide the analyses of the Catalan examples (15), (16) and (17) that were discussed in Section 2.

$$Odia\ el\ bròquil\ l'\text{AMO} \lhd s \rhd \text{HATE}(\text{THE}(\text{BROCCOLI}))(\text{THE}(\text{BOSS})) \tag{61}$$

As regards the all-focus example (15), *Odia el bròquil l'*AMO, it can be observed that the sign (61) is in the language of the lexicon $L = \{\text{odia} \lhd (s/n)/n \rhd \text{HATE}, \text{el} \lhd n/c \rhd \text{THE}, \text{bròquil} \lhd c \rhd \text{BROCCOLI}, l' \lhd n/c \rhd \text{THE}, \text{amo} \lhd c \rhd \text{BOSS}\}$, in view of the fact that $[[f \lhd (s/n)/n \rhd x\,'[g \lhd n/c \rhd y\,'h \lhd c \rhd z]]\,'[i \lhd n/c \rhd u\,'j \lhd c \rhd v]] \Rightarrow \langle\langle f\,'\langle g\,'h\rangle\rangle\,'\langle i\,'j\rangle\rangle \lhd s \rhd x(y(z))(u(v))$ is a derivable sequent: the type-logical part of its derivation is given in (62), and the prosodic and semantic interpretation of (62) are specified in (63) and (64), respectively:

$$\cfrac{c \Rightarrow c \quad n \Rightarrow n}{\cfrac{[n/c\,'c] \Rightarrow n}{[[(s/n)/n\,'[n/c\,'c]]\,'[n/c\,'c]] \Rightarrow s}[/L]} \quad \cfrac{\cfrac{c \Rightarrow c \quad n \Rightarrow n}{[n/c\,'c] \Rightarrow n}[/L] \quad s \Rightarrow s}{[s/n\,'[n/c\,'c]] \Rightarrow s}[/L] \tag{62}$$

$$\cfrac{h \Rightarrow h \quad g' \Rightarrow g'}{[g\,'h] \Rightarrow \langle g\,'h\rangle} \quad \cfrac{\cfrac{j \Rightarrow j \quad i' \Rightarrow i'}{[i\,'j] \Rightarrow \langle i\,'j\rangle} \quad f'' \Rightarrow f''}{[f'\,'[i\,'j]] \Rightarrow \langle f'\,'\langle i\,'j\rangle\rangle} \over [[f\,'[g\,'h]]\,'[i\,'j]] \Rightarrow \langle\langle f\,'\langle g\,'h\rangle\rangle\,'\langle i\,'j\rangle\rangle} \tag{63}$$

$$\cfrac{z \Rightarrow z \quad y' \Rightarrow y'}{[y\,'z] \Rightarrow y(z)} \quad \cfrac{\cfrac{v \Rightarrow v \quad u' \Rightarrow u'}{[u\,'v] \Rightarrow u(v)} \quad x'' \Rightarrow x''}{[x'\,'[u\,'v]] \Rightarrow x'(u(v))} \over [[x\,'[y\,'z]]\,'[u\,'v]] \Rightarrow x(y(z))(u(v))} \tag{64}$$

---

[8] As a consequence of this architecture, we have that performing a prosodic substitution in different prosodic terms may result in one and the same string, something which holds by virtue of possibility that $\varphi\{f_1 \to \varphi_1, \ldots, f_n \to \varphi_n\} = \varphi'\{f_1 \to \varphi_1, \ldots, f_n \to \varphi_n\}$. This can be exploited in an account of what is known as *focus projection*, that is: the fact that a single prosodic form such as *Kim likes* JIM can correspond to different information packagings, for example [F *Kim likes* JIM] (in answer to the question *What's new?*), *Kim* [F *likes* JIM] (in answer to the question *What about Kim?*) and *Kim likes* [F JIM] (in answer to the question *Who does Kim like?*). Discussion of this phenomenon will have to be resumed on another occassion.

The process of prosodic substitution is displayed in (65), where s is used to abbreviate the sequence $f \to$ odia, $g \to$ el, $h \to$ bròquil, $i \to$ l', $j \to$ amo, while (66) presents the result of performing the required semantic substitution:

$$\langle\langle f \, {}^{\backprime}\langle g\, {}^{\backprime} h\rangle\rangle\, {}^{\backprime}\langle i\, {}^{\backprime} j\rangle\rangle\{\, f \to \text{odia}, g \to \text{el}, h \to \text{bròquil}, i \to \text{l'}, j \to \text{amo}\,\} = \qquad (65)$$

$$\langle\langle f \, {}^{\backprime}\langle g\, {}^{\backprime} h\rangle\rangle\, {}^{\backprime}\langle i\, {}^{\backprime} j\rangle\rangle\{\, \text{s}\,\} = \langle f \, {}^{\backprime}\langle g\, {}^{\backprime} h\rangle\rangle\{\, \text{s}\,\}\langle i\, {}^{\backprime} j\rangle\{\, \text{s}\,\} =$$

$$f\{\, \text{s}\,\}\langle g\, {}^{\backprime} h\rangle\{\, \text{s}\,\}i\{\, \text{s}\,\}j\{\, \text{s}\,\} = f\{\, \text{s}\,\}g\{\, \text{s}\,\}h\{\, \text{s}\,\}i\{\, \text{s}\,\}j\{\, \text{s}\,\} =$$

$$f\{\, f \to \text{odia}\,\}g\{\, g \to \text{el}\,\}h\{\, h \to \text{bròquil}\,\}i\{\, i \to \text{l'}\,\}j\{\, j \to \text{amo}\,\} =$$

$$Odia \; el \; bròquil \; l'\text{AMO}$$

$$x(y(z))(u(v))[x \to \text{HATE}, y \to \text{THE}, z \to \text{BROCCOLI}, u \to \text{THE}, v \to \text{BOSS}] = \qquad (66)$$

$$\text{HATE}(\text{THE}(\text{BROCCOLI}))(\text{THE}(\text{BOSS}))$$

We now turn to the analysis of example (16), *L'amo odia el* BRÒQUIL, in which the link subject *l'amo* has been detached to the left. We can account for this example if we assume that the agreement morphology *-a* that has been suffixed to the verbal stem *odi-* may function as a 'defocusing' operator which affects the informational status of the subject by downgrading it to the rank of link (tail), while it also takes care of its concomitant left (right) detachment and deaccenting. Such an assumption should be uncontroversial, since it is also the verbal agreement morphology that is generally held responsible for an even more radical downgrading of the subject which can be attested in 'pro-drop' languages such as Catalan. Thus the subjectless (67) is a grammatical Catalan sentence, which means roughly something like '(s)he hates broccoli':

$$Odia \; el \; \text{BRÒQUIL} \qquad (67)$$

With respect to example (16), the above assumption involves the assignment of the higher-order functor category $((s/_{*}n)/_{*}n)\backslash((n\backslash^{*}s)/_{*}n)$ and the interpretation $\lambda R\lambda x\lambda y[\text{LINK}(y) \wedge R(y)(x)]$ to the suffix *-a*. (As announced in Section 1 above, we assume that our lambda terms figure in a type-theoretical version of DRT. We will not go further into the formal interpretation of the non-logical constants 'LINK' and 'TAIL' here. More detailed information is provided in Hendriks 1996b.) This creates the possibility of combining the suffix with the verbal stem *odi-*, which is of category $(s/_{*}n)/_{*}n$ and has the interpretation HATE.[9]

$$L'amo \; odia \; el \; \text{BRÒQUIL} \; \lhd s \rhd [\text{LINK}(\text{THE}(\text{BOSS})) \wedge \qquad (68)$$

$$\text{HATE}(\text{THE}(\text{BROCCOLI}))(\text{THE}(\text{BOSS}))]$$

As a result, the sign (68) can be shown to belong to the language of the lexicon $L' = \{\text{l'} \lhd n/_{*}c \rhd \text{THE}, \text{amo} \lhd c \rhd \text{BOSS}, \text{odi-} \lhd (s/_{*}n)/_{*}n \rhd \text{HATE}, \text{-a} \lhd ((s/_{*}n)/_{*}n)\backslash((n\backslash^{*}s)/_{*}n)\rhd \lambda R\lambda x\lambda y[\text{LINK}(y) \wedge R(y)(x)], \text{el} \lhd n/_{*}c \rhd \text{THE}, \text{bròquil} \lhd c \rhd \text{BROCCOLI}\}$, because the

---

[9] Example (15) can be accounted for along the present lines if it is assumed that the sign odi- $\lhd (s/_{*}n)/_{*}n \rhd$ HATE combines with the 'basic' all-focus guise -a $\lhd ((s/_{*}n)/_{*}n)\backslash((s/_{*}n)/_{*}n) \rhd \lambda R\lambda x\lambda y.R(x)(y)$ of the suffix.

sequent $[[f \triangleleft n/_{\!\!*}c \triangleright x \text{'}g \triangleleft c \triangleright y] \text{'} [[h \triangleleft (s/_{\!\!*}n)/_{\!\!*}n \triangleright z, i \triangleleft ((s/_{\!\!*}n)/_{\!\!*}n)\backslash((n\backslash s)/_{\!\!*}n) \triangleright u] \text{'} [j \triangleleft$
$n/_{\!\!*}c \triangleright v \text{'} k \triangleleft c \triangleright w]]] \Rightarrow \langle\langle f \text{'} g \rangle \text{'} \langle\langle h, i \rangle \text{'} \langle j \text{'} k \rangle\rangle\rangle \triangleleft s \triangleright u(z)(v(w))(x(y))$ is derivable:
(69) represents the type-logical part of its derivation; the prosodic and semantic
interpretation of (69) appear in (70) and (71), respectively; and the results of
performing the relevant prosodic and semantic substitutions are listed in (72)
and (73), respectively:

$$\frac{\begin{array}{c}\frac{c \Rightarrow c \quad n \Rightarrow n}{[n/_{\!\!*}c \text{'} c] \Rightarrow n}[/_{\!\!*}L] \quad \dfrac{\dfrac{\dfrac{c \Rightarrow c \quad n \Rightarrow n}{[n/_{\!\!*}c \text{'} c] \Rightarrow n}[/_{\!\!*}L] \quad s \Rightarrow s}{[[n/_{\!\!*}c \text{'} c] \text{'} n\backslash s] \Rightarrow s}[\backslash L]}{[[n/_{\!\!*}c \text{'} c] \text{'} [(n\backslash s)/_{\!\!*}n \text{'} [n/_{\!\!*}c \text{'} c]]] \Rightarrow s}[/_{\!\!*}L]\end{array}}{[[n/_{\!\!*}c \text{'} c] \text{'} [[(s/_{\!\!*}n)/_{\!\!*}n, ((s/_{\!\!*}n)/_{\!\!*}n)\backslash((n\backslash s)/_{\!\!*}n)] \text{'} [n/_{\!\!*}c \text{'} c]]] \Rightarrow s}[\backslash L]$$

with $(s/_{\!\!*}n)/_{\!\!*}n \Rightarrow (s/_{\!\!*}n)/_{\!\!*}n$ on the left branch. (69)

$$\frac{h \Rightarrow h \quad \dfrac{\dfrac{k \Rightarrow k \quad j' \Rightarrow j'}{[j \text{'} k] \Rightarrow \langle j \text{'} k \rangle} \quad \dfrac{\dfrac{g \Rightarrow g \quad f' \Rightarrow f'}{[f \text{'} g] \Rightarrow \langle f \text{'} g \rangle} \quad i''' \Rightarrow i'''}{[[f \text{'} g] \text{'} i''] \Rightarrow \langle\langle f \text{'} g \rangle \text{'} i'' \rangle}}{[[f \text{'} g] \text{'} [i' \text{'} [j \text{'} k]]] \Rightarrow \langle\langle f \text{'} g \rangle \text{'} \langle i' \text{'} \langle j \text{'} k \rangle\rangle\rangle}}{[[f \text{'} g] \text{'} [[h, i] \text{'} [j \text{'} k]]] \Rightarrow \langle\langle f \text{'} g \rangle \text{'} \langle\langle h, i \rangle \text{'} \langle j \text{'} k \rangle\rangle\rangle} \qquad (70)$$

$$\frac{z \Rightarrow z \quad \dfrac{\dfrac{w \Rightarrow w \quad v' \Rightarrow v'}{[v \text{'} w] \Rightarrow v(w)} \quad \dfrac{\dfrac{y \Rightarrow y \quad x' \Rightarrow x'}{[x \text{'} y] \Rightarrow x(y)} \quad u''' \Rightarrow u'''}{[[x \text{'} y] \text{'} u''] \Rightarrow u''(x(y))}}{[[x \text{'} y] \text{'} [u' \text{'} [v \text{'} w]]] \Rightarrow u'(v(w))(x(y))}}{[[x \text{'} y] \text{'} [[z, u] \text{'} [v \text{'} w]]] \Rightarrow u(z)(v(w))(x(y))} \qquad (71)$$

$$\langle\langle f \text{'} g \rangle \text{'} \langle\langle h, i \rangle \text{'} \langle j \text{'} k \rangle\rangle\rangle\{ f \rightarrow \text{l'}, g \rightarrow \text{amo}, h \rightarrow \text{odi-}, i \rightarrow \text{-a}, j \rightarrow \text{el}, k \rightarrow \text{bròquil} \} = \qquad (72)$$
$$\text{L'amo odia el BRÒQUIL}$$

$$u(z)(v(w))(x(y))[x \rightarrow \text{THE}, y \rightarrow \text{BOSS}, z \rightarrow \text{HATE}, \qquad (73)$$
$$u \rightarrow \lambda R \lambda x \lambda y[\text{LINK}(y) \wedge R(x)(y)], v \rightarrow \text{THE}, w \rightarrow \text{BROCCOLI}] =$$
$$[\text{LINK}(\text{THE}(\text{BOSS})) \wedge \text{HATE}(\text{THE}(\text{BROCCOLI}))(\text{THE}(\text{BOSS}))]$$

Furthermore, example (17), *L'amo l'ODIA el bròquil*, in which the link subject
has been detached to the left and, moreover, the tail direct object has been
detached to the right while a clitic has been prefixed to the verb, can be analysed
analogously, that is: provided that also the clitic *l'* is allowed to function as a
defocusing operator—this time one which affects the informational status of the
direct object. With respect to example (17), this involves the assignment of the
category $((n\backslash s)/n)/_{\!\!*}((n\backslash s)/_{\!\!*}n)$ and the interpretation $\lambda R \lambda x \lambda y[\text{TAIL}(x) \wedge R(x)(y)]$
to the expression *l'*.

$$\text{L'amo l'ODIa el bròquil} \triangleleft s \triangleright [\text{TAIL}(\text{THE}(\text{BROCCOLI})) \wedge \qquad (74)$$
$$\text{LINK}(\text{THE}(\text{BOSS})) \wedge \text{HATE}(\text{THE}(\text{BROCCOLI}))(\text{THE}(\text{BOSS}))]$$

Let $L'' = L' \cup \{l' \lhd ((n\backslash s)/n)/((n\backslash s)/n) \rhd \lambda R \lambda x \lambda y [\text{TAIL}(x) \wedge R(x)(y)]\}$, where L' is the lexicon listed above. Then the sign (74) is a member of the language of lexicon L'', because $[[f \lhd n/c \rhd x \, `g \lhd c \rhd y] \, `[[h \lhd ((n\backslash s)/n)/((n\backslash s)/n) \rhd z \, `[i \lhd (s/n)/n \rhd t, j \lhd ((s/n)/n)\backslash((n\backslash s)/n) \rhd u]], [k \lhd n/c \rhd v \, `l \lhd c \rhd w]]] \Rightarrow \langle\langle f \, `g\rangle \, `\langle\langle h \, `\langle i, j\rangle\rangle, \langle k \, `l\rangle\rangle\rangle \lhd s \rhd z(u(t))(v(w))(x(y))$ is a derivable sequent. The type-logical part of its derivation is given in (75), where α, β and γ abbreviate the respective categories $(s/n)/n$, $(n\backslash s)/n$ and $(n\backslash s)/n$; the prosodic and semantic interpretations of (75) are specified in (76) and (77), respectively; and the results of performing the relevant prosodic and semantic subsititutions can be found in (78) and (79).

$$
\cfrac{
\alpha \Rightarrow \alpha \quad
\cfrac{
\beta \Rightarrow \beta \quad
\cfrac{
\cfrac{c \Rightarrow c \quad n \Rightarrow n}{[n/c \, `c] \Rightarrow n}[/L] \quad
\cfrac{
\cfrac{c \Rightarrow c \quad n \Rightarrow n}{[n/c \, `c] \Rightarrow n}[/L] \quad s \Rightarrow s
}{[[n/c \, `c] \, `n\backslash s] \Rightarrow s}[\backslash L]
}{[[n/c \, `c] \, `[((n\backslash s)/n), [n/c \, `c]]] \Rightarrow s}[/L]
}{[[n/c \, `c] \, `[\gamma/\beta \, `\beta], [n/c \, `c]]] \Rightarrow s}[/L]
}{[[n/c \, `c] \, `[[\gamma/\beta \, `[\alpha, \alpha\backslash\beta]], [n/c \, `c]]] \Rightarrow s}[\backslash L] \tag{75}
$$

$$
\cfrac{
i \Rightarrow i \quad
\cfrac{
j' \Rightarrow j' \quad
\cfrac{
\cfrac{l \Rightarrow l \quad k' \Rightarrow k'}{[k \, `l] \Rightarrow \langle k \, `l\rangle} \quad
\cfrac{
\cfrac{g \Rightarrow g \quad f' \Rightarrow f'}{[f \, `g] \Rightarrow \langle f \, `g\rangle} \quad h''' \Rightarrow h'''
}{[[f \, `g] \, `h''] \rightarrow \langle\langle f \, `g\rangle \, `h''\rangle}
}{[[f \, `g] \, `[h', [k \, `l]]] \Rightarrow \langle\langle f \, `g\rangle \, `\langle h', \langle k \, `l\rangle\rangle\rangle}
}{[[f \, `g] \, `[[h \, `j'], [k \, `l]]] \Rightarrow \langle\langle f \, `g\rangle \, `\langle\langle h \, `j'\rangle, \langle k \, `l\rangle\rangle\rangle}
}{[[f \, `g] \, `[[h \, `[i, j]], [k \, `l]]] \Rightarrow \langle\langle f \, `g\rangle \, `\langle\langle h \, `\langle i, j\rangle\rangle, \langle k \, `l\rangle\rangle\rangle} \tag{76}
$$

$$
\cfrac{
t \Rightarrow t \quad
\cfrac{
u' \Rightarrow u' \quad
\cfrac{
\cfrac{w \Rightarrow w \quad v' \Rightarrow v'}{[v \, `w] \Rightarrow v(w)} \quad
\cfrac{
\cfrac{y \Rightarrow y \quad x' \Rightarrow x'}{[x \, `y] \Rightarrow x(y)} \quad z''' \Rightarrow z'''
}{[[x \, `y] \, `z''] \rightarrow z''(x(y))}
}{[[x \, `y] \, `[z', [v \, `w]]] \Rightarrow z'(v(w))(x(y))}
}{[[x \, `y] \, `[[z \, `u'], [v \, `w]]] \Rightarrow z(u')(v(w))(x(y))}
}{[[x \, `y] \, `[[z \, `[t, u]], [v \, `w]]] \Rightarrow z(u(t))(v(w))(x(y))} \tag{77}
$$

$$\langle\langle f \, `g\rangle \, `\langle\langle h \, `\langle i, j\rangle\rangle, \langle k \, `l\rangle\rangle\rangle\{f\to l', g\to \text{amo}, h\to l', i\to \text{odi-}, j\to \text{-a}, \tag{78}$$
$$k\to \text{el}, l\to \text{bròquil}\} = L'amo\ l'\text{ODIA}\ el\ bròquil$$

$$z(u(t))(v(w))(x(y))[x\to \text{THE}, y\to \text{BOSS}, z\to \lambda R\lambda x\lambda y[\text{TAIL}(x) \wedge R(x)(y)], \tag{79}$$
$$t\to \text{HATE}, u\to \lambda R\lambda x\lambda y[\text{LINK}(y) \wedge R(x)(y)], v\to \text{THE}, w\to \text{BROCCOLI}] =$$
$$[\text{TAIL}(\text{THE}(\text{BROCCOLI})) \wedge \text{LINK}(\text{THE}(\text{BOSS})) \wedge$$
$$\text{HATE}(\text{THE}(\text{BROCCOLI}))(\text{THE}(\text{BOSS}))]$$

5 English

Under the approach outlined above, every expression contains exactly one focal H* pitch accent, which is sufficient for representing the 'rather lame' part played by intonational structure in languages such as Catalan. Moreover, our present means are also sufficient for an analysis of the English all-focus example (9), *The boss hates* BROCCOLI.

$$\textit{The boss hates } \text{BROCCOLI} \triangleleft s \triangleright \text{HATE}(\text{THE}(\text{BROCCOLI}))(\text{THE}(\text{BOSS})) \qquad (80)$$

For note that (80) is in the language of the lexicon $L''' = \{$the $\triangleleft n/_c c \triangleright$ THE, boss $\triangleleft c \triangleright$ BOSS, hates $\triangleleft (n\backslash s)/_l n \triangleright$ HATE, broccoli $\triangleleft n \triangleright$ THE(BROCCOLI)$\}$, since $[[f \triangleleft n/_c c \triangleright x 'g \triangleleft c \triangleright y]' [h \triangleleft (n\backslash s)/_l n \triangleright z 'i \triangleleft n \triangleright v]] \Rightarrow \langle\langle f 'g\rangle ' \langle h 'i\rangle\rangle \triangleleft s \triangleright z(v)(x(y))$ is a derivable sequent, as shown by derivation (81) and its respective prosodic and semantic interpretations in (82) and (83). The results of performing the relevant prosodic and semantic substitutions are listed in (84) and (85), respectively.

$$\frac{n \Rightarrow n \qquad \dfrac{\dfrac{c \Rightarrow c \quad n \Rightarrow n}{[n/_c c 'c] \Rightarrow n}[/_c L] \qquad s \Rightarrow s}{[[n/_c c 'c]'n\backslash s] \Rightarrow s}[\backslash L]}{[[n/_c c 'c]'[(n\backslash s)/_l n 'n]] \Rightarrow s}[/_l L] \qquad (81)$$

$$\frac{i \Rightarrow i \qquad \dfrac{\dfrac{g \Rightarrow g \quad f' \Rightarrow f'}{[f 'g] \Rightarrow \langle f 'g\rangle} \qquad h'' \Rightarrow h''}{[[f 'g]'h'] \Rightarrow \langle\langle f 'g\rangle 'h'\rangle}}{[[f 'g]'[h 'i]] \Rightarrow \langle\langle f 'g\rangle ' \langle h 'i\rangle\rangle} \qquad (82)$$

$$\frac{v \Rightarrow v \qquad \dfrac{\dfrac{y \Rightarrow y \quad x' \Rightarrow x'}{[x 'y] \Rightarrow x(y)} \qquad z'' \Rightarrow z''}{[[x 'y]'z'] \Rightarrow z'(x(y))}}{[[x 'y]'[z 'v]] \Rightarrow z(v)(x(y))} \qquad (83)$$

$$\langle\langle f 'g\rangle ' \langle h 'i\rangle\rangle \{\, f \to \text{the}, g \to \text{boss}, h \to \text{hates}, i \to \text{broccoli}\,\} = \qquad (84)$$
$$\textit{The boss hates } \text{BROCCOLI}$$

$$z(v)(x(y))[x \to \text{THE}, y \to \text{BOSS}, z \to \text{HATE}, v \to \text{THE}(\text{BROCCOLI})] = \qquad (85)$$
$$\text{HATE}(\text{THE}(\text{BROCCOLI}))(\text{THE}(\text{BOSS}))$$

Nonetheless, we saw above that if an English transitive sentence such as *The boss hates broccoli* contains a link subject—for example because it answers the question *What about the boss?*—, then it will not only contain a focal H* pitch accent aligned with its prosodic head, that is: the direct object noun phrase of the transitive verb, but also an additional L+H* pitch accent aligned with the subject of the sentence. Within the domain of the subject of the sentence, the alignment of this L+H* pitch accent observes the same regularities as the alignment of H* pitch accent, in that it attaches to the prosodically most prominent expression. Thus if the subject of the sentence is the noun phrase *the boss*, it is the common noun of the noun phrase, rather than the determiner, that will be accented. In other words: both types of accent exploit the same notion of prosodic head.

In order to account for the occurrence of L+H* pitch accents in English, we enrich the sign-based calculus with the minimal logical rules of the operators $\Diamond$ and $\boxdot$ which can be found in Moortgat (1996) (where $\boxdot$ denotes Moortgat's $\Box^{\downarrow}$).[10] The type-logical rules for these operators are given in (86) and (87), and the sign-based versions appear in (88) through (91).

$$\frac{\Gamma\{A\} \Rightarrow B}{\Gamma\{[\boxdot A]\} \Rightarrow B} \; [\boxdot L] \qquad \frac{[\Gamma] \Rightarrow A}{\Gamma \Rightarrow \boxdot A} \; [\boxdot R] \tag{86}$$

$$\frac{\Gamma\{[A]\} \Rightarrow B}{\Gamma\{\Diamond A\} \Rightarrow B} \; [\Diamond L] \qquad \frac{\Gamma \Rightarrow A}{[\Gamma] \Rightarrow \Diamond A} \; [\Diamond R] \tag{87}$$

$$\frac{\Gamma\{a \triangleleft A \triangleright u\} \Rightarrow \beta \triangleleft B \triangleright \sigma}{\Gamma\{[a \triangleleft \boxdot A \triangleright u]\} \Rightarrow \beta[a \to \langle a \rangle] \triangleleft B \triangleright \sigma} \; [\boxdot L] \tag{88}$$

$$\frac{[\Gamma] \Rightarrow \langle \alpha \rangle \triangleleft A \triangleright \tau}{\Gamma \Rightarrow \alpha \triangleleft \boxdot A \triangleright \tau} \; [\boxdot R] \tag{89}$$

$$\frac{\Gamma\{[a \triangleleft A \triangleright u]\} \Rightarrow \beta \triangleleft B \triangleright \sigma}{\Gamma\{a \triangleleft \Diamond A \triangleright u\} \Rightarrow \beta[\langle a \rangle \to a] \triangleleft B \triangleright \sigma} \; [\Diamond L] \tag{90}$$

$$\frac{\Gamma \Rightarrow \alpha \triangleleft A \triangleright \tau}{[\Gamma] \Rightarrow \langle \alpha \rangle \triangleleft \Diamond A \triangleright \tau} \; [\Diamond R] \tag{91}$$

Because (88) through (91) introduce unary brackets, which constitute a new type of prosodic structure, we now extend the definition of prosodic substitution $\varphi\{ f_1 \to \varphi_1, \ldots, f_n \to \varphi_n \}$ that was given in (60) in the following way:

---

[10] Slightly different rules for unary modal operators were initially introduced by Morrill (1992) against the background of the class of so-called *functional* models, where the unary and binary operators are interpreted in terms of unary and binary functions, respectively. In the larger class of so-called *relational* models which is assumed by Moortgat (1996), on the other hand, the unary and binary operators are interpreted in terms of binary and ternary relations, respectively.

$$\langle \varphi, \psi \rangle \{ \mathbf{s} \} = \varphi \{ \mathbf{s} \} \ \psi \{ \mathbf{s} \} \tag{92}$$
$$\langle \varphi \, {}^{\backprime} \psi \rangle \{ \mathbf{s} \} = \varphi \{ \mathbf{s} \} \ \psi \{ \mathbf{s} \}$$
$$\langle \varphi \rangle \{ \mathbf{s} \} = \varphi \{ \mathbf{s} \}$$
$$a \{ \mathbf{s}, a \rightarrow \mathrm{term}, \mathbf{s}' \} = \mathrm{TERM}$$
$$\langle \varphi, \psi \rangle \{ \mathbf{s} \} = \varphi \{ \mathbf{s} \} \ \psi \{ \mathbf{s} \}$$
$$\langle \varphi \, {}^{\backprime} \psi \rangle \{ \mathbf{s} \} = \varphi \{ \mathbf{s} \} \ \psi \{ \mathbf{s} \}$$
$$\langle \varphi \rangle \{ \mathbf{s} \} = \varphi \{ \mathbf{s} \}$$
$$a \{ \mathbf{s}, a \rightarrow \mathrm{term}, \mathbf{s}' \} = \mathit{term}$$
$$\langle \varphi, \psi \rangle \{ \mathbf{s} \} = \varphi \{ \mathbf{s} \} \ \psi \{ \mathbf{s} \}$$
$$\langle \varphi \, {}^{\backprime} \psi \rangle \{ \mathbf{s} \} = \varphi \{ \mathbf{s} \} \ \psi \{ \mathbf{s} \}$$
$$\langle \varphi \rangle \{ \mathbf{s} \} = \varphi \{ \mathbf{s} \}$$
$$a \{ \mathbf{s}, a \rightarrow \mathrm{term}, \mathbf{s}' \} = \mathbf{term}$$

Note that the assignment of L+H* pitch accent indeed proceeds in such a way that it is always aligned with the prosodically most prominent subexpression of a given structure inside its domain, which is demarcated by the unary brackets that come with the operator $\Diamond$, since just as the assignment of H* pitch accents, the assignment of L+H* pitch accent consistently follows its path down via prosodic heads.

We will now provide analyses of the examples (11), *The* **boss** *hates* BROC-COLI, and (13), *The* **boss** HATES *broccoli*, in which we will assume that the linkhood of the subjects is taken care of by an 'abstract' defocusing operator, the lexical sign $\epsilon \triangleleft ((\Diamond n \backslash s)/n)/((n \backslash s)/n) \triangleright \lambda R \lambda x \lambda y [\mathrm{LINK}(y) \wedge R(x)(y)]$, where ϵ denotes the empty string. This operator is a higher-order functor that combines with the transitive verb and affects the intonational and informational interpretation of the sentence in which it occurs in the required way.

$$\text{The } \mathbf{boss} \text{ hates BROCCOLI} \triangleleft s \triangleright [\mathrm{LINK}(\mathrm{THE}(\mathrm{BOSS})) \wedge \tag{93}$$
$$\mathrm{HATE}(\mathrm{THE}(\mathrm{BROCCOLI}))(\mathrm{THE}(\mathrm{BOSS}))]$$

Let L''' be the lexicon assumed for example (80). Then sign (93) is in the language of $L'''' = L''' \cup \{\epsilon \triangleleft ((\Diamond n \backslash s)/n)/((n \backslash s)/n) \triangleright \lambda R \lambda x \lambda y [\mathrm{LINK}(y) \wedge R(x)(y)]\}$, because the sequent $[[[f \triangleleft n/c \triangleright x \, {}^{\backprime} g \triangleleft c \triangleright y]] \, {}^{\backprime} [[h \triangleleft ((\Diamond n \backslash s)/n)/((n \backslash s)/n) \triangleright z \, {}^{\backprime} k \triangleleft (n \backslash s)/n \triangleright v] \, {}^{\backprime} l \triangleleft n \triangleright w]] \Rightarrow \langle \langle \langle f \, {}^{\backprime} g \rangle \rangle \, {}^{\backprime} \langle \langle h \, {}^{\backprime} k \rangle \, {}^{\backprime} l \rangle \rangle \triangleleft s \triangleright z(v)(w)(x(y))$ is derivable: the type-logical part of its derivation is given in (94), and the prosodic and semantic interpretation of (94) are specified in (95) and (96), respectively:

$$
\cfrac{
  \cfrac{
    \cfrac{
      \cfrac{c \Rightarrow c \quad n \Rightarrow n}{[n/c \, {}^{\backprime} c] \Rightarrow n}[/L]
    }{[[n/c \, {}^{\backprime} c]] \Rightarrow \Diamond n}[\Diamond R] \quad s \Rightarrow s
  }{
    \cfrac{
      n \Rightarrow n \quad [[[n/c \, {}^{\backprime} c]] \, {}^{\backprime} \Diamond n \backslash s] \Rightarrow s
    }{[[[n/c \, {}^{\backprime} c]] \, {}^{\backprime} [(\Diamond n \backslash s)/n \, {}^{\backprime} n]] \Rightarrow s}[/L]
  }[\backslash L]
}{
  \cfrac{(n \backslash s)/n \Rightarrow (n \backslash s)/n \quad [[[n/c \, {}^{\backprime} c]] \, {}^{\backprime} [(\Diamond n \backslash s)/n \, {}^{\backprime} n]] \Rightarrow s}{[[[n/c \, {}^{\backprime} c]] \, {}^{\backprime} [[((\Diamond n \backslash s)/n)/((n \backslash s)/n) \, {}^{\backprime} (n \backslash s)/n] \, {}^{\backprime} n]] \Rightarrow s}[/L]
}[/L]
\tag{94}
$$

$$\cfrac{k \Rightarrow k \quad \cfrac{l \Rightarrow l \quad \cfrac{h''' \Rightarrow h''' \quad \cfrac{[[f\,`g]] \Rightarrow \langle\langle f\,`g\rangle\rangle}{[[f\,`g]] \Rightarrow \langle\langle f\,`g\rangle\rangle} \quad \cfrac{f' \Rightarrow f'}{[f\,`g] \Rightarrow \langle f\,`g\rangle}}{[[[f\,`g]]\,`h''] \Rightarrow \langle\langle\langle f\,`g\rangle\rangle\,`h''\rangle}}{[[[f\,`g]]\,`[h'\,`l]] \Rightarrow \langle\langle\langle f\,`g\rangle\rangle\,`\langle h'\,`l\rangle\rangle}}{[[[f\,`g]]\,`[[h\,`k]\,`l]] \Rightarrow \langle\langle\langle f\,`g\rangle\rangle\,`\langle\langle h\,`k\rangle\,`l\rangle\rangle}} \tag{95}$$

$$\cfrac{v \Rightarrow v \quad \cfrac{w \Rightarrow w \quad \cfrac{z''' \Rightarrow z''' \quad \cfrac{[[x\,`y]] \Rightarrow x(y)}{[[x\,`y]] \Rightarrow x(y)} \quad \cfrac{x' \Rightarrow x'}{[x\,`y] \Rightarrow x(y)}}{[[[x\,`y]]\,`z''] \Rightarrow z''(x(y))}}{[[[x\,`y]]\,`[z'\,`w]] \Rightarrow z'(w)(x(y))}}{[[[x\,`y]]\,`[[z\,`v]\,`w]] \Rightarrow z(v)(w)(x(y))} \tag{96}$$

The process of prosodic substitution is displayed in (97), where s is used to abbreviate the sequence $f\to$the, $g\to$boss, $h\to\epsilon$, $k\to$hates, $l\to$broccoli, while (98) presents the result of performing the required semantic substitution:

$$\langle\langle\langle f\,`g\rangle\rangle\,`\langle\langle h\,`k\rangle\,`l\rangle\rangle\{\,f\to\text{the}, g\to\text{boss}, h\to\epsilon, k\to\text{hates}, l\to\text{broccoli}\,\} = \tag{97}$$
$$\langle\langle\langle f\,`g\rangle\rangle\,`\langle\langle h\,`k\rangle\,`l\rangle\rangle\{\,\text{s}\,\} = \langle\langle f\,`g\rangle\rangle\{\,\text{s}\,\}\,\langle\langle h\,`k\rangle\,`l\rangle\{\,\text{s}\,\} =$$
$$\langle f\,`g\rangle\{\,\text{s}\,\}\,\langle h\,`k\rangle\{\,\text{s}\,\}\,l\{\,\text{s}\,\} = f\{\,\text{s}\,\}\,g\{\,\text{s}\,\}\,h\{\,\text{s}\,\}\,k\{\,\text{s}\,\}\,l\{\,\text{s}\,\} =$$
$$f\{\,f\to\text{the}\,\}\,g\{\,g\to\text{boss}\,\}\,h\{\,h\to\epsilon\,\}\,k\{\,k\to\text{hates}\,\}\,l\{\,l\to\text{broccoli}\,\} =$$
$$\text{The \textbf{boss} hates BROCCOLI}$$

$$z(v)(w)(x(y))[x\to\text{THE}, y\to boss, z\to\lambda R\lambda x\lambda y[\text{LINK}(y) \wedge R(x)(y)], \tag{98}$$
$$v\to\text{HATE}, w\to\text{THE}(\text{BROCCOLI})] = [\text{LINK}(\text{THE}(\text{BOSS})) \wedge$$
$$\text{HATE}(\text{THE}(\text{BROCCOLI}))(\text{THE}(\text{BOSS}))]$$

Finally, example (13), *The* **boss** HATES *broccoli*, which contains both a link subject and a tail object, can be analysed if another abstract defocusing operator is assumed: the sign $\epsilon \triangleleft ((\Diamond n\grave{\backslash}s)/n)/_{\!\!\star}((\Diamond n\grave{\backslash}s)/_{\!\!\star}n) \triangleright \lambda R\lambda x\lambda y[\text{TAIL}(x) \wedge R(x)(y)]\}$.

$$\textit{The }\textbf{boss}\textit{ HATES broccoli} \triangleleft s \triangleright [\text{TAIL}(\text{THE}(\text{BROCCOLI})) \wedge \tag{99}$$
$$\text{LINK}(\text{THE}(\text{BOSS})) \wedge \text{HATE}(\text{THE}(\text{BROCCOLI}))(\text{THE}(\text{BOSS}))]$$

We then have that sign (99) is in the language of the lexicon $L'''' = L'''' \cup$ $\{\epsilon \triangleleft ((\Diamond n\grave{\backslash}s)/n)/_{\!\!\star}((\Diamond n\grave{\backslash}s)/_{\!\!\star}n) \triangleright \lambda R\lambda x\lambda y[\text{TAIL}(x) \wedge R(x)(y)]\}$, where L'''' is the lexicon that was assumed for (93), since $[[[f \triangleleft n/_{\!\!\star}c \triangleright x\,`g \triangleleft c \triangleright y]]\,`[[h \triangleleft \tau \triangleright z\,`[i \triangleleft ((\Diamond n\grave{\backslash}s)/_{\!\!\star}n)/_{\!\!\star}((n\grave{\backslash}s)/_{\!\!\star}n) \triangleright u\,`j \triangleleft ((n\grave{\backslash}s)/_{\!\!\star}n \triangleright v]]\,, k \triangleleft n \triangleright w]] \Rightarrow \langle\langle\langle f\,`g\rangle\rangle\,`\langle\langle h\,`\langle i\,`j\rangle\rangle\,, k\rangle\rangle$ $\triangleleft s \triangleright z(u(v))(w)(x(y))$ is a derivable sequent, as illustrated by derivation (100), where α, β and γ abbreviate the respective categories $(n\grave{\backslash}s)/_{\!\!\star}n$, $(\Diamond n\grave{\backslash}s)/_{\!\!\star}n$ and $(\Diamond n\grave{\backslash}s)/n$. The prosodic and semantic interpretations of (100) are given in (101) and (102), respectively.

$$\cfrac{\cfrac{\cfrac{\cfrac{\cfrac{c \Rightarrow c \quad n \Rightarrow n}{[n/_\bullet c\,'\,c] \Rightarrow n}[/_\bullet L]}{[[n/_\bullet c\,'\,c]] \Rightarrow \Diamond n}[\Diamond R] \quad s \Rightarrow s}{[[[n/_\bullet c\,'\,c]]\,'\,\Diamond n\backslash_\bullet s] \Rightarrow s}[\backslash_\bullet L]}{n \Rightarrow n \quad \cfrac{[[[n/_\bullet c\,'\,c]]\,'\,[(\Diamond n\backslash_\bullet s)/n\,,\,n]] \Rightarrow s}{[[[n/_\bullet c\,'\,c]]\,'\,[\gamma/_\bullet\beta\,'\,\beta]\,,\,n]] \Rightarrow s}[/L]}{\beta \Rightarrow \beta \quad \cfrac{[[[n/_\bullet c\,'\,c]]\,'\,[[\gamma/_\bullet\beta\,'\,\beta]\,,\,n]] \Rightarrow s}{}[/_\bullet L]}}{\alpha \Rightarrow \alpha \quad \cfrac{}{}}}{[[[n/_\bullet c\,'\,c]]\,'\,[[\gamma/_\bullet\beta\,'\,[\beta/_\bullet\alpha\,'\,\alpha]]\,,\,n]] \Rightarrow s}[/L]} \qquad (100)$$

$$\cfrac{\cfrac{\cfrac{\cfrac{\cfrac{g \Rightarrow g \quad f' \Rightarrow f'}{[f\,'\,g] \Rightarrow \langle f\,'\,g\rangle}}{[[f\,'\,g]] \Rightarrow \langle\langle f\,'\,g\rangle\rangle \quad h''' \Rightarrow h'''}}{k \Rightarrow k \quad \cfrac{[[[f\,'\,g]]\,'\,h''] \Rightarrow \langle\langle\langle f\,'\,g\rangle\rangle\,'\,h''\rangle}{}}}{i' \Rightarrow i' \quad \cfrac{[[[f\,'\,g]]\,'\,[h'\,,\,k]] \Rightarrow \langle\langle\langle f\,'\,g\rangle\rangle\,'\,\langle h'\,,\,k\rangle\rangle}{}}}{j \Rightarrow j \quad \cfrac{[[[f\,'\,g]]\,'\,[[h\,'\,i']\,,\,k]] \Rightarrow \langle\langle\langle f\,'\,g\rangle\rangle\,'\,\langle\langle h\,'\,i'\rangle\,,\,k\rangle\rangle}{}}}{[[[f\,'\,g]]\,'\,[[h\,'\,[i\,'\,j]]\,,\,k]] \Rightarrow \langle\langle\langle f\,'\,g\rangle\rangle\,'\,\langle\langle h\,'\,\langle i\,'\,j\rangle\rangle\,,\,k\rangle\rangle} \qquad (101)$$

$$\cfrac{\cfrac{\cfrac{\cfrac{\cfrac{y \Rightarrow y \quad x' \Rightarrow x'}{[x\,'\,y] \Rightarrow x(y)}}{[[x\,'\,y]] \Rightarrow x(y) \quad z''' \Rightarrow z'''}}{w \Rightarrow w \quad \cfrac{[[[x\,'\,y]]\,'\,z''] \Rightarrow z''(x(y))}{}}}{u' \Rightarrow u' \quad \cfrac{[[[x\,'\,y]]\,'\,[z'\,,\,w]] \Rightarrow z'(w)(x(y))}{}}}{v \Rightarrow v \quad \cfrac{[[[x\,'\,y]]\,'\,[[z\,'\,u']\,,\,w]] \Rightarrow z(u')(w)(x(y))}{}}}{[[[x\,'\,y]]\,'\,[[z\,'\,[u\,'\,v]]\,,\,w]] \Rightarrow z(u(v))(w)(x(y))} \qquad (102)$$

Performing the relevant prosodic and semantic substitutions will finally result in (103) and (104):

$$\langle\langle\langle f\,'\,g\rangle\rangle\,'\,\langle\langle h\,'\,\langle i\,'\,j\rangle\rangle\,,\,k\rangle\rangle \{\,f \to \text{the}, g \to \text{boss}, h \to \epsilon, i \to \epsilon,$$
$$j \to \text{hates}, k \to \textit{broccoli}\,\} = \textit{The } \textbf{boss } \text{HATES } \textit{broccoli} \qquad (103)$$

$$z(u(v))(w)(x(y))[x \to \text{THE}, y \to \textit{boss}, z \to \lambda R\lambda x\lambda y[\text{TAIL}(x) \wedge R(y)(x)], \qquad (104)$$
$$u \to \lambda R\lambda x\lambda y[\text{LINK}(x) \wedge R(x)(y)], v \to \text{HATE}, w \to \text{THE}(\text{BROCCOLI})] =$$
$$[\text{TAIL}(\text{THE}(\text{BROCCOLI})) \wedge \text{LINK}(\text{THE}(\text{BOSS})) \wedge$$
$$\text{HATE}(\text{THE}(\text{BROCCOLI}))(\text{THE}(\text{BOSS}))]$$

6 Conclusion

We noted above that in expressing information packaging, different languages choose different structural means to spell out the same informational interpretations. Catalan, for example, has a constant prosodic structure and effectuates information packaging via word order permutations, whereas a language such as English structurally realizes information packaging by means of alternative intonational contours of identical strings. In English, one and the same string may be assigned different intonational phrasings in order to realize different informational interpretations: the focus is associated with an H* pitch accent, links are marked by an L+H* pitch accent, and tails are structurally characterized by being deaccented. In Catalan, focal elements remain within a core clause, but ground elements are detached to a clause-peripheral position. In particular, links are detached to the left, and non-link ground elements undergo right-detachment. In the process, clitics are left behind in the core clause. Intonational structure plays a restricted role: the last item of the core clause carries an H* pitch accent.

We also concluded above that such observations provide confirmation that information packaging involves syntax as well as prosody, and suggest that any attempt to reduce information packaging either to syntax or to prosody will be inadequate from a cross-linguistic point of view. Therefore, the present account of the range of variation in the structural realization of information packaging as displayed by Catalan and English deals with intonation and word order at one and the same level. In doing so, it does not employ 'focusing' operators but, instead, makes use of 'defocusing' operators. Both in Catalan and English, these defocusing operators are higher-order functions that combine with verbs in order to license the presence of links and tails. However, whereas in Catalan the defocusing operators are realized as clitics and verbal agreement morphology, expressions which take care of 'non-basic' word order as well as deaccenting of the dislocated constituents, in English they are abstract operators that do not affect word order but merely have intonational repercussions: tail-licensing operators induce deaccenting of the relevant phrase, while link-introducing operators are responsible for the presence of L+H* pitch accent.

References

Beckman, M., and J. Pierrehumbert (1986). 'Intonational Structure in Japanese and English'. *Phonological Yearbook* **3**, pp. 15–70.

Chafe, W.L. (1976). 'Givenness, Contrastiveness, Definiteness, Subjects, Topics and Point of View'. In C.N. Li (ed.), *Subject and Topic*. Associated Press, New York.

Dahl, Ö. (1974). 'Topic-Comment Structure Revisited'. In Ö. Dahl (ed.), *Topic and Comment, Contextual Boundedness and Focus. Papers in Text Linguistics* **6**. Helmut Buske, Hamburg.

Engdahl, E. (ed.) (1994). *Integrating Information Structure into Constraint-based and Categorial Approaches*. ESPRIT Basic Research Project 6852, Dynamic Interpretation of Natural Language. DYANA-2 Deliverable R1.3.B. ILLC, University of Amsterdam.

Erteschik-Shir, N. (1996). *The Dynamics of Focus Structure*. Cambridge University Press.

Heim, I. (1982). *The Semantics of Definite and Indefinite Noun Phrases*. Ph.D. Dissertation University of Massachusetts, Amherst. Published in 1989 by Garland, New York.

Heim, I. (1983). 'File Change Semantics and the Familiarity Theory of Definiteness'. In R. Bäuerle, C. Schwarze and A. von Stechow (eds.), *Meaning, Use and Interpretation of Language*. De Gruyter, Berlin.

Hendriks, H. (1996a). 'Intonation, Derivation, Information. A Proof-Theoretic Framework for the Representation of Information Packaging'. In: M. Abrusci and C. Casadio (eds.), *Proofs and Linguistic Categories. Proceedings of the Third Roma Workshop*. Editrice CLUEB, Bologna.

Hendriks, H. (1996b). 'Information Packaging: From Cards to Boxes'. In T. Galloway and J. Spence (eds.), *Proceedings of Semantics And Linguistic Theory VI*, CLC Publications, Ithaca, New York.

Hendriks, H. (1997). 'L+H* Accent and Non-Monotone Anaphora'. To appear in: R. Kager and W. Zonneveld (eds.), *Proceedings of the Utrecht Workshop on Phrasal and Prosodic Phonology*. Foris Publications, Dordrecht.

Hendriks, H. (1998). 'A Strong Theory of Topic and Focus Interpretation'. Manuscript.

Hendriks, H., and P. Dekker (1995). 'Links without Locations'. In P. Dekker and M. Stokhof (eds.), *Proceedings of the Tenth Amsterdam Colloquium*. ILLC, University of Amsterdam.

Hobbs, J., (1990). 'The Pierrehumbert and Hirschberg Theory of Intonation Made Simple: Comments on Pierrehumbert and Hirschberg'. In P. Cohen, J. Morgan and M. Pollack (eds.), *Intentions in Communication*, MIT Press, Cambridge (Mass.).

Hoffman, B. (1995). 'Integrating "Free" Word Order Syntax and Information Structure'. Manuscript, University of Pennsylvania.

Jackendoff, R. (1972). *Semantic Interpretation in Generative Grammar*. MIT Press, Cambridge (Mass.).

Jacobs, J. (1983). *Fokus und Skalen: Zur Syntax und Semantik von Gradpartikeln im Deutschen*. Niemeyer, Tübingen.

Kamp, H. (1981). 'A Theory of Truth and Semantic Representation'. In J. Groenendijk, T. Janssen and M. Stokhof (eds.), *Formal Methods in the Study of Language*. Mathematical Centre, Amsterdam. Reprinted in J. Groenendijk, T. Janssen and M. Stokhof (eds.) (1984), *Truth, Interpretation and Information. Selected Papers from the Third Amsterdam Colloquium*. Foris, Dordrecht.

Kamp, H., and U. Reyle (1993). *From Discourse to Logic. Introduction to Modeltheoretic Semantics of Natural Language, Formal Logic and Discourse Representation Theory.* Kluwer, Dordrecht.

Kraak, E. (1995). 'French object clitics: a multimodal analysis'. In G. Morrill and R. Oehrle (eds.), *Proceedings Formal Grammar Conference*, Barcelona, pp. 166–180.

Krifka, M. (1991). 'A Compositional Semantics for Multiple Focus Constructions'. *Linguistische Berichte, Suppl.* **4**, pp. 17–53.

Lambek, J. (1958). 'The Mathematics of Sentence Structure'. *American Mathematical Monthly* **65**, pp. 154–169.

Lambek, J. (1961). 'On the Calculus of Syntactic Types'. In R. Jakobson (ed.), *Structure of Language and its Mathematical Aspects.* Providence.

Linden, E.-J. van der (1991). 'Accent Placement and Focus in Categorial Logic'. In S. Bird (ed.), *Declarative Perspectives on Phonology.* Edinburgh Working Papers in Cognitive Science. Eccs, Edinburgh.

Moortgat, M. (1996). 'Multimodal Linguistic Inference'. *Journal of Logic, Language and Information* **5**, pp. 349–385.

Moortgat, M. (1997). 'Generalized Quantification and Discontinuous Type Constructors'. In H. Bunt and A. van Horck (eds.) (1997), *Proceedings of the Tilburg Symposium on Discontinuous Dependencies.* Mouton de Gruyter, Berlin.

Moortgat, M., and G. Morrill (1991). 'Heads and Phrases. Type Calculus for Dependency and Constituent Structure'. OTS Research Paper, University of Utrecht.

Morrill, G. (1992). 'Categorial Formalisation of Relativisation: Pied Piping, Islands, and Extraction Sites'. Report de Recerca LSI-92-23-R, Departament de Llenguatges i Sistemes Informàtics, Universitat Politècnica de Catalunya.

Morrill, G. (1994). *Type Logical Grammar: Categorial Logic of Signs.* Kluwer, Dordrecht.

Muskens, R. (1993). 'A Compositional Discourse Representation Theory'. In P. Dekker and M. Stokhof (eds.), *Proceedings of the Ninth Amsterdam Colloquium.* ILLC, University of Amsterdam.

Nooteboom, S.G., and J.M.B. Terken (1982). 'What Makes Speakers Omit Pitch Accents?'. *Phonetica* **39**, pp. 317–336.

Oehrle, R. (1988). 'Multidimensional Compositional Functions as a Basis for Grammatical Analysis'. In R. Oehrle, E. Bach and D. Wheeler (eds.), *Categorial Grammars and Natural Language Structures.* Reidel, Dordrecht.

Oehrle, R. (1991). 'Prosodic Constraints on Dynamic Grammatical Analysis'. In S. Bird (ed.), *Declarative Perspectives on Phonology.* Edinburgh Working Papers in Cognitive Science. Eccs, Edinburgh.

Oehrle, R. (1994). 'Term-labeled Categorial Type Systems'. *Linguistics and Philosophy* **17**, pp. 633–678.

Pierrehumbert, J. (1980). *The Phonology and Phonetics of English Intonation.* Ph.D. Disertation MIT, Cambridge (Mass.). Distributed by the IULC.

Pierrehumbert, J., and J. Hirschberg (1990). 'The Meaning of Intonational Contours in the Interpretation of Discourse'. In P. Cohen, J. Morgan and M. Pollack (eds.), *Intentions in Communication*, MIT Press, Cambridge (Mass.).

Pollard, C., and I. Sag (1987). *Information-Based Syntax and Semantics. Vol. 1: Fundamentals.* CSLI, Stanford.

Pollard, C., and I. Sag (1994). *Head-Driven Phrase Structure Grammar.* University of Chicago Press, Chicago, and CSLI, Stanford.

Prince, E. (1981). 'Toward a Taxonomy of Given-New Information'. In P. Cole, *Radical Pragmatics.* Academic Press, New York.

Reinhart, T. (1982). 'Pragmatics and Linguistics: An Analysis of Sentence Topics'. *Philosophica* **27**, pp. 53–94.

Rooth, M. (1985). *Association with Focus*. Ph.D. Dissertation University of Massachusetts, Amherst.

Rooth, M. (1992). 'A Theory of Focus Interpretation'. *Natural Language Semantics* **1**, pp. 75–116.

Steedman, M. (1991). 'Structure and Intonation'. *Language* **67**, pp. 260–296.

Steedman, M. (1992). 'Surface Structure, Intonation and "Focus" '. In E. Klein and F. Veltman (eds.) *Natural Language and Speech. Symposium Proceedings, Brussels*. Springer, Berlin.

Steedman, M. (1993). 'The Grammar of Intonation and Focus'. In P. Dekker and M. Stokhof (eds.), *Proceedings of the Ninth Amsterdam Colloquium*. ILLC, University of Amsterdam.

Vallduví, E. (1992). *The Informational Component*. Garland, New York.

Vallduví, E. (1993). 'Information Packaging: A Survey'. Report prepared for *Word Order, Prosody, and Information Structure*. Centre for Cognitive Science and Human Communication Research Centre, University of Edinburgh.

Vallduví, E. (1994). 'The Dynamics of Information Packaging'. In E. Engdahl (ed.).

Vallduví, E., and R. Zacharski (1993). 'Accenting Phenomena, Association with Focus, and the Recursiveness of Focus-Ground'. In P. Dekker and M. Stokhof (eds.), *Proceedings of the Ninth Amsterdam Colloquium*. ILLC, University of Amsterdam.

A Linear Logic Treatment of Phrase Structure Grammars for Unbounded Dependencies

Joshua S. Hodas

Computer Science Department
Harvey Mudd College
Claremont, CA, 91711
hodas@cs.hmc.edu

Abstract. A number of researchers have proposed applications of Girard's Linear Logic [7] to computational linguistics. Most have focused primarily on the connection between linear logic and categorial grammars. In this work we show how linear logic can be used to provide an attractive encoding of phrase structure grammars for parsing structures involving unbounded dependencies. The resulting grammars are closely related to Generalized Phrase Structure Grammars [4, 5]. As part of the presentation we show how a variety of issues, such as island and coordination constraints can be dealt with in this model.

1   Introduction

Over the last several years a number of researchers have proposed applications of Girard's Linear Logic [7] to computational linguistics. On the semantics side, Dalrymple, Lamping, Pereira, and Saraswat have shown how deduction in linear logic can be used to enforce various constraints during the construction of semantic terms [1, 2, 3]. On the syntax side, Hepple, Johnson, Moortgat, Morrill, Oehrle, Roorda, and others have related linear logic to formal grammars [8, 13, 20, 21, 23, 27]. The latter body of work has focused primarily on the connection between linear logic and categorial grammars. This is natural as the Lambek Calculus [17, 18, 29] can be seen as a non-commutative linear logic.

In this work we show how linear logic can be used to provide a straightforward, perspicuous encoding of phrase structure grammars for parsing structures involving unbounded dependencies. The resulting grammars are closely related to the Generalized Phrase Structure Grammars of Gazdar [4, 5]. This work builds on earlier work by Pareschi and Miller [24, 25]. Some of this work has been described previously in the proceedings of the 1992 JICSLP [9], and in the author's dissertation [10].

The outline of this paper is as follows: In Section 2 we will review the basic principals of unbounded dependencies and their treatment in GPSG. In Section 3 we will describe the standard techniques for implementing GPSG parsers using gap-threading Definite Clause Grammars (in Prolog). In Section 4 we will describe Pareschi and Miller's methodology for implementing GPSG grammars in λProlog, an extension of Prolog based on a richer fragment of intuitionistic logic. In Section 5 we will briefly introduce linear logic, and in Sections 6-11 we will present our proposal for representing these grammars using the operators of linear logic and implementing them in the extended DCGs provided by the language Lolli, based on linear logic.

2 Unbounded Dependencies and GPSG

It is common to view a relative clause as being formed by a relative pronoun followed by a sentence that is missing a noun phrase. For example, the sentence:

John wrote the book that Jane gave to Jill.

can be thought of as having the following structure, where *gap* marks the spot where the missing noun phrase would be, if the bracketed clause were a sentence:

John wrote the book that [Jane gave *gap* to Jill].

This sort of construction is called an *unbounded dependency*, because two features (in this case the filler, that, and the *gap*) which stand in a dependency relationship can be separated in a sentence by arbitrary grammatical structures, and with the extraction site in almost any position.

Generalized Phrase Structure Grammar (GPSG) proposes a simple technique for handling structures involving unbounded dependencies, such as relative clauses and **wh** questions, using a phrase structure grammar [4, 5].[1] For example, if sentences belong to the category **S**, and noun phrases to the category **NP**, then GPSG posits a rule for (one particular form of) relative clause as:

REL⟶ REL-PRON S/NP

where **S/NP** is the *derived category* of sentences missing a noun phrase. This requires, in turn, that rules be given for the derived category. These new rules are generated from the original grammar in a relatively straightforward manner. So, for instance, if the original grammar were:

$$\textbf{S} \longrightarrow \textbf{NP VP} \qquad \textbf{NP} \longrightarrow \textbf{PN} \qquad \textbf{VP} \longrightarrow \textbf{TV NP}$$
$$\textbf{NP} \longrightarrow \textbf{DET N} \qquad \textbf{VP} \longrightarrow \textbf{DTV NP NP}$$

then the new grammar, which allows relative clauses in noun phrases, would consist of those rules, augmented with the rules:

---

[1] Note that when we refer to 'GPSG' we will mean the simpler, earlier version cited. The later, 'modern' version [6] introduces a variety of changes that are orthoganal to our work. For instance, in spite of its name, it essentially drops the phrase-structure style of presentation in favor of so-called node admissibility rules. It is simply easier to describe our proposals in terms of the earlier style of presentation. The ideas presented, however, should be applicable to the modern presentation and its follow-ons, such as HPSG.

NP $\longrightarrow$ **DET N REL**
REL $\longrightarrow$ **REL-PRON S/NP**

S/NP $\longrightarrow$ **NP VP/NP**   **VP/NP** $\longrightarrow$ **TV NP/NP**
                              VP/NP $\longrightarrow$ **DTV NP/NP NP**
NP/NP $\longrightarrow$ ϵ **VP/NP** $\longrightarrow$ **DTV NP NP/NP**

In general, for each rule in the original grammar which defines a category that could dominate an **NP** (i.e., could occur above an **NP** in a parse tree) there will be a new version of that rule for each category on the right of the rule that could dominate an **NP**.

2.1   Island Constraints

Note, however, that we have not included the derived rule:

S/NP $\longrightarrow$ **NP/NP VP**

This was done in order to block extraction from within the subject noun phrase of the subordinate sentence, which is generally not allowed in English. For example, were the grammar extended to handle stative verbs and prepositional phrases, then this rule would incorrectly admit such sentences as:

* John wrote the book that [the story in *gap* is long].

This sort of restriction, in which certain constructions are disallowed in certain positions, is called an *island constraint* [28]. We will have more to say about this particular island constraint, which is sometimes called the *generalized left-branch condition*, below.

3   GPSG as Definite Clause Grammars

GPSG-style grammars may be implemented as Prolog Definite Clause Grammars in a variety of ways. Obviously, the grammar could be implemented directly as a DCG with rules defining the base categories as well as each of the derived categories. This is not an attractive option, however. Depending on the number of derived categories, the resulting grammar can be substantially (potentially quadratically) larger than the core grammar on which it is based. Gazdar points out, however, that since the rules for the derived categories are formed so uniformly from the original grammar, it is possible to use the original grammar on its own, together with switches controlling whether the parser uses a rule as is or in derived form [4, page 161].

To understand how this idea can be implemented in DCG grammars, consider for example the two rules:

S $\longrightarrow$ **NP VP**   **S/NP** $\longrightarrow$ **NP VP/NP**

If we think in terms of a switch variable named Gap that can have two values, gap and nogap, then these two rules can be mapped to the single DCG clause:

```
s(Gap) --> np, vp(Gap).
```

When the variable Gap is instantiated to nogap this clause corresponds to the first, core, rule. When it is instantiated to gap it corresponds to the second rule. Building on this idea, the grammar above can be implemented with the following DCG:

```
s        --> s(nogap).
s(Gap) --> np(nogap), vp(Gap).

np(gap)     --> [].
np(nogap)   --> pn.
np(nogap)   --> det, n.
np(nogap)   --> det, n, rel.

rel    --> rel-pron, s{gap}

vp(Gap) --> tv, np(Gap).
vp(Gap) --> dtv, np(Gap), np(nogap).
vp(Gap) --> dtv, np(nogap), np(Gap).
```

Each rule where the head is parameterized by the constant nogap corresponds to a rule in the core grammar only, while those with heads parameterized by gap are slashed rules only. Rules parameterized by the variable Gap act as core rules when the variable is instantiated to nogap, but as slashed rules when it is instantiated to gap. It is easy to see that this DCG implements the given GPSG grammar faithfully.

This implementation has problems though. First, as pointed out by Pereira and Shieber, because the two DCG rules for verb phrases with ditransitive verbs are identical when Gap is instantiated to nogap, simple sentences with ditransitive verbs will have two identical parses, depending on which rule is used in the parse [26]. In addition, the system of switches is too limited for grammars intended to handle multiple extractions from nested structures. (This problem is actually present in GPSG itself, since there is only a single level of slashing.) Therefore gap-threading parsers (as these are called) are typically implemented with a difference list of gaps in place of the simple toggle. In such an implementation, the DCG above becomes:

```
s              --> s([]-[]).
s(F0-F)        --> np([]-[]), vp(F0-F).

np([gap|F]-F) --> [].
np(F-F)        --> pn.
np(F-F)        --> det, np([]-[]).
np(F-F)        --> det, np([]-[]), rel.
```

```
rel              --> rel-pron, s([gap|F]-F).

vp(F0-F)         --> tv, np(F0-F).
vp(F0-F)         --> dtv, np(F0-F1), np(F1-F).
```

Although the difference list in this example will never grow beyond a single element, in more complex grammars it can. Notice, though, that there is now just a single rule for ditransitive verb phrases. The difference list of gaps is divided between the two object noun phrases; if there is just one gap in the list it can be used in only one of the two noun phrases. This technique for implementing GPSG parsers has been developed extensively by Pereira and Shieber [26] and others.

Unfortunately, while using a difference list to manage gap distribution solves the problems mentioned, the solution is still unsatisfactory. In particular, a problem common to both implementations is that they introduce a good deal of complexity in constructing the grammar. Insuring that gap distribution among substructures is handled correctly can be quite subtle. Precisely because the filler-gap dependency is unbounded, portions of the grammar that seem unconnected with the problem at hand require significant adjustment to insure that they do not interfere with the transmission of the gap information from the gap's introduction to its discharge, since the two may be separated by almost any structure.

4   GPSG in Intuitionistic Logic

Notice that the DCG implementation of the grammar includes the rule:

```
np(gap) --> [].
```

which, if we ignore the switch argument, corresponds to the grammar rule:

NP $\longrightarrow \epsilon$

This rule states that it is possible to have a noun phrase with no surface structure. In some sense the purpose of the switches, the difference lists, and even the slashes, is to control when this rule can be used. These machinations are necessary because DCG's and PSG's, like Horn clauses, are flat; all rules are global.

In his dissertation, and later in a paper with Miller, Pareschi proposed using the expanded formula language of λProlog (which is based on a larger fragment of intuitionistic logic than is Prolog) to enhance the expressiveness of DCG's [25]. In particular, Pareschi proposed using the $\supset$ operator to restrict the scope of the **NP** $\longrightarrow \epsilon$ rule to the derivation of the **S** that forms the body of the relative clause. The proof rule for $\supset$ is written:

$$\frac{\Gamma, A \longrightarrow B}{\Gamma \longrightarrow A \supset B} \supset R$$

If we take the λProlog view that logic programming is the bottom-up search for cut-free proofs in intuitionistic logic, then this rule states that in order to prove a formula of the form $A \supset B$, add the formula A to your assumptions and then attempt to prove the formula B. This limits the scope of the clause A to the search for the (sub)proof of the goal B [22].

We can imagine augmenting the standard DCG syntax with the '=>' operator to represent intuitionistic implication. Then, using Pareschi's ideas (which were stated in terms of raw λProlog clauses, not this extended DCG syntax) we arrive at the following implementation of the grammar in which the implication is used to restrict the scope (i.e. availability) of the rule for gap noun phrases:

```
s   --> np, vp.

np --> pn.
np --> det, n.
np --> det, n, rel.

rel --> rel-pron, (np --> []) => s.

vp --> tv, np.
vp --> dtv, np, np.
```

The key feature of this implementation is that the bulk of the grammar is unchanged from the core grammar. The only gap-related machinery is in the rule for relative clauses. It states that a string is a relative clause if it begins with a relative pronoun, and the remainder can be parsed as a sentence once we assume the presence of a rule for empty noun phrases. The newly assumed rule may be used to complete any rule looking for an **NP** during the parse of the subordinate **S**, but is available only during that sub-parse.

4.1   Island Constraints

In order to handle restrictions on where a gap is allowable (such as the restriction on extraction from a subject noun phrase already discussed), Pareschi proposed modifying the general scheme to load so-called "gap locator" rules rather than the gap noun phrase rules themselves. These gap locator rules are just partially interpreted versions of the rules that can use the gap. So for instance, rather than assuming a gap noun phrase rule, the rule for relative clauses might assume two appropriately modified verb phrase rules, as in:

```
rel --> rel-pron, (vp --> tv) => (vp --> dtv, np) => s.
```

While this technique works, it is roughly equivalent to defining the grammar to include rules for derived categories up front, and can become quite cumbersome if there are many categories immediately dominated by **S** which can dominate an **NP**.

4.2 Problems Due to Contraction and Weakening

A serious problem with this simple representation, which Pareschi recognized, is that, as mentioned above, the np --> [] rule can be used to complete *any* rule looking for an **NP** during the parse of the subordinate **S**. In particular, it could, for instance, be used to fill both the direct and indirect object positions in a ditransitive verb phrase. So, for example, the grammar above incorrectly admits:

* John wrote the book that [Jane gave *gap gap*].

Similarly, there is no method to require that an introduced gap be used. The grammar therefore admits:

* John wrote the book that [Jane read a magazine].

4.3 A Partial Solution

Pareschi's solution to the first problem was to take advantage of the fact that he was working with λProlog clauses rather than in the DCG syntax. These clauses include a difference list of words from the input stream as parameters to each terminal and non-terminal. By directly manipulating the quantification of the variables used for the difference lists it is possible to block the multiple extractions.

The solution relies on the fact that the intended translation of the augmented DCG syntax:

```
rel --> rel-pron, (np --> nil) => s.
```

is that the assumed rule is to have the same quantifier treatment as any other rule. So the translation into λProlog clauses would be:[2]

```
rel S0 S1 :- rel-pron S0 S2, (pi T0 \ (np T0 T0)) => s S2 S1.
```

Pareschi noted that if the explicit quantification of T0 is dropped, then it will be implicitly quantified at the outer limits of the clause for rel, and when the gap noun phrase rule is added to the program in an attempt to parse a relative clause, T0 will be an uninstantiated logic variable. The first time that rule is used to fill a noun phrase in the subordinate sentence structure the variable will become instantiated to that string position. After that the rule cannot be used to complete a different noun phrase, unless the parse fails back to some point before this. Unfortunately, this technique does not work to block double use of a gap if the presumed occurrences are next to each other (as in the example above) since the two gaps then have identical locator values.[3]

---

[2] For historical reasons, λProlog uses pi to denote universal quantification, and uses a curried syntax for application.

[3] This problem was pointed out by Fernando Pereira in private communication.

In the second case Pareschi's solution relied on the fact that his system builds semantic terms in conjunction with parse trees, and that the ungrammatical example in which the assumed gap noun phrase rule is ignored would have a vacuous abstraction —i.e. a term of the form $\lambda x.t$ where x is not free in t— in the semantic term constructed for the relative clause. Pareschi, therefore, discarded any parse that constructed a semantic term with a vacuous abstraction.

These solutions are not entirely satisfying. First, as pointed out, they are only partial solutions to the given problems. Equally seriously from a philosophical standpoint, it seems unfortunate that dual problems of multiplicity and relevance in the treatment of the assumed noun phrase rule should have such disparate solutions. The solutions feel a bit too close to "hacking" the grammar.

5   Linear Logic

In recognizing the limitations of his system, Pareschi suggested that a solution might be found in Girard's linear logic, which at the time had only recently been introduced [7].

The problem of allowing multiple extractions with a single gap introduction is due to the free availability of the *contraction* rule:

$$\frac{\Gamma, A, A \longrightarrow B}{\Gamma, A \longrightarrow B} \; C$$

in traditional logics. Similarly, the problem of vacuous gap introduction is due to the *weakening* rule:

$$\frac{\Gamma \longrightarrow B}{\Gamma, A \longrightarrow B} \; W$$

In linear logic, each of these rules is significantly limited in scope: they can each only be applied to assumptions that are marked with the modal operator '!'.

While the operator rules of intuitionistic linear logic are similar to those of ordinary intuitionistic logic, because of the restrictions on the structural rules there are two forms of conjunction, disjunction, and truth, which differ based on the way they treat the proof context. To understand the need for two conjunctions, for instance, consider two ways of specifying the right-hand conjunction in intuitionistic logic:

$$\frac{\Gamma \longrightarrow A \quad \Gamma \longrightarrow B}{\Gamma \longrightarrow A \wedge B} \; \wedge R \qquad \frac{\Gamma \longrightarrow A \quad \Delta \longrightarrow B}{\Gamma, \Delta \longrightarrow A \wedge B} \; \wedge R$$

In the presence of the contraction rule, these two formulations are equivalent, since the former rule can be replaced with the proof:

$$\frac{\dfrac{\Gamma \longrightarrow A \quad \Gamma \longrightarrow B}{\Gamma, \Gamma \longrightarrow A \wedge B} \; \wedge R}{\Gamma \longrightarrow A \wedge B} \; C^*$$

Figure 1 gives the rules for a fragment of intuitionistic linear logic which forms the foundation of the progrmaming language Lolli (named for the linear logic

$$\frac{}{B \longrightarrow B} \ \text{identity} \qquad \frac{}{\Delta \longrightarrow \top} \ TR$$

$$\frac{\Delta, B_i \longrightarrow C}{\Delta, B_1 \& B_2 \longrightarrow C} \ \&L \ (i = 1, 2) \qquad \frac{\Delta \longrightarrow B \quad \Delta \longrightarrow C}{\Delta \longrightarrow B \& C} \ \&R$$

$$\frac{\Delta, B_1, B_2 \longrightarrow C}{\Delta, B_1 \otimes B_2 \longrightarrow C} \ \otimes L \qquad \frac{\Delta_1 \longrightarrow B \quad \Delta_2 \longrightarrow C}{\Delta_1, \Delta_2 \longrightarrow B \otimes C} \ \otimes R$$

$$\frac{\Delta_1 \longrightarrow B \quad \Delta_2, C \longrightarrow E}{\Delta_1, \Delta_2, B \multimap C \longrightarrow E} \ \multimap L \qquad \frac{\Delta, B \longrightarrow C}{\Delta \longrightarrow B \multimap C} \ \multimap R$$

$$\frac{\Delta \longrightarrow C}{\Delta, !B \longrightarrow C} \ !W \qquad \frac{\Delta, !B, !B \longrightarrow C}{\Delta, !B \longrightarrow C} \ !C \qquad \frac{\Delta, B \longrightarrow C}{\Delta, !B \longrightarrow C} \ !D \qquad \frac{!\Delta \longrightarrow B}{!\Delta \longrightarrow !B} \ !R$$

$$\frac{\Delta, B[t/x] \longrightarrow C}{\Delta, \forall x.B \longrightarrow C} \ \forall L \qquad \frac{\Delta \longrightarrow B[y/x]}{\Delta \longrightarrow \forall x.B} \ \forall R,$$

provided that y is not free in the lower sequent.

Fig. 1. A proof system for a fragment of linear logic

implication operator, $\multimap$, known as lollipop). The applications and proof theory of this fragment have been discussed extensively in prior works [12, 11, 10]. Of crucial importance is that there is a straightforward bottom-up, goal-directed proof procedure (conceptually similar to the one used for Prolog) that is sound and complete for this fragment of linear logic.

6 GPSG in Linear Logic

The solution, then, is simple. The core rules of the grammar are represented by formulas (assumptions) marked with the modal !, meaning they can be contracted and weakened. That is, they can be used as many times as needed, or not at all. In contrast, The temporary rules for gap noun phrases are added as formulas without the modal marker. The introduced gap is thereby represented by a bounded resource, and it must be used exactly once in the subordinate sentence.

Thus if we augment DCG syntax with the operator $\multimap$ representing linear implication, then the rule for relative clauses becomes:

```
s    --> np, vp.


np  --> pn.
np  --> det, n.
np  --> det, n, rel.


rel --> rel-pron, (np --> []) -o s.
```

```
vp  --> tv, np.
vp  --> dtv, np, np.
```

In order to insure that the gap rules are managed correctly, we must assume that the comma and DCG arrow now stand for '⊗' and 'o−' respectively (as opposed to ∧ and ⊂). Each time a '⊗' conjunction goal is encountered during the parse of the subordinate S, the gap noun phrase rule is carried up into the proof of only one side of the conjunction. This eliminates the problem of the introduced gap being discharged more than once. Similarly, the relevance constraint on unmarked assumptions will insure that the assumed gap will be discharged.

7   Coordination Constraints

In addition to yielding solutions to the problems that Pareschi and Miller encountered, the linear logic setting affords simple treatments of other parsing issues. One particularly nice feature of this system is its ability to specify the management of gaps across coordinate structures, such as conjunctions. GPSG proposes that any category can be expanded by the conjunction of two or more structures of the same category. So, for instance:

S ⟶ S and S.

It is required, however, that any gaps discharged in one conjunct also be discharged in the other. If the language level conjunction is represented in the grammar by the second form of logical conjunction, '&', then such *coordination constraints* are handled automatically. Since the '&' goal duplicates the linear context into both branches of the proof, both of the subordinate parses must consume the same gaps. Thus, if the clause:

```
s   --> (s, [and]) & s.
```

is added to the grammar,[4] then the system will admit the sentences

[John wrote the book] and [Jane read the magazine].

and

John wrote the book that [[Jane read *gap*] and [Jill discarded *gap*]].

but will reject:

---

[4] In reality, since performing a parse in this setting corresponds to top-down parsing, we cannot add this or any similar rule to the proof as it would cause the parser to loop. Thus we must actually add a rule of the form:

```
s --> (np, vp, [and::nil]) & (np, vp).
```

but this is a technical issue only.

* John wrote the book that [[Jane read *gap*] and [Jill discarded the magazine]].

Of course this last will be accepted with the bracketing:

* [John wrote the book that [Jane read *gap*]] and [Jill discarded the magazine].

8 Island Constraints

Recall from Figure 1 that the proof rule for ! in a goal is:

$$\frac{!\Gamma \longrightarrow A}{!\Gamma \longrightarrow !A} \; !_R$$

This states that a !'ed goal can only be proven in a context where all the assumptions are !'ed.

It is possible to take advantage of this definition to specify restrictions on extraction in the grammar. A gap noun phrase rule, which is not marked with the ! modal, cannot be used during the parse of a substructure whose non-terminal is marked with the !. Thus, for example, in order to block extraction from subject noun phrases, the first rule of the grammar can be rewritten as:

```
s --> {np}, vp.
```

where the use of {} marks the goal as !'ed. [5]

If $!\Gamma$ is the grammar above, with the first rule modified as stated, together with lexical definitions for a sufficient set of words, then attempting to parse the relative clause:

that [Jane saw *gap*]

leads to a proof of the form shown in Figure 2. In contrast, attempting to parse the clause:

* that [the story in *gap* is long]

will fail, because the gap *np* formula will be unavailable for use in the branch of the proof attempting to parse the **NP** "*the story in *gap*", since the !'ed *np* goal forces the gap *np* in the linear context to the other side of the tree.

At first glance it might appear that using this method would then require that ordinary nouns have a type assignment of the form:

john : !**NP**

---

[5] Braces are used for this purpose in Lolli in order to allow the ! to be scoped over a compound goal. Note that this use conflicts with their existing use for embedding Prolog code in a DCG clause. An alternate syntax is therefore used for embedding Lolli code in Lolli DCG clauses.

$$\dfrac{\dfrac{!\Gamma \longrightarrow pn([jane, saw]), [saw])}{\dfrac{!\Gamma \longrightarrow np([jane, saw], [saw])}{!\Gamma \longrightarrow !np([jane, saw], [saw])} \, !_R} \ast \quad \dfrac{\dfrac{!\Gamma \longrightarrow tv([saw], []) \quad \dfrac{t_0 = []}{!\Gamma, \forall t_0.np(t_0, t_0) \longrightarrow np([], [])} \ast}{\dfrac{!\Gamma, \forall t_0.np(t_0, t_0) \longrightarrow tv([saw], []) \otimes np([], [])}{!\Gamma, \forall t_0.np(t_0, t_0) \longrightarrow vp([saw], [])} \ast} \otimes_R}{\dfrac{!\Gamma, \forall t_0.np(t_0, t_0) \longrightarrow !np([jane, saw], [saw]) \otimes vp([saw], [])}{\dfrac{!\Gamma, \forall t_0.np(t_0, t_0) \longrightarrow s([jane, saw], [])}{\dfrac{!\Gamma \longrightarrow (\forall t_0.np(t_0, t_0)) \multimap s([jane, saw], [])}{!\Gamma \longrightarrow rel([that, jane, saw], [])} \ast} \multimap_R} \ast} \otimes_R}$$

Fig. 2. The Parse/Proof of "that jane saw"

so that they might be used to satisfy the subject noun phrase. It is important to note, however, that, unlike categorial grammar and similar systems, we are not supposing that the words of the string being parsed are among the assumptions of the proof. Rather they occur at the term level in the implicit difference list arguments. The lexicon itself is among the !'ed assumptions and contains assignments of the form:

$$!(john : \mathbf{NP})$$

8.1 Problems With This Approach

Unfortunately, this technique is a bit too coarse-grained. For instance, it blocks the acceptance of

who [*gap* saw Jane]

which should be allowed —the restriction on extraction from the subject noun should not block extraction of the entire subject, only its substructures. This problem can be circumvented by having multiple rules for relative clauses: one, as we have already shown, which introduces a gap and attempts to parse for an **S**, and one which simply attempts to parse for a **VP**. The other choice would be to avoid the use of '!' entirely by using gap locator rules as in Pareschi's system; but this seems unattractive for reasons already cited.

A subtler problem is that the use of ! blocks all extractions from the subject, not just the extraction of noun phrases. This could become an issue if other types of gaps were introduced.

9 Pied Piping

An interesting construction related to relative clauses is the so-called "pied-piping" construction, in which the relative pronoun is not the filler, but rather is properly embedded as the rightmost constituent within the filler. An example of this, taken from Pareschi, is the relative clause:

the sister of whom [Paul married *gap*]

In this case, the filler can be seen as being formed by concatenating the relative pronoun onto an **NP/NP**, with the added restriction that the *gap* occur only as the rightmost element of the **NP/NP**. It is interesting that this sort of restricted extraction is exactly the sort that can be modeled well in Categorial Grammar, which cannot model arbitrary extraction well. In contrast, in our system, which handles arbitrary extractions easily, there is no straightforward way to restrict the location of the gap to one particular position.

If we are willing to leave the representation of grammar rules as propositional formulas, and move to the representation with explicit string lists and quantifiers (as Pareschi did) then we can also adopt Pareschi's solution to this problem. Consider the clauses:

```
rel  S0 S1 :- relf S0 S2, (forall T0 \ (np T0 T0)) -o s S2 S1.
relf S0 S1 :- (np S2 S2) -o np S0 S2, rel-pron S2 S1.
```

The first clause just replaces the clause for relative pronouns with one in which the filler is in the new category **RELF**. The second clause says that a **RELF** is either just a relative pronoun (if the assumed gap is used immediately to fill in for the noun phrase, in which case $s_2 = s_0$), or it is an **NP/NP** followed by a relative pronoun. Notice, though, that the rule assumed for the gap does not have its string position variables universally quantified. Rather they are pre-bound to the same position as the end of the **NP/NP**. Thus the gap can only be used in that position.

10 Parasitic Gaps

Historically, one of the most difficult filler-gap constructions to handle is the so-called "parasitic gaps" in which a single filler can be used to fill two gaps, but, unlike coordinate structures, the second gap is optional. For instance, both of the following standard examples are acceptable noun phrases:

The book that [I discarded *gap* [without reading *gap*]]
The book that [I discarded *gap* [without reading the index]]

Pareschi proposes parsing such constructions by introducing two gaps but relaxing the relevance constraint on the second. Unfortunately, in the fragment of linear logic used here there is no simple way to relax the relevance constraint. Another possible solution is to construct a special coordination constraint between the two verb phrases as in the following two clauses:

```
vp  --> (vp, [without]) &  vp.
vp  --> (vp, [without]) , {vp}.
```

The first rule is for the case in which the parasitic gap occurs, and the second for when it does not. In the second rule it is necessary to ensure that the gap is used in the first verb phrase and not the second, since otherwise the grammar would admit:

* The book that [I discarded the magazine [without reading *gap*]]

Thus the **VP** is marked with a ! to restrict extraction from within it.

11 Other Types of Filler-Gap Dependencies

While the examples have thus far dealt only with relative clauses, GPSG proposes similar treatments of other sorts of unbounded dependencies. For instance, given a category **Q** of non-**wh** questions, the category can be expanded to cover some **wh** questions with GPSG rules of the form:

Q $\longrightarrow$ **wh-NP Q/NP**

So that from questions like:

Did Jane read the book?

one gets:

What [did Jane read *gap*]?

It should be apparent that such extensions are easy to add in this setting. Figures 3 and 4 shows a larger grammar than those presented up till now that parses several forms of sentences and questions. This grammar is designed to return the parse tree it constructs as an argument of the non-terminal parsed. Only the grammar itself is shown, the pre-terminals and lexicon are removed for the sake of brevity. Figure 5 shows a sample interaction with the parser, with several examples like those from the paper properly parsed or rejected. Note that a translator (written in Lolli) from the augmented DCG syntax to Lolli syntax is included with the current Lolli distribution.

12 The Problem of Crossing Dependencies

Using linear logic as the foundation of this sort of system induces what may be considered either a bug or a feature, depending on one's point of view. In constructing a grammar designed to admit constructions with multiple extractions from nested structures, it is not possible to block the generation of parse trees in which the filler-gap pairs are allowed to cross. Thus, when asked to parse the question:

Which book [did you wonder who [john told *gap* that [you wrote *gap*]]]?

a version of the large grammar modified to mark gap introduction/discharge site pairs with unique names produces two distinct parse trees, shown in Figure 6. In the first parse tree, which is correct, the introduction/discharge pairs are nested. In the second pair they overlap, which is not allowed in English.

The problem is caused by the fact that linear logic is a commutative logic. Thus, once the gap rules are loaded into the linear context they can be rearranged

```
GRAMMAR big_grammar.

parse Str Tree :- explode_words Str Lst,
                  (sent Tree Lst nil ; quest Tree Lst nil).

sent (sent NP VP)  --> {np NP}, vp VP.
sent (and (sent NP1 VP1) (sent NP2 VP2)) -->
      {np NP1}, vp VP1, [and]   &   {np NP2}, vp VP2.

quest (quest VFA NP AP) --> vfa VFA, np NP, ap AP.
quest (quest VFA NP VP) --> vfa VFA, np NP, vp VP.
quest (quest NPWH Q)    --> npwh NPWH, np (np gap) -o quest Q.
quest (quest APW  Q)    --> apwh APW, ap (ap gap) -o quest Q.
quest (quest PPW  Q)    --> ppwh PPW, pp (pp gap) -o quest Q.
quest (quest NPWH VP)   --> npwh NPWH, vp VP.

npwh (npwh NWH) --> nwh NWH.
npwh (npwh which OptAP N) --> [which], optap OptAP, n N.

apwh (apwh AWH) --> awh AWH.

ppwh (ppwh PWH) --> pwh PWH.

sbar (sbar that S) --> [that], sent S.
qbar (qbar NPWH VP) --> npwh NPWH, vp VP.
qbar (qbar NPWH S)  --> npwh NPWH, np (np gap) -o sent S.
```

Fig. 3. A Large Lolli Definite Clause Grammar (Part I).

in any order. To solve this problem at the logical level will presumably require examining non-commutative variants of the logic. In the meantime, a simple extra-logical solution is available which relies on the ordering of the Lolli search procedure. First, modify the gap introductions to be of the form:

```
rel --> (npgap --> nil) -o s.
```

then, add rules of the form:

```
np -->  once npgap.
```

where once is a Lolli extralogical that tests its argument and lets it succeed at most once. This way when a gap is used, only the most recently introduced gap of the appropriate type can be used. The parse cannot re-succeed using an earlier gap. It is interesting to note that this reintroduces what GPSG calls *gap termination rules*, which were, until now, unnecessary in this setting.

It is worth noting, however, that crossing dependencies are allowed in a limited form in some languages. Until now there have been few formalisms that could admit such constructions.

```
np (np PNposs) --> pnposs PNposs.
np (np Det Nposs OptPP OptRel) -->
               det Det, nposs Nposs, optpp OptPP, optrel OptRel.

pnposs (pnposs PN) --> pn PN.
pnposs (pnposs PN s Nposs) --> pn PN, [s], nposs Nposs.

nposs (nposs OptAP N) --> optap OptAP, n N.
nposs (nposs OptAP N s Nposs) --> optap OptAP, n N, [s], nposs Nposs.

vp (vp DV NP PP)     --> dv DV,  np NP, pp PP.
vp (vp TV NP)        --> tv TV,  np NP.
vp (vp IV OptPP)     --> iv IV,  optpp OptPP.
vp (vp Stv Sbar)     --> stv Stv, sbar Sbar.
vp (vp TV NP Sbar) --> tv TV,  np NP, sbar Sbar.
vp (vp Qv Qbar)      --> qv Qv,  qbar Qbar.
vp (vp Vfa VP)       --> vfa Vfa, vp VP.
vp (vp Vfa AP)       --> vfa Vfa, ap AP.

optpp (optpp epsilon) --> nil.
optpp (optpp PP)        --> pp PP.
pp (pp P NP) --> p P, np NP.

optap (optap epsilon) --> nil.
optap (optap AP)        --> ap AP.
ap (ap A) --> a A.

optrel (optrel epsilon) --> nil.
optrel (optrel Rel)       --> rel Rel.
rel (rel that VP)    --> [that], {vp VP}.
rel (rel who VP)     --> [who],  {vp VP}.
rel (rel that S)     --> [that], {np (np gap) -o sent S}.
rel (rel whom S)     --> [whom], {np (np gap) -o sent S}.
rel (rel P whom S)   --> p P, [whom], {pp (pp gap) -o sent S}.
rel (rel P which S) --> p P, [which], {pp (pp gap) -o sent S}.
```

Fig. 4. A Large Lolli Definite Clause Grammar (Part II).

13 The Question of Complexity

When faced with a new grammar formalism, one of the first questions one wants
answered is what the computational complexity of the accepted languages is.
This is important both because it offers a lower bound on the efficiency of parsers
that can be built, and because it provides an immediate feel for how likely
an explanation of natural language the system might be. Interest is currently
focused on systems that are slightly more complex than context free, such as
Steedman's Combinatory Categorial Grammars [29] and Joshi's Tree Adjoining
Grammars [14, 15].

```
?- parse 'the program that john wrote halted' T.

T <- s (np (det the) (nposs (n program))) (optpp epsilon)
        (optrel (rel that (s (np (pnposs (pn john)))
                              (vp (tv wrote) (np gap)))))))
     (vp (iv halted) (optpp epsilon)).


?- parse 'i told mary that john wondered who jane saw' T.

T <- s (np (pnposs (pn i)))
       (vp (tv told) (np (pnposs (pn mary)))
          (sbar that (s (np (pnposs (pn john)))
                     (vp (qv wondered)
                        (qbar (npwh (nwh who))
                           (s (np (pnposs (pn jane)))
                              (vp (tv saw) (np gap)))))))))) .


?- parse 'i told that john wondered who jane saw sally' T.

no


?- parse 'which computer did john write the program on' T.

T <- q (npwh which (optap epsilon) (n computer))
       (q (vfa did) (np (pnposs (pn john)))
          (vp (dv write) (np (det the) (nposs (n program))
                              (optpp epsilon) (optrel epsilon))
             (pp (p on) (np gap)))) .
```

Fig. 5. A Sample Interaction With The Large Lolli Definite Clause Grammar.

It is a legitimate question to ask then, what is the computational complexity of the formalism underlying these parsers. At present we are prepared to provide only a partial answer. It is well known that fragments of propositional linear logic are far more complex than equivalent fragments of intuitionistic logic. Lincoln, et al. have shown that full propositional intuitionistic linear logic is undecidable [19]. More recently, Kanovich has claimed that if G is a formula built out of a single propositional letter, '$\multimap$', and '&', and Γ and Δ are multisets of such formulas, then the system in which sequents are of the form:

$$!\Gamma, \Delta \longrightarrow G$$

is also undecidable [16]. This is significant, since it is clearly a sublanguage of

```
quest (npwh which (optap epsilon) (n book) Gap_5492)
     (quest (vfa did)
            (np (pnposs (pn you)))
            (vp (qv wonder)
                (qbar (npwh (nwh who) Gap_30922)
                      (sent (np (pnposs (pn john)))
                            (vp (tv told) (np Gap_30922)
                                (sbar that (sent (np (pnposs (pn you)))
                                                 (vp (tv wrote)
                                                     (np Gap_5492))
     )))))))
```

```
quest (npwh which (optap epsilon) (n book) Gap_5492)
     (quest (vfa did)
            (np (pnposs (pn you)))
            (vp (qv wonder)
                (qbar (npwh (nwh who) Gap_30922)
                      (sent (np (pnposs (pn john)))
                            (vp (tv told) (np Gap_5492)
                                (sbar that (sent (np (pnposs (pn you)))
                                                 (vp (tv wrote)
                                                     (np Gap_30922))
     ))))))).
```

Fig. 6. Two parses of the question "Which book [did you wonder who [john told *gap* that [you wrote *gap*]]]?" demonstrating the problem of crossing dependencies.

the fragment we are considering here. This is not necessarily bad news, though. While the propositional variant of our fragment is apparently undecidable, the grammars we have constructed do not begin to utilize the full formula language. In particular, our grammar rules have had only a single level of nested implications. It seems likely that if we impose this as a formal restriction we may obtain a significantly less expressive (and complex) language.

References

1. Mary Dalrymple, John Lamping, Fernando Pereira, and Vijay Saraswat. Linear logic for meaning assembly. In *Proceedings of the Workshop on Computational Logic for Natural Language Processing*, 1995.
2. Mary Dalrymple, John Lamping, Fernando Pereira, and Vijay Saraswat. *A Deductive Account of Quantification in LFG*. Center for the Study of Language and Information, Stanford, California, 1996.
3. Mary Dalrymple, John Lamping, Fernando Pereira, and Vijay Saraswat. Quantifiers, anaphora, and intensionality. *Journal of Logic, Language, and Information*, 6(3):219 – 273, 1997.

4. Gerald J. M. Gazdar. Unbounded dependencies and coordinate structure. *Linguistic Inquiry*, 12(2):154–184, 1981.

5. Gerald J. M. Gazdar. Phrase structure grammar. In P. Jacobson and G. K. Pullum, editors, *The Nature of Syntactic Representation*, pages 131–186. Reidel, Dordrecht, 1982.

6. Gerald J. M. Gazdar, Ewan Klein, Geoffrey K. Pullum, and Ivan Sag. *Generalized Phrase Structure Grammar*. Harvard University Press, Cambridge, Mass., 1985.

7. Jean-Yves Girard. Linear logic. *Theoretical Computer Science*, 50:1–102, 1987.

8. Mark Hepple. Hybrid categorial logics. *Bulletin of the Interest Group in Pure and Applied Logics*, 3(2.3), 1995.

9. Joshua Hodas. Specifying filler-gap dependency parsers in a linear-logic programming language. In K. Apt, editor, *Proceedings of the Joint International Conference and Symposium on Logic Programming*, pages 622 – 636, 1992.

10. Joshua S. Hodas. *Logic Programming in Intuitionistic Linear Logic: Theory, Design, and Implementation*. PhD thesis, University of Pennsylvania, Department of Computer and Information Science, May 1994.

11. Joshua S. Hodas and Dale Miller. Logic programming in a fragment of intuitionistic linear logic. *Journal of Information and Computation*, 1994. To appear.

12. Joshus Hodas and Dale Miller. Logic programming in a fragment of intuitionistic linear logic: Extended abstract. In G. Kahn, editor, *Sixth Annual Symposium on Logic in Computer Science*, pages 32 – 42, Amsterdam, July 1991.

13. Mark Johnson. Resource-sensitivity in lexical-functional grammar. In *Proceedings of the Roma Workshop*, 1996.

14. A.K. Joshi. An introduction to tree adjoining grammars. In A. Manaster-Ramer, editor, *The Mathematics of Language*. Benjamins, 1986.

15. Aravind K. Joshi. Tree adjoining grammars: How much context-sensitivity is required to provide reasonable structural description? In David Dowty, Lauri Karttunen, and Arnold Zwicky, editors, *Natural language processing: psycholinguistic, computational and theoretical perspectives*, pages 206–250. Cambridge University Press, New York, 1983.

16. Max Kanovich. The expressive power of initial fragments of linear logic. A talk given at the Linear Logic Workshop, Cornell University, June 1993.

17. J. Lambek. The mathematics of sentence structure. *American Mathematical Monthly*, 65:154 – 169, 1958.

18. J. Lambek and P. J. Scott. *Introduction to Higher Order Categorical Logic*. Cambridge University Press, 1986.

19. P. Lincoln, J. Mitchell, A. Scedrov, and N. Shankar. Decision problems for propositional linear logic. Technical Report SRI-CSL-90-08, SRI International, 1990.

20. Michael Moortgat. Unambiguous proof representations for the lambek calculus. In *Proceedings of the 8th Amsterdam Colloquium*, 1991.

21. Glyn Morrill. Clausal proof nets and discontinuity. In *Proceedings of the London Workshop on Proof Theory and Linguistic Analysis*, 1994.

22. Gopalan Nadathur and Dale Miller. An Overview of λProlog. In *Fifth International Logic Programming Conference*, pages 810–827, Seattle, Washington, August 1988. MIT Press.

23. Richard T. Oehrle. Forms of labeled categorial type deduction. In *Proceedings of the London Workshop on Proof Theory and Linguistic Analysis*, 1994.

24. Remo Pareschi. *Type-driven Natural Language Analysis*. PhD thesis, University of Edinburgh, 1989.

25. Remo Pareschi and Dale Miller. Extending definite clause grammars with scoping constructs. In David D. H. Warren and Peter Szeredi, editors, *1990 International Conference in Logic Programming*, pages 373–389. MIT Press, June 1990.

26. Fernando C. N. Pereira and Stuart M. Shieber. *Prolog and Natural-Language Analysis*, volume 10. CLSI, Stanford, CA, 1987.

27. Dirk Roorda. *Resource Logics: Proof-Theoretical Investigations*. PhD thesis, University of Amsterdam, 1991.

28. John Robert Ross. *Constraints on Variables in Syntax*. PhD thesis, Massachusetts Institute of Technology, 1967.

29. Mark J. Steedman. Combinators and grammars. In Bach Oehrle and Wheeler, editors, *Categorial Grammars and Natural Language Structures*, 1988.

Underspecification in Type-Logical Grammars

Dirk Heylen

UiL-OTS

Abstract. We show how in a mixed multimodal categorial framework unary modalities can be used to represent morphosyntactic properties of expressions. The residuation logic for the unary connectives, $\Diamond_i, \Box_i$ is used to define a feature checking procedure. Each mode i represents some morphosyntactic feature. Underspecification is dealt with by assuming general modes that are related to specific instances by *inclusion postulates*. The distribution of features is regulated by means of *distribution postulates*. The mixed multimodal approach is compared to some other versions of extended categorial grammars that deal with morphosyntactic issues.

1 Classify and Compose

Our concerns in this paper are focussed on two central tasks of a grammar which involve the *classification* of expressions into categories and the specification of their *compositional structure*. More specifically, we will look at refinements of the classificatorial mechanisms in type logical grammars and on the effects of these extensions on the compositional dimension. A central and recurrent theme in this discussion is that of underspecification. In this introductory section we will make these general remarks more concrete in order to articulate in more detail the goals of this paper.

In context-free phrase structure grammars, the classification of expressions is defined partly by the lexicon where simplex (non-composed) expressions are assigned a category and partly by the rules. A rule like S → NP VP, classifies expressions composed out of a noun phrase followed by a verb phrases as being of the category sentence. As the example already shows, the compositional structure is defined by the rules which tell us which classes of expressions combine with which others and what the category of the combination is.

In a categorial grammar this information is expressed by functional categories. The familiar categorial types $A/B, A \bullet B$, and $B \backslash A$, are used to classify expressions along their combinatorial properties. Expressions of type A/B and $B \backslash A$ combine with expressions of type B to form expressions of type A. Expressions of type $A \bullet B$ are composed out of two expressions of type A and type B. In their common linguistic usage such categories thus assume the role of defining the syntactic 'constituent structure' of a language, as an alternative to the definition of such structures by phrase structure grammars ([14]).

It is common to assume a restricted set of basic categories. The information expressed by the types is thereby often restricted to part of speech and subcategorisation information. This way of using the categories does not pay attention to properties like case, number, person, etc., involving dependencies such as government and agreement that treat the morphological form of words rather than the pure syntactic construction. Though not a central concern, but still a recurrent theme in the literature on categorial grammar of the past two decades has been a treatment of these morphosyntactic aspects of linguistic descriptions (see [15] and [16] for overviews). One of the reasons why extensions to the calculus for morphosyntax have not received more attention is probably because of the general consensus that the basic categorial machinery can, in principle, handle the phenomenon as well by using more basic types in the grammar ([13]).

The motivation to look for extensions derives mainly from descriptive work. It parallels the need in phrase structure grammars, where atomic nonterminal categories are replaced by feature structures. These structures not only offer a perspicuous mechanism to represent multiple properties of linguistic expressions but they also come with a partial informativeness ordering defined on them that can be used to capture certain generalisations, or that make it possible to state grammars more economically ([4, Ch. 4], [5, p. 95-96]).

To illustrate this latter point, we consider some of the morphosyntax involved in a small set of Subject - Verb Phrase combinations in English. The difference between present tense forms like *walk* and *walks*, requires us to provide at least three basic types for noun phrases: NP_1 for third person singular nominative noun phrases (*he, she, the boy...*), NP_2 for the other nominative noun phrases (*I, they, the boys*), and NP_3 for the noun phrases that are not nominative (*him, her, the boy, me, them, the boys*). With these distinctions we can type the verbs as $NP_1 \backslash S$ for *walks* and $NP_2 \backslash S$ for *walk*. It is already apparent that some expressions must be assigned at least two types; *the boy* is both NP_1 and NP_3 and *the boys* is both NP_2 and NP_3. If we look at the traditional type for *the*, NP/N, in this context, we see that it has to be assigned the following types to account for all of its occurrences: NP_1/N_1, NP_2/N_2, NP_3/N_1 and NP_3/N_2; where N_1 and N_2 index singular and plural nouns respectively. We summarise the categories and their interpretation in the following table.

NP_1	$= $ 3-sg-nom	*he, she, the boy...*	
NP_2	$= \neg$(3-sg)-nom	*I, they, the boys*	
NP_3	$= $ 123-sgpl-acc	*him, her, the boy, me, them, the boys*	
N_1	$= $ sg	*boy*	
N_2	$= $ pl	*boys*	
$NP_1 \backslash S$	$= $ 3-sg-verb	*walks*	
$NP_2 \backslash S$	$= \neg$(3-sg)-verb	*walk*	

A first way to reduce the number of assignments consists of three steps (see also [7], [13]). (i) We introduce two new basic types NP_4 (*the boy*) and NP_5 (*the boys*), representing singular and plural noun phrases that can be both nominative and accusative (so it contains the full noun phrases and not the case marked pronouns). This also leads to a simplification for the types for *the*: NP_4/N_1 and NP_5/N_2. (ii) We introduce a partial ordering relation on the basic types: $NP_4 \leq NP_1, NP_5 \leq NP_2, NP_3 \leq NP_4, NP_3 \leq NP_5$. This relation corresponds to an inclusion relation on the set of expressions corresponding to the types. (iii) We change the rules of combination so that a functor A/B or $B \backslash A$ combines with an argument C if $C \leq B$. This allows us to combine *the boy*, NP_4, with the verb *walks*, $NP_1 \backslash S$, because $NP_4 \leq NP_1$.

In grammars using feature structures the same kind of reduction of assignments takes place. Here the ordering of information is taken care of by the subsumption ordering ($\sqsubseteq$, corresponding to $\geq$) and by changing the rule of application in terms of compatibility (or merging/unification) of the information in C and B. We could therefore define an alternative kind of categorial grammar in which the basic categories are replaced by feature structures.

$$
NP_1 : \begin{bmatrix} \text{CAT} & \text{NP} \\ \text{AGR} & \textit{3-sg} \\ \text{CASE} & \textit{nom} \end{bmatrix} \quad NP_2 : \begin{bmatrix} \text{CAT} & \text{NP} \\ \text{AGR} & \neg\textit{3-sg} \\ \text{CASE} & \neg\textit{nom} \end{bmatrix}
$$
$$
\{\textit{the boy, he}\} \qquad\qquad \{\textit{the boys, they}\}
$$

$$
NP_3 : \begin{bmatrix} \text{CAT} & \text{NP} \\ \text{CASE} & \neg\textit{nom} \end{bmatrix}
$$
$$
\{\textit{the boy, the boys, him, them}\}
$$

$$
NP_4 : \begin{bmatrix} \text{CAT} & \text{NP} \\ \text{AGR} & \textit{3-sg} \\ \text{CASE} & \textit{both} \end{bmatrix} \quad NP_5 : \begin{bmatrix} \text{CAT} & \text{NP} \\ \text{AGR} & \neg\textit{3-sg} \\ \text{CASE} & \textit{both} \end{bmatrix}
$$
$$
\{\textit{the boy}\} \qquad\qquad \{\textit{the boys}\}
$$

Fig. 1 *Information ordering*

First note that $\neg$ in $\neg\textit{3-sg}$ and $\neg\textit{nom}$ is not meant as a logical operator, but in both cases the whole should just be read as an atomic sort. The sort *both* is also special. Suppose *case* is the supertype of all possible CASE values. Then we now have the following subsumption ordering: $\textit{case} \sqsubseteq \textit{nom} \sqsubseteq \textit{both}$ and $\textit{case} \sqsubseteq \neg\textit{nom} \sqsubseteq \textit{both}$. This means that the feature structure corresponding to NP_4 does not subsume the feature structure corresponding to NP_1 but vice versa. This can easily be seen from the examples because $\{\textit{the boy}\} \subseteq \{\textit{the boy, he}\}$ and not vice versa.

The feature structure grammars allow for a second way to reduce the number of assignments. If we replace the basic types by their feature structure equivalents in the types we assigned to *the*, we get the following assignments.

$$
\begin{bmatrix} \text{CAT} & \text{NP} \\ \text{AGR} & \textit{3-sg} \end{bmatrix} / \begin{bmatrix} \text{CAT} & \text{N} \\ \text{AGR} & \textit{3-sg} \end{bmatrix} \text{ and } \begin{bmatrix} \text{CAT} & \text{NP} \\ \text{AGR} & \neg\textit{3-sg} \end{bmatrix} / \begin{bmatrix} \text{CAT} & \text{N} \\ \text{AGR} & \neg\textit{3-sg} \end{bmatrix}
$$

The determiner combines with both types of N and produces all types of NP, but there is an important dependency between the agreement values of the domain and of the range of the determiner. The determiner passes the values from the noun to the noun phrase so to speak. This distribution fact is accounted for in unification-based grammars by introducing reentrancies. In this case, they also reduce the number of assignments to just one.

$$
\begin{bmatrix} \text{CAT} & \text{NP} \\ \text{AGR} & \boxed{1} \end{bmatrix} / \begin{bmatrix} \text{CAT} & \text{N} \\ \text{AGR} & \boxed{1} \end{bmatrix}
$$

In a more precise notation of such a functional category in a categorial unification grammar this would read as follows (see [5]):

$$\left[\begin{array}{ll} \text{VAL} & \left[\begin{array}{ll} \text{CAT} & \text{NP} \\ \text{AGR} & \boxed{1} \end{array} \right] \\ \text{DIR} & / \\ \text{ARG} & \left[\begin{array}{ll} \text{CAT} & \text{N} \\ \text{AGR} & \boxed{1} \end{array} \right] \end{array} \right]$$

What we learn from this example are two things. (1) The informativeness ordering on the basic types allows us to reduce the number of type assignments through underspecification. (2) Reentrancies allow us to state distribution principles and help us to reduce further the number of assignments needed. They thereby allow for a more elegant presentation of the grammar. We can summarise our concerns in this papers as follows. In the context of a type-logical categorial grammar (a multimodal Lambek version) we want to:

- refine the classification structures,
- impose an information ordering (hierarchical classification) and use this to simplify the grammar (more specifically the lexicon in a categorial context),
- define distribution principles that help to reduce the number of assignments.

In the examples above we have replaced atomic categories by feature structures to allow for cross-classification of expressions along a number of dimensions. Such changes have been proposed in the literature by a number of authors, mostly for simple applicative categorial grammars ([1], [5], [20], [21] to mention a few). However, for Lambek-style categorial grammars such extensions pose specific problems. In the approach we present below a different strategy is adopted.

We opt for the use of modal decorations in a multimodal Lambek-style grammar to act as markers of morphosyntactic properties. These are specified as unary operators indexed by sorts. In the next section we will sketch and illustrate this strategy. In the other sections we will see how it copes with specific problems concerning underspecification and the distribution of morphosyntactic information in phrase structure.

2   Feature checking

Our proposals fit into a mixed, multimodal type-logical approach to categorial grammar. In fact, we will not use any new mechanisms to account for morphosyntax. We will now outline and illustrate the formalism and show how we use it to refine category structures.

2.1   The Framework

In the type of categorial grammar we are working with, a language is defined by assigning the atomic expressions of the language (the words) to different categories. The categories are formulas from a logical language. It is the task of the grammar to define which complex expressions are grammatical and in which category they are to be classified. In the type-logical approach this is taken care of by a proof-procedure. To show that an expression E is of some category C, we replace the words by their categories (as specified in the lexicon) and take these formulas as the assumptions from which we try to derive C by the logic governing the formulas. This sketches the general picture. We will now present the language and the rules of inference in some detail. For more details consult [15].

The formula language is defined by the following grammar, where $\mathcal{A}$ is a set of atomic symbols, called the basic categories. The indices i, are taken from some set of symbols $\mathcal{I}$.

$$\mathcal{F} ::= \mathcal{A} \mid (\mathcal{F}/_i\mathcal{F}) \mid (\mathcal{F}\backslash_i\mathcal{F}) \mid (\mathcal{F} \bullet_i \mathcal{F}) \mid \Box_i\mathcal{F} \mid \Diamond_i\mathcal{F}$$

A formula or category represents a set of expressions, or more generally, a set of 'linguistic resources'. The structure of the formula tells us something about the properties of the expressions they denote. For instance, we want to say that a resource in $A \bullet_i B$ is related (in mode i) to a resource in A and one in B. This relation between the three expressions will be interpreted as some kind of composition relation in our application. For a resource in $\Diamond_i A$ we could say that it is an i-marked version of a resource in A. We will distinguish between different types of composition and different types of markings, hence the indices. For our interpretation we will thus assume a set of linguistic resources W, a family of ternary and binary relations (both indexed by $\mathcal{I}$) used to interpret the binary ($/, \bullet, \backslash$) and unary ($\Box, \Diamond$) connectives, respectively. For the interpretation, we assume that the denotation of the basic categories is provided by some valuation function v. This is extended to cover the complex categories by the following clauses.

$$
\begin{aligned}
v(\text{A} \bullet_i \text{B}) &= \{w \mid \exists x \exists y [R_i^3 wxy \ \& \ x \in \text{A} \ \& \ y \in \text{B}]\} \\
v(\text{C}/_i\text{B}) &= \{x \mid \forall y \forall w [(R_i^3 wxy \ \& \ y \in \text{B}) \Rightarrow w \in v(\text{C})]\} \\
v(\text{A}\backslash_i\text{C}) &= \{y \mid \forall x \forall w [(R_i^3 wxy \ \& \ x \in \text{A}) \Rightarrow w \in v(\text{C})]\} \\
v(\Diamond_i\text{B}) &= \{w \mid \exists x [R_i^2 wx \ \& \ x \in v(\text{B})]\} \\
v(\Box_i\text{B}) &= \{x \mid \forall w [R_i^2 wx \Rightarrow x \in v(\text{B})]\}
\end{aligned}
$$

The clauses clearly express the dependencies between the connectives $/, \backslash$ and $\bullet$, and between $\Box$ and $\Diamond$. They also show the parallelism between the binary and the unary connectives. If the ternary relation is interpreted as composition ($R(wxy)$ means that w consists of an x and a y) than $A \bullet B$ denotes, as we already indicated, the 'composed' resource w. A/B denotes the resources related to the second argument of the relation (x): those that select B resources (y) to form A resoures (w). The unary connectives show the same duality, which will be exploited in our account of morphosyntactic features.

To represent the linguistic resources or linguistic structures in a more familiar form we use the following grammar to define expressions, where $\mathcal{W}$ are the 'words', $(\mathcal{E} \circ_i \mathcal{E})$ are expressions composed by R_i^3 and $\langle\mathcal{E}\rangle_i$ are expressions marked by R_i^2.

$$\mathcal{E} ::= \mathcal{W} \mid (\mathcal{E} \circ_i \mathcal{E}) \mid \langle\mathcal{E}\rangle_i$$

We want a notion of derivability between formulas $A \to B$ so that $v(A) \subseteq v(B)$, which respects this interpretation. The so-called pure residuation logic below, also known as the non-associative Lambek calculus, **NL** captures these requirements. It is sound and complete with respect to this interpretation.

(REFL) $A \to A$
(TRANS) if $A \to B$ and $B \to C$, then $A \to C$,
(RES) $A \to C/_i B$ iff $A \bullet_i B \to C$ iff $B \to A\backslash_i C$
         $A \to \Box_i B$ iff $\Diamond_i A \to B$

Instead of the axiomatic presentation in which derivability is considered as a relation between formulae, we will use a Gentzen sequent format to represent the linguistic derivations. In this case we are interested in proving statements (sequents) of the form $\Gamma \Rightarrow C$, where Γ is a term (antecedent) and C a category (succedent). Terms are built up from categories as follows.

$$\mathcal{T} ::= \mathcal{F} \mid (\mathcal{T} \circ_i \mathcal{T}) \mid \langle \mathcal{T} \rangle_i$$

The parallelism with the definition of expressions is obvious. They have an identical structure. To show that some expression E is of category C, we simply replace the words in E by a category (one assigned to the word in the lexicon). Leaving the structure of the expression intact we thus obtain a term, say T. If we can prove that $T \Rightarrow C$ by the rules below, then we have shown that $E \in v(C)$.

$$\frac{}{A \Rightarrow A} \; ax$$

$$\frac{\Gamma[A \circ_i B] \Rightarrow C}{\Gamma[A \bullet_i B] \Rightarrow C} \; L\bullet_i \qquad \frac{\Gamma \Rightarrow A \quad \Delta \Rightarrow B}{\Gamma \circ_i \Delta \Rightarrow A \bullet_i B} \; R\bullet_i$$

$$\frac{\Delta \Rightarrow B \quad \Gamma[A] \Rightarrow C}{\Gamma[A/_i B \circ_i \Delta] \Rightarrow C} \; L/_i \qquad \frac{\Gamma \circ_i B \Rightarrow A}{\Gamma \Rightarrow A/_i B} \; R/_i$$

$$\frac{\Delta \Rightarrow B \quad \Gamma[A] \Rightarrow C}{\Gamma[\Delta \circ_i B\backslash_i A] \Rightarrow C} \; L\backslash_i \qquad \frac{B \circ_i \Gamma \Rightarrow A}{\Gamma \Rightarrow B\backslash_i A} \; R\backslash_i$$

$$\frac{\Gamma[\langle A \rangle_i] \Rightarrow B}{\Gamma[\Diamond_i A] \Rightarrow B} \; L\Diamond_i \qquad \frac{\Gamma \Rightarrow A}{\langle \Gamma \rangle_i \Rightarrow \Diamond_i A} \; R\Diamond_i$$

$$\frac{\Gamma[A] \Rightarrow B}{\Gamma[\langle \Box_i A \rangle_i] \Rightarrow B} \; L\Box_i \qquad \frac{\langle \Gamma \rangle_i \Rightarrow A}{\Gamma \Rightarrow \Box_i A} \; R\Box_i$$

We have used the Gentzen sequent presentation because it shows very well the duality between the connectives. The rules can best be read from bottom to top. Consider the $L/_i$ rule. This says that an antecedent Γ that contains the substructure $A/_i B \circ_i \Delta$ in it is of type C provided that Δ is of type B and the sequent Γ with $A/_i B \circ_i \Delta$ replaced by A is of type C. Putting in the appropriate context, this expresses the behaviour of $A/_i B$: (i) look for some part (Δ) of the structure that reduces to B, (ii) the combination is of category A. Also important in the derivations below are the rules for $\Box$. The $R\Box$ rule says that in order to show that some structure Γ is in $\Box_i A$ we have to show that the 'marked' version $\langle \Gamma \rangle_i$ is in A. The $L\Box_i$ rule nicely shows how structural brackets check (and remove) the $\Box$-markings in the antecedent.

It is important to realise that we have a whole family of binary and unary connectives (indexed by $\mathcal{I}$) but that all of the binary and unary connectives are governed by the same logical rules which relate the bullet to the slashes and the diamonds to the boxes for each mode i. This relation is constant. The distinction between $\bullet_i$ and $\bullet_j$ or R_i and R_j in the model is not one of 'logic' but of 'structure'. R_i^3 can be an associative relation and R_j^3 non-associative, R_l^3 might be commutative but R_k^3 not. These characteristics are defined as frame conditions on the relations in the model theory. In the proof theory, they are defined by so-called structural rules.

$$\frac{\Gamma[\Delta_2 \circ_p \Delta_1] \Rightarrow C \quad \Gamma[(\Delta_1 \circ_a (\Delta_2 \circ_a \Delta_3))] \Rightarrow C}{\Gamma[\Delta_1 \circ_p \Delta_2] \Rightarrow C \quad \Gamma[((\Delta_1 \circ_a \Delta_2) \circ_a \Delta_3)] \Rightarrow C}$$

Besides structural postulates that fix the characteristics of single modes of composition and marking, we can also specify certain rules for the interaction of different modes.

$$\frac{\Gamma[\Delta_2 \circ_p \langle \Delta_1 \rangle_c] \Rightarrow C \quad \Gamma[\langle \Delta \rangle_y] \Rightarrow C \quad \Gamma[\langle \Delta_1 \rangle_z \circ_n \Delta_2] \Rightarrow C}{\Gamma[\langle \Delta_1 \rangle_c \circ_p \Delta_2] \Rightarrow C \quad \Gamma[\langle \Delta \rangle_x] \Rightarrow C \quad \Gamma[\langle \Delta_1 \circ_n \Delta_2 \rangle_z] \Rightarrow C}$$

In the first example, we see a composition relation where the components can commute provided the first component is marked c. In the second example, we see that an x-checking can be changed into a y-checking. This enables us to prove a sequent like $\Box_y A \Rightarrow \Box_x A$. We will call this an inclusion postulate, because from a semantic perspective it means that $v(\Box_y A) \subseteq v(\Box_x A)$.

$$\frac{\frac{\frac{A \Rightarrow A}{\langle \Box_y A \rangle_y \Rightarrow A}}{\langle \Box_y A \rangle_x \Rightarrow A}}{\Box_y A \Rightarrow \Box_x A}$$

In the third example, we see that a z-marking on an n-composite can be replaced by a z-marking on the first component of the composite.

Now that we have the formal machinery worked out it is time to be more precise about how it is used to define grammars. At this point we only look at the use of the logical operations and their potential to effect cross-classification. The use of postulates will be discussed in the following sections which will deal with underspecification and distribution of morphosyntactic information in phrase structure.

2.2 Cross-classification

The duality between $\Diamond$ and $\Box$ is similar to the duality between $\bullet$ and $/, \backslash$. We have seen an interpretation of these residuation duals in very general models. In the case of the binary connectives we make them refer to composition and selection operations (wholes and parts). A similar interpretation holds for the unary connectives. However because there is only one part, the operation of composition will be interpreted as some kind of marking on an intuitive level. If $\bullet_i$ represents the glue to combine parts, $\Diamond_i$

represents a shell around a part. We shall look at this as a specific kind of marking. As we already said, the models we presented are very general. For our linguistic application we will use the operations in a specific context with a less general interpretation to denote certain aspects of linguistic structure. In this case we use the duality to define the morphosyntactic properties of a language in terms of checking. An expression typed as $\Box_i A$ is similar to $B\backslash_i A$ and can be read as "requires mode i checking" parallel to "requires argument". The $\Diamond_i$ provides the checking. Just as $B \bullet_i B\backslash_i A \to A$ is valid so is $\Diamond_i \Box_i A \to A$. The $\Diamond$ cancels or checks the $\Box$. Metaphorically speaking we can also say that the $\Box_i$ functions as a lock that can be opened by a corresponding key $\Diamond_i$.

We take up the example of the introduction. We use unary operators to express the morphosyntactic distinctions.

$NP_1 \rightsquigarrow \Box_1 NP = 3\text{-sg-nom}$ *he, she, the boy...*

$NP_2 \rightsquigarrow \Box_2 NP = \neg(3\text{-sg})\text{-nom}$ *I, they, the boys*

$NP_3 \rightsquigarrow \Box_3 NP = 123\text{-sgpl-acc}$ *him, her, the boy, me, them, the boys*

Given these translations of the categories for the noun phrases, the categories for the verbs *walk* and *walks* correspond to the following.

$NP_1 \backslash S \rightsquigarrow \Box_1 NP\backslash S = 3\text{-sg-subject}$ *walks*

$NP_2 \backslash S \rightsquigarrow \Box_2 NP\backslash S = \neg(3\text{-sg})\text{-subject } walk$

Because we use only a single mode of composition, the binary connectives (both the logical and the structural ones) bear no index. To show that *he* ∘ *walks* is a sentence, we try to prove the sequent $\Box_1 NP \circ \Box_1 NP\backslash S \Rightarrow S$.

$$\frac{\dfrac{\dfrac{\dfrac{NP \Rightarrow NP}{\langle \Box_1 NP \rangle_1 \Rightarrow NP}}{\Box_1 NP \Rightarrow \Box_1 NP} \qquad S \Rightarrow S}{\Box_1 NP \circ \Box_1 NP\backslash S \Rightarrow S}}{}$$

What becomes immediately obvious when we take a closer look at this proof, is the balance of symbols in each sequent. Take the initial sequent at the bottom: there are two NP symbols, two S symbols and two $\Box_i$ symbols. The elements of each pair have opposite polarities: one NP symbol occurs positively in the antecedent term, the other negatively (in 'selection' position). Similarly for the pair of boxes. One S symbol occurs in the antecedent, the other in the succedent. The last dual pair involves the composition operator ∘ and the selection connective \. A similar pair of duals, i.e. of structural and logical operator is found in the sequent $\langle \Box_1 NP \rangle_1 \Rightarrow NP$, with $\langle \cdot \rangle_1$ and $\Box_1$.

2.3 Discussion

Our definition of grammar provides a deductive perspective on the characterisation of grammatical structures. We have classified expressions using logical formulas as categories and defined the typing relation of complex expressions in terms of logical deduction in a resource conscious grammar logic. We have used the connectives $/, \bullet, \backslash$ to define composition and selection (valence, subcategorisation, if you want). This covers the basic phrase structure component of the grammar. The classification potential of the formulas is refined by decorating categories with morphosyntactic properties. These are marked by the operators $\Box$ and $\Diamond$, whose logic defines a checking procedure.

Checking Procedure The checking theory of morphosyntactic properties bears a general resemblance to certain ideas in the minimalist program with respect to the cancellation of features. We can make this a bit more precise by taking a closer look at some reconstructions of minimalism by Stabler (for instance [19]). A grammar consists of a lexicon and a pair of generating functions: merge and move. The lexicon is a set of feature terms which are simply strings of features. Different types of features can be distinguished.

Selected categories c, t, d, n, v, p, ...
Selector features =c, =t, =d, =n, =v, =p, ...
Licensors +wh, +case, +focus, ...
Licensees -wh, -case, -focus, ...
Phonetic features every, some, student, ...

Expressions are either lexical items (strings of features) or binary trees: $\Delta_1 < \Delta_2$ or $\Delta_2 > \Delta_1$, where Δ_1 and Δ_2 are either binary trees themselves or lexical items. If we talk about the features of a tree, we mean the features of its head, which is the 'bigger' element of the pair. For our purposes of illustration here, we can simply ignore them and we will use the $\circ$ operator to denote structure.

The operation merge is defined on two expressions.

from $= x\Delta_1$ and $x\Delta_2$ make $\Delta_1 \circ \Delta_2$

This should be read as follows: two expressions (lexical or phrasal) can merge into a tree provided the first feature of one is $= x$ and the first feature of the other is x. In the resulting tree these features are cancelled (erased). The effects of the move function are as follows.

from $(+x\Delta_1 \circ (\Delta_2 \circ (-x\Delta_3 \circ \Delta_4)))$ make $((\Delta_3 \circ \Delta_4) \circ (\Delta_1 \circ \Delta_2))$

Note again, that in this case, the movement is triggered by a pair of opposing features, which are cancelled after the operation has taken place. We illustrate this with a simple grammar. If the lexicon consists of the items $d - x$ *he* and $= d + x$ *walks*. We can apply a merge step followed by a move step, Δ_2 and Δ_4 are empty.

from $= d + x$ *walks*   and $d - x$ *he*   make $(+x$ *walks*$) \circ (-x$ *he*$)$
from $(+x$ *walks*$) \circ (-x$ *he*$)$ make *he* $\circ$ *walks*

The idea that feature checking defines a kind of agreement-matching is thus not unique to the approach we have sketched here. We should also mention the work by Johnson [12] that deals with a resource conscious perspectives on grammatical description in LFG. Such an approach is, however, quite different from the more common feature structure based approaches.

Feature Structures We started out this paper by pointing out the benefits of feature structures: cross-classification, simplification of grammars by the information ordering, feature distribution, etc. We have now made a start with adding more structure to the categories in a type-logical grammar to account for multiple properties. However, it is important to see that what we have ended up with are not feature structures.

First of all, it is important not to confuse the models and the logic of type-logical and constraint-based theories despite superficial similarities. In a modal perspective on feature structures, the structures are also taken to be Kripke structures and a mixed multi-modal logic is used to talk about the structures (see [3] for example). But the common factor to both approaches is restricted to this meta-level of the common use of the same logical tools. The way the tools are used to characterise aspects of linguistic structure is different. For instance, the elements that populate the models are clearly different. In typical feature structure models there are many kinds of objects. Most of them are not linguistic resources. Only elements of sort *sign* could count as such in a theory like HPSG. The others are reified properties like *nom* or *boolean*. In our type-logical set-up such properties are not expressed as nodes in the model, but rather as relations between linguistic resources.

It is also important to see that the grammars work differently. In the categorial case there is a need to check and cancel morphosyntactic features. For this we need a balance between boxes and diamonds or negative and positive positions and the logical duality that holds between these operators. In the constraint-based theories there is no need to check features. In particular cases we may require a compatibility check (or unification) but features are not cancelled. This has further repercussions on how we deal with underspecification as we will see in the following sections.

In constraint-based theories as they are usually presented, a language is specified by a logical formula, consisting of subformulas describing the feature structures that model words (the lexicon) and subformulas that describe certain aspects of phrasal construc-tions (head-feature principle, etc.). A language is defined by such a grammar as the collection of feature structures (models) that satisfy this formula. In the type-logical grammar, the basic statements are sequents that have to be proven. Semantically, this pours down to validity: truth in all models. This technical difference poses specific problems for combinations of constraint-based approaches with type-logical ones as has been pointed out by, for instance, [6] and [7] and [8].

3 Underspecification

In the introduction we discussed how an information ordering on the categories, corre-sponding to a hierarchical classification of the expressions, can be used to simplify a grammar by reducing the number of assignments to lexical expressions. Now that we have defined a more refined notion of classification in the previous section, we want to discuss the definition of such an ordering for the system we have just presented. We will see how inclusion postulates can be used to define an information ordering on the morphosyntactic properties.

3.1 Inclusion

In the simple example from the introduction, we presented the advantages of having an information ordering defined on the categories. This provides a way to refer to classes of expressions and also to subclasses and superclasses ($NP_1 \leq NP_3$ means that $v(NP_1) \subseteq v(NP_3)$). In the example, we used it to reduce the number of assignments. Note that the calculus as we have presented it, also defines an ordering relation on categories: if $A \rightarrow B$ this means that $v(A) \subseteq v(B)$ as we saw above. Logical derivability thus corresponds to an inclusion relation or to an information ordering. This ordering depends on the properties of the logical connectives. However, we can also define an order on the non-logical vocabulary. In our case this consist of the basic categories $\mathcal{A}$ and the indices $\mathcal{I}$. We can view these orderings as part of the signature that comes with the specification of the grammatical vocabulary used in a specific grammar. When we want to account for the ordering in a proof-theoretical way we can add non-logical axioms for each ordered pair of basic categories as follows.

$$\frac{}{A \Rightarrow B} \; A \leq B$$

For the indices we use inclusion postulates. Again we can simplify this by having a general schema with a side-condition that mentions the ordering on the indices.

$$\frac{\Gamma[\langle \Delta \rangle_y] \Rightarrow C}{\Gamma[\langle \Delta \rangle_x] \Rightarrow C} \; y \leq x$$

In using the ordering relation we have to take into account the position where a diamond or box occurs in a category, i.e. its polarity. In order to be able to derive $\Box_i A \circ \Box_j A \backslash B \Rightarrow B$, it must be the case that $i \leq j$ and not vice versa. This has important consequences for our view on underspecification. This is best explained by a very basic example. We take a tiny fragment of Dutch. Note that we write $[i]$ for $\Box_i$.

Zij	she/they	$[Num]$NP
zingt	sings	$[sg]$NP$\backslash$S$/[num]$NP
zingen	sing	$[pl]$NP$\backslash$S$/[num]$NP
liedjes	songs	$[pl]$NP

The type assignment to *Zij* captures both a singular and plural assignment. For the verbs, the assignments also abbreviate two options. The *num* decoration on the object noun phrase tells us that the verb does not care whether its object is singular or plural. The difference between $[Num]$ and $[num]$ is due to the polarity. In terms of feature checking we want $[Num]$NP to be able to be checked by either a singular or a plural verb. We want $[num]$ to check both singular and plural noun phrases. We first present a derivation for *zij zingt* (she sings). We leave out the object for the sake of simplicity.

$$\frac{\dfrac{\dfrac{\dfrac{\overline{NP \Rightarrow NP}}{\langle [Num]NP \rangle_{Num} \Rightarrow [sg]NP}}{\langle [Num]NP \rangle_{sg} \Rightarrow [sg]NP}}{[Num]NP \Rightarrow [sg]NP} \quad \overline{S \Rightarrow S}}{[Num]NP \circ [sg]NP\backslash S \Rightarrow S}$$

For this derivation to work we need the following inclusion relation.

$$\frac{\Gamma[\langle\Delta\rangle_{Num}] \Rightarrow C}{\Gamma[\langle\Delta\rangle_{sg}] \Rightarrow C} \; Num \leq sg$$

As we already said, we want $([sg]\text{NP}\backslash\text{S})/[num]\text{NP}$ to check both singular and plural objects. Because we are only interested in the checking of the object, we abbreviate $[sg]\text{NP}\backslash\text{S}$ to VP. The derivation for *zingt liedjes* (sings songs).

$$\frac{\dfrac{\dfrac{\dfrac{\text{NP} \Rightarrow \text{NP}}{\langle[pl]\text{NP}\rangle_{pl} \Rightarrow \text{NP}}}{\langle[pl]\text{NP}\rangle_{num} \Rightarrow \text{NP}}}{[pl]\text{NP} \Rightarrow [num]\text{NP} \quad \text{VP} \Rightarrow \text{VP}}}{\text{VP}/[num]\text{NP} \circ [pl]\text{NP} \Rightarrow \text{VP}}$$

$$\frac{\Gamma[\langle\Delta\rangle_{pl}] \Rightarrow C}{\Gamma[\langle\Delta\rangle_{num}] \Rightarrow C} \; pl \leq num$$

3.2   The Status of Underspecified Categories

Before we turn to a discussion of distribution principles in this framework, we want to pay some attention to the status of the underspecified categories. In the introduction to this paper, we briefly illustrated a version of categorial grammar in which the basic categories are replaced by feature structures. This is essentially the move that is proposed by Bach ([1]). Let us consider this option within an applicative system (one that has only left rules, no right rules). The rules of application can be formulated as follows:

$$\begin{array}{cc} A & A \\ \overset{\frown}{B \quad B\backslash A} & \overset{\frown}{A/B \quad B} \end{array}$$

If we use feature structures we can use the following variant.

$$\begin{array}{cc} A & A \\ \overset{\frown}{C \quad B\backslash A} & \overset{\frown}{A/C \quad B} \\ B \sqsubseteq C & \end{array}$$

The extra condition says that B has to subsume C, i.e. C must be more specific in the information ordering than B or $v(C) \subseteq v(B)$ $(C \leq B)$. This allows us to work with underspecified information while deriving a sentence. In this sense it is similar to our approach which we sketched above. We will call this a 'derivational view on underspecification'. However, Bach presents another view on underspecified structures which is worth to mention to show that other options are available. Bach uses underspecified categories only in the lexicon, as abbreviations for a collection of the possible expansions. Grammatical derivations only deal with fully specified entries so there is no need to change the definition of application. This could be called a 'lexical view on underspecification'. The question here is whether the choice makes any difference. The common analysis of coordination of unlike type constructions seems to point out that some kind of derivational underspecification is necessary.

In feature structure grammars like GPSG and HPSG it has been assumed that subsumption of feature structures plays an important role in these constructions ([17] and [18]). In Bayer and Johnson's work ([2]) this has been picked up as an argument in favour of type-logical approaches to grammar because there the derivational relation $\Rightarrow$ corresponds essentially to subsumption. We shall not go into that argument here but only provide a simple example that shows the use of a derivational perspective on underspecification, where a strictly lexical perspective as we have sketched it would fail. In [9] and [10] the limitations of the derivational approach are sketched.

To account for the grammatical coordination *became wealthy and a republican*, we need the verb to combine with an adjectival and a nominal phrase. We can take the underspecified category XP to account for this. The reader can construct the proof for the verb phrase given the following assignments.

became	VP/XP
wealthy	AP
and	XP\XP/XP
a republican	NP

We make use of the following axioms that implement the idea that both AP and NP are categories denoting subsets of $v(\text{XP})$.

$$\overline{\text{AP} \Rightarrow \text{XP}} \quad \overline{\text{NP} \Rightarrow \text{XP}}$$

However, in a lexical approach to underspecification the 'underspecified' verb category will be expanded to its two instantiations. Neither of these will however be able to account for the correct derivation. The derivation goes through only, if we allow the underspecified category in it.

Note that this example involves the ordering of basic categories, but other examples can be provided which involve other morphosyntactic properties and hence the ordering on the morphosyntactic indices.

4 Distribution

In our approach we have special operators for morphosyntactic properties instead of more complex basic categories. The advantages of having morphosyntactic information decoupled of the basic categories will become clear in this section, in which we discuss the distribution of morphosyntactic information in phrase structure.

4.1 Distribution Postulates

The decomposition of syntactic and morphosyntactic information of categories in terms of features structures as worked out in theories like GPSG and HPSG, offers the possibility to consider the distribution of each feature or group of features in phrase structure separately (head feature principle, foot feature principle, etc.). In feature structures grammars, like HPSG, feature distribution principles are expressed through reentrancies that indicate that the values in two parts of the structures have to be identical.

In a categorial grammar, the phrase structural properties of expressions are projected from the lexicon. More specifically, they are determined by the selectional requirements expressed by functional categories. These categories provide the information that is expressed by phrase structure rules in theories like HPSG. In the example of the introduction we therefore presented an example of feature distribution as some kind of constraint on functional categories: agreement in specifier categories is accounted for by the reentrancy between the domain and the range part of the functor. But this categorial encoding of a feature distribtution principle is not possible in the type-logical language that we have presented because in the formal language that we are working with, we have no means to express reentrancies.

The solution we will present does not involve an extension of the language to express reentrancies. Instead of stating distribution principles as constraints on categories, we formulate them as principles that relate morphosyntactic decorations and phrase structural composition. Consider, for instance, the distribution postulate that we presented earlier.

$$\frac{\Gamma[\langle\Delta_1\rangle_z \circ_n \Delta_2] \Rightarrow C}{\Gamma[\langle\Delta_1 \circ_n \Delta_2\rangle_z] \Rightarrow C}$$

In a linguistic setting this distribution postulate can be interpreted as fixing the behaviour of head features. The combination mode $\circ_n$ should be interpreted as a mode in which the linguistic head appears as the first component. A head feature like z has the property that when it has to check a phrase, it means that it has to check the head of that phrase. Now consider the following distribution rule:

$$\frac{\Gamma[\langle\Delta_1\rangle_w \circ_m \langle\Delta_2\rangle_w] \Rightarrow C}{\Gamma[\langle\Delta_1 \circ_m \Delta_2\rangle_w] \Rightarrow C}$$

In this case the mode w distributes over both parts of an m-composed structure. Linguistically speaking this captures the essence of an agreement configuration. We illustrate this with a simple Italian fragment.

i	the (pl)	$[pl](NP/_sN)$
pomodori	tomatoes	$[pl]N$
rossi	red	$[pl](N\backslash_mN)$

With the help of the structural rules we can distribute the check for $[pl]$ over both parts so that agreement on this feature is forced on the parts.

$$\frac{\cdots}{NP/_sN \circ_s N \circ_m N\backslash_mN \Rightarrow NP}$$
$$\frac{}{\langle[pl](NP/_sN)\rangle_{pl} \circ_s \langle[pl]N\rangle_{pl} \circ_m \langle[pl](N\backslash_mN)\rangle_{pl} \Rightarrow NP}$$
$$\frac{}{\langle[pl](NP/_sN)\rangle_{pl} \circ_s \langle[pl]N \circ_m [pl](N\backslash_mN)\rangle_{pl} \Rightarrow NP}$$
$$\frac{}{\langle[pl](NP/_sN) \circ_s ([pl]N \circ_m [pl](N\backslash_mN))\rangle_{pl} \Rightarrow NP}$$
$$\frac{}{[pl](NP/_sN) \circ_s ([pl]N \circ_m [pl](N\backslash_mN)) \Rightarrow [pl]NP}$$

4.2 Distribution and Inclusion

We will now consider the use of such distribution postulates and their interaction with inclusion relations. The example we used in the introduction provides us with a good starting point. Here we showed that the reentrancies in the entry for the determiner, reduced the number of assignments. The determiner can combine with both a singular and a plural noun, but the properties of the resulting noun phrase co-vary with each choice. This idea of co-variation will be enforced in our account of agreement by having the agreement postulates be defined only for fully specified morphosyntactic values.

$$
\begin{array}{ll}
the & [Num](\mathrm{NP}/_s\mathrm{N}) \\
boy & [sg]\mathrm{N} \\
walks & [sg]\mathrm{NP}\backslash_h\mathrm{S}
\end{array}
$$

$$
\cfrac{\cfrac{\cfrac{\cfrac{\cfrac{\cfrac{\cdots}{\mathrm{NP}/_s\mathrm{N} \circ_s \mathrm{N} \Rightarrow \mathrm{NP}}}{\langle[Num](\mathrm{NP}/_s\mathrm{N})\rangle_{Num} \circ_s [sg]\mathrm{N}\rangle sg \Rightarrow \mathrm{NP}}}{\langle[Num](\mathrm{NP}/_s\mathrm{N})\rangle sg \circ_s [sg]\mathrm{N}\rangle sg \Rightarrow \mathrm{NP}}}{\langle[Num](\mathrm{NP}/_s\mathrm{N}) \circ_s [sg]\mathrm{N}\rangle sg \Rightarrow \mathrm{NP}}}{[Num](\mathrm{NP}/_s\mathrm{N}) \circ_s [sg]\mathrm{N} \Rightarrow [sg]\mathrm{NP} \qquad \overline{\mathrm{S} \Rightarrow \mathrm{S}}}}{[Num](\mathrm{NP}/_s\mathrm{N}) \circ_s [sg]\mathrm{N} \circ_h [sg]\mathrm{NP}\backslash_h\mathrm{S} \Rightarrow \mathrm{S}}
$$

The agreement postulate takes care of the correct distribution of the morphosyntactic information in phrase structure. The use of special decorations, i.e. separate logical operators for the morphosyntactic properties ensures this kind of treatment.

Consider what would happen if we had an ordering only on the basic categories as in the extended Lambek calculus proposed by [2]. In this case, the basic categories are replaced by simple propositional formulas and the axiom schema is changed so that $A \Rightarrow B$ is derivable in case it is a theorem of propositional logic. A possible assignment to the words from the previous fragment could look like this. We also consider an alternative characterisation using our morphosyntactic modalities. The difference with the previous lexicon is the assignment to *the*.

$$
\begin{array}{lll}
the & (\mathrm{SG} \wedge \mathrm{PL} \wedge \mathrm{NP})/_s\mathrm{N} & [Num]\mathrm{NP}/_s[num]\mathrm{N} \\
boy & (\mathrm{SG} \wedge \mathrm{N}) & [sg]\mathrm{N} \\
boys & (\mathrm{PL} \wedge \mathrm{N}) & [pl]\mathrm{N} \\
walks & (\mathrm{SG} \wedge \mathrm{NP})\backslash_h\mathrm{S} & [sg]\mathrm{NP}\backslash_h\mathrm{S}
\end{array}
$$

There is only a single assignment to *the*. This captures the fact that it combines with both singular and plural nouns (underspecification in negative positions), and the fact that it gives rise to both singular and plural noun phrases (overspecification). However the problem with this assignment is that it does not relate the choices of argument and result. We can derive the expression *the boy* as a singular noun phrase.

$$
\cfrac{\cfrac{\cdots}{\mathrm{SG} \wedge \mathrm{PL} \wedge \mathrm{NP} \Rightarrow \mathrm{SG} \wedge \mathrm{NP}} \qquad \cfrac{\cdots}{\mathrm{SG} \wedge \mathrm{N} \Rightarrow \mathrm{N}}}{((\mathrm{SG} \wedge \mathrm{PL} \wedge \mathrm{NP})/_s\mathrm{N}) \circ (\mathrm{SG} \wedge \mathrm{N}) \Rightarrow \mathrm{SG} \wedge \mathrm{NP}}
$$

But the problem is that we can also derive the *the boys* to be a singular noun phrase.

$$\frac{\dfrac{\cdots}{\mathrm{SG} \wedge \mathrm{PL} \wedge \mathrm{NP} \Rightarrow \mathrm{SG} \wedge \mathrm{NP}} \quad \dfrac{\cdots}{\mathrm{PL} \wedge \mathrm{N} \Rightarrow \mathrm{N}}}{(\mathrm{SG} \wedge \mathrm{PL} \wedge \mathrm{NP})/_s \mathrm{N}) \circ (\mathrm{PL} \wedge \mathrm{N}) \Rightarrow \mathrm{SG} \wedge \mathrm{NP}}$$

The same goes for the alternative analysis with unary modalities.

$$\frac{\dfrac{\dfrac{\dfrac{\mathrm{NP} \Rightarrow \mathrm{NP}}{\langle [Num]\mathrm{NP}\rangle_{Num} \Rightarrow \mathrm{NP}}}{\langle [Num]\mathrm{NP}\rangle_{sg} \Rightarrow \mathrm{NP}}}{[Num]\mathrm{NP} \Rightarrow [sg]\mathrm{NP}} \quad \dfrac{\dfrac{\dfrac{\mathrm{N} \Rightarrow \mathrm{N}}{\langle [pl]\mathrm{N}\rangle_{pl} \Rightarrow \mathrm{N}}}{\langle [pl]\mathrm{N}\rangle_{num} \Rightarrow \mathrm{N}}}{[pl]\mathrm{N} \Rightarrow [num]\mathrm{N}}}{[Num]\mathrm{NP}/_s[num]\mathrm{N} \circ [pl]\mathrm{N} \Rightarrow [sg]\mathrm{NP}}$$

Conclusion What this specific example shows is that we are not dependent on the use of reentrancy to define distributional information. The structural rules enforce a regime of feature percolation that enforces the sharing of information, or more precisely, identical checking of information in different parts of the structure.

On a more general level, it is worth to note the following. The specification of morphosyntactic properties as modal operators, governed by their own logic, allows us to modularise the grammar. We can fix the distributional behaviour of each property or group of properties in a separate component of the grammar (the structural rule package). Not only has this advantages for expressing generalisations, it also makes the distribution of information less dependent on the function/argument structure of the functional categories $A/B, A\backslash B$.

Above we have only presented the basic machinery and illustrated its use. We will now suggest a few refinements and alternatives that exploit more fully the potential offered by this approach.

5 Refinements and Alternatives

In the introduction we summarised our concerns in this papers as follows. In the context of a type-logical categorial grammar (a multimodal Lambek version) we want to: refine the classification structures, impose an information ordering (hierarchical classification) and use this to simplify the grammar (lexicon), and finally, define distribution principles to reduce further the number of assignments. In the previous sections we have discussed the outlines of how unary residuated operators can be used to add morphosyntactic decorations onto the familiar category structure and how inclusion and distribution postulates take care of the other concerns. In this final section we want to point out some further refinements and alternatives to these proposals. The first concerns the issue of having more than one modal decoration. The second explores the use of alternative ways to fix the polarity duality required for the checking procedure.

Multiple Modalities In all of the examples above, we have used a single modal decoration to carry morphosyntactic information. In most cases we have simplified the analysis considerably by taking this decoration to refer to a single morphosyntactic property, say number, ignoring all the other properties like person, case, or gender. Of course, this is not a principled restriction. There are several options available to arrive at a more realistic description.

One option is simply to let the indexes stand for complexes of information. In fact, this is what we did in the example of the introduction which we took up in Section 2.2. Here we used categories like $\Box_1 \text{NP}$, where $\Box_1$ stands for 'third person, singular, and nominative'. As an alternative, we could make this structure visible and replace the set of atomic symbols $\mathcal{I}$ by, for instance, simple feature structures or perhaps more accurately by formulas from some feature description language:

$$\begin{bmatrix} \text{NUMBER } 3 \\ \text{PERSON } sg \\ \text{CASE } \quad nom \end{bmatrix} \text{NP or, } \Box_{(\langle\text{NUMBER}\rangle 3 \land \langle\text{PERSON}\rangle sg \land \langle\text{CASE}\rangle nom)} \text{NP}$$

Note that the square brackets $[\cdot]$ represent our residuated $\Box$ operator, whereas the $\langle\cdot\rangle$ brackets represent $\Diamond$ operators of a Blackburn-like modal feature logic. Of course, this use of a logical language for the inscriptions suggests further exploitation of its potential.

$$\frac{\Gamma[\langle\Delta\rangle_y] \Rightarrow C}{\Gamma[\langle\Delta\rangle_x] \Rightarrow C} \, y \leq x \qquad \frac{\Gamma[\langle\Delta\rangle_y] \Rightarrow C}{\Gamma[\langle\Delta\rangle_x] \Rightarrow C} \, y \to x$$

Note that here, in a structure like $\langle\Delta\rangle_x$, the angular brackets represent the structural counterpart of the $\Diamond$ operator. The y and x variables represent feature description formulas and $\to$ represents derivability in an appropriate logic for these formulas. One could say that we have here a special case of a layered logic. For more suggestions see [11].

Our formula language allows another option to decorate categories along multiple dimensions. Instead of complicating the inscriptions on the operators, we can also multiply the number of operators, one for each dimension, and use simplex inscriptions as before.

$$\Box_3 \Box_{sg} \Box_{nom} \text{NP}$$

This is a very simple solution, comparable to the list of features of the minimalist analysis above. It does not require an extension to our basic set-up. The most important advantage of this option is that it allows us to differentiate between the behaviour of individual features with respect to their distribution in phrase structure. That means that we can have a collection of distribution postulates that express per feature and construction mode how the morphosyntactic properties distribute. Some may act as head features (identity between the whole and the head daughter) others as agreement features (identity between the whole and daughters) according to the kind of construction that is involved.

Of course, it is possible to mix the two options and to group together in one complex inscription all the features that behave in the same way ('head' vs. 'agreement', or 'government' features for instance). There are many options here, and the choices may be different for individual grammars.

Polarities Our presentation of morphosyntactic description is couched in terms of a feature checking theory using markings that have to be checked parallel to the selection / composition duality. Both are governed by the logic of residuation. In order for a construction to be grammatical there has to be a balance between decorations of opposite polarities just as there has to be a balance between selection and composition operations. In the examples so far the opposition was of two (related) kinds, illustrated by the following schema:

$$\Box_i^+ A \circ \Box_i^- A \backslash B \Rightarrow B, \text{ or}$$
$$\Box_i^+ A \Rightarrow \Box_i^- A$$

This does not, however, cover all the options. In the cases above, we have used pairs of the same operator $\Box$ in the sequent each in an opposite position. However, it is also possible to exploit the opposition between the operators. Schematically, this can be represented as follows.

$$\Box_i^+ A \circ \Diamond_i^+ (A \backslash B) \Rightarrow B$$

Let us see what we need for a proof of this sequent to succeed.

$$\frac{\cdots}{\cfrac{A \circ_n A \backslash B \Rightarrow B}{\cfrac{\langle \Box_i A \rangle_i \circ_n A \backslash B \Rightarrow B}{\cfrac{\Box_i A \circ_n \langle A \backslash B \rangle_i \Rightarrow B}{\Box_i A \circ_n \Diamond_i (A \backslash B) \Rightarrow B}}}}$$

In this proof we have used a postulate that looks like this.

$$\frac{\langle \Box_i A \rangle_i \circ_n A \backslash B \Rightarrow B}{\Box_i A \circ_n \langle A \backslash B \rangle_i \Rightarrow B}$$

It is not difficult to imagine a more concrete setting for such a postulate. For instance, the construction mode $\circ_n$ could represent a subject-verb combination (or more generally a specifier-head construction). The postulate then moves the morphosyntactic requirements of the verb to check the features on the subject. Of course, this movement is conditioned by the precise identity of the features and of the construction mode.

The advantage of this way of fixing the opposite polarities is that the relation between the morphosyntactic distribution and the selectional requirements is loosened even further. In fact, in this case one is no longer committed to put checking features on the domain position of functional categories. One could, for instance, inverse the situation (as expressed by the postulate below) or go even further and define checker/checkee relations through distribution postulates between categories that are not in a direct selection relation.

$$\frac{\Box_i A \circ_n \langle A \backslash B \rangle_i \Rightarrow B}{\langle \Box_i A \rangle_i \circ_n A \backslash B \Rightarrow B}$$

In this last section, we have tried to indicate how the basic procedure which we defined before can be modified to provide a fine instrument that can be used in the description of natural language grammars. Although the list of options is far from complete, we hope to have provided the reader with an idea of how the basic techniques can be refined for actual linguistic description.

Conclusion

In this paper we have looked at the application of the basic apparatus assumed in current versions of type-logical categorial grammars to deal more adequately with the description of morphosyntactic properties of expressions. We have used the residuated unary operators $\Box$ and $\Diamond$ to decorate categories with morphological information and have used their logic to define a checking procedure. We have also looked at the issue of how underspecification can reduce the amount of information that has to be stated in the lexicon and the number of lexical assignments that need to be entered in it. Besides the specification of morphosyntactic properties on lexical items it is also important to see how such properties distribute in grammatical structures (how and where are features checked, how do they move through constituent structure, etc.). The use of the multimodal calculus with inclusion and distribution postulates provides the possibility to fine-tune this relation in a linguistically contentful manner.

References

1. Emmon Bach. On the relationship between word-grammar and phrase grammar. *Natural Language and Linguistic Theory*, 1:65–89, 1983.
2. Sam Bayer and Mark Johnson. Features and agreement. In *ACL-95*, 1995.
3. Patrick Blackburn. Structures, languages and translations: the structural approach to feature logic. In C.J. Rupp, M. A. Rosner, and R.L. Johnson, editors, *Constraints, Language and Computation*, pages 1–27. Academic Press, London, 1994.
4. Robert D. Borsley. *Syntactic Theory, a unified approach.* Edward Arnold, London, 1991.
5. Gosse Bouma. *Nonmonotonicity and Categorial Unification Grammar.* PhD thesis, R.U. Groningen, The Netherlands, 1993.
6. Jochen Dörre, Dov Gabbay, and Esther König. Fibred semantics for feature-based grammar logic. *Journal of Logic, Language, and Information*, 5(3-4):387–422, October 1996.
7. Jochen Dörre and Suresh Manandhar. On constraint-based Lambek calculi. In Patrick Blackburn and Maarten de Rijke, editors, *Logic, Structures and Syntax.* Reidel, Dordrecht, 1997.
8. Nissim Francez. On the direction of fibring feature logics with concatenation logics. Nancy, LACL 1997.
9. Dirk Heylen. On the proper use of booleans in categorial logic. In *Formal Grammar*, pages 71–84, Prague, 1996.
10. Dirk Heylen. Generalisation and coordination in categorial grammar. In *Formal Grammar*, pages 101–111, Aix-en-Provence, 1997.
11. Dirk Heylen. Modalities and morphosyntax. In *Proceedings of Roma-4 Workshop*, page (to appear). -, 1997.
12. Mark Johnson. A resource-sensitive interpretation of lexical functional grammar. In *Proofs and Linguistic Categories. Proceedings 1996 Roma Workshop*, 1997.
13. Joachim Lambek. Type grammar revisited. unpublished manuscript, 1997.

14. Michael Moortgat. *Categorial Investigations. Logical and Linguistic Aspects of the Lambek Calculus.* GRASS. Foris, Dordrecht, 1988. diss. Amsterdam.
15. Michael Moortgat. Categorial type logics. In Johan van Benthem and Alice ter Meulen, editors, *Handbook of Logic and Language*, pages 93–177. Elsevier, 1996.
16. Glyn Morrill. *Type Logical Grammar.* Kluwer Academic Publishers, Dordrecht, 1994.
17. Ivan Sag, Gerald Gazdar, Thomas Wasow, and Steven Weisler. Coordination and how to distinguish categories. *Natural Language and Linguistic Theory*, 3:117–171, 1985.
18. Stuart M. Shieber. *Constraint-Based Grammar Formalisms.* The MIT press, 1992.
19. E.P. Stabler. Derivational minimalism. In Christian Retoré, editor, *Logical Aspects of Computational Linguistics*, pages 68–95. Springer Verlag, 1996.
20. Hans Uszkoreit. Categorial unification grammar. In *Proceedings of the 11th International Conference on Computational Linguistics*, Bonn, 1986.
21. Henk Zeevat, Ewan Klein, and Jo Calder. Unification categorial grammar. In Nicholas Haddock, Ewan Klein, and Glyn Morrill, editors, *Categorial Grammar, Unification Grammar and Parsing.* Centre for Cognitive Science, University of Edinburgh, 1987. Volume 1 of Working Papers in Cognitive Science.

On Fibring Feature Logics with Concatenation Logics

Nissim Francez[*]

Computer science dept., Technion-IIL, Haifa, Israel

Abstract. A dual-fibring of a feature-logic and a concatenation-logic is proposed, in which syntactic categorial types "live in" feature terms, in contrast to current fibring, in which feature-terms "live in" types. The dual-fibring contains also arrow-introduction rules for hypothetical reasoning. It is used to explain some "privileged features" in HPSG and their non-unification manipulation.

keywords *Feature-Logic, Lambek-calculus, unification, fibring, categorial-grammar, natural language*

1 Introduction

Recent advances in the 'parsing as deduction' paradigm are advocating the combination of two logics, a "concatenation-logic" and a "feature-logic", as the adequate means of implementing this paradigm, in view of the advent of 'unification-based grammar-formalisms'. Two recent examples of this approach are [3] and [4]. The combination of the logics is called 'fibring' in [3], and we retain this name generically in this paper. Both papers consider the Lambek logic $\mathcal{L}$ [5] as the concatenation-logic, but differ in several respects regarding the way $\mathcal{L}$ should be fibred with a feature-logic:

1. Should the operators of $\mathcal{L}$ be applied directly to atomic elements of the feature-logic, or should the latter be embedded within atomic $\mathcal{L}$-types (as arguments)?

2. Should the feature-logic be based on unification or on subsumption?

3. Should the restrictions imposed by the feature-logic be localized (to derivation-steps), or kept globally?

However, one common implicit assumption in both approaches is that in the fibring (in spite of its symmetric definition w.r.t. the fibred logics), the feature-logic should be embedded within the concatenation-logic, no matter how the above differences are to be resolved. Thus, the focus is on extended-types, in such a way that feature information "lives-within" types. In particular, this view induces a role of feature information as a *partitioning* of types into subtypes, or a refinement of the type-structure. For example, the basic type np (denoting noun-phrases) can be partitioned into[2] $np(num : sg)$ and $np(num : pl)$, denoting, respectively, singular and plural noun-phrases.

---

[*] Most of the work was carried out during a Sabbatical leave at CWI, 413 Kruislaan, Amsterdam, and OTS, Utrecht university.

[2] In the introduction, the notation is supposed to be self-explanatory. It is properly introduced in the body of the paper.

In this paper, a dual fibring is proposed, that embeds the concatenation-logic within the feature-logic, by which categorial information is made to "live-within" feature-terms. It seems that this kind of dual fibring fits better the practice of grammar writers, in particular in the HPSG framework [7], and explains the role of "privileged features" such as 'cat', 'subcat', 'dtrs' etc., a role stipulated in HPSG without any theoretical justification, except for the clear linguistic need and adequacy of its use. Often, such privileged features have values the manipulation of which exceeds unification, again, without an explicit justification. The latter phenomenon is mentioned in [8] (p. 295) as a general characteristic of many unification-based grammar-formalisms. The dual fibring suggested here may constitute a common explanation and justification for many such "deviations" from unification, and explains the privileged features as arising from the interface-rules used in the fibring of two logics, while the deviation from unification in handling the values of these features reflects the proof-rules of the concatenation-logic. This view induces a dual role of features and types; the types are now seen as partitioning feature-structures (or refining them) according to categorial information. For example, the class of feature-structures satisfying (in AVM-notation) $T = [vform : finite]$, denoting all entities with a finite verb-form feature, can be partitioned into $T[np \to s]$ and $T[np \to (s \leftarrow np)]$, denoting, respectively intransitive verbs (or object-saturated verb-phrases) and transitive verbs. Here $T[A]$ denotes an encoding of an extended-type (explained below) as a sub-feature-term within a feature-term T. The resulting logic has a lot in common with CUG ([2], [1]). However, it is, according to the classification of [6], a second-generation logic, due to the presence of *residuation-rules* for hypothetical reasoning, while CUG is classified as first-generation system in the absence of such rules. It still remains to be investigated what is the logic arising when neither of the entities "lives-within" the other, applying the fully-recursive definition of fibring as given in [3].

Many simplifications are assumed in the current paper. The uncovering of the fibred-logics structure of "full HPSG" remains an issue for further research. For example, there is by now no logical distinction between the various schemes employed in HPSG grammars for combining phrases. In particular, the notion of *head*, central to HPSG, has no logical counterpart capturing its full content. A gross approximation is presented in the paper. As another example, having multiple valency lists (in contrast to the single subcategorization list used in the current paper) has no logical basis. Maybe a more elaborate system of arrows, the introduction-rules for which are not based solely on directionality, might be a step towards capturing multiple valency lists.

2 The base-logics

The following definitions are basically extracted from [3].

The feature-term logic

The syntax of FL (over a signature $\langle \mathcal{F}, \mathcal{P} \rangle$ of feature-names and node-predicate-names, respectively) is described in Figure 1. Terms of the feature-logic FL

$$T ::= \quad p \qquad\qquad\qquad \text{(sorts, } p{\in}\mathcal{P})$$
$$\qquad |x \qquad\qquad\qquad \text{(variables, } x{\in}\mathcal{V})$$
$$\qquad |f : T_1 \qquad\qquad \text{(features, } f{\in}\mathcal{F})$$
$$\qquad |T_1{\wedge}T_2 \mid \neg T_1 \qquad \text{(propositional} - \text{logic connectives)}$$

Fig. 1. The syntax of FL

are interpreted over *feature-structures* $\mathcal{A} = \langle \mathcal{D}^\mathcal{A}, \{f^\mathcal{A} : f{\in}\mathcal{F}\}, \{p^\mathcal{A} : p{\in}\mathcal{P}\}\rangle$, where: $\mathcal{D}^\mathcal{A}$ is a non-empty set of *nodes*, for each $f{\in}\mathcal{F}$, $f^\mathcal{A}$ is a partial function on $\mathcal{D}^\mathcal{A}$, and for each $p{\in}\mathcal{P}$, $p^\mathcal{A}$ is a subset[3] of $\mathcal{D}^\mathcal{A}$. The *satisfaction* of an FL term T over a feature structure $\mathcal{A}$ w.r.t. a variable assignment $g : \mathcal{V}{\to}\mathcal{D}^\mathcal{A}$ (mapping each variable $x{\in}\mathcal{V}$ to $g[x]{\in}\mathcal{D}^\mathcal{A}$ and taking care of reentrancy) and a node $d{\in}\mathcal{D}^\mathcal{A}$, denoted by $\langle \mathcal{A}, g, d\rangle{\models}_{FL}T$, is presented in Figure 2. To express reentrancy btween, say, the paths $< f\ g >$ and $< h >$ in some feature structure, the structure would have to satisfy the term $f : g : x \wedge h : x$. A term T_2

$$\langle \mathcal{A}, g, d\rangle{\models}_{FL}p \text{ iff } d{\in}p^\mathcal{A}$$
$$\langle \mathcal{A}, g, d\rangle{\models}_{FL}x \text{ iff } d = g[x]$$
$$\langle \mathcal{A}, g, d\rangle{\models}_{FL}f : T_1 \text{ iff there exists a } d' \text{ s.t. } d' = f^\mathcal{A}(d) \text{ and } \langle \mathcal{A}, g, d'\rangle{\models}_{FL}T_1$$
$$\langle \mathcal{A}, g, d\rangle{\models}_{FL}T_1{\wedge}T_2 \text{ iff both } \langle \mathcal{A}, g, d\rangle{\models}_{FL}T_1 \text{ and } \langle \mathcal{A}, g, d\rangle{\models}_{FL}T_2$$
$$\langle \mathcal{A}, g, d\rangle{\models}_{FL}\neg T_1 \text{ iff } \langle \mathcal{A}, g, d\rangle{\not\models}_{FL}T_1$$

Fig. 2. The semantics of FL

is an FL-consequence of a term T_1, denoted by $T_1{\models}_{FL}T_2$, iff for all $\mathcal{A}, g, d$: if $\langle \mathcal{A}, g, d\rangle{\models}_{FL}T_1$, then $\langle \mathcal{A}, g, d\rangle{\models}_{FL}T$.

The concatenation logic

As for the concatenation logic, we also consider $\mathcal{L}$, Lambek's basic logic, over a set $\mathcal{B}$ of *basic types*. The syntax of $\mathcal{L}$ is given in Figure 3. Terms of $\mathcal{L}$ (types) are interpreted over string structures (models) $(\mathcal{S}, \cdot^\mathcal{S})$, consisting of a non-empty set $\mathcal{S}$ ("words"), and an interpretation that assigns to each basic category $b{\in}\mathcal{B}$ a non-empty set $b^\mathcal{S} \subseteq \mathcal{S}^+$ (strings over $\mathcal{S}$). The denotations of syntactic types are presented in Figure 4. The deductive calculus is defined over *(declarative) units* $U \rhd A$, where A is a $\mathcal{L}$-type and U is a sequence of $\mathcal{L}$-types that keeps track of the resource management over assumptions in proofs. The proof-rules are presented in Figure 5. The reader is referred to [3] for the definition of the

---

[3] In many applications, it is useful to require that these subsets be pairwise disjoint.

$$A ::= \quad b \qquad\qquad (b \in \mathcal{B}, \text{ basic types})$$
$$|C \to B \qquad\qquad (\text{leftward type})$$
$$|B \leftarrow C \qquad\qquad (\text{rightward type})$$

Fig. 3. The syntax of $\mathcal{L}$

$$[b]^{S} = b^{S}$$
$$[C \to B]^{S} = \{t | \forall t' \in [C]^{S} : t't \in [B]^{S}\}$$
$$[B \leftarrow C]^{S} = \{t | \forall t' \in [C]^{S} : tt' \in [B]^{S}\}$$

Fig. 4. The denotation of $\mathcal{L}$-types

fibred logic $\mathcal{L}(FL)$, the fibred structure over which this logic is interpreted, and a complete calculus for deriving valid declarative units.

$$(\text{ax}) \; A \triangleright A$$
$$(\to E) \; \frac{U_1 \triangleright B, \quad U_2 \triangleright (B \to A)}{(U_1 U_2) \triangleright A} \qquad (\leftarrow E) \; \frac{U_2 \triangleright (A \leftarrow B), \quad U_1 \triangleright B}{(U_2 U_1) \triangleright A}$$
$$(\to I) \; \frac{(BU) \triangleright A}{U \triangleright (B \to A)} \qquad\qquad\quad (\leftarrow I) \; \frac{(UB) \triangleright A}{U \triangleright (A \leftarrow B)}$$

Fig. 5. The type calculus for $\mathcal{L}$

3 The dual fibring logic

We now show how to dual fiber the concatenation-logic $\mathcal{L}$ into the feature-terms logic FL. The dual fibred logic is referred to as FL($\mathcal{L}$), in analogy with $\mathcal{L}$(FL) in [3]. The corresponding calculus is also based on fibring satisfiability of feature-terms with validity of types, as in the usual fibrings. For the interfacing the two logics, we assume that $\{cat, lsub, rsub, dtrs, hdtr, cdtr\} \cap \mathcal{F} = \emptyset$, and extend the $\mathcal{F}$-component of the signature of FL($\mathcal{L}$) by these feature-names. To save space, the feature names 'rsubcat' and 'lsubcat' are abbreviated to 'rsub' and 'lsub', respectively. The first three features accomodate the directionality of $\mathcal{L}$-types similarly to the way *subcat* and *cat* act[4] in HPSG. Similarly, the last three

---

[4] We ignore here multiple complements on the subcat list in HPSG and consider a "binary version" of it. Also, we ignore here HPSG's multiple valency lists. As

encode the hierarchical structure of signs (strings), similarly to the use of the 'DTRS' (daughters), head-daughter and complement daughter in HPSG. As we are simplifying a lot here, the special role of heads is not fully reflected. The functor is the head, and the argument - the complement (in the right linear-order imposed by the directionality of the functor). In addition, we assume that $\mathcal{P} \cap \mathcal{B} = \emptyset$, and extend the $\mathcal{P}$-component of the signature with the elements of $\mathcal{B}$ (the basic types of $\mathcal{L}$) as new sort-names.

For defining the syntax of $FL(\mathcal{L})$, we use some auxiliary definitions. Wherever convenient, we use the AVM-notation for feature terms. First, *extended types* are defined by extending the arrow-operators to feature-terms encoding type as values of dedicated features. Let T be an FL-term and $b \in \mathcal{B}$. An extended type EA is defined by BNF as follows.

$$EA ::= \; T[b] \mid T[EA_1 \rightarrow EA_2] \mid T[EA_2 \leftarrow EA_1].$$

With each extended-type EA we can naturally associate its underlying $\mathcal{L}$-type, "stripping" all its feature information, so to speak, denoted $\tau(EA)$, by letting

$$\tau(EA) = \begin{cases} b & EA = T[b] \\ (\tau(EA_1) \rightarrow \tau(EA_2)) & EA = (T[EA_1 \rightarrow EA_2]) \\ (\tau(EA_2) \leftarrow \tau(EA_1)) & EA = (T[EA_2 \leftarrow EA_1]) \end{cases}$$

We use an extended type EA for denoting the extension of a feature-term T with an extended type EA, defined by $T[EA] =_{\text{df.}} T \sqcup \theta[EA]$, where $\theta[EA]$ is a function encoding[5] an extended-type as an $FL(\mathcal{L})$-term, using the new feature-names and new type-sorts in the extended signature, defined as follows:

$$\theta[EA] =_{\text{df.}} \begin{cases} T \sqcup \begin{bmatrix} cat : b \end{bmatrix} & EA = T[b] \\ T \sqcup \begin{bmatrix} cat : \begin{bmatrix} cat : & \theta[EA_2] \\ lsub : & \theta[EA_1] \end{bmatrix} \end{bmatrix} & EA = (T[EA_1 \rightarrow EA_2]) \\ T \sqcup \begin{bmatrix} cat : \begin{bmatrix} cat : & \theta[EA_2] \\ rsub : & \theta[EA_1] \end{bmatrix} \end{bmatrix} & EA = (T[EA_2 \leftarrow EA_1]) \end{cases}$$

By this construction, the categorial information "lives-within" feature-terms as desired, leaving the denotation of extended types to be a feature-structure. The dependence on the embedded categorial type is reflected in the definition of the validity of a declarative-unit as defined below, and in the preservation of this va-lidity by the rules of the $FL(\mathcal{L})$-calculus presented in the sequel. This specific way of encoding types allows feature-information everywhere, not only in conjunction with basic types, or heads. The linguistic motivation for such encodings may be found in [2] and [1]. For example, assuming that $\{num, pers, vform, sform\} \subseteq \mathcal{F}$, $\{sg, 3rd, fin, affirm\} \subseteq \mathcal{P}$ and $\{np, s\} \subseteq \mathcal{B}$, and letting $T_1 = \begin{bmatrix} num : sg \\ pers : 3rd \end{bmatrix}$,

---

mentioned in the introduction, a full exposition of HPSG as a fibred logic should deal with both issues.

[5] Similarly to the encoding in CUG ([2], [1]).

$T_2 = \big[\, sform : affirm \,\big]$ and $T_3 = \big[\, vform : fin \,\big]$, we have:

$$T_3[T_1[np] \to T_2[s]] = \begin{bmatrix} cat : & \begin{bmatrix} cat : & \begin{bmatrix} cat : & s \\ sform : affirm \end{bmatrix} \\ lsub : & \begin{bmatrix} cat : & np \\ pers : & 3rd \\ num : & sg \end{bmatrix} \end{bmatrix} \\ vform : fin \end{bmatrix}$$

as an $FL(\mathcal{L})$-term. Note that it has feature information at all levels. Under this view, lexical entries assigned to words are extended-types. In a fibring notation in which, contrary to dual fibring, the "arrows" *are* available, the same information might be encoded as follows.

$$[vform : fin] \sqcap ((np \sqcap [pers : 3rd] \sqcap [num : sg]) \to (s \sqcap sform : affirm))$$

Before embarking on the full presentation of $FL(\mathcal{L})$, we make a small detour to explain more of HPSG's privileged features. One can make a distinction between two kinds of logics expressing grammars: *recognition-logics* and *parsing-logics*. In a recognition logic, derivability of a suitable term signals membership of a certain string in the language defined by the grammar encoded by the logic. However, no extra information about the member string is present. On the other hand, in a parsing-logic, the derived term expresses (in addition to membership in the language) some syntactic structure attributed to the member string by the grammar, e.g., a phrase-structure. This reflects the known distinction between weak generative power and strong generative power; usually, the latter is of more interest in computational linguistics.

As it turns out, the role of HPSG's features like 'DTRS' (daughters), 'HDTR' (head-daughter), 'CDTRS' (complement-daughters) and the like, is an encoding of the information needed for a parsing-logic. In defining a dual fibring for that purpose, we use $\delta(T[EA], T_1[EA_1], T_2[EA_2])$ to denote the hierarchical embedding of two (extended types) feature terms T_1, T_2 in (extended type) feature-term T, using the daughters features. Thus,

$$\delta(T[EA], T_1[EA_2 \leftarrow EA_1], T_2[EA_1]) =_{\mathrm{df.}} T[EA] \sqcup \begin{bmatrix} dtrs : & \begin{bmatrix} hdtr : T_1[EA_2 \leftarrow EA_1] \\ cdtr : & T_2[EA_1] \end{bmatrix} \end{bmatrix}$$

To maintain a simpler notation, we focus in the rest of this paper on a dual fibring variant of $FL(\mathcal{L})$ reflecting a recognition-logic only. The extension to a full parsing-logic is not hard. Thus, the syntax of $FL(\mathcal{L})$ consists of extended type feature terms $T[EA]$ as defined above.

We now turn to the denotation of $FL(\mathcal{L})$-terms and declarative-units. Both are interpreted in *dual fibred* structures $\mathcal{M} = (\mathcal{S}, \mathcal{A}, g, \{R_b : b \in \mathcal{B}\})$, where $\mathcal{S}$ is a string-model, $\mathcal{A}$ is a feature-structure, g is a variable-assignment $\mathcal{V} \to \mathcal{D}^{\mathcal{A}}$, and $R_b \subseteq \mathcal{D}^{\mathcal{A}} \times b^{\mathcal{S}}$ is a family (indexed by basic types) of fibring-relations[6], such

---

[6] Note the difference in the direction of the relation compared to the fibring-relations in [3].

that whenever $\langle \mathcal{A}, g, d \rangle \models cat : b$ (for some $b \in \mathcal{B}$), there exists some string $t \in \mathcal{S}^+$ such that $dR_b \tau$. For the definition of a String model and a feature structure, see Section 2.

The denotation $[T[EA]]^{\mathcal{M}}$ of an FL($\mathcal{L}$)-term $T[EA]$ has already been fixed via satisfaction in $\mathcal{A}$. To take the categorial type into account, we associate with every FL($\mathcal{L}$)-term $T[EA]$ a language $L[T[EA]]^{\mathcal{M}}$, as presented in Figure 6. Thus, the "privileged" features are related to the denotations of $\mathcal{L}$-types in a fibred-structure. Note that by this definition we have for every FL($\mathcal{L}$)-term $T[EA]$ and $\mathcal{M}$

$$L[T[EA]]^{\mathcal{M}} \subseteq [\tau(T[EA])]^{\mathcal{M}}.$$

As for the denotation of the resources ("structured databases"), these are a

---

$L[T[b]]^{\mathcal{M}} =_{df.} \{t| \ \exists d \in \mathcal{D}^{\mathcal{A}}(\langle \mathcal{A}, g, d \rangle \models T \wedge cat : b \text{ and } dR_b t)\}$

$L[T[EA_1 \rightarrow EA_2]]^{\mathcal{M}} =_{df.} \{t| \ \exists d \in \mathcal{D}^{\mathcal{A}}(\langle \mathcal{A}, g, d \rangle \models T \wedge cat : cat : EA_2 \wedge cat : lsub : EA_1$
$\text{and } \forall t' \in L[EA_1]^{\mathcal{M}} : t't \in L[EA_2]^{\mathcal{M}})\}$

$L[T[EA_2 \leftarrow EA_1]]^{\mathcal{M}} =_{df.} \{t| \ \exists d \in \mathcal{D}^{\mathcal{A}}(\langle \mathcal{A}, g, d \rangle \models T \wedge cat : cat : EA_2 \wedge cat : rsub : EA_1$
$\text{and } \forall t' \in L[EA_1]^{\mathcal{M}} : tt' \in L[EA_2]^{\mathcal{M}})\}$

Fig. 6. The language associated with extended type feature-terms

natural extension of feature-structures called *multi-rooted structures* (MRSs), described[7] in detail in [9]. Basically, these are sequences of feature-structures with possible sharing (reentrancy) of substructures between elements of a sequence. We use sequences of FL($\mathcal{L}$)-terms (with possibly shared variables) to denote them. The definition of the language associated with an extended type feature-term is naturally extended by letting

$$L[T_1[EA_1], T_2[EA_2]]^{\mathcal{M}} =_{df.} L[T_1[EA_1]]^{\mathcal{M}} \cdot L[T_2[EA_2]]^{\mathcal{M}}.$$

namely, the concatenation (in $\mathcal{S}^+$) of the respective languages. Note that by this definition, the inclusion of languages to the denotations of the underlying type is preserved, i.e.,

$$L[T_1[EA_1], T_2[EA_2]]^{\mathcal{M}} \subseteq [\tau(T_1[EA_1], T_2[EA_2])]^{\mathcal{M}}.$$

Finally, a declarative-unit $(U_1, ..., U_m) \triangleright T[EA]$ is *valid* iff for all dual fibred structures $\mathcal{M}$,

$$L[(U_1 ..., U_m)]^{\mathcal{M}} \subseteq L[T[EA]]^{\mathcal{M}}.$$

---

[7] Only rooted, connected, finite feature-structures are considered in [9], but all definitions extend naturally to the more relaxed definition employed here.

Following the HPSG convention, we represent also the lexical input words (and the generated concatenations thereof) as the value of yet another (new) feature, *phon*.

For the presentation of the fibred calculus, we use $\mathbf{u}(T_1, T_2)$ to denote that the (satisfiable) $\mathrm{FL}(\mathcal{L})$-terms T_1, T_2 are *unifiable*, and $T_1 \sqcup T_2$ for the (satisfiable) outcome of their unification. We do not present here the well-known full definition of unification (of FL-terms). Just note that its main effect can be seen in

$$f : p \sqcup f : x = f : p \wedge x$$

Thus, satisfying assignments are restricted to assign x a value from p^A. As x may appear as a conjunct elsewhere in a term, this restriction represents what is usually referred to as (part of) the "side-effect" of unification. The form of an axiom now becomes as follows.

$$\frac{T}{T[EA] \rhd T[EA]}$$

meaning that any satisfiable extended type term derives itself. The new form of the elimination rule $\leftarrow E$ now becomes:

$$(\leftarrow E) \quad \frac{U_1 \rhd T_1[T_{1.2}[EA_{1.2}] \leftarrow T_{1.1}[EA_{1.1}]], \ U_2 \rhd T_2[EA_{2.1}], \mathbf{u}(T_1, T_{1.2}), \mathbf{u}(T_{1.1}[EA_{1.1}], T_2[EA_{2.1}])}{(U_1, U_2) \rhd \sqcup(T_1, T_{1.2})[EA_{1.2}]}$$

The unifiability requirement is a side-condition of the rule, and is placed as assumptions for notational convenience only. This rule reflects a simplified version of the subcategorization-principle, as well as the head-feature principle of HPSG.

In Figure 7 is a sample derivation of a highly simplified representation for **Mary loves John**, where the only syntactic restriction present is number-agreement between the subject and the verb.

Next, we turn to the new form of a residuation-rule. The feature percolations for such rules are not explicitly discussed in the literature. The main property of the new form of the residuation-rules is, that feature-information present in the assumption is preserved, to be made use of after the discharge of the assumption. The new form of the ($\leftarrow I$) rule is as follows.

$$(\leftarrow I) \quad \frac{(U, T_1[EA_1]) \rhd T_2[EA_2]}{U \rhd T_2[(EA_2 \leftarrow T_1[EA_1])]}$$

To exemplify the particular feature percolation employed by the rule, we consider in the next section an example from Hebrew. The full calculus is presented in Figure 8. The following lemma ensures the soundness of the $\mathrm{FL}(\mathcal{L})$-calculus, based on the soundness of the $\mathcal{L}$-calculus.

Lemma: (type-restriction)
If U_i, $i = 1, n$ are satisfiable, and $\vdash_{\mathrm{FL}(\mathcal{L})} (U_1, ..., U_m) \rhd T[EA]$, then $T[EA]$ is satisfiable, and furthermore, $\vdash_{\mathcal{L}} (\tau(U_1), ..., \tau(U_m)) \rhd \tau(T[EA])$.

Proof: By a simple inductive argument on the structure of proofs. Satisfiability is preserved by the proof-rules due to the unifiability tests. The inclusion of the associated languages in the denotations of the underlying types was observed before, and the proof-rule mimic the categorial manipulation of these languages.

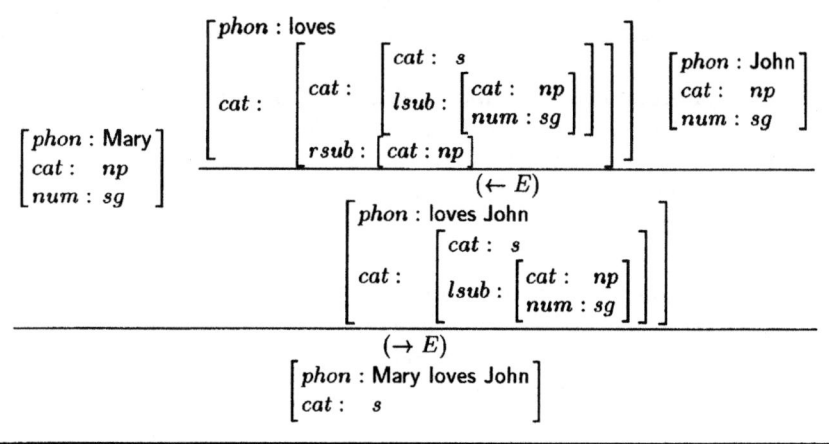

Fig. 7. A derivation of Mary loves John

$$(\text{Ax}) \quad \frac{T}{T[EA] \triangleright T[EA]}$$

$$(\leftarrow E) \quad \frac{U_1 \triangleright T_1[T_{1.2}[EA_{1.2}] \leftarrow T_{1.1}[EA_{1.1}]], \ U_2 \triangleright T_2[EA_{2.1}], \mathbf{u}(T_1, T_{1.2}), \mathbf{u}(T_{1.1}[EA_{1.1}], T_2[EA_{2.1}])}{(U_1, U_2) \triangleright \sqcup(T_1, T_{1.2})[EA_{1.2}]}$$

$$(\rightarrow E) \quad \frac{U_1 \triangleright T_1[EA_{1.1}], \ U_2 \triangleright T_2[T_{2.1}[EA_{2.1}] \rightarrow T_{2.2}[EA_{2.2}]], \ \mathbf{u}(T_2, T_{2.1}), \mathbf{u}(T_{2.1}[EA_{2.1}], T_1[EA_{1.1}])}{(U_1, U_2) \triangleright \sqcup(T_2, T_{2.1})[EA_{2.1}]}$$

$$(\leftarrow I) \quad \frac{(U, T_1[EA_1]) \triangleright T_2[EA_2]}{U \triangleright T_2[(EA_2 \leftarrow T_1[EA_1])]}$$

$$(\rightarrow I) \quad \frac{(T_1[EA_1], U) \triangleright T_2[EA_2]}{U \triangleright T_2[(T_1[EA_1] \rightarrow EA_2)]}$$

Fig. 8. The FL($\mathcal{L}$) calculus

4 An application of residuation

First, recall the derivation of John whom Mary likes slept in [3], using the residuation rule ($\leftarrow I$) of $\mathcal{L}$. The category assigned to whom is $(np \rightarrow np) \leftarrow (s \leftarrow np)$, which triggers the introduction of an assumption $[np]_1$ (with a null string value), later discharged by the residuation rule. We now show how the corresponding FL($\mathcal{L}$) rule can be used to solve elegantly a generalization of relativizing in English.

In Hebrew, many categories, including NPs, VPs and APs, are marked for gender, being either feminine or masculine. In particular, according to some

syntactic analysis[8] of Hebrew, there are two relative pronouns of the two corresponding genders, ota (feminine) and oto (masculine), similarly to German and
Russian, for example. One of the agreement rules in Hebrew calls for a gender
agreement between a relative pronoun (in a relative clause), and the relativized
NP (in addition to subject-verb gender agreement). Note that the first person
singular pronoun any (i.e., I) is underspecified for gender, and agrees with both
genders. Thus, we have[9]:

(1) hayeled oto ani ohev shar
namely
the boy$_m$ whom$_m$ I love$_m$ sings$_m$,
but
(2) (*) hayalda oto ani ohev shara
namely
(*) the girl$_f$ whom$_m$ I love$_m$ sings$_f$.
Similarly,
(3) hayalda ota ani ohev shara
namely
the girl$_f$ whom$_f$ I love$_m$ sings$_f$,
but
(4) (*) hayeld ota ani ohev shar
namely
(*) the boy$_m$ whom$_f$ I love$_m$ sings$_m$.
Actually, as there are also plural versions of these relative pronouns (otam for
masculine-plural and otan for feminine-plural), we end up in four similar, though
different, lexical entries. Let us ignore for this example all other featural distinctions as number, person, etc., as well as their agreement rules. One way of en-
forcing the gender agreement in relativization is to assign the following extended
categories to oto and ota, using a gender feature *gen* with atomic values m (for
masculine) and f (for feminine). This way, the specific gender expected by each
relative pronoun is built-in in its lexical entry.

$$
\begin{bmatrix}
phon : oto \\
cat : \begin{bmatrix}
cat : \begin{bmatrix}
cat : \begin{bmatrix} cat : np \\ gen : [1] \end{bmatrix} \\
lsub : \begin{bmatrix} cat : np \\ gen : [1] \end{bmatrix}
\end{bmatrix} \\
rsub : \begin{bmatrix}
cat : s \\
rsub : \begin{bmatrix} cat : np \\ gen : [1]m \end{bmatrix}
\end{bmatrix}
\end{bmatrix}
\end{bmatrix}
\qquad
\begin{bmatrix}
phon : ota \\
cat : \begin{bmatrix}
cat : \begin{bmatrix}
cat : \begin{bmatrix} cat : np \\ gen : [1] \end{bmatrix} \\
lsub : \begin{bmatrix} cat : np \\ gen : [1] \end{bmatrix}
\end{bmatrix} \\
rsub : \begin{bmatrix}
cat : s \\
rsub : \begin{bmatrix} cat : np \\ gen : [1]f \end{bmatrix}
\end{bmatrix}
\end{bmatrix}
\end{bmatrix}
$$

The generated assumption now carries gender information, that has to be perco-
lated when a residuation-rule is applied (otherwise this information disappeares
with the discharged assumption). Figure 9 shows the main part of the derivation
corresponding to hayeled oto ani ohev shar. The rest of the derivation combines

---

[8] Other analyses regard these examples as having a phonologically-empty relative-
pronoun, and a dislocated resumptive pronoun.

[9] To simplify, we ignore the fact that Hebrew is written from right to left.

with the subject, matching the masculine gender, and then the relativized NP combines with the intransitive verb sings, again with the right gender agreement.

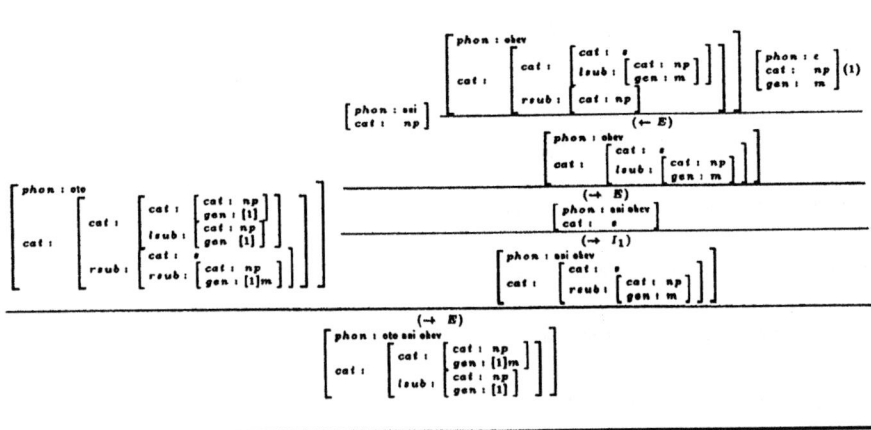

Fig. 9. A derivation of oto ani ohev

Note that the lexical value associated with the verbs ohev/ohevet right-subcategorizes for a (gender-underspecified) np, being ready to combine with noun-phrases of both genders. The gender of the generated assumption "dictates" the way the derivation proceeds. A similar derivation exists for (3), where the generated assumption has $[gen : f]$ as the extra-categorial initial feature-information, to match that assigned to ota. On the other hand, there is no way to generate assumptions that will cause the wrong gender matching with the relative pronoun, thus blocking (4) and (2). The structure of the above derivation can be viewed as a logical counterpart of a typical use of the SLASH feature in HPSG's treatment of object relativization. Similar use of hypothetical reasoning in other cases of long-distance dependencies suggests itself.

5 Conclusions

The paper presented a dual-fibring of feature-logics and concatanation-logics, by which types "live within" feature-terms, in contrast to previously suggested fibrings, in which feature-terms "live within" types. In particular, arrow-introduction rules (for hypothetical reasoning) in the dual-fibring calculus are presented. The main benefit of this approach is that it models better actual practice in computational linguistics, as embodied in formalisms such as HPSG. In that, such a dual-fibring is a first step towards a more comprehensive logical formalisation of formalisms like HPSG.

6 Acknowledgments

Most of this research was carried out under a grant B 62-443 from Nederlandse Organisatie voor Wetenschappelijk Onderzoek (NWO). I wish to thank NWO for their support. I thank Jan van Eijck and Michael Moortgat, as well as the OTS students in a seminar on the categories and features, for various discussions and an oppurtunity to present these ideas while in the making. I thank Gosse Bouma, Mark Johnson and Esther König-Baumer for various comments on earlier drafts. The (anonymous) referees of this volume are thanked for several suggestions that led to an improvement of the presentation. Ranni Nelken spotted an error in the Hebrew example in a previous draft. In the Technion, my work was partially funded by the fund for the promotion of research in the Technion.

References

1. Goose Bouma. Modifiers and specifiers in categorial unification grammar. *Linguistics*, 26:21 – 46, 1988.
2. Gosse Bouma. *Nonmonotonicity and Categorial Unification grammar*. PhD thesis, Groningen university, The Netherlands, 1988.
3. Jochem Dörre, Esther König, and Dov Gabbay. Fibred semantics for feature-based grammar logic. *J. of Logic, Language and Information*, 5, October, 1996.
4. Jochen Dörre and Suresh Manandhar. On constraint-based Lambek calculi. In Patrick Blackburn and Martin de Rijke, editors, *Specifying Syntactic Structures*, Studies in Logic, Language and Information (SiLLI). CSLI, Stanford, CA 94305, to appear. available from http://xxx.lanl.gov/cmp-lg/9508008.
5. Joachim Lambek. The mathematics of sentence structure. *American mathematical monthly*, 65:154 – 170, 1958.
6. Michael Moortgat. Categorial type logics. In Johan van Benthem and Alice ter Muelen, editors, *Handbook for Logic and Language*. Elsevier, 1997.
7. Carl Pollard and Ivan Sag. *Head-Driven phrase structure grammar*. Chicago university press and CSLI publications, 1994.
8. Stephen G. Pulman. Unification encodings of grammatical notations. *Computational Linguistics*, 22:295 – 328, 1996.
9. Shuly Wintner and Nissim Francez. Parsing with typed feature structures. In *Proceedings of the 4th International workshop on parsing technologies (IWPT)*, pages 273–287, Prague, Czech republic, September, 1995.

An Operational Model for Parsing Definite Clause Grammars with Infinite Terms

Manuel Vilares[1], Miguel A. Alonso[1], and David Cabrero[2]

[1] Department of Computer Sciences
Faculty of Informatics, University of A Coruña
Campus de Elviña s/n, 15071 A Coruña, Spain
e-mail: {vilares,alonso}@dc.fi.udc.es
[2] Ramón Piñeiro Research Center for Humanities
Estrada Santiago-Noia km 3, A Barcia,
15896 Santiago de Compostela, Spain
e-mail: dcabrero@cirp.es

Abstract. Logic programs share with context-free grammars a strong reliance on well-formedness conditions. Their proof procedures can be viewed as a generalization of context-free parsing. In particular, definite clause grammars can be interpreted as an extension of the classic context-free formalism where the notion of finite set of non-terminal symbols is generalized to a possibly infinite domain of directed graphs. In this case, standard polynomial parsing methods may no longer be applicable as they can lead to gross inefficiency or even non-termination for the algorithms. We present a proposal to avoid these drawbacks, focusing on two aspects: avoiding limitations on the parsing process, and extending the unification to composed terms without overload for non-cyclic structures.

1 Introduction

Grammar formalisms based on the encoding of grammatical information in unification-based strategies enjoy some currency both in linguistics and natural language processing. Such formalisms, as is the case of *definite clause grammars* (DCGs), can be thought of, by analogy to context-free grammars, as generalizing the notion of non-terminal symbol from a finite domain of atomic elements to a possibly infinite domain of directed graph structures.

Although the use of infinite terms can be often avoided in practical applications, the potential offered by cyclic trees is appreciated in language development tasks, where a large completion domain allows the modeling effort to be saved. Unfortunately, in moving to an infinite non-terminal domain, standard methods of parsing may no longer be applicable to the formalism. Typically, the problem manifests itself as gross inefficiency or even non-termination of the algorithms.

One approach guaranteeing termination that has been investigated is based on restricting to some extent the parsing process, for example:

- mandating a non-cyclic context-free backbone and using only major category information in the original grammar to filter spurious hypotheses by top-down filtering [1].
- coupling grammar and parsing design, which is the case of some works based on constraint logic programming [12]. Since linguistic and technological problems are inherently mixed, this approach magnifies the difficulty of writing an adequate grammar-parser system.
- parameterizing parsing algorithms with grammar dependent information, that tells the algorithm which of the information in the feature structures is significant for guiding the parse [11]. Here, the choice for the exact parameter to be used is dependent on both the grammar and the parsing algorithm, which produce results that are of no practical interest in a grammar development context.

Another approach has been to extend the unification in order to provide the capability of traversing cyclic trees, for example:

- substituting resolution by another unification mechanism. This is the case of Haridi and Sahlin in [4], who base unification on natural deduction [9]. Here, pointers are temporarily replaced in the structures, requiring undoing after execution, and unification of non-cyclic structures is penalized.
- considering functions and predicates as elements with the same order as variables as is shown by Filgueiras in [3]. Essentially, the idea is the same as that considered by Haridi and Sahlin, and the drawbacks are extensible to this case.
- generalizing an available algorithm for traversing cyclic lists, as is the case of Nilsson and Tanaka in [7]. These strategies require some past nodes in structures to be saved and compared to new nodes. So, computational efficiency depends heavily on the depth of the structures.

Our goal is to combine the advantages of the preceding approaches, eliminating the drawbacks.

In Sect. 2 of this paper, we present our parsing model for DCGs, a summary of the results described in [14]. An example of parsing is shown in Sect. 3. Section 4 describes our strategy for detecting and traversing cyclic terms. Sect. 5 compares our work with preceding proposals. In Sect. 6 we characterize the application domain of the algorithm. Sect. 7, includes a general consideration of the quality of the system. Finally, Sect. 8 is a conclusion regarding the work presented.

2   A parsing Strategy for DCGs

Strategies for executing *definite clause grammars* (DCGs) are still often expressed directly as symbolic manipulations of terms and rules using backtracking, which does not constitute an adequate basis for efficient implementations. Some measures can be put into practice in order to make good these lacks: firstly, to orientate the proof procedure towards a compiled architecture. Secondly, to improve the sharing quality of computations in a framework which is naturally not deterministic. Finally, to restrict the computation effort to the useful part of the search space.

2.1 Logical Push-Down Automata as Operational Formalism

Our operational formalism is an evolution of the notion of *logical push-down automaton* (LPDA) introduced by Lang in [5], a push-down automaton that stores logical atoms and substitutions on its stack, and uses unification to apply transitions.

For us, an LPDA is a 7-tuple $\mathcal{A} = (\mathcal{X}, \mathcal{F}, \Sigma, \Delta, \$, \$_f, \Theta)$, where: $\mathcal{X}$ is a denumerable and ordered set of *variables*, $\mathcal{F}$ is a finite set of *functional symbols*, Σ is a finite set of *extensional predicate symbols*, Δ is a finite set of predicate symbols used to represent the *literals* stored in the stack, $\$$ is the *initial predicate*, $\$_f$ is the *final predicate*; and Θ is a finite set of *transitions*. Transitions are of three kinds:

- *horizontal:* $B \longmapsto C\{A\}$. Applicable to stacks $E.\rho \, \xi$, iff there exists the *most general unifier* (mgu), $\sigma = \mathrm{mgu}(E, B)$ such that $F\sigma = A\sigma$, for F a fact in the extensional database. We obtain the new stack $C\sigma.\rho\sigma \, \xi$.
- *push:* $B \longmapsto CB\{A\}$. We can apply this to stacks $E.\rho \, \xi$, iff there is $\sigma = \mathrm{mgu}(E, B)$, such that $F\sigma = A\sigma$, for F a fact F in the extensional database. We obtain the stack $C\sigma.\sigma \, B.\rho \, \xi$.
- *pop:* $BD \longmapsto C\{A\}$. Applicable to stacks of the form $E.\rho \, E'.\rho' \, \xi$, iff there is $\sigma = \mathrm{mgu}((E, E'\rho), (B, D))$, such that $F\sigma = A\sigma$, for F a fact in the extensional database. The result will be the new stack $C\sigma.\rho'\rho\sigma \, \xi$.

where B, C and D are items, and A is in $T_\Sigma[\mathcal{F} \cup \mathcal{X}]$ representing the control condition.

In bottom-up evaluation strategies, we can exploit the possibilities of dynamic programming taking S^1 as dynamic frame [13,2], by collapsing stacks on its top. In this way, we optimize sharing of computations in opposition to the standard dynamic frame S^T, where stacks are represented by all their elements, or even S^2 using only the last two elements. To replace the lack of information about the rest of the stack during pop transitions, we redefine the behavior of transitions on items I in a dynamic frame S^1, as follows:

- *horizontal case:* $(B \longmapsto C)(I) = C\sigma$, where $\sigma = \mathrm{mgu}(I, B)$.
- *push case:* $(B \longmapsto CB)(I) = C\sigma$, where $\sigma = \mathrm{mgu}(I, B)$.
- *pop case:* $(BD \longmapsto C)(I) = \{D\sigma \longmapsto C\sigma\}$, where $\sigma = \mathrm{mgu}(I, B)$, and $D\sigma \longmapsto C\sigma$ is the *dynamic transition* generated by the pop transition. This is applicable to the item resulting from the pop transition, and also probably to items to be generated.
  The number of dynamic transitions can be limited by grouping items in *itemsets* that refer to the analysis of a same word in the input string, and completing in sequence these itemsets. So, we can guarantee that a dynamic transition can be used to synchronize a computation to be done in this

itemset if and only if the itemset is not locally deterministic and an empty reduction has been performed on it [13]. That establishes a simple criterion to save or not these transitions.

where we have omitted the use of control conditions, $\{A\}$, in order to simplify the exposition.

2.2 LALR Parsing in Dynamic Programming

Experience shows that the most efficient evaluation strategies seem to be those bottom-up approaches including a predictive phase in order to restrict the search space. So, our evaluation scheme is a bottom-up architecture optimized with a control provided by an LALR(1) driver, that we shall formalize now.

Assuming a DCG of clauses $\gamma_k : A_{k,0} : -A_{k,1}, \ldots, A_{k,n_k}$, we introduce: the vector $\boldsymbol{T}_k$ of the variables occurring in γ_k, and the predicate symbol $\nabla_{k,i}$. An instance of $\nabla_{k,i}(\boldsymbol{T}_k)$ indicates that all literals from the ith literal in the body of γ_k have been proved.

The *stack* is a finite sequence of *items* $[A, it, bp, st].\sigma$, where the top is on the left, A is a category in the DCG, σ a substitution, it is the current position in the input string, bp is the position in this input string at which we began to look for that configuration of $\mathcal{A}$, and st is a state for a driver controlling the evaluation. We choose as driver the LALR(1) automaton associated to the context-free skeleton of the logic grammar, by keeping only functors in the clauses to obtain terminals from the extensional database, and variables from heads in the intensional one. We can now describe the transitions:

1. $[A_{k,n_k}, it, bp, st] \longmapsto [\nabla_{k,n_k}(\boldsymbol{T}_k), it, it, st] [A_{k,n_k}, it, bp, st]$
   $\{\text{action}(st, \text{token}_{it}) = \text{reduce}(\gamma_k^f)\}$

2. $[\nabla_{k,i}(\boldsymbol{T}_k), it, r, st_1]$
   $[A_{k,i}, r, bp, st_1] \longmapsto [\nabla_{k,i-1}(\boldsymbol{T}_k), it, bp, st_2]$
   $\{\text{action}(st_2, \text{token}_{it}) = \text{shift}(st_1)\}, \ i \in [1, n_k]$

3. $[\nabla_{k,0}(\boldsymbol{T}_k), it, bp, st_1] \longmapsto [A_{k,0}, it, bp, st_2]$
   $\{\text{goto}(st_1, A_{k,0}) = st_2\}$

4. $[A_{k,i}, it, bp, st_1] \longmapsto [A_{k,i+1}, it + 1, it, st_2] [A_{k,i}, it, bp, st_1]$
   $\{\text{action}(st_1, \text{token}_{it}) = \text{shift}(st_2)\},$
   $\text{token}_{it} = A_{k,i+1}, \ i \in [0, n_k)$

5. $[A_{k,i}, it, bp, st_1] \longmapsto [A_{l,0}, it + 1, it, st_2] [A_{k,i}, it, bp, st_1]$
   $\{\text{action}(st_1, \text{token}_{it}) = \text{shift}(st_2)\},$
   $\text{token}_{it} = A_{l,0} \neq A_{k,i+1}, \ i \in [0, n_k)$

6. $[\$, 0, 0, 0] \longmapsto [A_{k,0}, 0, 0, st] [\$, 0, 0, 0]$
   $\{\text{action}(0, \text{token}_0) = \text{shift}(st)\}$

where *action*(*state*, *token*) denotes the action of the driver for a given *state* and *token*, γ_k^f denotes the context-free rule in this driver corresponding to the clause γ_k, and expressions between brackets are conditions to be tested for the driver before applying transitions. Briefly, we can interpret these transitions as follows:

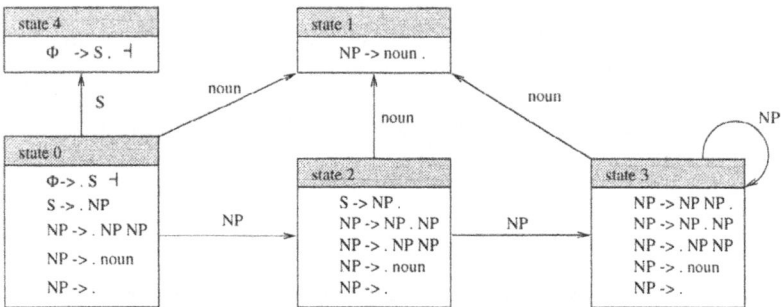

Fig. 1. Characteristic finite state machine for the running example

1. select the clause γ_k whose head is to be proved, then push $\nabla_{k,n_k}(T_k)$ on the stack to indicate that none of the body literals have yet been proved.
2. the position literal $\nabla_{k,i}(T_k)$ indicates that all body literals of γ_k following the ith literal have been proved. Now, all stacks having $A_{k,i}$ just below the top can be reduced and in consequence the position literal can be incremented.
3. the literal $\nabla_{k,0}(T_k)$ indicates that all literals in the body of γ_k have been proved. Hence, we can replace it on the stack by the head $A_{k,0}$ of the rule, since it has now been proved.
4. The literal $A_{k,i+1}$ is pushed onto the stack, assuming that it will be needed for the proof.
5. The literal $A_{l,0}$ is pushed onto the stack in order to begin to prove the body of clause γ_l.
6. As a special case of the previous transition, the initial predicate will only be used in push transitions, and exclusively as the first step of the LPDA computation.

The parser builds items from the initial one, applying transitions to existing ones until no new application is possible. An equitable selection order in the search space ensures fairness and completeness. Redundant items are ignored by a subsumption-based relation. Correctness and completeness, in the absence of functional symbols, are easily obtained from [13, 2], based on these results for LALR(1) context-free parsing and bottom-up evaluation, both using S^1 as dynamic frame. Our goal now is to extent these results to a larger class of grammars.

3 Parsing a Sample Sentence

To illustrate our work we consider as running example a simple DCG to deal with the sequentialization of nouns in English, as in the case of *"North Atlantic Treaty Organization"*. The clauses, in which the arguments are used to build the abstract syntax tree, could be the following

$$\gamma_1: \ \mathrm{s(X)} \ \rightarrow \mathrm{np(X)}. \qquad \gamma_2: \ \mathrm{np(np(X,Y))} \ \rightarrow \ \mathrm{np(X)\ np(Y)}.$$
$$\gamma_3: \ \mathrm{np(X)} \ \rightarrow \ \mathrm{noun(X)}. \quad \gamma_4: \ \mathrm{np(nil)}.$$

In this case, the augmented context-free skeleton is given by the context-free rules:

$$(0)\ \Phi \ \rightarrow \ \mathrm{S} \ \dashv \qquad (1)\ \mathrm{S} \ \rightarrow \ \mathrm{NP} \qquad (2)\ \mathrm{NP} \ \rightarrow \ \mathrm{NP\ NP}$$
$$(3)\ \mathrm{NP} \ \rightarrow \ \mathrm{noun} \qquad (4)\ \mathrm{NP} \ \rightarrow \ \varepsilon$$

whose characteristic finite state machine is shown in Fig. 1.

We are going to describe the parsing process for the simple sentence "*North Atlantic*" using our running grammar. From the initial predicate \$ on the top of the stack, and taking into account that the LALR automaton is in the initial state 0, the first action is the scanning of the word "*North*", which involves pushing the item $[noun(\text{"}North\text{"}), 0, 1, st_1]$ that indicates the recognition of term $noun(\text{"}North\text{"})$ between positions 0 and 1 in the input string, with state 1 the current state in the LALR driver. This configuration is shown in Fig. 2.

$$\begin{array}{|c|}\hline [\$, 0, 0, st_0] \\ \hline \end{array} \vdash \begin{array}{|c|}\hline [noun(\text{"}North\text{"}), 1, 0, st_1] \\ \hline [\$, 0, 0, st_0] \\ \hline \end{array}$$

Fig. 2. Configurations during the scanning of "*North*".

At this point, we can apply transitions 1, 2 and 3 to reduce by clause γ_3. The configurations involved in this reduction are shown in Fig. 3.

$$\vdash \begin{array}{|c|}\hline [\nabla_{3,1}(X), 1, 1, st_1] \\ \hline [noun(\text{"}North\text{"}), 1, 0, st_1] \\ \hline [\$, 0, 0, st_0] \\ \hline \end{array} \vdash \begin{array}{|c|}\hline [\nabla_{3,0}(\text{"}North\text{"}), 1, 0, st_0] \\ \hline [\$, 0, 0, st_0] \\ \hline \end{array}$$

$$\vdash \begin{array}{|c|}\hline [np(\text{"}North\text{"}), 1, 0, st_2] \\ \hline [\$, 0, 0, st_0] \\ \hline \end{array}$$

Fig. 3. Configuration during the reduction of clause γ_3.

We can now scan the word "*Atlantic*", resulting in the recognizing of the term $noun(\text{"}Atlantic\text{"})$ between positions 1 and 2 in the input string, with the LALR driver in state 1. As in the case of the previous word, at this moment we can reduce by clause γ_3. This process is depicted in Fig. 4.

After having recognized two *np* predicates, we can reduce by clause γ_2 in order to obtain a new predicate *np* which will represent the nominal phrase "*North Atlantic*". This reduction is shown in Fig. 5.

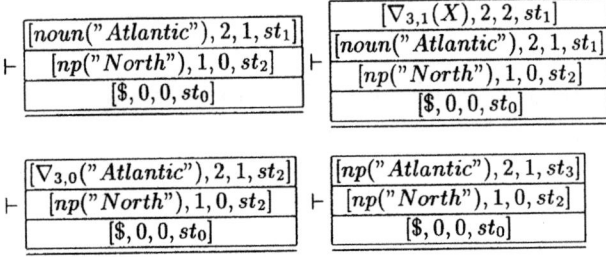

Fig. 4. Configurations during the processing of the word "*Atlantic*".

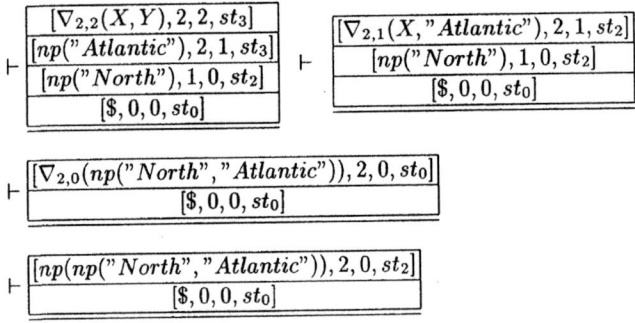

Fig. 5. Recognition of the nominal phrase "*North Atlantic*".

The recognition of the complete sentence ends with a reduction by clause γ_1, obtaining the term

$$s(np("North","Atlantic"))$$

representing the abstract parse tree for the sentence "*North Atlantic*". The state of the LALR driver will now be 4, which is the final state, meaning that the processing of this branch has finished. The resulting configurations are depicted in Fig. 6.

4 Traversing Cyclic Terms

Although structures that generate cyclic terms can be avoided in final systems, they usually arise during the development of grammars. For example, in the previous example we have shown the parsing process for only one branch, but the grammar really defines an infinite number of possible analyses for each input sentence. If we observe the LALR automaton, we can see that in states 0, 2 and 3 we can always reduce the clause γ_4, which has an empty right-hand side, in addition to other possible shift and reduce actions. In particular, in state 3 the predicate np can be generated an unbounded number of times without consuming any character of the input string.

$$\vdash \frac{\boxed{\begin{array}{c} [\nabla_{1,1}(X), 2, 2, st_2] \\ [np(np("North","Atlantic")), 2, 0, st_2] \\ [\$, 0, 0, st_0] \end{array}}}{}$$

$$\vdash \frac{\boxed{\begin{array}{c} [\nabla_{1,0}(np(np("North","Atlantic"))), 2, 0, st_0] \\ [\$, 0, 0, st_0] \end{array}}}{}$$

$$\vdash \frac{\boxed{\begin{array}{c} [s(np("North","Atlantic")), 2, 0, st_4] \\ [\$, 0, 0, st_0] \end{array}}}{}$$

Fig. 6. Configurations for the recognizing of the sentence "*North Atlantic*".

Our parsing algorithm has no problems in dealing with non-determinism. It simply explores all possible alternatives in each point of the parsing process. This does not affect the level of sharing, which is achieved by the use of S^1 as dynamic frame, but it can pose problems with termination due to the presence of cyclic structures. Therefore, a special mechanism for representing cyclic terms must be used. At this point, it is important to remark that this mechanism should not decrease the efficiency in the treatment of non cyclic structures. In this context, we have separated cyclic tree traversal in two phases:

- cycle detection in the context-free backbone.
- cycle traversing for predicate and function symbols by extending the unification algorithm to these terms.

We justify this approach by the fact that the syntactic structure of the predicate symbols represents the context-free skeleton of the DCG. As a consequence, it is possible to efficiently guide the detection of cyclic predicate symbols on the basis of the dynamic programming interpretation for the LALR(1) driver. In effect, for cycles to arise in arguments, it is first necessary that the context-free backbone given by the predicate symbols determines the recognition of a same syntactic category without extra work for the scanning mode. It should be pointed out that the reciprocal is not always true. This is, for example, the case of the DCG defined by the following clauses:

$$\gamma_1 : \text{a(nil)}. \qquad \gamma_2 : \text{a(f(Y,X))} \rightarrow \text{a(X)}.$$

whose context-free skeleton is given by the rules

$$(1)\ A \rightarrow \varepsilon \qquad (2)\ A \rightarrow A$$

where the presence of cycles is clear. On the other hand, one look at the DCG is sufficient to detect the refutation of non-cyclic infinite structures of the form

$$\text{a(nil), a(f(Y}_1,\text{nil)), } \ldots, \text{ a(f(Y}_{n+1},\text{f(Y}_n, .\overset{n}{.}. \text{ f(Y}_1,\text{nil) } .\overset{n}{.}.))), \ldots$$

4.1 Searching for a Condition to Loop

From the previous discussion, we apply the first phase in our traverse strategy to detect cycles in context-free grammars in a dynamic frame S^1, using an LALR(1) parser. This problem has previously been studied in [13]. Given that we have indexed the parse, it is sufficient to verify that in a same itemset the parsing process re-visits a state. In effect, this implies that an empty string has been parsed in a loop within the automaton. This can be shown in the context-free backbone of our running example. Following with our example, we can see in the left-hand drawing of Fig. 7 a cycle in the context-free skeleton produced by successive reductions by rules 2 and 4 in state 3. In this figure, boxes represent the recognition of a grammar category in a given state of the LALR(1) driver.

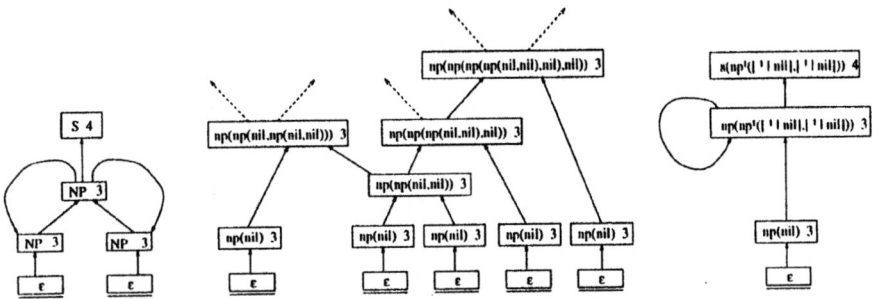

Fig. 7. Cycles in the context-free skeleton and within terms.

To verify now that we can extend cycle detection to predicate symbols, we shall test for unification of the terms implicated. In particular, we must generalize unification to detect cyclic terms with functional symbols.

4.2 Extending Unification and Subsumption

To prevent the evaluation looping, the concept of substitution is generalized to include function and predicate symbol substitution. This means modifying the unification and subsumption algorithms so that these symbols are treated in the same way as for variables.

Looking for Cycles. After testing the compatibility of name and arity between two terms, the algorithm establishes if the associated non-terminals in the driver have been generated in the same state, covering the same portion of the text, which is equivalent to comparing the corresponding back-pointers. If all these comparisons succeed, unification could be possible and we look for cycles, but only when these non-terminals show a cyclic behavior in the LALR(1) driver. In this case, the algorithm verifies, one by one, the possible occurrence of repeated terms by comparing the addresses of these with those of the arguments of the other predicate symbol. The optimal sharing of the interpretation guarantees that cycles arise if and only if any of these comparisons succeed. In this last case, the unification algorithm stops on the pair of arguments concerned, while continuing with the rest of the arguments.

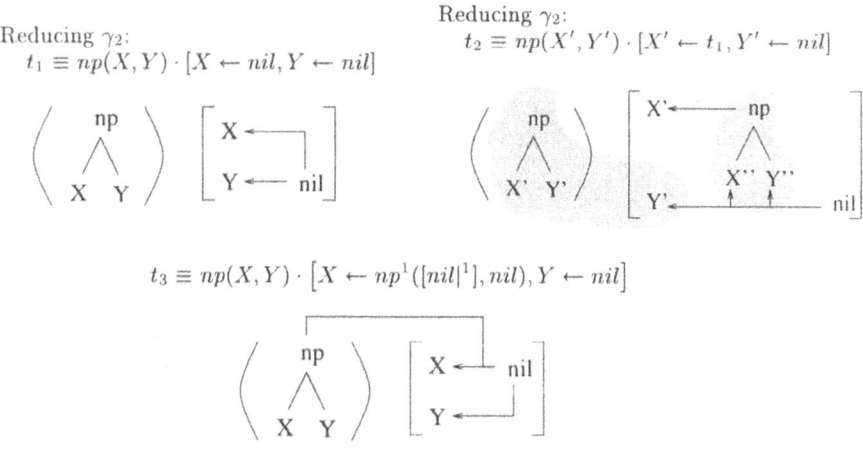

Reducing γ_2:
$$t_1 \equiv np(X,Y) \cdot [X \leftarrow nil, Y \leftarrow nil]$$

Reducing γ_2:
$$t_2 \equiv np(X',Y') \cdot [X' \leftarrow t_1, Y' \leftarrow nil]$$

$$t_3 \equiv np(X,Y) \cdot \left[X \leftarrow np^1([nil|^1], nil), Y \leftarrow nil\right]$$

Fig. 8. Cyclic tree traversing (1)

Returning to Fig. 7, once the context-free cycle has been detected, we check for possible cyclic term in the original DCG. The center drawing in that figure shows how the family of terms

$$np(nil), np(np(nil, nil)), np(np(np(nil, nil), nil)), \ldots, np(np^1([nil|^1], nil))$$

is generated. In an analogous form, the family

$$np(nil), np(np(nil, nil)), np(np(nil, np(nil, nil))), \ldots, np(np^1(nil, [nil|^1]))$$

can be generated. Due to the sharing of computations the second family is generated from the result of the first derivation, so, by means of the successive applications of clauses γ_2 and γ_4, we will in fact generate the term on the right-hand side of the figure, $np(np^1([nil|^1], [nil|^1]))$, which corresponds exactly to the internal representation of the term[1]. We shall now describe how we detect and represent these types of construction. In the first stages of the parsing process, two terms $np(nil)$ are generated, which are unified with $np(X)$ and $np(Y)$ in γ_2, and $np(np(X,Y))$ is instantiated, yielding $np(np(nil, nil))$. In the following

---

[1] it must be pointed out that we could collapse structures $np(nil)$ and $np(np^1([nil|^1], [nil|^1]))$ from the right-hand side of Fig. 7 in $np(^1[nil|np(^1,^1)])$, but this would require a non-trivial additional treatment.

Reducing γ_2:

$$t_4 \equiv np(X,Y) \cdot \begin{bmatrix} X \leftarrow np^1([nil|^1], nil), \\ Y \leftarrow nil \end{bmatrix}$$

Reducing γ_2:

$$t_5 \equiv np(X,Y'') \cdot \begin{bmatrix} X \leftarrow np^1([nil|^1], nil), \\ Y'' \leftarrow t_4 \end{bmatrix}$$

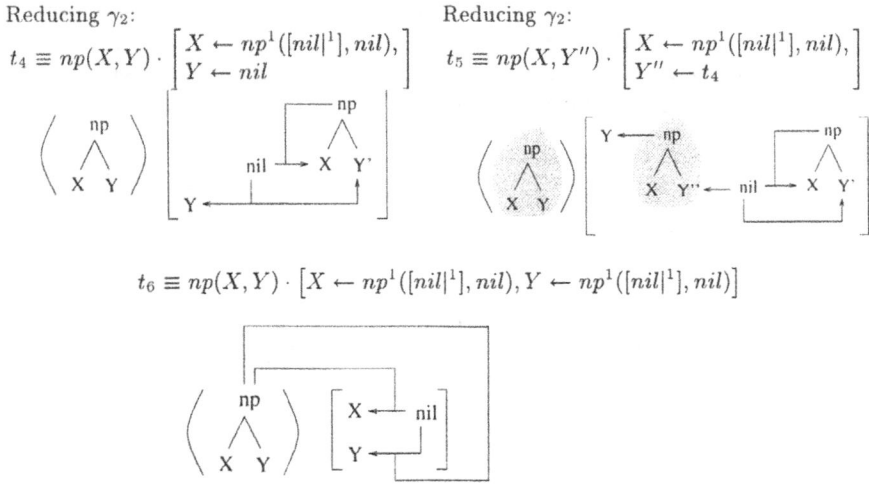

$$t_6 \equiv np(X,Y) \cdot \begin{bmatrix} X \leftarrow np^1([nil|^1], nil), Y \leftarrow np^1([nil|^1], nil) \end{bmatrix}$$

Fig. 9. Cyclic tree traversing (2)

stage, the same step will be performed over $np(np(nil, nil))$ and $np(nil)$, yielding $np(np(np(nil, nil), nil))$. At this point, we consider that:

- there exists a cycle in the context-free backbone,
- we have repeated the same kind of unification twice, and
- the latter has been applied over the result of the former.

Therefore this process can be repeated an unbounded number of times to give terms with the form $np(np^1([nil|^1], nil))$. The same reasoning can be applied if we wish to unify with the variable Y. The right-hand drawing in Fig.7 shows the compact representation we use in this case of cyclic terms. The functor np is considered in itself as a kind of special variable with two arguments. Each of these arguments can be either nil or a recursive application of np to itself. In the figure, superscripts are used to indicate where a functor is referenced by some of its arguments.

The unification is explained in detail in Fig. 8. The terms to be unified are intermediate structures in the computation of the proof shared-forest associated to the successive reductions of rules 2 and 4 in the context-free skeleton. So we have to compare the structures of the arguments associated to predicate symbol np, and in order to clarify the exposition, we have written them as term-substitution. The second term, t_2, is obtained after applying a unification step over the first one, t_1. To show that this step is the same we applied when building t_1, they are shadowed. Now, t_1 and t_2 satisfy the conditions we have established to detect a cycle, namely a cycle exists in the context-free backbone, and we have repeated the same kind of unification twice, the latter over the result of the former. t_3 is the resulting cyclic term. In Fig. 9 we show an analogous operation over t_3.

Cyclic Subsumption and Unification. Now, we will see some examples of how the presence of cyclic terms affects the unification and subsumption operations.

In general, a function subsumes ($\preceq$) another function if it has the same functor and arity and its arguments either are equal or subsume the other function's arguments. When dealing with cyclic terms, one or more arguments can be built from an alternative: another term, or cycling back to the function. Such an argument will subsume another one if it is subsumed by at least one alternative.

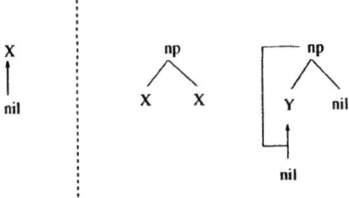

Fig. 10. mgu of substitutions involving cyclic terms.

Returning to the example of Fig. 8, we can conclude that $np^1([nil|^1],^1)$ subsumes $np^1([nil|^1], nil)$. Functor and arity, $np/2$ are the same, and so are the first arguments, $[nil|^1]$, and for the second ones, $[nil|^1] \preceq nil$ because of the first alternative, clearly $nil \preceq nil$.

On the other hand, when calculating the mgu we also have to consider each alternative in the cyclic term, but discarding those that do not match. Thus:

$$\text{mgu}(\{Y \leftarrow [a|b]\}, \{Y \leftarrow a\}) = \{Y \leftarrow a\}$$

and therefore, following the latter example:

$$\text{mgu}(np(X, X), np^1([nil|^1], nil)) = \{X \leftarrow nil\}$$

which is graphically shown in Fig. 10. Finally, we must not forget that variables are the most general terms and so they subsume any term, even alternatives in cyclic terms. For example:

$$\text{mgu}(np(X), np^1([a|^1])) = \{X \leftarrow [a|np^1([a|^1])]\}$$

5 A Comparison with Previous Works

In relation to systems forcing the primacy of major category [1], we only consider the context-free skeleton of a DCG as a guideline for parsing, but without omitting information about sub-categorization. So, we apply constraints due to unification as soon as rules are applied, rather than considering a supplementary filtering phase after a classic context-free parsing.

The strategy described does not couple the design of descriptive and operational formalisms [12], nor even limit them [11]. In particular, we do not split up the infinite non-terminal domain into a finite set of equivalence classes that can be used for parsing. The only practical constraint is the consideration of monotonous DCGs, that we justify for their practical linguistic interest. This allows us to conceive their use in a grammar development context.

In comparison with algorithms based on the temporary replacement of pointers in structures [4], our method does not need main memory references for pointer replacements. In addition, the absence of backtracking makes it unnecessary to undo work after execution, which facilitates the sharing of structures.

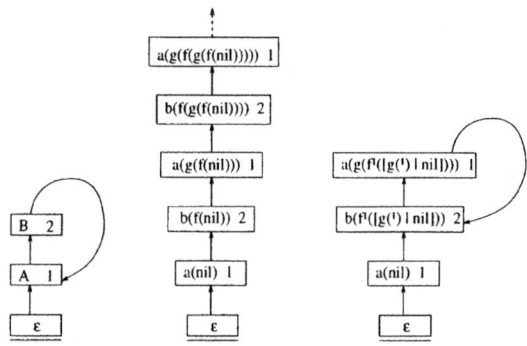

Fig. 11. Cycles in a conjunctive context

Focusing now our attention on methods extending the concept of unification to composed terms [3], the overload for non-cyclic structures is often great. In our case, we minimize this cost factor by a previous filtering phase to detect cycles in the context-free backbone. In the same way, the treatment of monotonous programs in a bottom-up evaluation scheme simplifies the unification protocol.

Finally, we can make reference to algorithms based on the memoization of nodes and comparison to new ones [7]. Here, the disadvantage is that these algorithms, to the best of our knowledge, cannot be optimized in order to avoid overload on non-cyclic structures.

6 The Domain of Application

This question has a practical sense since, as has already been established [8], DCGs are only semi-decidable when functional symbols are present and, in consequence, any evaluation strategy dealing with cycles is at stake. To simplify our explanation we shall work in the frame of monotonic first-order logic. We shall prove that our proposal is capable of detecting and traversing cycles with a regular syntactic structure. If this is not the case, the strategy does not guarantee

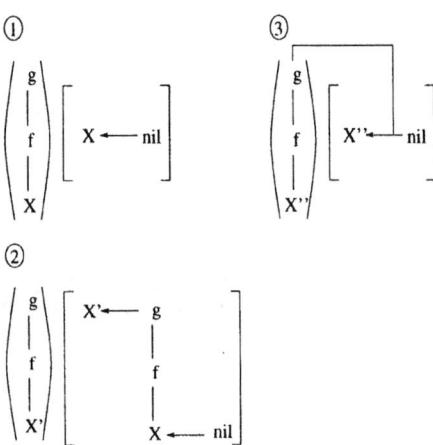

Fig. 12. Cycle traversing in a conjunctive context

termination, which in practical terms is equivalent to saying that the algorithm is equivalent to classic evaluation schema in the worst case.

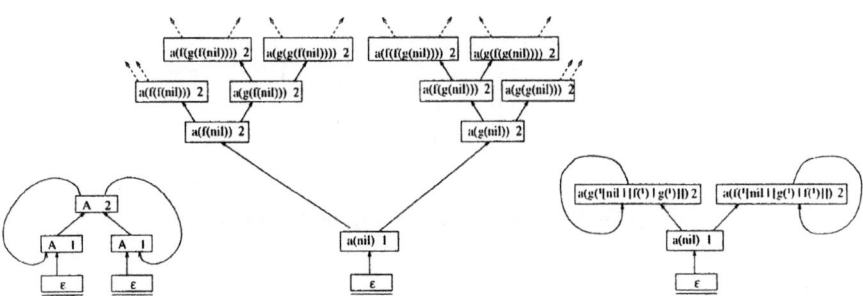

Fig. 13. Cycles in a disjunctive context

Although the technique described could be extended to more complex cycles, our interest in regular ones is justified by the difficulty of representing useful information about non-regular structures in an interactive programming environment, which would reduce the interest of this study to a theoretical one.

To facilitate understanding, and given that technical points have been studied in much greater detail before, we shall informally describe the behavior of our proposal over representative examples covering all possible cases in cycles with a regular structure.

6.1 Conjunctive Terms

This is the simplest case, when all terms included in the cycle are generated from the refutation of clauses without common bodies. This is, for example, the case of the following DCG:

$$\gamma_1 : \ a(nil). \qquad \gamma_2 : \ a(g(X)) \ \rightarrow \ b(X). \qquad \gamma_3 : \ b(f(X)) \ \rightarrow \ a(X).$$

Here, we have a cycle such as is shown in Fig. 11, one for predicate a and another for predicate b; both with depth two. Cycle traversing is illustrated in Fig. 12 for predicate a.

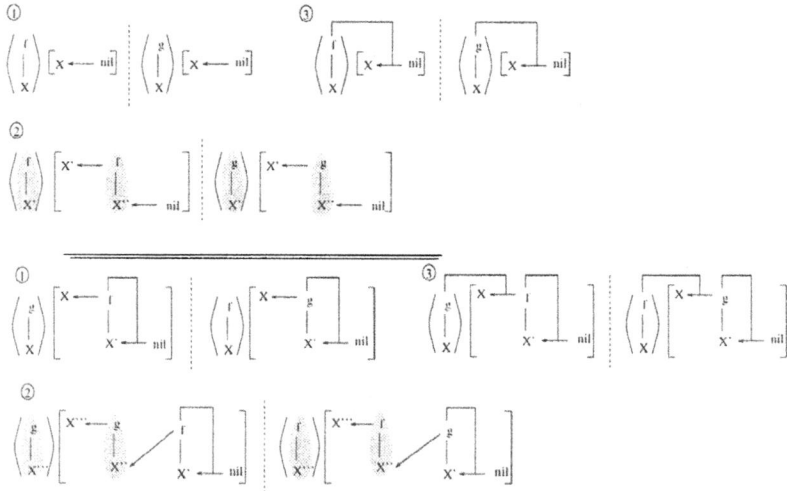

Fig. 14. Cycle traversing in a disjunctive context

6.2 Disjunctive Terms

In this case, we consider that there exist terms in the cycle that have been generated from the refutation of clauses with common bodies. A simple example is given by the DCG defined by the following clauses:

$$\gamma_1 : \ a(nil). \qquad \gamma_2 : \ a(f(X)) \ \rightarrow \ a(X). \qquad \gamma_3 : \ a(g(X)) \ \rightarrow \ a(X).$$

which presents two cycles on predicate a with a disjunction on functions f and g, as is shown in Fig. 13. The cycle traversing is succinctly described in Fig. 14, due to lack of space, only formely steps are shown.

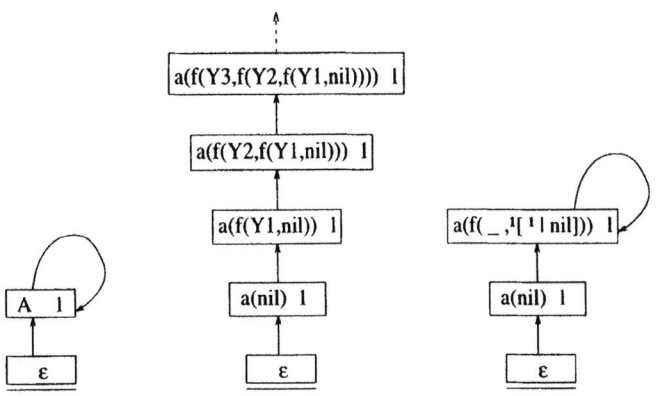

Fig. 15. An infinite structure

6.3 Non-Cyclic Infinite Structures

Finally, our proposal allows us sometimes, but not always, to detect and traverse non-cyclic infinite structures. This is, typically, the case of the presence of anonymous variables in the clauses. Here, we re-take the DCG defined by the clauses:

$$\gamma_1 : \ a(nil). \qquad \gamma_2 : \ a(f(Y,X)) \ \rightarrow \ a(X).$$

in which each time the second rule is refuted, the variable Y takes a new value. As a consequence, it is possible to enter the evaluation in an infinite loop in order to generate all possible answers to the request of the type $\rightarrow$ a(X), as is shown in Fig. 15. However, once these anonymous variables have been located[2], it is possible to detect and traverse this kind of structures as we can see in Fig. 16.

7 Experimental Results

For the tests we take our running example. Given that the grammar contains a rule NP $\rightarrow$ NP NP, the number of cyclic parses grows exponentially with the length, n, of the phrase. This number is:

$$C_0 = C_1 = 1 \quad \text{and} \quad C_n = \binom{2n}{n} \frac{1}{n+1}, \text{ if } n > 1$$

We cannot really provide a comparison with other DCG parsers because of their problems in dealing with cyclic structures. We can however consider results on S^T as a reference for non-dynamic SLR(1)-like methods [6, 10], and naïve dynamic bottom-up methods [5, 2] can be assimilated to S^1 results without synchronization. This information is compiled in Figs. 18 and 17. The former

---

[2] a simple static study of the DCG is sufficient.

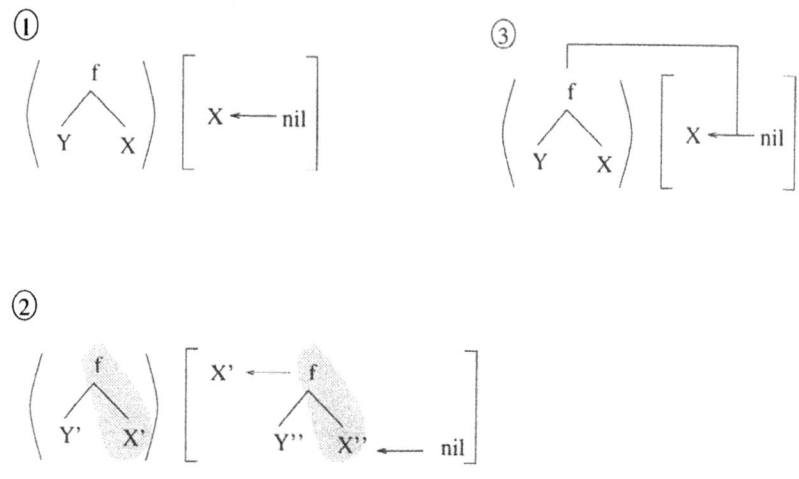

Fig. 16. Traversing a non-cyclic infinite structure

compares the generated items in S^1, S^2 and S^T, the actual number of dynamic transitions generated in S^1 and the original number to be considered if no optimization is applied. The latter compares the variables instantiated in S^1, S^2 and S^T as well as the gain of computational efficiency due to the use of the LALR(1) driver to detect cycles.

8   Conclusion

We have described an efficient strategy for analyzing DCG grammars which is based on a LPDA interpreted in dynamic programming, with a finite-state driver and a mechanism for dealing with cyclic terms. The evaluation scheme is parallel bottom-up without backtracking and it is optimized by predictive information provided by an LALR(1) driver. The system ensures a good level of sharing at the same time as it guarantees correctness and completeness in the case of monotonous DCGs. In this context, we exploit the context-free backbone of these logic programs to efficiently guide detection of regular cyclic constructions without overload for non-cyclic ones.

9   Acknowledgments

This work has been partially supported by projects XUGA 10505B96 and XUGA 20402B97 of the Autonomous Government of Galicia (Xunta de Galicia), project HF97-223 by the Government of Spain, and project 1FD97-0047-C04-02 by the European Community.

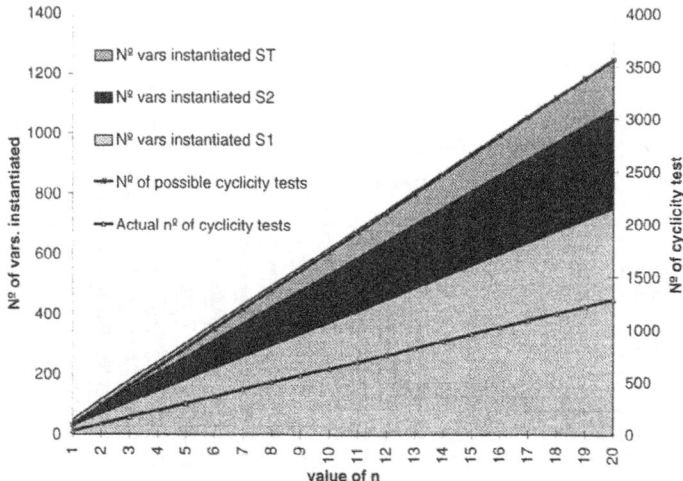

Fig. 17. Some experimental results

References

1. Bresnan, J., Kaplan, T.: Lexical-Functional Grammar: a formal system for grammatical representation. In J. Bresnan (ed.): the Mental Representation of Grammatical Relations (1982) 173–281. MIT Press
2. De la Clergerie, E.: Automates à piles et programmation dynamique. DyALog: une application à la Programmation en Logique. PhD thesis. University of Paris 7 (1993)
3. Filgueiras, M.: A PROLOG interpreter working with infinite terms. In *Implementations of* PROLOG (1985)
4. Haridi, S., Sahlin, D.:. Efficient implementation of unification of cyclic structures. In *Implementations of* PROLOG (1985)
5. Lang, B.: Towards a uniform formal framework for parsing. In M. Tomita (ed.): Current Issues in Parsing Technology (1991) 153–171. Kluwer Academic Publishers
6. Nilsson, U.: AID: an alternative implementation of DCGs. New Generation Computing **4** (1986) 383–399
7. Nilsson, M., Tanaka, H.: Cyclic tree traversal. Lecture Notes in Computer Science **225** (1986) 593–599. Springer-Verlag
8. Pereira, F.C.N., Warren, D.H.D.: Parsing as Deduction. Proc. of the 21st Annual Metting of the Association for Computational Linguistics (1983) 137-144. Cambridge, Mass.
9. Prawitz, D.: Natural Deduction, Proof-Theoretical Study (1965). Almqvist & Wiksell, Stockholm, Sweden
10. Rosenblueth, D. A., Peralta, J. C.: LR inference: inference systems for fixed-mode logic programs, based on LR parsing. International Logic Programming Symposium (1994) 439–453. The MIT Press
11. Shieber, S. M.: Using restriction to extend parsing algorithms for complex-feature-based formalisms. 23th Annual Meeting of the ACL (1985) 145–152

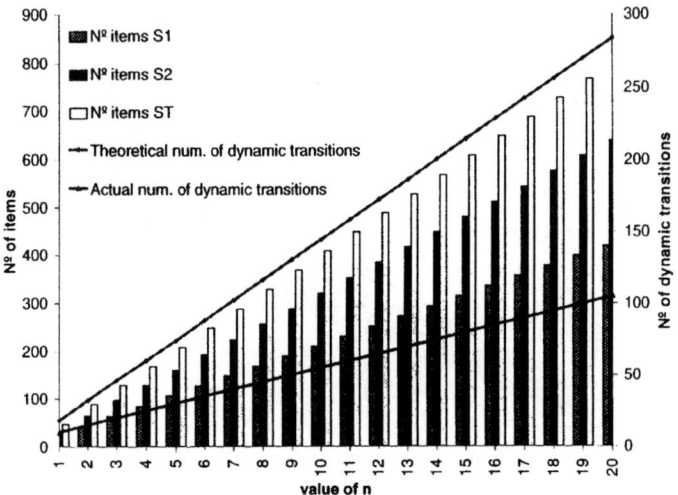

Fig. 18. Some experimental results

12. Stolzenburg, F.: Membership-constraints and some applications. Technical Report Fachberichte Informatik **5/94** (1994). Universität Koblenz-Landau, Koblenz
13. Vilares, M.: Efficient Incremental Parsing for Context-Free Languages. PhD thesis. University of Nice (1992)
14. Vilares, M., Alonso, M. A.: An LALR extension for DCGs in dynamic programming. In C. Martín Vide (ed.): Mathematical Linguistics II (1997). John Benjamins Publishing Company

Mathematical Vernacular and Conceptual Well-Formedness in Mathematical Language[*]

Zhaohui Luo and Paul Callaghan

Department of Computer Science, University of Durham,
South Road, Durham DH1 3LE, U.K.
{Zhaohui.Luo, P.C.Callaghan}@durham.ac.uk

Abstract. This paper investigates the semantics of mathematical concepts in a type theoretic framework with coercive subtyping. The type-theoretic analysis provides a formal semantic basis in the design and implementation of Mathematical Vernacular (MV), a natural language suitable for interactive development of mathematics with the support of the current theorem proving technology.

The idea of semantic well-formedness in mathematical language is motivated with examples. A formal system based on a notion of conceptual category is then presented, showing how type checking supports our notion of well-formedness. The power of this system is then extended by incorporating a notion of subcategory, using ideas from a more general theory of coercive subtyping, which provides the mechanisms for modelling conventional abbreviations in mathematics. Finally, we outline how this formal work can be used in an implementation of MV.

1 Introduction

By *mathematical vernacular* (MV), we mean a mathematical and natural language which is suitable for developing mathematics, has a formal semantics, and is implementable for interactive mathematical development based on the technology of computer-assisted formal reasoning and Natural Language Processing. In a research project on MV at the University of Durham, a type-theoretic approach is being considered: we are developing an MV language together with its type-theoretic semantics and the associated techniques to implement MV based on existing theorem proving technology. Such technology is represented by type theory based proof development systems such as ALF [MN94], Coq [Coq96], and Lego [LP92].

One of the motivations of our work reported here is to study the *linguistic structure* of mathematical language based on which MV is to be designed and implemented. In particular, we are interested in how various linguistic aspects

---

[*] This work is supported partly by the Durham Mathematical Vernacular project funded by the Leverhulme Trust (see http://www.dur.ac.uk/~dcs7ttg/mv.html) and partly by the project on Subtyping, Inheritance, and Reuse funded by UK EPSRC (GR/K79130, see http://www.dur.ac.uk/~dcs7ttg/sir.html).

of mathematical language, such as its conceptual structure, may be analysed in a framework of constructive type theory. Note that, though being a semantic language in our discussion, a type theory is a syntactic language manipulated by a proof development system. Therefore, a type-theoretic analysis of the linguistic structure is an important step in the development and implementation of MV.

In this paper, we study the conceptual structure of mathematical language by studying a notion of conceptual category [NPS90, Luo94]. An important issue in this analysis is that of well-formedness and meaningfulness of expressions in MV. Mathematicians attach importance to the criterion of semantic well-formedness, as well as to grammatical well-formedness. Conceptual categories play an important role not only in correctness checking (ie, deciding whether an expression or a sentence is well-formed and meaningful) but also in capturing the generative nature of concept composition in MV.

Focussing on the conceptual structure reflected in the use of substantives (or common noun phrases) and adjectives – the key linguistic entities used to represent mathematical concepts (cf., [dB94]), we consider fine-structured categories that allow advanced treatment of deciding whether an expression is well-formed. With our type-theoretic semantics, checking semantic well-formedness is supported by type-checking (MV will be implemented around a type-checker) on the one hand, and helps to produce proof obligations in the interactive process of using MV, on the other.

Another contribution of this paper in studying the conceptual structure of MV is the treatment of the inheritance relation between conceptual categories based on *coercive subtyping* – a general theory of subtyping and inheritance in type theory [Luo97, Luo98, SL98]. It is interesting to see that coercive subtyping, a theory developed in a rather different context, can be successfully applied to understanding the linguistic structure of MV.

In Section 2, we shall briefly elaborate the background of this work, giving a general discussion of informal mathematical language and MV, and outlining the approach to developing MV based on type theory. Then, in Section 3, conceptual well-formedness is informally discussed. In Section 4, a formal notion of conceptual category is discussed and used to give a type-theoretic analysis of the issues of syntactic and semantic correctness in MV. Section 5 introduces coercive subtyping and discusses how its abbreviational mechanisms can be used in studying the conceptual structure of MV and providing mechanisms such as overloading for more flexible and productive analysis of meaningfulness of expressions. Section 6 considers some implementation issues of MV, and discusses related work.

2 Developing Mathematical Vernacular: a Type-theoretic Approach

In the following, we consider the idea of informal mathematical language, and then our notion of a mathematical vernacular, ending with background information on type theory and its automation.

2.1 Informal Mathematical Language

Mathematicians communicate with a mixture of natural language and symbols. However, the NL used is restricted, and certain idioms appear frequently. We call it "Informal Mathematical Language" (IML). IML has important differences from unrestricted natural language: many complications from the unrestricted natural language, such as tense and metaphor, do not occur. Furthermore, there are problems which are specific to, or assume a greater importance in the context of, IML. Note that IML has never been defined: it is not a formal language in any sense. It arose in an ad hoc way as a means to describe mathematical development in a convenient fashion. Consequently, there is no "universal" IML. However, one can identify many important characteristics; these include

- **Correctness**: Applications must not make mistakes. Users must not be allowed to believe they have proved a false theorem, and likewise must not be prevented from proving a true one.
- **Introduction of New Concepts**: Much mathematics consists of defining new concepts and investigating the consequences of the definitions. Concepts are usually referenced by NL phrases which are chosen to convey some of the meaning of the concept. Such phrases are not always used as fixed entities, eg one may understand "finite Abelian group" having only seen definitions of the individual concepts. This introduction of new phrases and their link to underlying meaning is a key part of IML.
- **Informality**: Proofs in IML do not contain the low-level detail that a formal mathematician or proof checker would require. Such steps are considered obvious, and hence often omitted, to concentrate on the important steps. Any competent mathematician should be able to provide the missing details. Some of this inference would be needed in interpreting IML, in the form of automated reasoning. Note that informality includes use of abbreviations like "finite group".
- **Idioms**: Certain set phrases exist with definite meanings, for example those used in statements of quantification ("for all X such that Y, P holds"). In a sense, such phrases have acquired a meaning independent of the constituent words, and are most easily analysed as phrases rather than word by word.
- **Mix with Symbolic Expressions**: Expressions using mathematical symbols must be understood to some degree, in order to understand the surrounding IML. These expressions may themselves be informal, compared to the detail required in a completely formal language. For example, in "$f(x, y)$ is finite", we must know what $f(x, y)$ produces, so we can understand the whole sentence.

2.2 Mathematical Vernacular

In order to mechanise any aspect of mathematics which involves IML, such as our long-term aim to implement an interactive system based on MV, we need a good *formal* understanding of the language. As mentioned above, there are quite a lot of interesting and novel problems attached to IML. Given the prime need for correctness in implementing IML, we believe it is necessary to identify successful parts of IML together with good practices suggested by our experience of formal mathematics, and fully formalise that, rather than attempt to formalise "all" of IML, a concept which we find hard to define precisely.

We therefore characterise this language as one which has a formal, type-theoretic semantics, and is implementable with current CAFR. Naturally, the language should be as close as possible to good IML, in the sense of allowing the richness of IML without having too many restrictions. For convenience, we will call it "mathematical vernacular" (MV). This term underlines the informality of the language relative to formal mathematics, but reminds that formality is still important. Similarly to IML, note that there is no "universal" MV: naturally there will be limitations of applicability for this MV language.

Our view is that MV will be *developed* by formalising the essential 'core' of mathematical language, without which no useful mathematics may be done – even if the means of expression are cumbersome, then by extending this core to make the language more flexible without losing the formal properties. The material in section 4 considers one part of this core: the "well-formedness" of mathematical concepts.

A further constraint on MV is the limits of type theory and its associated technology, which we introduce below. But MV can also make new demands on them, and show new ways of looking at them. One need we have identified is for better 'meta-variable' facilities, which will allow a user to omit parts of his proofs temporarily – such as details he considers trivial. This 'feedback' of ideas can also occur for IML: studying it in order to create MV will help to identify good parts and bad parts, showing a way to improvements in IML.

Thus, we can regard development of MV as a constraint satisfaction problem – MV sits between mathematics and its realisation in IML, and mathematics and its realisation in type theory and its implementations; MV will have implications for all of those areas.

Related work includes that of de Bruijn [dB94], the Mizar group [Miz], and Ranta [Ran94, Ran96]; see section 6.2.

2.3   Type-theoretic Approach

Our type-theoretic approach to the study of MV builds on existing work on computer-assisted formal reasoning, represented by the use of proof assistants based on type theory in the formal development of mathematical theories and proofs. One motivation in studying MV is to investigate how to implement a suitable natural language interface for interactive development of mathematics with the support of such mechanised theorem proving. We give a brief introduction to formalising and checking mathematics using type theory, and to its associated proof assistants.

Type theory was chosen because of its properties of decidable checking and flexible representation. (This decidability was also a consideration in our decision to produce a type-theoretic semantics for MV.)

Proof Checking with Type Theory A type theory is a language which allows representation of types and objects, with a judgement form of when an object belongs to a certain type, and inference rules for constructing judgements. The notion of *dependent* types, and the addition of types to represent logic and data structures allows complex reasoning. Propositions are represented by types, and a proof of a proposition as a term which inhabits the type representing the proposition. Theorems are typically expressed as propositions, and proved by a term of suitable type; this term can then be used as a function in proofs of other propositions. We can also have algebraic structures, eg groups – which can be represented as a (dependent) tuple of a set, a binary operator over that set, an identity element, and an inverse function over the set, plus a proof that the data items satisfy the axioms[2].

Type theory and its associated technology is a developing field. Novel ways of using and presenting type theory are being investigated, and aspects of representation are being studied: equality is a particular issue that needs careful consideration. A lot of serious mathematics has already been done based on type theory, eg Ruys' work on the Fundamental Theorem of Algebra [Ruy], or the formalism of type checking of certain type systems [vBJMP93], or Alex Jones' work on the Decidable Dependency Theorem in Linear Algebra [Jon95]. A good source of further information is Bailey's thesis [Bai98], which contains much discussion on how to formalise maths with type theory and how to make the formalised version more understandable, followed by the formalisation of a substantial example (parts of Galois Theory).

Mechanised Type Theory Here we outline the current "tool support" for type theory. This is in the form of *proof assistants*, such as Lego [LP92] or Coq [Coq96], which help with several aspects of proof production: managing the details of representing a piece of maths (definitions of concepts); storing proved theorems and assumptions (which comprise a 'context', together with the definitions); guiding the process of proof construction; and checking whether a given term proves the statement it is claimed to.

Construction of proofs is by 'refinement'. For example, a proof of $A \wedge B$ is achieved by finding proofs of A and of B separately, at which point the proof assistant will combine them appropriately to prove the main goal. There is currently little automation in these proof assistants: most of the work is done by the user, although there are some simple mechanisms to prove basic propositions, eg simple logic or to help with repetitive operations in induction proofs.

There are obviously quite a few differences between doing conventional maths and using a proof assistant. Some of these will need attention to support interactive work with MV, most importantly to allow *holes* or meta-variables in proof development that will allow representation of statements from the user that are incomplete in a formal sense. We discuss this further in section 6.

---

[2] Actually, dependent tuples are represented with a Σ type constructor. $\Sigma(A, B)$ is the type of dependent pairs whose first element is of type A, and whose second element is of type $B(x)$ where x is the first element. Other representations are possible.

3 Mathematical concepts and meaningfulness of expressions

3.1 Meaningfulness of expressions

Meaningfulness, or *semantic acceptability*, as opposed to syntactic acceptability, can be illustrated by Chomsky's example, "Colourless green ideas sleep furiously". His observation is that this sentence is perfect as far as (pure) syntax is concerned, and that its unacceptability lies in the domain of conceptualisation (although it can be meaningful in some imaginative context).

In mathematics, semantic acceptability presumes a distinguishably important role. Semantically ill-formed expressions and meaningless sentences are strictly unacceptable. This is partly because that rigour and correctness are the basic requirements for mathematical development. A formal analysis of mathematical concepts is important in understanding how to exclude ill-formed constructions such as "Abelian set" on the one hand, and why we should accept the more flexible uses such as "finite group" and the generative uses such as "finite Abelian group" even if no explicit definitions of such phrases have been given, on the other.

In the development of mathematical vernacular, such an analysis (a type-theoretic analysis in our case) gives us guidance to the design and implementation of MV. For example, checking semantic acceptability involves type-checking, verification of presuppositions, generation of proof obligations; these can trigger proof search and system-user interactions. (See Section 6 for a further discussion.)

3.2 Mathematical Concepts: an Informal Discussion

Before considering a formal treatment in the next two sections, we first give an informal discussion of mathematical concepts, their formation, and relationships between them[3].

Objects, Basic Classes, and Properties A starting point is to observe that in IML, as in NL, the terms of description are oriented towards human thinking. Mathematical objects, including primitive ones, are naturally organised into different basic classes, objects in each of which may share common structures. These basic classes correspond to primitive types in type theory (eg, the inductive type of natural numbers). Objects have properties and a property is defined over a class of objects. In logical terms, properties are expressed by means of predicates over objects of a type (eg, 'even' and 'odd' over natural numbers).

---

[3] Our discussion on mathematical concepts is largely independent of surface linguistic details. For example, the phrases "group which is Abelian" and "Abelian group" are just regarded as different ways of describing the same conceptual entity. Note that we only use natural language phrases to denote concepts as a matter of convenience.

Mathematical Concepts Denoting Classes of Objects Mathematical concepts, typically represented by means of substantives (common noun phrases) such as 'group' and "finite set", denote classes of objects. Introduction of a new mathematical concept is done by giving an explicit definition. For example, "A semigroup is a set together with an associative binary operation over the set." Forming a class of objects introduces abstraction in the sense that one can assume a hypothetical member of the class, and define and study properties of the objects in the class (eg, by means of quantification and generalisation).

Existing concepts may be combined to form new concepts. Typical ways to do this include structural composition (eg, set together with a binary operation) and specification of logical properties or constraints (eg, associativity) shared by the objects in the class denoted by the concept. The distinction between structure and logical constraints is usually conceptually clear, though it may sometimes be blurred in practice.[4] Logical constraints alone result in concepts denoting more restricted classes, often labelled by a qualified name (eg "finite set"). In some cases, especially when new *structure* is postulated, the new class is treated as a distinguished concept with a new name (eg, 'semigroup' obtained from 'set', 'field' defined by means of 'ring'), rather than being qualified by some property.

Generative Formation of Concepts Because of the generative nature of IML, not every concept used in mathematics has to be introduced by explicit definition, and our study of MV should reflect this.[5] Defining a concept also introduces many other composite concepts by linguistic convention. Linguistic mechanisms for this include, at the surface level of IML, the use of adjectives and their combinations in syntactically valid constructs to form substantives representing concepts. For instance, having defined 'cyclic' and 'Abelian' over groups, we can also use "cyclic Abelian group" without having to define it explicitly; having to do so would be unproductive at least.

Inheritance between mathematical concepts In general, it is semantically invalid to use a property to qualify a concept over whose objects the property is undefined. For example, just as "green ideas" is unacceptable, so is "odd group", if 'odd' is a property defined over natural numbers rather than groups.

However, though naturally rejecting obviously meaningless constructions, mathematicians do allow a considerable flexibility into their practice in communicating mathematical ideas and proofs. Many of these are based on special

---

[4] Sometimes, especially in classical mathematics, a property can suggest additional structure of objects through existential statements, especially those with uniqueness property. A good example is of an element in a group which is an identity of the associated operator; this can easily be proven unique, so one usually refers to 'the' identity element.

[5] This is a different view from that taken by Prof de Bruijn in his study of MV, where he correctly identifies the importance of definitions in mathematical development, but considers that everything should be introduced by explicit definitions [dB94].

relationships between different mathematical concepts. Examples of such relationship include concept implication (or class inclusion), structural inheritance, and their combinations. For instance, although 'finite' is a property defined over sets, "finite group" is usually regarded as valid in expressing "group whose carrier set is finite". As another example, one often says "for all elements in [the carrier set of] group G, ...", with the phrase in the bracket omitted. Such abbreviations are regarded as tacit conventions and are not expected to cause problems.

Other issues concerning mathematical concepts

- *Transformations between Concepts.* Expressions that denote transformations or operations between concepts (eg, union of two sets) constitute an important class of entities to be studied. An interesting issue is to study what properties they preserve and how we represent such a notion of preservation of properties, eg as in the union of two finite sets being automatically finite.
- *Non-restrictive adjective-noun modification.* Not every use of an adjective to modify a concept results in a more restricted concept. A good example is "left monoid". (A left monoid is a similar structure to a monoid which has only a left identity.) A left monoid is not a monoid (cf, a fake gun is not a gun.) General analysis and treatment of such phenomena are out of the scope of this paper.
- *Lexical ambiguity.* In mathematics, truly ambiguous expressions and sentences are regarded as unacceptable, or a bad practice at the best. However, overloading of terminology and notation does occur quite often for the sake of abbreviation or simplicity. When this happens, a term is used to have multiple meanings with contrasted ambiguity (homonymy). For example, 'finite' in "finite set" and "finite sequence" may have formally different (though informally related) meanings.
- *Redundant information.* Whether expressions such as "finite finite set" are semantically acceptable is debatable. It is certainly desirable to avoid but it seems difficult to find logical disciplines to deal with it. A more interesting example is "Abelian left monoid", which is logically a monoid because commutativity implies that the left and right identities are the same.

4 Conceptual categories: a type-theoretic analysis

In this section, we introduce and study a notion of category. This is used to investigate the semantics of expressions denoting mathematical concepts. We do not consider syntactic issues at this stage; the semantic details are studied independently of such issues[6]. We also ignore (for the moment) issues concerning instances of mathematical concepts, such as the meaning of the claim that a particular object x is an instance of concept C.

---

[6] Moreover, the work here does not force a particular approach to syntax, so any comments we make would be provisional, and not add to the theoretical content of this paper. The same applies to other related issues.

The basic formal theory we use has been studied in several contexts, including the subset theory developed by Nordström, Petersson and Smith in Martin-Löf's type theory [NPS90], the specification calculus by Luo in the Extended Calculus of Constructions and UTT [Luo93], and the related (but different) framework on deliverables [BM92, McK92] and mathematical theories [Luo91a]. Here, we apply this theory to mathematical concepts and the related well-formedness issues. In the next section, we shall extend this to introduce a notion of subcategory based on the theory of coercive subtyping.

Our presentation below will be precise but informal in that type theory is used informally as the semantic language to define the meanings of categories and category constructors. The underlying type theory is UTT, which consists of an impredicative type universe of logical propositions ($Prop$), predicative type universes, inductive types including type constructors for functional types $A \to B$, dependent functional types $\Pi(A, B)$, types of dependent pairs $\Sigma(A, B)$, and types of natural numbers, lists, trees, etc. (See [Luo94] for details.) UTT is implemented in the proof system Lego [LP92].

4.1 Conceptual categories

A *(conceptual) category* represents a mathematical concept. We shall use the judgement form $C : \text{CAT}$ to denote that C is a category.

In general, a category C consists of two components: the syntactic category of C, $\text{SYN}(C)$, and the logical constraint of C, $\text{LOG}(C)$. The syntactic category $\text{SYN}(C)$ is a type, representing the structure of the objects of the represented concept and the logical constraint $\text{LOG}(C)$ is a predicate over the syntactic structures (ie, $\text{LOG}(C)$ is of type $\text{SYN}(C) \to Prop$).

Another form of judgement is $e : C$, asserting that the expression e is of category C. The meaning of this judgement is defined as:

- $e : C$ if, and only if,
  - e is of type $\text{SYN}(C)$, and
  - $\text{LOG}(C)(e)$ is true (provable in the type theory).

We introduce the following notions of well-formedness and logical correctness.

Definition (well-formedness and logical correctness)

- M is *well-formed* (more precisely, an expression that denotes M is well-formed) if either $M : \text{CAT}$ or $M : \text{SYN}(C)$ for some $C : \text{CAT}$.
- e is *logically correct wrt* C if $\text{LOG}(C)(e)$ is true.

Note that logical correctness of an object e wrt C presupposes the well-formedness of category C and the well-formedness of e itself. Since type checking is decidable, we can automatically check whether an expression, either denoting a category or an object, is well-formed. Of course, this is not the case for logical correctness of objects.

We note that many of the cases traditionally discussed for semantic (un)acceptability are incorporated into the notion of well-formedness and some require checking logical correctness. For example, "odd group" is not well-formed, while "finite set" and "finite group" are (see below). Therefore, checking semantic acceptability (meaningfulness in the traditional sense, as discussed in section 3) can be helped by (decidable) type-checking. In addition, checking logical correctness incorporates verification obligations (eg, verification of presuppositions).

Remark. We have taken the view that proof terms (proofs of logical propositions) should not be regarded as explicit objects. Effectively, an object of the category denoted by "finite set" (we name it $FSet$) is just a set that is finite, as opposed to a set together with a proof of its finiteness. This allows a direct analysis of sentences such as "If A is a finite set, then ...", where A denotes an object of category *set*. Note that the hypothesis of the sentence corresponds to the judgement $A : FSet$. If an object of $FSet$ were required to be a structure which contains the set and a proof term rather than just a set, the if-clause would have been trivially false (ie, ill-typed and not derivable)[7]. We omit further specific discussion of how objects and proof terms will be treated under this strategy (see [CL98] for more information).

4.2 Category Constructors

Categories can either be base categories or the result of applying a category constructor. A category or a category constructor is defined by giving only its formation rule and definitions of its syntactic category and logical constraints.

Category of Logical Sentences An example of base category is S, the category of logical sentences. The syntactic category of S is the type of logical propositions and the logical constraint of S is the true predicate:

- $\text{SYN}(S) = Prop$
- $\text{LOG}(S)(e) = true$, for any $e : \text{SYN}(S)$.

A base category is isomorphic to its syntactic category, since its logical part is always true (ie, there are no logical constraints). In the following, for notational convenience, we shall just write S for the syntactic category of S.

Syntactic categories Besides the other category constructors, one can consider SYN as a category constructor as well. We have:

- $\text{SYN}(\text{SYN}(C)) = \text{SYN}(C)$
- $\text{LOG}(\text{SYN}(C))(e) = true$, for any $e : \text{SYN}(C)$

---

[7] To manipulate structures that contain proof terms requires some non-trivial operations to ensure that expressions remain well-typed. For example, if a binary relation R is said to be symmetric, reflexive, and transitive, then to show that it is transitive and symmetric requires some unpacking and rebuilding of R.

That is, the syntactic category of $\text{SYN}(C)$ is itself and the logical constraint is always true, ie, there are no logical conditions on a plain syntactic object.

Δ-categories The Δ-operator creates a new category by attaching to a category C a logical predicate on the syntactic structure of C. Its formation rule is:

$$\frac{C : \text{CAT} \quad p : \text{SYN}(C) \to S}{\Delta(C, p) : \text{CAT}}$$

The syntactic category of $\Delta(C, p)$ is the same as that of C and its logical constraint is the logical conjunction of that of C and the extra constraint p.

- $\text{SYN}(\Delta(C, p)) = \text{SYN}(C)$
- $\text{LOG}(\Delta(C, p))(e) = \text{LOG}(C)(e) \wedge p(e)$

For example, if *set* is the category of sets and *finite* is the finiteness predicate defined over sets, the category of finite sets can be represented by $\Delta(set, finite)$. Similarly, with *Abelian* and *cyclic* defined over group structures, "cyclic Abelian group" can be represented as $\Delta(\Delta(group, Abelian), cyclic)$. Note that, conversely, the calculus does not allow the ill-formed concepts such as "Abelian set" or "transitive group" since their representations fail to type-check.

Σ-categories The formation rule for Σ-categories is

$$\frac{C : \text{CAT} \quad f(x) : \text{CAT} \; [x{:}\text{SYN}(C)]}{\Sigma(C, f) : \text{CAT}}$$

which says that, if C is a category and f is a family of categories indexed by C-structures, then $\Sigma(C, f)$ is a category. The definitions of the corresponding syntactic category and logical constraint are:

- $\text{SYN}(\Sigma(C, f)) = \Sigma(\text{SYN}(C), \text{SYN} \circ f)$
- $\text{LOG}(\Sigma(C, f))(e) = \text{LOG}(C)(\pi_1 e) \wedge \text{LOG}(f(\pi_1 e))(\pi_2 e)$

where Σ on the RHS of the first equation is the Σ-type constructor (types of dependent pairs) with the projection operators π_1 and π_2, and $\text{SYN} \circ f$ is the composition of SYN and f. The above definitions indicate that the syntactic component of an object of a Σ-category is a pair of the base structure and its extension, and that the logical component is a combination of those from the base with those from the extension. Note that we have overloaded Σ for both the type constructor and the category constructor (this is for notational convenience).

As Σ-types can be used to represent types of structures (tuples), Σ-categories can be used to represent mathematical structures of algebraic theories etc. Note that properties of such structures can only be added by using the Δ constructor (otherwise, explicit proof terms will appear in the system, which we wish to avoid). A simple example of structure is the formation of the concept of monoid from that of set by adding a binary operator and an identity with their properties. A more sophisticated example would be to form the concept of ring by combining the concepts of group and monoid by adding extra logical constraints; this involves sharing of the common carrier set, and we omit the details here (see [Luo93, Luo91a]).

Functional categories We can form the functional category of two categories:

$$\frac{C : \text{CAT} \quad D : \text{CAT}}{C \Rightarrow D : \text{CAT}}$$

The corresponding syntactic category and logical constraint are defined as:

- $\text{SYN}(C \Rightarrow D) = \text{SYN}(C) \rightarrow \text{SYN}(D)$
- $\text{LOG}(C \Rightarrow D)(f) = \forall c{:}\text{SYN}(C). \ \text{LOG}(C)(c) \supset \text{LOG}(D)(f(c))$

That is, the objects of a functional category are the functions that preserve the logical constraints.

Objects of a functional category represent operations or transformations between concepts. Here is an example. Let B be a set, the concept "subset of B" can be represented as $Sub(B) = \Delta(set, sub_B)$, where $sub_B(A) = A \subseteq B$. Then, "complement of ... wrt B", the operation that takes a subset of B and returns its complement, is defined to be of category $Sub(B) \Rightarrow set$. Note that the logical correctness of "complement of A wrt B" requires that A be a subset of B – a presupposition to be verified. If A is not a subset of B, the phrase is logically incorrect.

There are other category constructors that can be introduced and used to analyse well-formedness and logical correctness of expressions and sentences, but we omit their discussion here.

4.3 Equivalence between categories

Another important notion is the equivalence between categories. A category C is *equivalent* to category D if $\text{SYN}(C) = \text{SYN}(D)$ (computational equality) and $\text{LOG}(C)$ and $\text{LOG}(D)$ are equivalent, ie, $\forall x{:}\text{SYN}(C). \ \text{LOG}(C)(x) \Leftrightarrow \text{LOG}(D)(x)$ is true. For example, the concept of symmetric, transitive relation is equivalent to that of transitive, symmetric relation.

Note that this notion of equivalence between categories is extensional. This reflects the fact that a mathematical concept can be defined in intensionally different ways. For example, the concept of "prime number smaller than 3" is equivalent to that of "number that is equal to 2".

5 Coercive subtyping, subcategories, and sense selection

As discussed in Section 3, structural inheritance and conceptual implication are important relationships between mathematical concepts. Many linguistic conventions, in particular, abbreviational conventions, are based on them. In this section, we extend our study of conceptual categories to investigate such relationships between categories.

In particular, we shall study how coercive subtyping [Luo97, Luo98], a new theory of subtyping and inheritance in type theory, can be applied in our type-theoretic analysis of mathematical language. The benefits are to provide adequate abbreviational mechanisms, to understand the inheritance relationships between mathematical concepts, and to deal with contrastive lexical ambiguity by means of the overloading mechanism.

5.1 Coercive subtyping

We first give an informal introduction to the underlying theory of coercive subtyping and then show how it allows abbreviations such as "finite group".

The basic idea is to consider subtyping as an abbreviational mechanism. A is a subtype of B, notation $A \leq B$, if either $A = B$ (computational equality) or A is a proper subtype of B (notation $A < B$) such that there is a unique implicit coercion from A to B. Any function from A to B can be specified as a coercion, as long as the coherence property holds for the overall system (in particular, there cannot be two different coercions from any A to any B).

This idea generalises both the traditional notion of inclusion-based subtyping (eg, between types of natural numbers and integers) and that of inheritance-based subtyping (eg, between record types). Anthony Bailey has implemented coercion mechanisms in Lego (and Saibi in Coq [Sai97]), and considered its applications to formal development of mathematics (Galois theory) based on type theory [Bai98]. For some meta-theoretic results of coercive subtyping, see [JLS97, SL98].

The mechanism with which coercive subtyping works can be explained informally as follows. If A is a proper subtype of B with coercion c, $a : A$, and $C[\_]$ is a context where an object of type B is required, then a can be used in that context — $C[a]$ stands for (more precisely, is computationally equal to) $C[c(a)]$.

For example, based on the usual formalisation of algebraic structures in type theory, the types of structures of groups and sets (ie, SYN(*group*) and SYN(*set*) in our notation) are Σ-types, with the former having the latter as a substructure. One can define a coercion *carrier* from groups to sets which extracts the type corresponding to the carrier set of a group. Then, if G : SYN(*group*), the logical proposition $\forall(G, P)$ (ie, $\forall x{:}G.\ P(x)$ in a more usual notation), which is not well-typed without subtyping, is well-formed and actually stands for $\forall(carrier(G), P)$, because $\forall$ requires a type as its first argument.

Similarly, if we interpret the conceptual categories of the previous section in UTT, and assume that SYN(*group*) is a proper subtype of SYN(*set*) with the forgetful map κ as coercion, then the category *Delta(group, finite)* (for "finite group") is well-formed because

- $finite$: SYN(*set*) $\rightarrow S$
- (SYN(*set*) $\rightarrow S$) $\leq$ (SYN(*group*) $\rightarrow S$)[8]

---

[8] Note that we have lifted the coercion between group and set to the function level; hence the use of function composition o as part of the coercion applied to *finite*.

In particular, we have the following computational equality: $\Delta(group, finite) = \Delta(group, finite \circ \kappa)$. With the coercion made explicit, "finite group" means literally "group whose carrier set is finite".

Coercions may be propagated over data structures, extending the usefulness of simple coercions. More technically, subtyping relations can generalise to various type constructors by default rules, unless the defaults are overridden. For example, if $A' \leq A$ and $B \leq B'$, then $(A \to B) \leq (A' \to B')$ (ie, subtyping is contravariant wrt functional types). The subtyping relation generalises to Σ-types (types of dependent pairs): if $A \leq A'$ and $B(x) \leq B'(x)$ for $x : A$, then $\Sigma(A, B) \leq \Sigma(A', B')$. The expected composite coercions with respect to these generalisations can be easily constructed from the component coercions, but we omit the details here (see [Luo98]).

5.2   The subcategory relation

We can use the notion of coercion *directly* in the calculus of section 4 by developing a notion of *subcategory relation* as a lifted version of the subtyping relation. We say C is a subcategory of D, written $C \preceq D$, if and only if:

- $\text{SYN}(C) \leq \text{SYN}(D)$, and
- $\forall x{:}\text{SYN}(C).\ \text{LOG}(C)(x) \supset \text{LOG}(D)(x)$ is true (provable in type theory).

In other words, C is a subcategory of D if $\text{SYN}(C)$ is a subtype of $\text{SYN}(D)$ and the corresponding coercion preserves the logical constraints. Structural inheritance is reflected in the subtyping relationship between the syntactic categories, and conceptual implication in the relationship between logical constraints.

Also, we introduce the following terminology and notations.

- If $C \preceq D$ and $\text{SYN}(C) < \text{SYN}(D)$ with coercion c, we say that C is a *proper subcategory* of D (with coercion c), notation $C \prec D$.
- If $C \preceq D$ and the syntactic categories of C and D are computationally equal, we say that C *implies* D, notation $C \supset D$.

Note that, because we require the subtyping relation to be coherent, if $C \preceq D$ and $D \preceq C$, then it must be the case that C and D are equivalent.

It is easy to check that the subcategory relation is reflexive and transitive, and furthermore it has the expected properties concerning various category constructors. For instance, assuming the default coercive subtyping rules concerning Σ-types and functional types and the well-formedness of the categories concerned, the following are derivable judgements or rules that represent the typical subcategory relationships concerning the category constructors discussed in Section 4.2.

- $C \supset \text{SYN}(C)$.

Furthermore, subtyping is contrapositive over functions, ie $A \leq A', B \leq B'$, then $B' \to A' \leq A \to B$.

- $\Delta(C,p) \supset C$.
- $\Delta(C,p') \preceq \Delta(C',p')$, if $C \preceq C'$.
- $\Sigma(C,f) \preceq \Sigma(C',f')$ if $C \preceq C'$ and $f(x) \preceq f'(x)$ for all $x : \text{SYN}(C)$.
- $(C \Rightarrow D) \preceq (C' \Rightarrow D')$ if $C' \preceq C$ and $D \preceq D'$.

Therefore, the mechanisms for abbreviation and inheritance provided by coercive subtyping are lifted to categories in a uniform way. For instance, if f is of category $D \Rightarrow D'$, c is of category C and $C \preceq D$, then $f(c)$ is of category D'.

5.3 Lexical ambiguity, overloading and sense selection

As discussed in Section 3, ambiguity is not desirable in mathematical texts. However, forms of local ambiguity which are resolvable in a wider (linguistic) context do occur frequently and naturally, thus should be allowed in MV. An example is of contrasted ambiguity, eg, "finite" in "$finite_1$ set" and "$finite_2$ sequence". Coercive subtyping allows a satisfactory treatment of this phenomenon through overloading of unit types (types containing only one object). This idea first appeared in [Luo97], where overloading pairs of Σ-types and product types is considered, and is further developed in Bailey's thesis [Bai98], where he makes extensive use of coercions and overloading.

The technique is to use several coercions from a unit type Unit (inductive type with only one object) to encode the multiple senses of an expression. The expression (eg, "finite") is represented by the object in the unit type, while the images of the coercions are its different senses (eg, "$finite_1$" and "$finite_2$"). When the expression is used in a context, its appropriate sense is selected, according to the coercive subtyping mechanism. For example, we shall have "finite sequence" = "$finite_2$ sequence" and, "finite set" = "$finite_1$ set".

Note that in using this mechanism, coherence must be maintained. So one must ensure that coherence is maintained (by having acceptable coercions) when the types of two different senses are related by the subtyping relation[9]. In our example concerning "$finite_1$ set" and "$finite_2$ sequence", we have that $finite_1 : set \Rightarrow S$ and $finite_2 : sequence \Rightarrow S$, and overloading coercions $\kappa_1 : Unit \rightarrow \text{SYN}(set \Rightarrow S)$ and $\kappa_2 : Unit \rightarrow \text{SYN}(sequence \Rightarrow s)$. If, for example, $sequence \prec set$ with some coercion, then we have $(set \Rightarrow S) \prec (sequence \Rightarrow S)$ by some coercion κ; in this case, we have to ensure $\kappa \circ \kappa_1 = \kappa_2$ to preserve coherence.

5.4 Related work on lexical semantics and remarks

It is not surprising that some of the phenomena discussed above have their counterpart in ordinary natural language. For example, one can consider the similarity between the following two examples:

---

[9] One possibility in an implementation is to suspend the subtyping relations that are oriented towards checking well-formedness of categories when performing the type checking necessary for sense disambiguation on the input text.

- a finite group = a group whose carrier set is finite
  ≠ an algebraic structure that is a group and that is finite
- a fast typist = someone who types fast
  ≠ someone who is a typist and who is fast

However, the NL example is defeasible – further information may affect which interpretation is chosen (eg a race between typists and accountants, [CB96]). This situation does not occur in IML: mathematical terms must have been given precise definitions, and the same meaning must result in all contexts.

Very recently, the work by Pustejovsky [Pus95] on generative lexicon and the work by Jackendoff on enriched composition [Jac97] have come to our attention. They have studied the conceptual structure and lexical semantics of natural language based on an idea of coercion. It would be interesting to study the connections of their work and the work reported here; in particular, we believe that the theory of coercive subtyping may have its application in the wider context as well.

A remark on methodology of our research may be worth making. We have taken an approach of componential analysis in our study of the conceptual structure (and lexical semantics). We argue that this is a suitable approach to the study of MV (and IML in general). This is partly because terms in mathematics are (or, can be) precisely defined and partly because mathematical terms can be considered to be defined from some basic concepts such as those in a foundational language. For these reasons, the traditional arguments against componential analysis in lexical semantics (cf, [Lyo95]) do not apply to mathematical language.

6 Implementing MV: Discussion and Related Work

As stated in Section 2, one of our research objectives is to develop the implementation technology of MV based on type theory. The long-term research aims include development of interactive systems with MV as the user language, that support productive communications between the user and the system. We are currently studying basic but crucial techniques such as more advanced treatment of meta-variables and multi-thread proof development techniques. A prototype is being developed for exploring these ideas; it is based on the typed logical framework LF introduced in Chapter 9 of [Luo94], which allows specification of different type theories suitable for different applications (such as the formal system of section 4).

In the following, we first consider how the type-theoretic analysis of mathematical concepts considered above can be used in implementing MV, and discuss related work.

6.1 Applications of Conceptual Categories in Implementation

In implementing MV based on type theory, the formal analysis reported in this paper supplies not only important theoretical ideas, but practical guidance on how to represent and reason about mathematical concepts, and how to check well-formedness and logical correctness of expressions and sentences in MV. In fact, we regard this analysis as one of the key steps in developing and implementing MV as it deals with objects, classes, and properties in mathematics.

First, the formal framework of conceptual categories is a basis for a type-theoretic semantics of MV (ie, how to translate MV expressions and sentences into type theory). Although working in a type-theoretic framework, we believe that explicit use of proof terms (or expressions of proofs) in mathematical language is unnatural to most of the mathematicians (even for constructive mathematicians doing informal mathematics). The system of conceptual categories provides a suitable framework based on type theory that allows direct and natural interpretations of MV expressions and sentences.

Secondly, the framework not only relates checking of well-formedness and correctness to type-checking, but provides a basis for more intelligent system-user interaction. For example, the categories of expressions such as "complement of ... wrt B" (of category $Sub(B) \Rightarrow set$) capture the presuppositions of sentences involving such expressions (eg, the logical correctness of "complement of A wrt B" presupposes that "A is a subset of B"). Among other things, this would enable a system that implements MV to make use of the subtle difference between presuppositions and unproven claims (eg, 'facts' explicitly claimed by the user without proof, and which can't always be proven automatically by the system) to produce more reasonable response in system-user interaction. Claims will be left as gaps in the development, while phrases or sentences with unverified presuppositions would require justification, by a mixture of automatic reasoning and further interaction with the user.

Furthermore, combined with coercive subtyping, the formal framework gives flexible mechanisms that allow a systematic treatment of abbreviations, direct inheritance, and multiple sense selection. For example, dealing with words such as "finite" that can be used to qualify many different but related concepts (set, group, ...), a system based on coercive subtyping does not have to consider all of these possible meanings when processing a text, but just consider very few essentially different meanings of the word, with the rest subsumed by the subtyping relations. Another practical benefit is that the abbreviational mechanisms allow compression of formal expressions (semantic denotations in type theory of MV expressions) and hence promote clearer communication with the user.

The notion of conceptual category is defined by interpretation into the underlying type theory (UTT in our case), which is a relatively sophisticated system. It would be very interesting to see whether it is possible to design an independent but simpler system of categories that can be used to capture the need in correctness checking of MV. The benefit of such a system is twofold. In theory, it would make it clear what basic mechanisms are needed for checking well-formedness and correctness for MV. In practice, it may provide simpler ways to perform independent well-formedness checking without having to consider unnecessary details of formalisation. We can both study and implement this using the implementation of LF mentioned above.

6.2 Related Work on Mathematical Vernacular

There have been several research efforts to study, to design, and to implement mathematical vernaculars in the general sense of the term. Some of them are more closely related to our research in their objectives and methods than others; among the more related are de Bruijn's work on mathematical vernacular [dB94], Ranta's work on type-theoretic grammar [Ran94] and his research on informal mathematical language based on type theory [Ran95] and its implementation [Ran97][10], Coscoy's work on proof explanation in Coq [CKT95], and the Mizar project [Miz], where a mathematical vernacular has been defined and implemented in a batch system whose logic is based on set theory, and subsequently used to formalise an impressive amount of mathematics.

Our work on mathematical vernacular has been substantially influenced and improved by general discussions in the works above, and by communications with Aarne Ranta. In particular, Prof de Bruijn's pioneering work on MV (and Automath [dB80]) has significantly influenced the research field and our work. His work on MV offers many insights in designing mathematical vernaculars, which we very much believe are deserving of further investigation and development.

Acknowledgements

We would like to thank the following for many useful discussions: Peter Aczel, James McKinna, Aarne Ranta, and members of the Computer Assisted Reasoning Group in Durham.

References

[Bai98]   A. Bailey. *The Machine-checked Literate Formalisation of Algebra in Type Theory*. PhD thesis, University of Manchester, 1998.

[BM92]   R. Burstall and J. McKinna. Deliverables: a categorical approach to program development in type theory. LFCS report ECS-LFCS-92-242, Dept of Computer Science, University of Edinburgh, 1992.

[CB96]   A. Copestake and T. Briscoe. Semi-productive polysemy and sense extension. In J. Pustejovsky and B. Boguraev, editors, *Lexical Semantics: The Problem of Polysemy*. Clarendon, 1996.

[CKT95]   Y. Coscoy, G. Kahn, and L. Théry. Extracting texts from proofs. Technical Report 2459, INRIA, Sophia-Antipolis, 1995.

[CL98]   P. Callaghan and Z. Luo. Mathematical vernacular in type theory-based proof assistants. In R. Backhouse, editor, *User Interfaces for Theorem Proving, UITP '98*, July 1998.

[Coq96]   Coq. *The Coq Proof Assistant Reference Manual (version 6.1)*. INRIA-Rocquencourt and CNRS-ENS Lyon, 1996.

---

[10] One function of this system is to translate simple expressions in mathematical language to expressions in a type theory. We have adapted this system to produce expressions in the Lego type theory (UTT): this involved working around a few important technical differences in the type theories concerned.

[dB80]   N.G. de Bruijn. A survey of the project AUTOMATH. In J. Hindley and
           J. Seldin, editors, *To H. B. Curry: Essays on Combinatory Logic, Lambda
           Calculus and Formalism.* Academic Press, 1980.

[dB94]   N. G. de Bruijn. The mathematical vernacular, a language for mathemat-
           ics with typed sets. In R. P. Nederpelt, J. H. Geuvers, and R. C. de Vrijer,
           editors, *Selected Papers on Automath.* North Holland, 1994.

[Jac97]   R. Jackendoff. *The Architecture of the Language Faculty.* MIT, 1997.

[JLS97]   A. Jones, Z. Luo, and S. Soloviev. Some proof-theoretic and algorithmic
           aspects of coercive subtyping. *Proc. of the Annual Conf on Types and
           Proofs (TYPES'96)*, 1997. To appear.

[Jon95]   A. Jones. The formalization of linear algebra in LEGO: The decidable
           dependency theorem. Master's thesis, University of Manchester, 1995.

[LP92]   Z. Luo and R. Pollack. LEGO Proof Development System: User's Man-
           ual. LFCS Report ECS-LFCS-92-211, Department of Computer Science,
           University of Edinburgh, 1992.

[Luo91a]   Z. Luo. A higher-order calculus and theory abstraction. *Information and
           Computation*, 90(1), 1991.

[Luo91b]   Z. Luo. Program specification and data refinement in type theory. *Proc.
           of the Fourth Inter. Joint Conf. on the Theory and Practice of Software
           Development (TAPSOFT), LNCS 493*, 1991. Also as LFCS report ECS-
           LFCS-91-131, Dept. of Computer Science, Edinburgh University.

[Luo93]   Z. Luo. Program specification and data refinement in type theory. *Math-
           ematical Structures in Computer Science*, 3(3), 1993. An earlier version
           appears as [Luo91b].

[Luo94]   Z. Luo. *Computation and Reasoning: A Type Theory for Computer Sci-
           ence.* Oxford University Press, 1994.

[Luo97]   Z. Luo. Coercive subtyping in type theory. *Proc. of CSL'96, the 1996 An-
           nual Conference of the European Association for Computer Science Logic,
           Utrecht. LNCS 1258*, 1997.

[Luo98]   Z. Luo. Coercive subtyping. *Journal of Logic and Computation*, 1998. To
           appear.

[Lyo95]   J. Lyons. *Linguistic Semantics.* Cambridge University Press, 1995.

[McK92]   J. McKinna. *Deliverables: a categorical approach to program development
           in type theory.* PhD thesis, Department of Computer Science, University
           of Edinburgh, 1992.

[Miz]   Mizar. Mizar home page. Δhttp://mizar.uw.bialystok.pl/Δ.

[MN94]   L. Magnusson and B. Nordström. The ALF proof editor and its proof
           engine. In *Types for Proof and Programs, LNCS*, 1994.

[NPS90]   B. Nordström, K. Petersson, and J. Smith. *Programming in Martin-Löf's
           Type Theory: An Introduction.* Oxford University Press, 1990.

[Pus95]   J. Pustejovsky. *The Generative Lexicon.* MIT, 1995.

[Ran94]   A. Ranta. *Type-theoretical Grammar.* Oxford University Press, 1994.

[Ran95]   A. Ranta. Type-theoretical interpretation and generalization of phrase
           structure grammar. *Bulletin of the IGPL*, 1995.

[Ran96]   Aarne Ranta. Context-relative syntactic categories and the formalization of
           mathematical text. In S. Berardi and M. Coppo, editors, *Types for Proofs
           and Programs.* Springer-Verlag, Heidelberg. 1996.

[Ran97]   A. Ranta. A grammatical framework (some notes on the source files), 1997.

[Ruy]   Mark Ruys. *Formalizing Mathematics in Type Theory.* PhD thesis, Com-
           puting Science Institute, University of Nijmegen. (to be submitted).

[Sai97]   A. Saibi. Typing algorithm in type theory with inheritance. *Proc of POPL'97*, 1997.

[SL98]   S. Soloviev and Z. Luo. Coercive subtyping: coherence and conservativity, 1998. In preparation.

[vBJMP93]   L. van Benthem Jutting, James McKinna, and Robert Pollack. Type-checking in pure type systems. submitted for publication, 1993.

Author Index

Springer
and the
environment

At Springer we firmly believe that an
international science publisher has a
special obligation to the environment,
and our corporate policies consistently
reflect this conviction.

We also expect our business partners –
paper mills, printers, packaging
manufacturers, etc. – to commit
themselves to using materials and
production processes that do not harm
the environment. The paper in this
book is made from low- or no-chlorine
pulp and is acid free, in conformance
with international standards for paper
permanency.

Lecture Notes in Artificial Intelligence (LNAI)

Lecture Notes in Computer Science